"We're going down there and start
a little war of our own."

—JOHN PAINE
Hashknife cowboy, August, 1887

A LITTLE WAR OF OUR OWN

The Pleasant Valley Feud Revisited

By Don Dedera
Foreword by C. L. Sonnichsen

 Northland Press

Frontispiece: First and most consistent in telling the story of the Pleasant Valley War was the small but enterprising staff of the Phoenix *Herald,* here posing for a group portrait in front of newspaper headquarters. *Courtesy Arizona Photographic Associates*

Designed by Lisa Dunning

Typeset in Goudy by Messenger Graphics, Phoenix, Arizona

Printed by Northland Printing Company, Flagstaff, Arizona

Cover art © 1988 by Bill Ahrendt

Contents

Editor's note: When quoting original documents, all spelling, punctuation, and other eccentricities of the times have been retained as recorded. The reader will notice many variants, particularly in the spelling of names.

*Dedicated to the women
of the Pleasant Valley War,
among them:*

Mary Blevins, who in the space of six weeks lost a husband missing in action, four sons shot to death, and a fifth son wounded . . .

Hannah Stott, whose bright, venturesome boy was hanged by lawless vigilantes . . .

Mary Ann Tewksbury, who, great with child, guarded the body of her murdered husband eleven days . . .

Braulia López, whose girlish dreams dissolved into war's nightmares: separation, waiting, disease, death, loneliness, want . . .

Duette Ellison, Arizona's first "first lady," but not without price . . .

Annie and Estella Graham, doomed by one deed to twenty-five thousand days of despair . . .

They, and others, sisters of sorrow.

Foreword

Feud situations—little wars in which two families or factions take turns killing each other—are more common than you might think. They happen when the law is absent or powerless and conditions become intolerable. In the American West, the post–Civil War period was particularly productive of these social eruptions and every state west of the Mississippi can boast of—or apologize for—a few episodes. Texas was the leader in this department with as many as a hundred examples, while the region between San Antonio and Houston was once known as the Pure Feud Belt.

Only one major feud broke out in Arizona—the Pleasant Valley War or the Graham-Tewksbury feud—but it was big enough and bloody enough to command national attention. It helped persuade the rest of the country that Arizona Territory was uncivilized and therefore unfit for statehood. With only one such episode to its discredit, however, Arizona was by no means a chief offender.

It is possible to argue, furthermore, that these firestorms of uncontrolled violence are not, strictly speaking, lawless. They are really invocations of the earliest criminal law of all, the law of an eye for an eye.

In earlier times, it was a family obligation to avenge the murder of a kinsman. Anglo-Saxons could substitute money for blood *(wergeld)* and thus prevent the killing, but Englishmen had to wait until the Middle Ages for murder to be defined as a crime against the state. Relics of the old attitudes still appear in more civilized times and places. Some Southerners still feel that it is unmanly to see a lawyer when one has been personally abused. They believe in do-it-yourself justice—that is, self-redress or folk justice. Lynch laws and frontier vendettas were direct results of these attitudes. Mark Twain found the old beliefs alive along the Mississippi in the lethal rivalry between the Grangerfords and the Shepherdsons, described in *Huckleberry Finn*.

As a matter of fact, all feuds, including the Pleasant Valley War, follow well-marked trails and evolve in similar patterns. They can happen in centers of population among people of some education and culture, but they are more likely to occur in isolated areas where the old folk ways and attitudes still persist. If law courts and peace officers are far away, the risk of serious trouble is greater; it was a two-day ride from Pleasant Valley to the county seat at Prescott and the sheriff did not appear in the valley unless he had to. Another factor in feud production was the fact that in pioneer times, everybody was armed. The settlers killed game to live and sometimes killed Indians for the same reason. They were thus prepared to kill each other.

The presence and persistence of outlawry was also a critical element. In the years after the Civil War, when law and order were in short supply, fugitives of many sorts drifted to the frontier and made life hard, if not impossible, for the bona-fide settlers. For several generations, people who got in trouble in Georgia or Alabama headed west, usually ending up in Texas. The letters G.T.T. (Gone to Texas) were posted on many a door, explaining that the bird had flown. These fugitives often joined gangs of thieves and bandits who preyed on borderland settlements, sometimes posing as Indian raiders to throw pursuers off the track. A story once heard in Texas told of a man who had killed a neighbor in Alabama and headed west. Arriving in Texas he promptly got in trouble again and killed somebody else.

"You will have to get out," his new friends advised him. "They will lynch you if you don't."

"But where can I go?" he inquired plaintively. "Ain't I in Texas now?"

By the time of the Pleasant Valley War, Arizona was the place to go. Rough characters from Texas had arrived in such numbers that something had to be done about it. In 1901, the Arizona Rangers were organized to put a stop to outlawry; many of the men pursued were former Texans. The Tewksburys and the Grahams were not Texans, but they lived by the same code and, as Dedera points out, many of the others involved were migrants from Texas. Some of them had guns for hire and gravitated to troubled areas. Tom Tucker of the Hashknife gang, for example, was a Texan who headed east after leaving Pleasant Valley and took a prominent part in the Lee-Fall-Fountain feud in New Mexico in the 1890s.

Given suitable time, place, and characters, how does a feud get started? Contrary to popular belief, it takes more than a disagreement about the ownership of a razorback hog or stray cow to begin the killing. A trivial event may trigger the first shot, but a buildup of intolerable conditions will provide the tinder for the spark. Usually somebody has been taking something that does not belong to him. Life and livelihood are endangered. Patience ceases to be a virtue. The authorities, if any, are no help and the aggrieved parties feel they have to fight fire with fire. They organize, arm themselves, and go after the bad guys. In Texas in the 1840s, wholesale stealing and rustling by organized gangs was at the root of the war of the "Regulators" and "Moderators." The good people felt they had to defend themselves, and a group of regulators—vigilantes— was assembled. The catchword in Texas was "mob." Sometimes these mobs traded work. The Llano River mob would break a horse thief out of jail somewhere else and hang him, and expect a mob from that place to do the same for them.

Other causes besides stealing could ignite a feud. Texans, who would fight about anything, feuded over politics, racial issues, family disagreements, local option—even religion. Stealing, however, was the major cause.

The problem was that once a regulator group got things in hand, it was likely to assume too much power and lynch the wrong people, with the result that a counter-organization of Moderators would be assembled to "moderate" the Regulators, and a full-scale feud would be under way. A vigilante group did not appear in Pleasant Valley until the end of the trouble, but, as Colonel Jesse Ellison said of such situations, "There has to be a cleanup," and the final hangings were perpetrated by a mysterious group who felt they had a right to protect themselves.

Feuds did not always develop. Texans had a word for a situation in which somebody got killed without retaliation. They called it a "difficulty." If there were repeated killings, however, a true vendetta was the result, and it followed standard procedures.

In the first place, all charity, all compassion, all Christian sentiments were sloughed off like old clothes. Each side felt an unrelenting hatred for the other and was convinced that there would be no peace or safety unless they wiped out the enemy. Ambush was not only tolerated, it was encouraged (they called it "laywaying" in Texas). If a man was warned to leave the country and he didn't go, he was considered to have committed suicide. When a member of the other side was disposed of, his killers rejoiced and celebrated as if they had eliminated a nest of rattlesnakes under the house. The Tewksburys and the Grahams felt this consuming hatred for each other and killed each other from ambush and without compassion. That was the way it was done.

Given these bitter hatreds, it is not surprising that a true feud had no brakes. Sam Houston stopped the War of the Regulators and Moderators in Texas by calling in the principals and giving them a fatherly talking-to as he sat whittling on a local woodpile, but as a rule, one side either left the country or stayed and was exterminated. In Arizona, the feud had only one survivor. In Zane Grey's words it was a war *To the Last Man*.

Typically also, feuds do not stay in the area of their origin. They move to town, at least to courts of law and often to prisons and jails. In Texas, the townspeople sometimes were drawn into the feud. In Arizona, nothing quite like that happened, but there is strong suspicion that peace officers were somehow involved in the later killings. In killing times, the infection is likely to spread.

One function of feuds is to produce local celebrities, who sometimes, as in the case of Billy the Kid, evolved into folk heroes. The Pleasant Valley War made its own contribution. Ed Tewksbury, the last man left alive, could not qualify though he was notorious enough. Shooting an unarmed man from ambush, even though he was arch-enemy Tom Graham, kept Tewksbury out of the hero class. Sheriff Commodore Perry Owens, however, made the grade. He was the long-haired sharpshooter who wiped out the Blevins clan singlehandedly at Holbrook in 1887. Many have felt that Owens's killings were unnecessary, but his exploit made him a little larger than life in the minds of others, then and since.

We sometimes forget that women were involved in these bloody encounters. In Texas they often encouraged their men to fight. Before the final battle in front of the Fort Bend County courthouse in Richmond, Texas, in 1889, between the Jaybird and Woodpecker factions, the Jaybird women are said to have distributed little sacks of sand to their men, subtly suggesting that a little grit was needed on their side. The women in Pleasant Valley, so far as is known, made no such lethal gestures, but they illustrated amply the fact that there are no winners in a full-fleged feud—only victims and mourners.

Don Dedera makes this fact sufficiently plain. He is admirably impartial in his depiction of the conflict. He feels that a feud situation like the Pleasant Valley War is really a Greek tragedy and the web of circumstance in which the Grahams and the Tewksburys were caught dooms them to defeat and death, with no one left at the end but the mourners.

C. L. Sonnichsen
Tucson, Arizona

Introduction

Much of this book's text was completed across a progression of hundred-year anniversaries of noteworthy episodes in what has come to be called the Pleasant Valley War of Arizona. Genesis of this classic human conflict dates possibly from as early as the 1870s, when certain combatants-to-be reportedly became acquainted in California.[1] The most sensational assassination in Arizona's territorial history occurred some fifteen years later in 1892. And retaliation may have carried well into the twentieth century. But 1887 was the year of heaviest losses for both camps of this protracted American vendetta.[2]

Conservatively, thirty deaths were attributed to the Pleasant Valley War. Fatalities may have numbered fifty. A Pleasant Valley battle correspondent wrote, "Outside of the Apache Indian troubles, there has been, in all the events of Arizona's history, no series of incidents that have attracted such wide attention, or has kept a good-sized section of the state in such a reign of terror as this Pleasant Valley feud during 1887 and 1888."[3]

Bloody 1887 began with the slaughter of a shepherd employed by one faction and ended with the hanging of a cattleman/leader of the opposing faction. Between those two deaths, terror and violence marred all the months of the year. So for those of us close to this true story of the frontier West, 1987, day-by-day, presented centennials of exquisite suffering, unquenchable hatred, and unspeakable violence.

Make no mistake. The battles and assassinations of Pleasant Valley amounted to a war. Though small in scale, it cost its people relative to engagements of nations. One of the Pleasant Valley War's women, in the course of ten weeks, lost her husband (missing in action) and four sons (shot to death). Another son was seriously wounded. These were losses to rival those of America's Sullivan family (five dead in a ship sinking) of World War II. Yet another Pleasant Valley woman well into her last month of pregnancy was obliged to guard her husband's unburied body for eleven days. One youth disemboweled by gunshot managed to gather his entrails into his arms and ride horseback to his home where his brothers stitched him up with needle and thread. He died. A lad who replaced him in ranks in turn was wounded in the buttocks; he had to sit a horse sidesaddle one hundred fifty miles through mountainous wilderness to the nearest medic.

Fortunes of war were sought, gained, and abandoned in and around Pleasant Valley. Campaign schemes went awry. Fate intervened— unfairly. Turns of events attracted cynical opportunists. Neutrals suffered as belligerents. Conspirators masqueraded as uninvolved. Moneyed people invested in the war. Brutes took charge. Innocents died. Professed peacekeepers exacted a dreadful toll. Spectators from safe distances followed battlefield communiqués with morbid fascination. Insipid, gratuitous advice from afar abounded. And ultimately, no clear victor prevailed. In fact, possession of contested territory drifted by default away from the more notorious contestants. Thus, in many ways, Pleasant Valley reinvented an ageless metaphor. War at once can be horrible and dehumanizing—and obscenely senseless.

The universal nature of Arizona's "little war" did not assert itself for me right away. To the contrary, my own beginning interest was avocational, even therapeutic. Not long graduated from Arizona State University's journalism school, I was assigned in the early 1950s to the night police beat of The Arizona Republic, the state's largest circulation newspaper then, as it is now. The job: monitor and chronicle crimes, calamities, and emergencies for the capital city, Phoenix, and all 113,000 square miles of Arizona plus adjacent regions, including Mexico. The responsibility was infinite; so was the stress. During one extraordinary Sunday stint I produced the entire front page news budget, including both banner stories, a human-interest feature, several photographs, plus two dozen lesser items inside. Worth a bonus, I hoped. (My pay was $40 a week.) And the following evening, in my office mailbox, from City Editor Gene McLain, was a memo affixed to a trivial, two-paragraph item clipped from our afternoon rival.

"When you missed this story," McLain (in mock displeasure) demanded to know, "what bar stool were you sleeping under?"

The nominal quitting time for the night shift was two AM, when the last of five editions was tucked abed. But I, bludgeoned by scenes of awful accident and sleazy sin, would be wide awake. For escape, I tarried in our library (then nicknamed "the morgue") to browse microfilms of territorial newspapers, mainly the *Phoenix Herald,* the *Arizona Gazette,* and the *Republican,* forerunner of our more modern *Republic.* The old publications with their formal tombstone headlines over generous columns of intercity exchanges served as quaint lenses illuminating the late-nineteenth-century West—far more compelling for me than pulp fiction. How did the *Tombstone Epitaph* crime writer cover the shootout at the O K Corral, anyway? Who-when-where reported what-why-how about Geronimo? Did a skeptical newsman unravel the Spanish land grant swindle perpetrated by James Addison Reavis, Baron of Arizona?

Heady stuff, for a callow fellow already hooked on journalistic adventure and regional nostalgia. I thought it must have been more moving, more romantic, more theatrical for journalists way back when. After all, no copy editor of the modern *Republic* was embellishing *my* stories with headlines such as: "CARNIVAL OF CRIME! A Bloody Week in Phoenix Ends with a Grand Neck-tie Party. Six Persons Launched on Their Journey Down the Dark River. Reckless Romero Madly Rushes to His Doom. Takes Three Pistol Balls with Him. John La Bar Stabbed Fatally by a Drunken Ruffian. Jesus Figero Pistoled on the Gila and Another Mexican Knifed at Seymour. McClosky and Keller Hurried Hellward at the End of a Rope."[4]

Not even my obituaries withstood comparison with those of frontier Arizona newsman Herbert E. Wilcox: "Dr. Woods did all that medical skill could do, but the mechanism of nature's works was too far impaired to be renewed through the agency of medical science, and the breast of Charles Keefe ceased to heave, and nothing but the inanimate form was left. What we call life is gone. Where? We know not."[5]

An impressionable cub reporter suffered no shortage of favorites. At one end of the territory, in Tombstone, there was John P. Clum showing newsmen how to bid farewell with class: "On this bright spring evening [1882], while the birds are singing in the grease wood bush and Apaches are howling through the mountains, the *Epitaph* wraps itself in an American flag and dies like a son of a gun. Ta, ta! We shall meet again, Clemantha. . . ."[6]

Northward, curmudgeonish A.H. Hackney of the *Arizona Silver Belt* admonished his readers, ". . .the general use of the electric light is liable to prove injurious to the eyesight of the public. It is so bright that ordinary eyes will not be able to bear it without pain, and the whole nervous system, it is thought, will be unduly harmed. . . . "[7] My prim and proper *Republic* of 1955 would have rejected it, but in 1875, William J. Berry inserted this classified advertisement in his Yuma, *Arizona Sentinel:* "Wanted: A nice, plump, healthy, good natured, good looking, domestic and affectionate lady to correspond with. Object—Matrimony. . . . If anybody doesn't like our way of going about this interesting business, we don't care. It's none of their business."[8] About the middle of Arizona Territory, at Prescott, Buckey O'Neill alternately outraged and delighted patrons of his *Hoof and Horn* livestock industry journal. But nobody in or out of Prescott exceeded John H. Marion of the *Prescott Courier* in editorial ire: as regarding a newly appointed, conciliatory Indian agent: "We ought, in justice to our murdered dead, to dump the old devil into the shaft of some mine, and pile rocks upon him until he is dead. A rascal who comes here to thwart the efforts of military and citizens to conquer a peace from our savage foe, deserves to be stoned to death, like the treacherous black-hearted dog that he is."[9] But Marion nearly met his match in attacking *The Apache Chief*, an "Anti-Mormon Journal Devoted to the Interests of Apache County, Arizona Territory." The *Chief* publisher George A. McCarter countered:

Poor, weak old John Marion of the *Prescott Courier* is very anxious about the editorial status of the *Chief*. Since he edits the *Courier* without brains there is no reason why he should not publish it without ink and ship it to some cholera-stricken district where the sheet can be put to its only appropriate and useful service.[10]

What fun. But over the weeks and months of my idle perusal, a true tragedy impinged, if only by persistence. The Pleasant Valley War of east-central Arizona coursed through territorial journals like an intermittent but robust stream along a western waterway, perhaps disappearing here and there, but rising to the surface again and again. As a self-styled New Wave reporter, I was favorably impressed by the thoroughness and overall accuracy achieved by my professional forebears. At least once, it seemed to me, the Pleasant Valley War was fairly well particularized—in the territorial press. In fact, I thought then, and still do, that a dandy book could be drawn from the carefully crafted columns of the *Herald* alone—an isle of literacy marooned in desert doldrums.

My reporter's nose sniffed out a shelf of uneven novels and narratives: Zane Grey's *To The Last Man*, Earle R. Forrest's *Arizona's Dark and Bloody Ground*, Dane Coolidge's *Man Killers*, Will Croft Barnes's *Apaches and Longhorns*; and the memoirs of McKinney, Flake, Horton, Voris, Burnham, Schute, Colcord, and others. In time, my interest assumed a force of its own, more than a hobby, not quite an obsession.

When, for fifteen years, a daily human-interest column became my career, my freedom of subject and travel led to interviews with surviving witnesses and relatives. Transcripts of testimony and other court records turned up in county seats. Diaries, letters, and depositions surfaced. Thanks to progress in photographic technology in the late 1800s, and the devotion of clever image-makers, the life and times of Pleasant Valley characters and enterprises were caught on glass plate and film. Limited physically, and thus not quite the battlefield Matthew Brady of Pleasant Valley, Miss Lena Ellison tested the length of her physical tether (she had been cruelly crippled by a fall when a child) to photograph Tonto ranch life toward the turn of the century.

If an introduction may serve as something of a confessional, I would ask the reader's understanding of another of the author's motivations. Just about midway between those early days of reporting the police beat and the present, I twice went to Vietnam as a war correspondent, in 1966 and 1969, sponsored by my maternal *Republic*. Expectations, including my own, ran high. But the Southeast Asia quagmire early and late gummed up every American goal—military, political, journalistic. A frontline analyst indicted us of the press: "Here is Telestar out in space distributing the phenomena of our day around the world at the speed of light. . . . In Saigon there are three hundred fifty correspondents supposedly assigned to making the war and its issues understandable to people, everywhere, a group thrice the size of the press gallery of the Korean War. Yet despite all this elaboration, the struggle in Vietnam is the most wretchedly reported war in the fane of our history since old Zach Taylor fought at Buena Vista. Never before have men and women in such numbers contributed so little to so many."[11] Frankly, I saw merit in the criticism. Few but intimates much understood what I meant in writing, "In 1966 I was off corresponding peacefully in Vietnam, losing too many good Arizona friends, half my sanity, three-fourths of my career, and all of the war." Unfortunately, not an uncommon fortieth birthday present for Americans in charge of the 1960s: failure.

Thereafter, in patching together a new livelihood as a free-lance journalist, I rediscovered my old Pleasant Valley War files. Again, but in different ways, the long-ago, small-scale, abstracted conflict presented both comforting busywork and manageable challenge. Belated as was my second scrutiny of the story, I was struck again by an enduring secretiveness, and pervasive caution among survivors, descendants, and witnesses. No interviewee of my neophyte's crime beat or grownup's Asia war seemed more bitter than elderly Bertha Acton, who as a girl three years of age, descried the molestation of her daddy's remains by swine. Mollie McTaggert, a full seventy years after she put her finger on a murderer, hugged her cat and lowered her voice and glanced furtively as she retold her tale to me. Then

Rose Maret, well into her nineties, frail and blind, vehemently insisting: "Grandpa Ellison *never* took a part in the war! He was a neutral, caught in the middle! Now you get that right!" In the mid-1950s, emotions still ran so strong, all but a dozen copies of a hardbound edition of a book about the Pleasant Valley War were meekly destroyed when banned from public distribution by court order. This—in America—land of the First Amendment to the Bill of Rights? In 1987, the gag order *still stood* uncontested. Individuals five generations removed from Pleasant Valley violence steadfastly refused to talk about it.

As these words are written, the rock-shielded grave of the first-fallen shepherd saddens a glade in the Tonto National Forest. The weathered walls of the cabin of a lynched rancher sag, empty but for the droppings of birds. Only a scrap of cryptic handwriting from an invincible widow is bequeathed to a multitude of great-grandchildren and their progeny. The mutter of musketry, which, in less than a minute, massacred most of the males of a family, now may be restaged from time to time as a historical curiosity for the entertainment of tourists.[12] The tree upon which three lads sprinted into eternity was by another generation logged for lumber in 1964. With few exceptions, today's names of Pleasant Valley are not of the land. The people of the war are gone. No one hundred-twenty-year-old veterans convene to revisit atrocities and reinforce loyalties. Yet obliquity of opinion strangely endures. Why? This writer is neither the first nor likely the last to wonder.

An admirable archivist, Clara Woody, staked a considerable share of her cherished historical reputation on the side of her Tewksbury townsmen. I came to converse and correspond with Earle Forrest, runaway Pennyslvania romanticist, for whom the war afforded a simplistic western morality play: Grahams the unsullied heroes and Tewksburys the unredeemed villains. Roscoe Willson, forester/journalist/historian for decades until his death in 1976, was my generously kind mentor. Yet Roscoe, in his lengthy series of articles in the 1950s and 1960s, could not or would not recognize his chief informant, William Colcord, as one of the Tewksbury "friends who make salt sweet and blackness bright." Jess G. Hayes, longtime Gila County school superintendent and valued research partner, authored boldly enlightening works on the Apache Kid and Sheriff Thompson, but restraint tempered Jess's writings about the Pleasant Valley War. Jess one day grasped my arm on Globe's Broad Street, waved his other hamlike hand at the Gila courthouse, and exclaimed, "It's all in there, and I know where, but I don't want to hurt my neighbors!" Drusilla Hazelton might have said as much, but instead she chronicled her pioneer forebears, the Burches and Hazeltons. Drusilla's unpublished typescript at the Arizona Historical Society presents dependable, straightforward family history, and (alas!) makes no bones about championing a patently Tewksbury point of view. Robert Allison, unexcelled in his sports editorship of the *Gazette,* in an earlier year crafted with diligent enterprise an essay amounting to a Blevins family white paper.

These were and are writers I came to know in person. With others, through their published works and papers, I sought a second-hand acquaintanceship. Zane Grey ostensibly employed a qualified historian and professed a faithful pursuit of facts himself for several years; but Grey's fictional treatment of the Pleasant Valley War bore little relationship to the record. Taken together, prediliction ran as denominator through reflective writings about the war. The authors came to feel comfortable with biased versions which they more or less privately buttressed and publicly put forth.

To my mind, the Pleasant Valley War, if it deserved another work at all, needed not another advocacy. A century ago, the maturing Arizona legal system had its chance with thirty to fifty cases of homicide, wholesale murderous assaults, several instances of arson, and rampant livestock rustling, perjury, mayhem, conspiracy, burglary, contempt, fraud, extortion, and flight from and obstruction of justice. Yet, through more than two decades of examination and prosecution, the territory failed to obtain a single Pleasant Valley War conviction. Not even for a misdemeanor. By default, the enigmas were left to historians. More sensible to me was the ideal of Robin W. Winks, who, in a provocative anthology[13] defined a discipline: history reduced to its purest essence is "the memory of things said and done." It so happened that my journalistic instincts jibed with that ideal. For this book, then, the effort has been to limit reportage of the war's happenings to things provably said and done, as documented in journals, diaries, court and government records, memoirs, letters, and transcribed interviews. Over a span of thirty-five years, I literally filled rooms with findings: stray magazine articles, letters to editors, photograph albums, family trees, rough maps, autograph books, court proceedings, bills of sale, estate inventories, artifacts. Among a hundred of my interviews, three were of theretofore silent witnesses to murder. My most helpful informant, at age seventy-six, was the daughter of the last man exterminated by "The Last Man." My greatest regret: I was unsuccessful in convincing the elderly Miss Ola Young to have her overflowing boxes of photographic portraits copied by the University of Arizona Library. Like Mehitebel's kittens, Miss Ola kept her precious gallery in Campbell's Soup cartons, next to her wood stove.

"Every boy in the war," she told me. "I have a picture of every boy and every boy's family. I'm keeping them safe with me, thank you."

Two years later, Miss Ola's cabin and everything in it burned to the ground, lost forever. But in the oil business, a saying goes, "The best

geologist is Dame Fortune." So, too, in the history business. Whereas
fiery fate deprived us of Ola Young's portfolio, sheer luck delivered to
me a hitherto unpublished contract.[14] One day in Prescott, the document
fell into my lap from where it had been *misfiled* for more than a century.

If this avocational exercise has taught me one lesson, it is respect for
professional historians. In topical, superficial journalism, bits of information may swiftly fill a satisfying mosaic—all that reasonably can be
expected within a short time. Journalists find a stray button and stitch a
whole suit onto it. But in the measured pace of historical inquiry, every
established fact seems to lead only to more mystery. A door kicked down
presents two more. Thanks in part to the man's maddeningly convoluted
and conflicting press reports, I feel that I know less about Charley
Duchet at the end than I did at the beginning. Some of my most treas-
ured Arizona rim country friends are named Flake, Mormons who *never*
throw anything away, yet they have been unwilling or unable to produce
from the Flake family archive the meticulously kept tally book which
might tell us whether James Stott was a justly hanged horsethief or a
cynically strangled innocent. Somewhere in the Payson country, it is said,
an early Haught diary would clarify many questions, but it was not made
available to me. The serious part-time historian shares the humbling certainty known so well to the career historian: nobody *ever* knows *all* there
is to know.

Much of this book deals with the practice of one human conflict. But
over a thirty-year span, I've sought theories addressing the "irrational and
unconscious forces that drive people to make war." Not long ago
Andrew Schmookler published *The Parable of Tribes: The Problem of
Power in Social Evolution*. He writes: "Imagine a group of tribes living
within reach of each other. If all choose the way of peace, then all may
live in peace. But what if all but one choose peace. . .?" A brief excerpt
suggests that Schmookler has synthesized insights into the causes of war
in general, and for "the little war of our own":

A society, when confronted with a powerful neighboring society that is bent on
vengeance, has only four options. One, it can be destroyed. Two, it can be absorbed
and transformed through conquest. Third, it can retreat, run away. And the fourth
option is, it can decide to defend itself. But to defend itself, it would have to have the
power to do so. It would have to become more like the society it is resisting. The
struggle for power says only those cultural forms, only those ways of organizing life
that make a society able to compete effectively against other societies will survive
and spread. And other ways of life, however humane or viable, will be eliminated. If
power is introduced anywhere in the system, anyplace that power is introduced will
spread the wave of power throughout the system.

Reprinted, with permission, from *Globe, Arizona: Early Times in a Little World of Copper and Cattle* by Clara T. Woody and Milton L. Schwartz, © 1977 by the Arizona Historical Society.

BOOK
ONE

Ed Tewksbury's pocket watch,
a gift from George Newton.

I. Blood on the Barley

Night before last, a sandstorm toppled a row of cottonwood trees across the earthen lane bordering the Bud Cummings farm. Now the four-horse team trudges past the treetops, finding constricted passage without urging, as if all is well with Tom Graham, as if the driver's hand still grips the reins, as if he still wants them to draw his wagon of barley to the mill.

Time: 7:20, an hour and thirty-nine minutes after sunrise, Tuesday, August 2, 1892.[1]

Tom Graham's blood-flecked buff hat lies in the middle of Double Buttes Road. Heavy, humid billows of dust envelop the wagon, and silver sunrays illuminate Graham's gray, unblinking face. His body sprawls upon the sacks of grain. His arms jiggle to the sway and jounce of the wagon. His feet flop in front of the dashboard. A heavy, blunt rifle ball has pierced his back two inches leftward of the seventh vertebra, severed the spinal cord, coursed upward, and emerged a bit to the right of the larynx.

J.P. Brooks, ten years old, holds a fishing pole while standing on a small bridge spanning a drainage canal near the intersection of two unpaved farm roads southwest of Tempe. His attention is fixed on a school of minnows flashing in shallow pools. A wagon approaches from the west, heading for Tempe, driven by a friend, Tom Graham. Mr. Graham just yesterday delighted a knot of Tempe children by letting them ride a ways on his grain wagon. Now Tom reins in again, to visit with a child. The boy would wait seventy years to tell what he saw:

At that time an adobe school house was on the southeast corner. . .a fence enclosed ten acres; all except a small playground was white sage brush six to ten feet high. . . .He stopped for a minute, waved, asked if I wanted to ride to town. No thanks, I told him. He was on a high-seated wagon, grain bags as high as the back of the seat. He drove on. I heard a shot. Turned. Tom was just falling slowly back on the grain bags. He pulled the horses to a stop as he went back; I saw three men on horses, smoke from two guns. . . .[2]

Miss Mollie Cummings, seventeen, also is abroad this muggy morning. She is showing off her buggy and freshly broken pony to her houseguest, (Grace Griffith.) Just as the girls turn out of the Cummings yard onto the road they hear the report of a firearm. Though muffled by fallen foliage, the sound makes Mollie's horse flinch. But to children of Arizona Territory, gunfire is commonplace, and Mollie drives on, due west, toward the nearest blown-down tree. She skirts it.)

A hundred yards westward Tom Graham's wagon hoves into view.

Behind and to the left of the wagon, a swarthy, keg-chested man of middle years sits on a big bay horse. As the man aims a rifle toward Tom Graham, the girls intrude upon his line of sight. The man lowers his rifle deliberately. At the touch of a spur, the horse bounds, drawing even with the wagon. The horseman stands his stirrups, leans over, and gazes down into the face of Tom Graham. If there are words, the girls thirty paces away do not hear them above the thump of hoof and ring of wheelrim and squeak of harness. Seemingly satisfied with what he sees, the horseman urges his mount into a lope. Mollie later will recall:

I took him for a Mexican. He was a tolerably large man. Heavy set. He wore a large, light-colored hat with a red band around it. He had a black mustache and something of a black cloth at his throat. He didn't frown or make any kind of remark, and we certainly didn't say anything to him. We sat there, too stunned to move. He first tried to go between us and the fallen tree, but he had to check his horse.

He bumped my buggy as he went by. He looked directly at me, and I stared back. I could have touched him.[3]

Then he is gone, the dark cowboy.)

M.A. Cravath, forty-three, schoolteacher by profession and Cummings's summertime hired man, is bent toward the east, hoeing cockleburrs in a pasture adjacent to the Double Buttes Road when he hears a shot to his left behind him. He, too, at first thinks little of it. Then in less than a minute "a tall man. . .very dark-complexioned. . .a very broad-shouldered man. . .very thick-chested or thick man. . . . " gallops eastward on a good-sized, light bay horse. Now curious, Cravath makes mental notes. The man is wearing a wide-brimmed, light-colored (maybe straw) hat with a wide red band, and seems to be dressed in blue. He either carries in a hand or has fastened to the saddle horn a long arm. In growing apprehension Cravath drops his hoe and strides into the road—there to intercept the wagon. Cravath will testify in court:

I met the team and led them along a few rods and turned them out of the road . . . . When I got upon the wagon I saw that he was not dead, that he was alive. . . . I had some water brought to me, and first I gave him a drink of water in a cup. . .and then he asked me to wash his face.[4]

Adjoining the Cummings farm on the east is the country place of John Gregg. Doctor Gregg makes the money, his wife is fond of saying, and Farmer Gregg spends it. Bettie Gregg, sixteen, baby of the family, steps onto her polished, black, two-wheel cart behind Lady, her spirited mare. Bettie clucks the horse into a trot. She will have to hurry to keep an appointment to give a music lesson to a child at a neighboring farm. On Double Buttes Road, only a quarter of a mile from the ambush, she hears a shot. Presently a horseman draws near. Half a century later her memory is vivid:

He was going full speed. He was dark, rather fleshy. Couldn't say if he had a beard or not. He rode a big bay horse, big for a saddle horse. Something in his manner frightened me. He seemed so stern, with his gaze straight ahead. His hat had an unusual scarlet band. He was such a powerful figure, and me—just a frail girl. I was no more than ten feet from him as he passed, and after he went by, I was a little put out that he did not pay any attention to my rig which was my pride and surely the fanciest in the Valley.[5]

Eastward presses the horseman.

Robert White, Doctor Gregg's man, looks up from chores to admire the large, bright bay loping on Double Buttes Road. White is only a hundred feet from the rider, whose white felt hat not only is decorated with a red band but is held with a black chinstrap an inch wide.[6]

Near the intersection with Farmer Avenue, near the single track of the Maricopa & Phoenix Railroad, Emma Sears, eighteen, fusses in her mother's flower garden, plucking fresh rose petals for a fragrance pillow. Seventy years will pass before she finds courage to tell an investigator:

I heard a horse running, so I looked up and saw a man coming real fast. After he saw me he leaned over on the right side of his horse. He had hold of the saddle horn with his left hand. I thought he had dropped his reins. He never sat erect in his saddle until after he crossed the railroad track, which would be the distance of one block. I didn't get to see his face. Soon people from town and around began coming in wagons, in buggies, and on horseback, and afoot. My brother-in-law, J.H. Harris, was in the crowd. I waved to him. He told me Tom Graham had been killed, and they were after the killer. I said, "I guess I saw him." And he told me to go into the house and not say a word to anyone.[7]

Unchallenged, the gunman on the bay horse flees through the Valley.

William McGrew, a cattleman, takes particular notice of the horseman he meets on the Double Buttes Road about a half mile east of Gregg's near the railroad crossing. Three miles east of Cummings's, E.G. Frankenburg meets the rider. Frankenburg is on a business trip to Tempe, agricultural center and crossing of the Salt River. Frankenburg will state:

Double Buttes Road is about two miles south of town. Where Double Buttes Road crosses Mill Avenue I met a man on a bay horse, or maybe more of a sorrel, that was streaked with sweat. I would say the horse was sweating abundantly. I took the man to be a Mexican. He was riding at a gallop. He had on a new alpaca coat, light-colored. He had on a light straw hat with a wide red band around it. I never saw the man before. I saw no gun on him.[8]

Orley Stapley runs a one-man dairy, and his placement of the murder day is solidly connected with the date he routinely fetches his payment for a month of milk deliveries. Close to eight o'clock the morning of August 2, having collected his money, he is eating a watermelon while standing alongside the eastward extension of Tempe's Double Buttes Road. A horseman appears from the west. He wears a light-colored coat, has no firearm in view, and makes no effort to obscure his face. In fact, his hatbrim is tilted up revealing a black chinstrap about the width of two fingers. The dark bay horse maintains an easy dog-trot, and Stapley has half a minute to study the man's features. One month later, Stapley cannot be shaken at a preliminary hearing:[9]

Q.: Now, do I understand you to say when a man's life is at stake that you are swearing to that proposition: that you identify this defendant as the identical man that you saw?

A.: Yes, sir; I do think he is the man I saw that morning.

Q.: You do?

A.: Yes, sir.

Q.: There is no doubt in your mind?

A.: I have no doubt at all. If I had—

Q.: Would you be willing to risk your own neck to swing on a statement like that: are you as positive as that?

A.: Yes, sir.

At her home in Goldman Addition, Mrs. E.M. Rumberg scatters a flock of hens with a pan of dishwater. She pauses, wiping her hands on her apron, and follows the progress of a rider. Her recognition is instantaneous, and under oath later she will state:

He was riding at an easy gallop. He had a light cowboy's hat on. He was dressed regular cowboy style with a heavy saddle. He was wearing two revolvers in sight. He had a rifle in a scabbard on the righthand side. I know the man. I have known him for years.

The man does not return her glance. He rides on purposefully. In Mesa City, six miles to the east of Tempe, half the town seems aware that a murderer is heading that way. Shortly after 8:00 A.M., at his home on Main Street, Deputy Sheriff William A. Kimball receives a telegram from Sheriff John Montgomery. The message tells of the shooting of Tom Graham, and includes a description of a suspect. Later, when asked for an accounting:

I went into the stable and saddled up my horse and went into my house and went out on the front porch. And the message said the man had a red band on his hat. I went out into the street from the house, and the man came along riding a bay horse, riding pretty fast; and I saw he had a high-crowned hat, sombrero, and had a red handkerchief, as I supposed, tied around in front with the ends behind. . . . He rode by, and I saw he wasn't the man I wanted, and I went back into the house.[10]

Into the open desert, toward Willow Spring, the cowboy rides, now alternately trotting and walking his horse.

A.J. Howell, fifty-three years of age, bosses the Cross Seven Land and Cattle Company headquartered at Tonto Basin. On the afternoon of August 2, 1892, he is mounted and driving two young dray horses down the Pleasant Valley trail a dozen miles northeast of Fort McDowell. As his animals round a bend, they are spooked by the abrupt appearance of another horseman. Howell must rein and spur his own horse leftward to drive his loose team back to the road, yet he has moments to steal glances. The stranger cradles a shotgun or a Winchester across his saddle. The horse presents something of a mystery of color—mostly light bay, but on the rump seemingly marked with spots of roan. Maybe, thinks Howell, dried sweat on a horse ridden hard on a hot day a long distance. Howell places his encounter with the lone horseman a good thirty-five miles from Tempe, some time between four and five o'clock. Howell adds:

I couldn't describe him to save my life. . . . My horses that I had ahead of me, they sprung off to the left, and my attention was drawed turning them back into the road more than anything else. . . . Just as he come around so he saw me, he taken out I think a kind of red handkerchief and he commenced wiping his face in this way [showing], and he kept wiping his face until he passed me; so I didn't see his face so as to recognize him at all.[11]

And quickly, the horseman rounds a bend in the trail, and is gone.

With much sound and fury, a posse of Salt River Valley citizens organizes to pursue the eastward-fleeing assassin. Samuel W. Finley, fulltime bartender at Bowen's Saloon in Tempe, declines an invitation to join the posse. Firstly, Finley says, the posse effort is futile. Secondly, if Edwin Tewksbury is indeed the wanted man, Finley tells the press, he could be summoned "with a postal card. If he knows that John Rhodes is in jail, Tewksbury will surrender himself of his own accord."[12] The remark is seized upon for derision and sarcasm. A newsman predicts that Finley will go to bed with Tewksbury, and when Ed sleeps, Finley will slip the handcuffs on him. Alas, "Ed Tewksbury returned that postal card unopened."[13]

Finley shrugs off the abuse. He studies the tracks of the suspects' horses at the Double Buttes School, swears himself in as a special deputy to Sheriff Montgomery, takes pains to pack carefully for a five-hundred-mile trailride, and on the evening of August 2, strikes out for the Reno Road. On the trail, he meets A.J. Howell, who informs him that a rider fitting Tewksbury's description had spooked his broncs in a sand wash near Sugarloaf, east of the Adams Ranch. Later, Finley will explain:

Being advised of the passage of a horseman ahead of me, I followed the trail carefully. The horse tracks were those of a large horse, wearing about a Number Two and smooth. The rider passed Bassett's Goat Ranch, this side of Reno Hill, about dusk on the second. He then took the short cut from Moore's to Crawford's, going north over the mesa to avoid passing the Cross Seven Store; thence north about ten miles to the junction of Wild Rye and Tonto Creek, where I dropped it. The unknown rider was met by a Mexican who described him as a short man wearing a regular cowboy hat, having a rifle in hand, and mounted on a large roan horse with no brands visible.[14]

Thereupon Finley realizes that he is not only following a substitute horse but by now, a decoy rider. Finley accepts the trick philosophically. No matter. Sheriff's Deputy Finley doesn't need an unbroken trail to know precisely where he can find Ed Tewksbury.

II. Drinkers of the Wind

Ten things Ed Tewksbury believed would now help save his neck from the noose. Foremost, his relay of swift, hardy horses.

Then, second, his Winchester. Third, the infinite impotency of Arizona law even as late as 1892. Certainly fourth, whatever his future, Ed could draw strength from the satisfaction of putting his despised enemy Tom Graham six feet into the ground for good.[1] Fifth, Ed counted upon steadfast friends and family. Sixth, if Ed ever had to stand trial, it would be before a jury of sodbusters and merchants who had forgotten (if they ever knew) the feeling of a real mountain cowhorse at the peak of its age and condition between your legs. Seventh, although possessing little money of his own, Ed had access to plenty. Eighth, his watch. Ninth, whiskey. And not necessarily last, himself. With his lathered horse still pushing a fast walk, Tewksbury cleared the outskirts of Mesa and wryly smiled to himself: Ed Tewksbury was still one formidable man, as big in real life as in reputation. Not to be messed with.

Did you see the expression on the face of that ridiculous Mesa lawman? He must have been told I was heading his way, but the fool never dreamed I'd ride right down the middle of Main Street. So he sees me coming, and rushes out onto the porch with a double-barreled shotgun I'll bet charged with enough buckshot to blow me to hell, and I just keep my horse in a walk, and stare that lawman right in the eye. And he doesn't have the guts to even raise the gun. Just lets me ride by. . .doesn't dare shoot even when my back is to him.[2]

When he shot Tom Graham, Ed Tewksbury was riding a horse named Jack. Getaway was Jack's part, and the big gelding gave its all through ten miles of loping and trotting. At the first relay station north of Mesa, Tewksbury threw his saddle on another borrowed horse. The next relay was waiting thirty miles north by east near Otero's. The next, fifteen miles more, at the western portal to Reno Pass. It was twelve miles then to abandoned Fort Reno, and another sixteen to Bouquet's Ranch. At Bouquet, Ed had stashed his stallion, Sockwad, a full brother to Jack. Bred and foaled around 1883 on the Tewksbury Ranch, both were deep-chested sorrels with white hind feet and other markings so similar that even family members had difficulty telling them apart standing side by side.[3] Now across the flat Salt River Valley farm fields, Ed pushed his remount for distance.

Most of these flatlanders can't imagine what a man and a horse can do. Alf DeVore heard in Globe that Mama had newmonia. He forked his pony and headed for his ranch—sixty-mile ride that day. Changed horses and lit out after dark for Medicine Camp. . . .He covered the fifteen mile by midnight but found we was gone, so followed the trail to Pole Corral. We'd left thar. He lit matches to find our sign. When he got to our camp we was out on the trapline, so he fixed himself some coffee and jerky and spuds and cold biskits, and left me a note. It was thirty miles back to his ranch. He'd rode one hundred thirty mile horseback in thirty hours without rest. . . .

Such was workaday. But Tewksbury horses were among the best of the Southwest's native-bred stables. Fifty years later, some of Sockwad's hot blood might course the veins of the founding registry of the American Quarter Horse Association. From Arab, Turk, and Barb studs bred with a band of English mares in American colonial times, the cross resulted in the compact, muscled, balanced steed unexcelled in the world for covering any distance from a standing start up to a quarter of a mile. The horse of Revere, Washington, Lee. But other qualities endeared the breed to American westerners. Expansive arenas of work and play required a type of horse with dependable common sense, catlike agility, gentle disposition, pleasing conformation (including a practical saddle back), a willingness to make do with just about any food available, self-cleaning, durable hooves, and marvelous endurance. In short, the most versatile breed of horse the world has ever known. Such prepotent bloodlines spread from the mid-Atlantic to anywhere humans needed a deft and doughty equine partner in battle or work: New England, Missouri Valley, Texas, Colorado, California. They'd plow, climb, soldier, draw, trail, pack, and rein all day, and go out and win an evening race. But their shining destiny was to outmaneuver an unpenned calf, and two years later outlast the resulting grown steer all the way to a railtown. Such a horse progenitor was Sockwad.[5]

Good riders, good horses. How far can they go? I guess we'll find out today, even if I have to kill a couple of each. The only way I can preserve my hide is to cover a hundred seventy miles in less than a day. A hot day. Maybe the hottest day of the year.

Yesterday I made sure I was seen near Pleasant Valley. Tomorrow morning I have to show myself as far east as Newton's, away on the the other side of Pleasant Valley. Every piece of this plan has to fit together. It better. . . .[6]

Here's how Tewksbury's relay was set up: "Louis Naegelin said that Tewksbury had a relay of horses, from Mesa or Tempe to Pleasant Valley. Jess Mullen said that Abe and Frank Watkins and another fellow had a corral in Mesa and they managed a relay of horses for Ed. . . .It is strongly believed that Ed was back in the Valley on the second of August, all right. . . .But it was entirely possible to ride across country on horseback if you knew the trails in the time Tewksbury had to do it in, about twelve hours."[7] On the first of August, Ed made himself obvious riding Sockwad, buying fruit, passing time around Pleasant Valley. Then go! He might have taken the most direct dash by Buzzard Roost or under Greenback Peak to Bouquet's, where he hid out Sockwad; thence by relay horses across Tonto Creek, over Reno pass, Sunflower, Dos Esses ranch, Sycamore Creek to the Verde, past Fort McDowell to the Salt River Valley where Jack was waiting.[8]

My, my! I wonder what color horse they'll swear I was riding? Let's see—there are a half dozen bays, that many more chestnuts, and at least that number of sorrels. Plus the duns and browns and roans—all mixed up with spots and paints and blazes. Ol' Jack's hind sox coulda been muddy, too. Same horse looks black when it's sweaty, might be called an appaloosa when the sweat dries to alkali. . . .Yep, there'll be somebody to take an oath on the Bible I was on a green hoss with six purple feet—ha![9]

If indeed the assassination plot sought to clutter eyewitness reports with contradiction, it worked masterfully. There's sound reason also to conclude that Tewksbury intended to encourage confusion regarding his own appearance. His wife-to-be helped camouflage him. "Ella [Ed's daughter] said that her mother's marriage to Ed was delayed by the trouble and that her mother had helped disguise Ed in readiness for the trip when he killed Graham."[10]

Now, the heat intensified as Ed drove his relay horse away from the murder scene. When the horse smelled or heard the Salt River running, Ed had only to give the eager animal its head due north, to a crossing under the brush dams the farmers maintained for diverting water into their irrigation canals. Ed allowed the horse to drink. . .not too much . . .and thus refreshed, with a belly wet inside and out, the horse stepped smartly along the old military supply road toward Fort McDowell. Here and there in the braided gravel bars of the Verde River the shade of towering cottonwoods afforded respite from the brass sun. From the watch pocket of his Levi's, Ed dug out a possession dearer to him than his .45-90.

Warm. Smooth. Glowing. Like a petite breast, sensually convex. Press the stem. A clamshell of eighteen-karat gold springs away from the ivory face of Waltham time-piece, Serial Number Q 2034. Tap the button. Nine hours. Twenty-one minutes. Thirteen seconds. Six tenths. Forty one-hundredths. God, that George Newton and I were friends. A man is lucky to have five friends like him in a lifetime, and me only a rancher and him an educated businessman—a jeweler! But we both admired fast horses, and the day he gave me this stopwatch, specially engraved with a mountain scene and a gaited stud and my name in calligraphy like spiderweb—that maybe was the tenderest moment I ever had with any man. We'd breed the best bloods we could buy, and train them up on Racehorse Flat above my old man's place, and I can hear George yelling, "How fast, Ed? What was the time, Ed?" Our horses built bottom on thin air with mother's milk, and when they were old enough to race, we'd challenge and beat horses that had reputations, but didn't know how to drink the mountain wind. Then, down at our old man's place—what a party we'd have with roasted pig and buttermilk and sweet corn and the women in print dresses and the men with pints in their boots![11]

Ed blinked away his reverie. The last of the army troops had been pulled out of Fort McDowell a couple of years ago. Then the federal commissioners decided the twenty-five-year-old post was too dilapidated and remote for an Indian school. But maybe the telegraph line to the fort was still working—and Ed couldn't run the risk that some of the ranchers along the Verde or some ambitious Indian agent might be planning a reception for him.[12] As usual in August, the Verde surged with flash-flood, but Ed's horse swam the fifty yards without difficulty while Ed held aloft his weaponry. Safely across, Ed took a deep pull from his whiskey flask.

Head hurts. Drank too much last night, this morning. Damn! It was dumb of me to get my shoes shined, and it was even stupider to go into Bowen's and grab that dude's cocktail off the bar and toss it down. I wasn't thinking very straight. Why is that for some men a shot of whiskey starts some of their sweetest memories, and the same shot of whiskey leads to some of their sorriest mistakes? Well, if it took likker to kill Tom Graham, drink can't be all bad. Either I had to do it or Johnny Rhodes was determined to do it.[13] My friends had set it all up. I had promised them to do it. Promised my family. Promised John's widow. Promised Braulia. But the whiskey. . .it gave me the nerve, but it made me too careless, too bold. The Rumberg woman saw me, knows me, and I let too many kids on the road get a look at my face. . .But how could we know Graham would be late? Three cigarets we rolled and smoked before he showed up. By then, young'uns were everywhere. Fishin'. Pickin' flowers. Ridin' buggies. Couldn't even see most of them until too late.

Well, it's done, and I've still got some whiskey to drink and a good hundred twenty miles to put behind me. I'll just keep in mind what ol' Buckey O'Neill put in his newspaper over in Prescott about the politician's speech about whiskey: "If you refer to that evil brew that softens the brains, ruins the kidneys, distorts the judgment, wrecks marriages, obliterates moral values and turns man into animal, I'm against it. But if, on the other hand, you refer to that magic potion that puts spring in the old man's step, stimulates conversation, enhances social contact, promotes the appetite and gives surcease of sorrow, then I am for it. That is my position on whiskey, gentlemen."

Ed Tewksbury managed a wry smile, even though he was tired to the gristle—not just from riding with almost no sleep for two days—but from weeks of screwing up his courage, and devising a plan, and positioning horses, and going without rest or decent chuck to see the assassination through. One unforeseen betrayal. . .one thrown horseshoe. . .could precipitate disaster. And Ed was not a well man. His Shoshone mother probably had died of it and his brothers had died of it and if a bullet or rope didn't get him first. . .quick or slow, it was still consumption, and despite what the newspapers advertised, no medicine helped it. What made tuberculosis worse was skulking around cold canyons and lying out in a soggy bedroll without a warm supper. That's when the hacking coughs wouldn't stop, and that's when the blood came up to dye a man's spit and close a cold hand at his throat. Ed once was whippet wiry; now he tended fleshy from the wracking, retching attacks, and from the whiskey that fought the fear. The labored heaving of his horse as it climbed up Sycamore Creek, around Romo Ranch by Sugarloaf, intruded on Ed's hearing. Not as often as knew he should, Ed let the pony stop and blow to repay the oxygen debt to the extremities and protect the horse's lungs from rupture.

But heat and alcohol and nerves conjured specters of pursuit, and as never before, Ed abbreviated the rest stops. "Horse," Ed said with unabashed sympathy, "when this wicked ride is done, I hope you and I don't have something awful in common."

At least I'm heading home. Four Peaks over there on the right, and rising the left, they call Mount Ord. Don't ask me how they measure it, but a government man once told me it was seven thousand feet above the ocean. The plants know. The greasewood gives up to the mesquite, and the palo verde thins out to the sycamore, and the Spanish bayonet makes way for the pinyon. At the base of Ord I can show you where the last giant cactus grows north. You almost know exactly how high you are in a cypress copse. Up on top of Ord once, eating hail stones mixed with wild strawberries, I could see all the way to Tucson to the south and all the way to Navajo Mountain to the north, and about as much east and west, damn near the length and breadth of the whole territory from one mountain top. . .whups!

In a sharp, blind bend under Sugarloaf, Ed Tewksbury came face to face with another lone rider—this one driving before him two half-broke colts. At the sight of Ed, the colts shied left and headed uphill. Cursing at this unexpected complication, the drover spurred and reined his saddle horse upslope and parallel to the stampede to prevent the colts from doubling back. Tewksbury recognized the man in an instant, and instinctively reined off his left side of the trail, and in so doing, he raised a hand and kerchief to his face. As quickly as the little rodeo began, it was over, and during the commotion the other man could only glance sideways a time or two. Then the two horsemen lost sight of one another altogether.

Judge A.J. Howell! How long were my odds, that on the day I murder a man in broad daylight, and need to establish an alibi, on maybe the hottest afternoon of the year when all sane livestock men are letting their animals doze as much as possible, I meet a well-acquainted justice of the peace pushing a pair of colts down my trail? And him! A sheep-hating cowman, to boot![14] Maybe I should have...no, I couldn't just shoot a man like that who never did anything against me. But dammit, I'm running into too many unexpected people.

Sun almost feels good on my back. The heat goes out of this country in a hurry, when the down-canyon breeze takes hold. ... I'll say this, when those army boys built a road, they meant for it to stay![15] I don't hate the army; don't much like it, either. But when I scouted for the army back in '82, it was because those Indians had stole Dad's horses. I didn't even hold hard thoughts against the Indians—hell, my first Maw was Indian. People think I'm a Cherokee, and I tell 'em if I was a Cherokee I'd be a *good-looking* Indian, but we were Shoshone, not very *good-looking* Indians![16] No, I just don't think I'd ever get used to being cooped up, or hearing some sergeant yelling, " 'Toon, count off by fours! Ones and twos dismount and hold horses. Threes and fours, forward. . .!" At the battle of Big Dry Wash the calvary was so badly mounted, they had to ride home on Indian ponies! Mostly, though, I don't want to be told where to stay and what to eat and how to act. I think, almost, I'd rather hang than that.

This passage of Ed's flight may have been most precarious. Over Reno Pass and past the ruins of the sutler's and spring, the horse Ed rode for this leg of the relay faltered. Any number of misfortunes may have overtaken the ambitious plan. The horse may have wedged a sharp stone in the frog of a hoof. Or overheated, it may have suffered cramps fording the chill flood of Tonto Creek. On the thinnest of lingering evidence: Ed purposely elected to sacrifice the future of the horse in his own need for salvation. . .his requirement to reach Bouquet Ranch and his waiting Sockwad. Mercilessly, he raked the horse with his spurs, whipped it with reins, cursed it, kicked it up, urged it, denied it breath. For decades engraved in the lore of the Tonto, old men and children told and retold of the pitiful sight of a splendid horse, standing spraddle-legged in Bouquet's pasture, trembling, heaving strings of saliva and blood. That horse, as they always ended the tale, was never worth a damn after that.[17]

There is the union with a woman, and for men who ride well, something of that embrace between me and this great horse. My stepmother Lydia had words for sentiments of this kind. She was a lady of education and from books she could tell us about the importance and sculpture and spirit of good breeding lines of horses. She is the one who told me of the Arabian, the foundation of the light breeds, and it was Lydia who could quote Keats and Byron and Macaulay. Arab blood heats thoroughbreds and our good cutting horses and roping horses. Lydia told us Napoleon's *Morengo*, an Arab, traveled 50,000 miles in its lifetime. Such, the progenitor, of what moves with such strength and grace beneath me. Lydia would tell me: *My horse is black like a night without moon or stars./He was foaled in immense solitudes/He is a drinker of the wind/A son of a drinker of the wind/His dam was also of a noble breed/Our warrior horsemen have named him Sabok/The very lightning cannot overtake him/May God save him from the Evil Eye.*[18]

"How did it go?"

"He is killed. The hole came out of his throat. There was blood on everything. His hat was in the road. I looked into his face. His eyes were rolled up white. It was fatal."

"Did anybody see you?"

"Everybody saw me. We always said secrecy would be difficult. Tempe overflows with people. All along the Salt there are people. Near Adams Ranch I met Judge Howell driving colts."

"Sorry-ass luck."

"Maybe not. He was busy chasing colts. He may see the wisdom of not seeing what he saw."

"Anything else?"

"I killed a horse getting over Reno. It's at Bouquet's."

"No matter."

"What do you want me to do today?"

"Go to work. Show yourself about. Talk about the time and the date. Remember today's just the second, and we can prove you were here on the first. Go down to the Tanks, and if I hear anything, I'll let you know."

There is never an hour of any day that some sort of bird is not calling. Listen, now, to that poorwill singing in the dark. Earlier, as I was falling asleep, the horned owl came into the Tanks to hunt. Now in first light, the titmice are peeping through the trees, and way off there I hear a flock of ravens complaining about the eagle. I see that golden eagle polish a bluff, soaring, peering, free, perfectly controlled, deadly, selfish, above it all. It is as I am, with my Winchester. With my six-shooter. Old man Horton was there the night the black man wouldn't serve me in the saloon at Globe. Insulted me. I shot him. Put a white crease right down the center of that black man's scalp, and I'm sort of glad I didn't kill him, because as old man Horton would go on telling it the rest of his life, "Ed Tewksbury? You mean he was Ed Tewksbury? Why, if I knew it was Ed Tewksbury, he could have had the whole damn place!"[19]

And my old man—he was practically a press agent for me. That time I tangled with that mama bear two years ago. The paper wrote, "Ed Tewksbury had a perilous encounter with a bear one day last week near Berranger's ranch on Cherry Creek. . . .Panthers had been killing colts and Ed started out for their scalps. He struck a fresh trail on rocky ground but couldn't tell what kind of animal he was following until having gone a short distance, he came suddenly upon a she-bear of the Silver Tip variety, with cubs. Mrs. Bruin resented his intrusion and charged fiercely upon Ed, who met the attack with a shot from his Winchester, which, however, did not stop the bear. Attempting to throw a second cartridge into place, it was flung to the ground and before another could be adjusted Tewksbury was in the embrace of the savage beast. He was bitten in the left hand and right knee and was reaching for his knife when the bear released him . . . .Two well-directed shots finished her. Mr. J.D. Tewksbury, our informant, stated that his son's wounds while painful were not thought to be dangerous.[20]

Bert Pratt was another one to make me eight feet tall. He used to tell everybody, "Ed was a remarkable marksman. He practiced a fast draw. He wore his gun under his vest and always had the vest unbuttoned. . .kept his hand folded across his breast, and almost upon the handle of the gun. If you were riding with him and he saw a crow or a buzzard, there would be a flash, and a shot, and the bird would drop dead, but no one would see the gun drawn. Then there was the day Ed shot the burro. We were camped at Salt River diving to find George Newton's body, and a burro got into our camp and stole our food, spilling flour everywhere. We had to go to a ranch to get more food. As we went along the trail, Ed called my attention to a burro looking down from a shelf above. The critter's head was covered with flour. Ed said, 'Watch me mark the rascal.' Ed brought his pistol to his hip, two quick flashes, no aiming, no outstretched arm. Then as we passed the animal the next day Ed said, 'Let's see what I did to the beast.' We looked and in the tip of each ear there was a little round hole, the marks that Ed had put on him."[21]

George Wilson, twenty-one years of age in 1892 yet Ed Tewksbury's nominal ranch boss, male successor to the economic leadership of his sister's considerable estate, ramrod of the Flying V, and involved up to his handsome eyebrows in the management of the horse relay, whistled self-consciously as he walked his horse down-canyon to the little lean-to lineshack where he had sent Ed Tewksbury to recuperate.

"You know something?"

"Finley's here. He says Tom Graham identified you."

"He couldn't! Graham's dead."

"Finley asked for you, and I said you'd come in, and if you did that, he would protect your life until the trial."

"You're still with me?"

"No matter what."

"I'm about packed. I've been expecting you."

III. "Ma, Do You Have Scissors?"

By the middle of the 1880s, the American West was filling fast. Although the game of golf had not yet crossed the Atlantic, California was prospering through its fourth decade of statehood. The boundaries of states and states-to-be of the nation largely were scribed. Not one building anywhere in America exceeded ten stories, but the Brooklyn Bridge was nearing completion, and well over a hundred thousand miles of railroad stitched together a union of fifty-five million Americans. Geronimo, symbolic of aboriginal resistance, had not yet surrendered. Already there were a million and a half Texans, and the population center of the United States was traversing Ohio, hurrying to Illinois.

On a four-color map ambitiously published as a companion to the leather-bound *Elliott's History of Arizona Territory 1884*,[1] the cartographer dutifully located literally hundreds of places of occupation: the territorial capital of Prescott, the Spanish pueblo of Tucson, the fabulous silver strike dubbed Tombstone, and the paddle wheel steamship port called Yuma. And not so obviously, the mapmaker also entered a dot for each and every tiny Charming Dale, Fort Defiance, and Chloride City.

Yet, in all the expansive watershed of Cherry Creek and other drainages

27

associated with Pleasant Valley and Tonto Basin, in a stretch of country encompassing some five thousand square miles and more—not one settlement was deemed worthy of inclusion in that map of 1884. Not one.

Even the minute names tucked into the perimeters of the Tonto country were tentative: Green Valley then, to become Payson later; Robinson's Grove, doomed to be drowned by another generation's irrigation reservoir; Forest Dale, not even to appear on a future official map of Arizona. This was the arena of the bloodletting that would begin as the Graham-Tewksbury Feud and end as the Pleasant Valley War.

On enormous scale, the setting was mindful of a geographical poker table: a horizon-wide sensuous green circle around which growing communities of gigantic ambition pulled up chairs for no-limit jackpot. Globe could have tossed in the first ante from its tall stacks of silver and copper chips (". . . in 1886 the camp bragged that all the copper coins minted by the United States Government were being made from bullion extracted at Globe.") Phoenix was more adept at dealing docile desert Indians out of their water rights; Prescott, wise to the worth of fawnskin sacks of gold dust, knew more of price than value of humanity; into another seat slumped Holbrook, reeking of cheap whiskey and cheaper perfume; most of St. Johns created wealth from communal sweat, but one element got rich financing at a premium a government purposely balanced on the brink of bankruptcy. The economic stakes were enormous for Tonto Basin, of greater area than some Atlantic states. By the time the last hand was dealt, the gamble attracted distant players—Albuquerque and Salt Lake City and Tucson and Los Angeles, for example—and kibitzers even farther off like San Francisco, Tacoma, Dallas, Boston, and Washington.

Pleasant Valley was settled late for good reason. The broad, open avenues easily sprawled east-west across Arizona; north-south travel would remain comparatively adventuresome even into an era when men frolicked on the moon. When Kearny's dragoons dashed from Santa Fe to San Diego in 1846 to secure the Southwest for America, they descended the west-flowing Gila River. When surveyors sought ways to turn wheels between California and the national middle, an attractive option was a vast chord of the Colorado Plateau that forms the northern one-third of Arizona. Again, the gentler natural grades extended east and west. Those back-and-forth sweeps, difficult though they were, were the logical routes for troops, forty-niners, mule-skinners, camel-drivers, and track-layers.

Not so easy was travel aligned with the compass needle. Beaver trapper James Ohio Pattie called Grand Canyon "horrid." He wanted to get across. The two-hundred-fifty-mile-long abyss so thwarted explorers, the Colorado River through the Inner Gorge wasn't navigated by white boatmen until after the Civil War. The other grand-scale geographical feature oriented east-west was the abrupt southern edge of the Colorado

Plateau. The Mogollon Rim confronted travelers not only with its own series of immense canyons, but with rocky ramparts extending nearly from Arizona's Grand Canyon deep into central New Mexico. Little wonder that Coronado, testing a northward path through Arizona in 1540, called it "a way worse than ever."[2]

Hard to get to. That was the reality of nineteenth-century central Arizona. The tablelands perched at five, six, seven thousand feet, with peaks above twelve. The escarpment of the Mogollon Rim here and again plunged fifteen hundred feet. Passes were few. Pleasant Valley—pristine and prime—was positioned almost dead center in the transition zone from rim to the low-lying Sonoran Desert.

In a day's ride, a horseman experienced the climate change from Mexico to Canada: cacti to conifers, roadrunners to snow geese, sand dunes to cinder cones, dust devils to driving blizzards, putrid pot holes to springs nectarous as chill wine, buried firewood to mile-high seashells, daylit desert mirages to magnified nighttime starscapes. In such a topographical spectrum, one could make a list of two hundred species of birds and six hundred kinds of plants. Included in forms of life would be a rat that never drinks, a dwarf cactus sitting atop a hundred-pound bulb, a giant cactus that sucks a ton of water from a summer shower, a toad that sleeps a year, a poorwill that hibernates with bated breath and heartbeat, a lizard that blows up like a balloon, and symbiotic moths and lilies.

Yet another extraordinary life form worked its will through Pleasant Valley as late as the 1880s. While foreign players shuffled themselves hands in the Tonto Basin play, the wild card for a while remained the wily, wiry, whimsical Apache. They were not a chivalrous enemy. When the Christian Cline family drove in one of Tonto's first cattle herds from California, they passed the startling figure of a white man, quite dead, lashed to a tree, his penis amputated and stuffed in his mouth.[3]

The Apaches themselves were relative newcomers—southwestern people for only a few centuries. Of Athabascan lineage, the Apaches drifted down from the north and appropriated as hunting grounds the upland home of less aggressive tribes. Evidence of human occupation for thousands of years, prehistoric ruins dotted the cliffs and vales of Pleasant Valley.

Ceding of lands by Mexico to the United States meant nothing to the Apaches. "No Indian had more virtues and none has been more truly ferocious when aroused."[4] Apaches knew every arbor and gulch of their broken, varied range. They were as at home on the desert floor as in the "steepest, highest, rockiest mountains where one would not believe a bird would dare to fly."[5] By the time Americans moved in, the Apaches represented the most effective human resistance from West Texas to Central Arizona, from Colorado to Chihuahua. Few homelands were as highly prized by the Apaches as the Eden white men began to call Pleasant Valley.

How was Pleasant Valley named? The conventional assumption: "descriptive."[6] Perhaps, although no shred of written record seems to survive to support that theory. There does repose in the National Archives a map of one of the early United States cavalry sorties from Fort McDowell, September 27-October 6, 1866. This bold invasion of *Apacheria* crossed to the eastern drainage of Tonto Creek and pushed due east from "North Masatzal Mtn.," probably Mount Ord. The scale and geometry of the hand-inked map suggests a penetration of thirty or forty miles beyond Tonto Creek along such long-forgotten landmarks as "Bedrock Creek" and "Mt. Titty" and curiously, "Crescent Cr." running through the large "Crescent Valley." The smudged and scratchy script of the anonymous army chart maker at some official level may have been misread as "Pleasant" instead of "Crescent," a supposition at least as valid as the wholly unsupported claim of "descriptive" for Pleasant. For Pleasant Valley was also crescent-shaped, and as long as the Apaches held title, the valley was not particularly pleasant for white squatters.[7]

Consider the agonies inflicted upon the Meadows and Middleton ranches. Neither family was first in Tonto Basin, but they both tried to take possession of a corner of Apacheland before the original tenants were permanently evicted. The dire results made only minor footnotes to the larger saga: for three decades an Apache nation of five thousand disrupted the expansion of a nation of fifty million; toward the end of one of humankind's classic guerrilla wars, a few hundred Apache braves were tying down one-half the combat troops of the United States. A general newly in command of these troops reported to Washington: "A more terror-stricken class of people than the citizens of these territories I have never found. . . . "[8]

In the 1880s, banished to reservations headquartered at hot, dry San Carlos and high, lonesome Fort Apache, the once free-roaming sub-tribes chafed under the often-conflicting orders of the civilian Indian agents and military commanders, restricted movement, a demeaning dole of marginal rations, corrupt white management, loss of choice lands, and forced residency with traditional Indian enemies.

Usually all it took to incite rebellion was a *tiswin* (intoxicating native drink) party, a hopeful dream of a medicine man, or an Anglo's bad administrative judgment. All three factors—plus the heady power of several thousand rounds of stolen army ammunition—put Nan-tia-tish on the warpath through Pleasant Valley in the summer of 1881.

Six years earlier, on a small tributary of Canyon Creek near the western boundary of the White Mountain Apache reservation, William Middleton built a small log cabin with a shake roof and shuttered, unglazed windows. Middleton's herd of milk cows from California may have been the first sizeable herd in Pleasant Valley.[9] For the Middleton butter-making enterprise, a log dugout milk-house anchored an angle of a fenced back yard.

Of twelve Middleton children, six younger ones still lived at the ranch. On September 6, all hands were busy with chores—rounding up horses, nailing together butter cartons, churning cream. Two young neighbor men, George Turner and Henry Moody, rushed in from Globe with news that Indian raiders were on the loose after a battle afield with soldiers, followed by an assault on Fort Apache. Though forewarned, most of the Middletons resumed work after their midday dinner. A few Indians appeared. Peaceful conversation ensued: a wish to borrow a cook pot, a request for food. Mrs. Middleton was obligingly handing a loaf of bread through the milk-house window when one of the braves yelled, "Now!" and a volley of rifle fire raked the yard.

Turner, walking to get a cup of buttermilk, fell dead. Moody, seated on the porch, also died instantly, a bullet in the eye. Father William Middleton and son Willis, thirteen, scampered from the milk-house to the main cabin. Eighteen-year-old Henry Middleton grabbed up the family's only weapon, a rifle, and was looking for a target when another Indian fusillade peppered the cabin. A bullet zipped through a crack in the log wall and smacked Henry in the shoulder above the heart. Now Mrs. Middleton and the rest of her children fluttered across the courtyard through another volley and miraculously tumbled unhurt into the cabin. For the Middletons, there followed an afternoon of blistering battle, a harrowing night hiding in brush, a brutal hike to Globe. The raid cost the Middletons seventy-five good horses.

Late next spring, Henry Middleton's shoulder was about healed when Nan-tia-tish again bolted the reservation, raided here and there, and again beset the Middleton Ranch, this time not only stealing the Middleton horses, but unmounting a heavily armed troop of the irregular Globe Rangers. That was enough for the Middletons. They moved to town and sold the ranch to George Newton and J.J. Vosburgh.

Now well-mounted, Nan-tia-tish and company thundered through Pleasant Valley. They stole more horses from the Tewksbury and Rose families.[10] They surprised and slew prospectors [Charles] Sixby and [Louis] Houdon on Haigler Creek

. . . and attacked Bob Sixby as he was entering his cabin with a bucket of water. He was shot through the lungs but managed to bar the door and brace himself up against one of the gunholes of the cabin, put up a desperate resistance—pools of blood indicated that he killed no less than a dozen of the renegades."[11]

Sixby survived, not so much by his grit than by pure chance. A trooper on the trail of Nan-tia-tish wrote in his diary:

. . . the Indians rushed the cabin and set it afire. Instead of coming out, Bob Sixby clambered up inside the large fireplace chimney. H Troop, also on the trail of the erring Indians, happened along and sighted the smouldering ruins of the cabin. The Indians had gone, thinking their victim had perished in the flames.

In rummaging through the debris of the cabin we saw a movement in the fireplace and, on closer investigation, we saw that it was a man wedged in the chimney. Only his feet were visible. We pulled him out with some difficulty. He came out fighting but soon heaved a sigh of relief when he saw that it was us rather than the Indians.

... The Indians' next stop was a ranch, owned by a Frenchman on Tonto Creek. The owner saw the Apaches coming and escaped to a hiding place on a nearby mountain side. He watched the savages set the buildings afire and saw all his belongings go up in smoke. He was lucky.

... We found Houdon and [Charles] Sixby alongside the trail, about a mile from the Frenchman's ranch.... Both men were naked, lying face up, and bore many marks of torture inflicted on them before they died. Their feet and hands were burned. One had a large rock on his stomach. The other had been hacked wide open....[12]

And so on. Nan-tia-tish could afford his own losses. By some official estimates he led as many as two hundred fifty adults on his rampage northward through Tonto Basin. The route of the raiders then aimed directly for the homestead of the John Meadows family near Diamond Point some fifteen miles northeast of Payson.

More prudent Rim Country settlers had by now heeded the army's advice and retreated to Fort McDonald, a flat-topped hillock abutting the hamlet of Payson.[13] But assuming the danger past, Meadows took his wife, four sons, and daughter, and even a young woman house guest, back to the Diamond Point ranch on July 14. Hard to believe, the Meadows family possessed perhaps only one and no more than two reliable firearms. Next day, according to Mrs. Meadows' oft-told account:

It was early in the morning and we heard the dogs barking. My husband said, "My dogs are baying a bear. I'll take my gun and go over there and kill it." I saw him pass that bare spot [a bit of open ground] and just as he entered those vines on the other side, the Indians opened fire. I saw him fall. They kept up one continuous war whoop and a continual rain of bullets were falling on the house and yard. The boys rushed out with guns to save their pa. The kicking up of the sand around them showed how thick the bullets were falling. I could not see how they got back to the house without being shot all to pieces. [Henry], the oldest, always directed all the works. He had us pile up sacks of flour or any other sacks in such a way as to furnish protection from any stray bullet.

... During that time I was so excited ... but I noticed that the boys looked pale. John came to me and said, "Ma, can you get me some splints?"

"Yes, what's the matter?"

"My arm is all shot to pieces."

... A little later Henry came to me and said, "Ma, have you a pair of scissors?"

"Yes, here they are."

He made a quick movement and I saw something fall to the floor. It was part of his entrails. He said afterward that he knew he could not live long, and that he wanted to save his mother and the children before he passed on.[14]

Thanks to a neighbor's alarm, Payson learned of the siege at about the time another son, Charley, arrived on the Globe stage. Charley joined forces with Marion Derrick, veteran Tonto freighter and Indian fighter, and several other local men, including Carter Hazelton, to ride to the rescue. They reached the cabin about simultaneously with the cavalry, sixty loyal Apache Indian scouts, and their famous and infamous leaders, Al Sieber, Tom Horn, and Mickey Free.[15]

Now in pursuit of Nan-tia-tish a formidable army converged. Feeling invincible, the defiant Indians dawdled along, but soon fifteen troops of cavalry were about to drum down upon them "like a lead storm."[16] By the sixteenth of July, soldiers from five Arizona army posts pressed the renegades up the Tonto Rim on the Old Navajo Trail. Suspecting a trap at an ideal defensive position near General Springs, the soldiers set one of their own. With Major Adna R. Chaffee as battle commander, the troops on July 17 baited the Indians with a column of cavalry on white horses, and then outflanked the distracted natives. In the ensuing close-quarter Battle of Big Dry Wash, the last significant pitched struggle of the Arizona Indian wars, Apache fatalities numbered about twenty-two. On the army side, one Apache scout was killed and several soldiers wounded. Had a severe, high-country thunderstorm not obscured the battlefield for twenty minutes, Indian losses surely would have been greater.[17]

The proximate cause of catastrophe is seldom anticipated. Neither are good times predictable. But gradually people realized that the days of Indian depredation were about done, and that Pleasant Valley again promised paradise. A few hardy individuals and families took the chance and did well. Then, word of the valley's seemingly inexhaustible grass and timber spread. Settlement accelerated.[18]

David Harer may have been the first to acquire a trouble-free *Apacheria* meadow of his own, in Greenback Valley in 1875. He went to the Indians, made friends, promised to share his fruit and beef at harvest time, and kept his word. The Indians let him be. "Old Man" Gentry went Dave one better. . .married an Apache woman and gained the whole Athabascan race as in-laws. William Burch, in putting down roots in 1876, was so remote in the Payson area that his brand served as the only place name for a while. Not long afterward, David Gowan was hunting horses when he stumbled onto quite a rock formation: Tonto Natural Bridge, the largest travertine arch in the world.

The Gordons came, froze out, and moved to a warmer clime, but their name remained on a canyon. L.J. Horton's rhapsodic recollection of Pleasant Valley's early days literally sings of a land of grapevines and black walnuts, acres of wild iris and pools of watercress, flowing milk and free honey—and unflagging, neighborly dairy folks peddling butter at a dollar a pound and bee nectar at a dollar a quart to the well-paid miners of Globe. Dutch bachelors Louis and William Naegelin put their name on a rim-like mountain which would never be famous—yet taller than the highest elevations of thirty-six of America's eventual fifty states. Lost in the Tonto country, Naegelin Rim, at 7,117 feet above sea level, would qualify as a national park if it had occurred in New York.

Florance A. Packard earned his first Tonto Basin pocket money hunting mountain lions—for which the government paid him twenty dollars bounty each. George Allen, near the mouth of Tonto Creek, raked wild hay into windrows, and he milked a herd of Devonshire cows. Revilo (Oliver spelled backward) Fuller, as early as 1877, freighted off the rim into Tonto Basin by dragging a braking log on a chain behind his wagon. Christopher C. Cline, his five sons, and four hundred cows from San Diego caused a population explosion of both bovines and humans on the lower Tonto. Andrew and Samuel Houston, six miles east by north of Payson, felt bad when Old Man Star died, so when they fenced Star Valley they made sure the grave was on the *cienega* side and wouldn't be trampled by livestock. Levi Berger had two partners at his spread on Little Green Valley: his brother-in-law, and a bull brought all the way from England. William O. St. John, at his mining claim south of Payson, caroused with his old army buddies, and built up a herd of goats to five thousand. J.H. Baker went up on Aztec Mountain, raised twenty-two tons of potatoes one summer, built a trail over a mountain range to Silver King, and sold the spuds for half a cent a pound. Ike Lothian, a Missourian, didn't have any cattle in 1877, but he had two mules and a horse, so he plowed the virgin Strawberry Valley, brought off a bumper crop of corn, fed it to his hogs, butchered them, cured the meat, and packed it off for sale to several army posts.

LaTereatte, January, McDonald. The names of the Tonto were the roster of America. *Roundtree, Freeman, Randall.* They were English and everything else. *Pyeatt, Haught, Nebuchar.* The names went upon the peaks, and down the draws. *Clark, Willis, Sanders, Gowan, Ward.* Lemmings on the rebound from California, gone broke Oklahomans halfway to the Promised Land. *Ashur, Sears, Mullen, Booth, Connelly.* Many were Mormons far from a temple; some were Roman Catholics even farther from a cathedral. *Conway, Protero, Boyd, Lawler.* They'd drag all of their possessions to a clearing, raise a tent, and call it home forever. *Dudley, Felton, Watkins.* Some had a belly-full of the war between brothers; others just wanted a Second Chance. *Craig, Hicks, Weber, Vogel, Griffin.* They had the peculiar courage to put down a dug well, straight sides, and stand at the bottom staring up forty feet to daylight. *Hazelwood, Armer, Crouch, Church, Drew, Nash, Haigler.* Women brought rose canes, tomato seeds, and Kentucky pole beans in a sack marked hope. *Cole, Chase, Higden, Hill.* Kids went to school by horse, with maybe a pistol in a saddlebag. *Fisk, Stahl, Robbins, Donohue, Christopher.* "The cowards stayed home," they'd laugh about their Eastern forebears. "And the weak died on the way." *Coler, McClintock, Chilson, Lazon, Fain.*

Irvin M. House began prowling the Tonto country in 1876 in search of valuable minerals—and indeed he discovered the Golden Waif Mine four miles southwest of Payson. But his strangest assignment was surveying a Globe-Flagstaff railroad that put down thirty-five miles of track before the scheme went broke. *Pyle, Gibson, Thompson.* Al Fulton was a cowboy, just passing through, in September, 1888, and up on the Rim at Lake Number One he was shot and killed for no known reason. Folks buried him decent, and put up a marker at Al Fulton Point. At least they remembered that he lived, and that he died. *Peach, Gray, Colcord.*[19] S.A. Haught said, "I started May 1, 1885, for Arizona from a point fifteen miles east of Dallas City, and was driving a hundred fifteen head of cattle. The Texas Panhandle had a quarantine on cattle south of the Texas and Pacific Railroad and I went through Indian Territory, thence through no mans' land to New Mexico, crossed the Rio Grande River at Albuquerque, then to Holbrook and Tonto Basin. It was four hundred fifty miles out my way . . . but I never lost a cow."[20] *Belluzzi, Packard, Boardman, Bonacker.* They arose before daylight and made fire and fetched water and slopped hogs and mended fence; they hitched teams, trapped wolves, fought fires; they filled lamps, carried ashes, scrubbed clothes; they watched their children die of diseases without names. *Robbins, Webb, Bowman, See.* They also experienced autumn in the Southwest, about 'a mile high: seemingly overnight the aspen turned flaxen, sumac to scarlet, oak to russet; bulbous pumpkins and dry pole beans; chill mornings and shirtsleeve afternoons; goodbye white-wing doves, hello Oregon juncos; split cedar, smoked pork, apple butter. Isadore Christopher twice was burned out by Indians, and he rebuilt with logs chinked with clay and hog's hair. *Franklin, Hilligas, Hise, Callahan.* If life became unbearable, there was Pieper's Dance Hall, an adobe saloon complete with gunports.

And if it should happen that you were Thomas Beach taking the hand of Maggie Meadows, and Charley Cole marrying Julia Hall, in the middle of an August day in Payson, and your new brother-in-law was the irrepressible Arizona Charley Meadows, he would announce to the wedding parties as they filed from the office of the justice of the peace:

It is my pleasure to offer, as my present to these newlyweds, that if all the parties in attendance will saddle up with their lariats and ride over my ranges, the brides and grooms can have any of my unbranded calves you can catch![21]

Eehah! Bridal bouquets and wishbook neckties were flung aside in favor of Stetsons and spurs. And away Payson rode in a twenty-mile calf scramble. By dusk, thirty-six head of Charley's dogies were roped and branded as starter stock for the newlyweds. Then Payson whacked the dust from its britches and powdered its sunburnt cheek, and danced the night away. Any wonder that the first organized cowboy tournament, or rodeo, occurred at Payson to be repeated as the August Doin's every year without fail for the next century and more?

When they came into the Tonto country, there were no subdivision plats or boundary markers. Most of the convoluted panoramas would not be surveyed until after the turn of the century; not an acre of Pleasant Valley could be tied to civilization's cornerstone: legal title to land. Newcomers attached to a relative or ally, looked about, espied an appealing dell, and moved in. Possession. Nine-tenths. By habit and handshake, metes would come together at three-hundred-year old oak trees, and bounds would take angle from Polaris, and length would derive from men's paces. A corner could be a boulder in a creek subject to flood, or—where no natural feature existed—a spot of soil blackened by a huge bonfire.[22]

Not until 1884 did Payson qualify for a post office, and that was a hard, two-day ride by horseback from Pleasant Valley. Fifteen miles northwest of Payson was the nearest law: a lanky Missouri pig farmer and magistrate only marginally literate. The railroad along the Southern Route did not enter Arizona until 1880, was not completed until 1882. Several years later, far to the north the Atlantic & Pacific's steel tracks energized four towns of note: the Holbrook shipping center, the Winslow railroad maintenance burg, the Flagstaff lumbering town, and the St. Johns county seat. Between, on faith and sometimes flawed vision, the Saints from Utah designated their agricultural villages: Snowflake, Woodruff, Eagar, Shumway, Taylor. Mormon influence at St. Johns was a sometimes-thing, for adjacent Concho made headquarters for gentile sheepmen and Hispanic herders. For some years after the railroad went by, the main street of St. Johns doubled as a demarcation—Mexicans to one side, Texans to the other, and God help a Mormon caught in the middle. The cattle-ranching Greer family fought its own range war with sheep interests funded from New Mexico.[23]

The convoluted trek of James Dunning Tewksbury to his Pleasant Valley was both unique, and typical of late nineteenth century-westering.[24] Perhaps of English or Welsh birth around 1823,[25] and assuredly with a quintessential old English name, Tewksbury was a Bostonian who may have married his lissome Shoshone Indian bride when she was a student in an Eastern school.[26] More likely, he was a bachelor argonaut—maybe a forty-niner over the Oregon Trail, or, as he told one man, one who came to the West Coast by sailing vessel via Cape Horn.[27] In Oregon, a staircase of dark, clean-limbed, striking Tewksbury children were born. By certain recollections, the elder Tewksbury brought west his passion for breeding and racing fine horses. The Tewskbury family in Oregon were considered propertied, wealthy, solid citizens, and were well-liked.[28]

But Tewksbury's foot itched. He cashed out in Oregon, and sought elsewhere his western dream. In San Francisco, Tewksbury, a devoted Mason, maintained membership in Mt. Moriah Lodge Number 44 from 1854 to 1866, when he withdrew and presumably moved on. He was a charter member in 1876 in a lodge in Battle Mountain, Nevada, where he listed his occupation, "miner."[29] A man who knew the Tewksburys at the Western Pacific Railroad junction of Battle Mountain in 1872 was struck by the beauty of Mrs. Tewksbury and the handsomeness of the children: John, about fourteen; Edwin, about twelve; James, about ten; and Elvira, about eight. A younger son was Frank. Tewksbury and his older boys were regulars at the horse races, where they entered some of their own steeds.[30]

Absent evidence, the cause of the Indian mother's death is left to latter-day speculation. When grown, three of her children would die prematurely of tuberculosis—possibly she breathed into her offspring not only life, but death. Tewksbury seemed never to mention his first wife's demise, but death set him drifting again, this time to Prescott, Arizona, in 1877. His children accompanied him.[31]

No doubt his horses did, too. According to descendants, "James D. Tewksbury first saw the Pleasant Valley from the Mogollon Escarpment when he and a group of men were following a herd of stolen stock. Tewksbury's party stopped there, deciding not to pursue the cattle. The stock would have been scattered among the trees in the direction of the White Mountain Apache Reservation."[32]

Not unusual for America and its western region, Tewksbury, with a large family of motherless youngsters, was attracted to a widow with a fatherless brood. The union November 6, 1879, of Tewksbury and Lydia Ann Shultes, a native of Wales and resident of Globe,[33] was conducted before a justice in Tempe, where Lydia owned cattle. Lydia had three children by two husbands now deceased. In time, the offspring could be categorized "his'n, her'n, and our'n."[34] The vaunted Tewksbury reputation for conviviality got a boost from the reporter who not only covered the news, but made some:

Mr. J.D. Tewksbury was married at 4 o'clock p.m. yesterday afternoon to Mrs. Lydia Shultes. The ceremony was performed by Justice H. Dunham. After the wedding the company partook of a fine repast, and then adjourned to the schoolhouse where dancing was kept up until midnight. The *Expositor* man got into the fun about 8 o'clock and the way he made that schoolhouse floor quake was something new to Tempe's terpsichorean bands.[35]

For a while, the older couple resided in Tempe. The four Tewksbury boys took the horse herd to Pleasant Valley, and on a Cherry Creek site likely selected by their father, built a cabin and bunkhouse, corrals, a smithy, and stables. The romance of the eldest boy, John, and Lydia's daughter, Mary Ann Crigger, culminated in their marriage in 1882. But for the occasional Indian outbreak, the idyllic life sought by Old Man Tewksbury for his clan seemed within reach. He and Lydia joined the boys at Pleasant Valley. The first of two sons born to James Sr. and Lydia arrived in 1881. The family set out an orchard of clingstone peach saplings. Lydia's green Welsh thumb nurtured rose bushes that continued to bloom and bristle along fence rows more than a century later.[36] While work reigned as the universal human lot, at Pleasant Valley, a party spirit eased the toil.

James D. Tewksbury Sr., who had lived for many years in California had grown accustomed to the Spanish custom of "Fiestas," and sponsored a yearly Fiesta at his ranch in Pleasant Valley. It was a gala affair, a beef was barbecued, horse races were matched and run, matched ropings were the order of the day, dancing, feasting and an all around pleasurable get-together for the settlers of lonely and isolated Pleasant Valley. The men loaded their families in wagons and came from far and near, the women bringing their most prized gourmet dish, and a fabulous time was had by all . . . .[37]

Four tranquil and productive years passed. But according to pioneer G.W. Shute, a fateful meeting occurred in the summer of 1882. Pleasant Valley could be a boring backwoods for young people, and when relief from duties permitted, the Tewksbury boys, by now in or approaching their twenties, would ride into Holbrook, Prescott, or Globe for a few days' recreation. On the agenda: drinking and gambling in some of the better saloons. Edwin Tewksbury, lithe and swarthy, on such occasions affected starched shirts, tie pins, and gloves; the man enjoyed being clean and neat.[38]

Ed Tewksbury left his mountain home and proceeded to the little mining town of Globe. Here, while walking up and down the single street that made up the business part of town, he met a tall, handsome young fellow who turned out to be Tom Graham.

Graham told Tewksbury that he was prospecting for a place to locate a herd of cattle. Tewksbury told Graham of a wonderful place where he had his own range with the result that when Tewksbury returned to Pleasant Valley, Tom went with him . . . .

Graham was greatly pleased at what he saw and stayed with the Tewksburys a few days, leaving with a promise to return as soon as he could with his outfit.[39]

This tale "that passed from man to man during and immediately after the trouble" does not differ greatly from that handed down in writing from the pen of Mary Ann, John Tewksbury's wife. Her version identifies Ed's visiting Graham as John, not Tom:

... Uncle Ed Tewksbury met John Graham in Globe and Graham was looking for a location as he and his brother wanted to start in the cattle business. Ed told him about Pleasant Valley for at that time there was not many ranchers there. Graham became very interested and came out to see the valley, he liked it so much he went back to Globe and sent for his brother Tom Graham to come on as he had found just what they wanted. They met in Globe, they had some money, not very much, and they bought a small bunch of cows and drove them out to the valley and settled. . . .[40]

And so the Grahams staked a segment of the broad, open, inclined main valley, just a mile or two up Cherry Creek from their new friends, the Tewksburys. That close-knit clan sized up the Graham boys, helped them build their first shelter, and gave them sound advice in livestock husbandry. The Tewksburys agreed . . . it would be downright pleasure-some, having some new neighbors.

IV. Who Are You Hunting?

Cold Arizona. Oxymoronic to the minds of many a newcomer, the hard truth hurt: Arizona winters bitterly chill the thin blood of unclimatized settlers. This country, which might swelter in 105 degrees in August, could drop below zero in December. At high altitudes, beginning usually in late autumn, frigid air masses from the North Pacific rolled along the wind-raked rims and soaked the shaded hollows and crept down chimneys into the very marrow. Marvelously adapted creatures, the nuthatches and the gray squirrels and the black bears might feast and frolic and slumber through frosty spells, but humans had no hair or humor for seasons that commonly shifted from balm to blizzard overnight. A mile above sea level, in central Arizona Territory, the winter of 1882-1883 helped establish the everfresh paradox: Arizona, hot and dry, could in reality turn cold and wet.

It was the first winter in the Tonto wilds for Tom and John Graham. They had made their home in Pleasant Valley only since September. They knew ninety-degree afternoons, tropical nights, and fruited morns of Indian summer. They indulged their doomsaying friends to the degree that they felled and squared great ponderosa pine logs and interlocked them around a little chimney. In these labors the Tewksburys helped.[1] Then, one November day, winter mugged the Grahams—rushed out of the cedars and wrapped a soggy arm around their one-room cabin, and pierced their flesh with frost. Every small duty in the high country turned into a cold-fingered chore. The Grahams sought relief from the cabin fever of their simple hut; they relished the companionship, advice, and aid of the Tewksburys, who by now oversaw a variety of houses, outbuildings, improvements. At Tewksburys', too, resided attractive women and amusing children, elements altogether lacking in the Graham cabin. The Graham boys and the Tewksbury colony, day by day, forged friendships that with better luck, might have sustained shared dreams.

Tewksbury enterprises assured an abundance and diversity of food for themselves and neighbors. Their bands of half-wild hogs provided sausage, bacon, lard. With Apaches, the Tewksburys traded for dried corn and beans. Apples, apricots, plums, cherries, nuts flourished in the Pleasant Valley climate. For enjoying fresh, for canning, and for bartering, the Tewksburys specialized in cling peaches.[2] Coffee, sugar, tobacco, liquor, salt, flour from town spiced and complemented the cornucopia of the land. Much could be put by as jerky, dried fruit, dehydrated squash, cold stored roots and butter. If butchering a beef seemed too rich a luxury, the hunt began at a threshold: deer, elk, bear, rabbit, squirrel, beaver, coon, javelina, turkey, three kinds of quail, two of dove, duck, goose. Streams ran with trout. Prospering amid plenty, the Tewksburys welcomed the new year of 1883 with the erection of a new house, a forge, extended corrals.

At mid-morning, January 12, all four Tewksbury brothers, John and Tom Graham, and Mary Ann Tewksbury, busied themselves at the northernmost Tewksbury residence on Cherry Creek. They were chinking logs, brewing coffee, hammering metal. . .hardly preparations for trouble. But trouble, spelled Gilleland, was on the way.

John C. Gilleland, at age twenty-four, already qualified as a genuine Tonto Basin pioneer cattleman. A refugee plowman from the black furrows of central Texas, John found footloose Arizona to his liking in 1879. He quickly hired on as a cowboy for James H. Stinson, the first American to run cattle in Pleasant Valley. Now well-off, Stinson kept his own comfortable home near lowland Phoenix, where his young stepson could go to school. Gilleland was entrusted with the day-to-day management of Stinson's high country ranch and herds.[3]

It's likely that Elisha Gilleland on this day experienced enough true-West excitement to last him the rest of his life. Also from Texas, he was visiting his uncle, O.C. Felton, a prominent rancher at the confluence of Rye and Tonto creeks. The youngster, yearning for adventure, was handed off another fifty miles eastward by "Potash" Ruiz to his older cousin, John.

The identity of Epitacio Ruiz was whittled in both directions. Arizona North Americans shortened his name to *"Pitac,"* pronounced *Pee-tass.* That must have struck Texan emigrés as a tad effeté; they dubbed the hombre "Potash." Although bearing one of Hispanic Arizona's venerable surnames (he himself wrote it at least once "Ruis" while Anglo officials spelled it "Ruiz"), he generally was obliged by authorities and bosses to answer to the nickname Potash.

On a mission perhaps never to be certified, this unlikely trio arrived horseback at Tewksbury headquarters. Mary Ann, John Tewksbury's wife, whose decades of terror and tragedy were just beginning, swore later in court to facts here condensed:

Her occupation, "ranch woman." She knew John Gilleland and Potash. She was just stepping into the doorway of the old house, near a new house then under construction. Inside the old house was her brother-in-law, Edwin Tewksbury. When she first saw the Gillelands and Potash coming down the trail, Ed was affixing an explosive cap to a piece of fuse in preparation for blasting a foundation in the frozen earth for the forge. Ed immediately went out to meet Gilleland. A sack of guns customarily hung above the door. She saw Ed take no firearms with him. She peered out the door, and from a distance of some fifty feet, heard Ed and John Gilleland "talking very low—they did not seem mad. I then saw Mr. Gilleland drawing his pistol and fired. I got back into the house. I saw no more."[4]

Assuming she told the truth, Mary Ann missed witnessing a real-life scene that, as fictional drama, would mesmerize mid-twentieth-century American audiences over and again. . .angry men in confrontation. . . curses. . .hands groping for weapons. . .horses wheeling. . .guns blazing . . .blood flowing.

In a country eighty miles from the nearest telegraph line, a hundred fifty miles from the closest rudimentary telephone, news of the shooting traveled with surprising speed. No doubt by mounted messenger, the word flew across mountain ranges and canyons quickly and convincingly enough to cause the issuance of the following handwritten in ink:

Territory of Arizona vs Tewks Berry + Tewks Berry / Warrant
Strawberry Valley Yavapai Co Arizona Territory Jan 14 1883 to Wm Burch Special Constable greeting Whers Complaint has been made in this office by Wm Mc Donald against John and Ed Tewks Berry and others charging them with Murder as hee Verily believes you are hereby Commanded to Arrest them and bring them before me at my office in Strawberry Valley Yavapai Co A Y in this the said Tewks Berry and others are here by commanded to not Resist under the Penalty of law
Witness my hand and seal done at my office this 14th day of January 1883
Isaac Louthian J P
Pinecreek Precinct Yavapai Co A Y

The charge was murder. The dirty work fell to Constable Burch, in the first rank of Tonto settlers. Two weeks went by, and Burch filed his written report—a remarkable document indeed—with Justice Louthian:

Having a warrent of Arrest for the Tewksberrys and others on a charge of Mur-der, acting as special constable, I started with a force of nine Men to make the arrest of the above named persons having proceded as far as within one Mile of Hudon Ranch and a Distance of nine Miles from Feltons Ranch We met Felton Broide and others with ther Wounded young Man that was suposed to have bin killed in the Shooting affair at Tewksberys Ranch Mr Felton and Broidy told to me that there was a force of armed Men from 14 to 20 and was in a Strong Posi-tion of defence at Tewksburys Not having suficient Men to cope With the num-bers reported there it was thought best to increas the Number of Our Men Strong Enough to make the arrest in a few days after I returned with a force of 18 men found Tewksberys and others willing to Submit to the Law.

Burch put down (rather casually and phonetically spelled) the names of some of his posse: "Alfred Peach, Andrew Piatt, Poley Chilson, Enos Cole, Marion Deric, Henry Sidler, Wm Henry, Joseph Gibson, Epham Blake, John Davis, W Th Dickinson." They brought in John, James, and Frank Tewksbury, and Tom Graham. But "Edward Tewskbery and John Graham could not be found. Was informed by the above Named prisoners that they Was on their Way to Prescott to Diliver their Selfs to the Law."

From the considerable documentation surviving more than a century fol-lowing the Gilleland/Tewksbury gunfight—from a large body of country gossip—and from articles of faith indelible yet as erroneous as the report of Elisha Gilleland's death—historians, descendants, and vicarious allies have derived a diversity of conclusions. At opposites:

• Gilleland-the-villain theory. Stinson knew his herds were being rustled, and he demanded that his foreman, John Gilleland, stop the thievery. Fortified with a few fingers of whiskey, Gilleland, known for his quick temper, mustered his adolescent nephew (so tender a foot that he had never so much as shot at a deer or turkey in all his life), and the vaquero Ruis into a hostile reconnoiter of Tewksbury headquarters. This troop, armed with two six-shooters and a small-calibre rifle in the hands of the boy, mounted up, rode to the Tewksbury ranch, and boldly inspected brands of animals penned in a Tewksbury corral within plain view of the Tewksburys and their cronies. Directly the Gilleland patrol walked horseback to the knot of men working at Tewksburys'. Unpro-voked, John Gilleland jerked free his revolver and snapped off a shot at Edwin Tewksbury. Tewksbury reacted in self-defense. He easily could have killed Gilleland and company. Instead, Ed drew his own pistol, which by chance reposed in his hip pocket, and elected to inflict rela-tively harmless wounds upon his tormenters.[5]

• Tewksbury-the-villain theory. Elisha, newly arrived from Texas, nagged his uncle into leading a hunt for game. The men entrusted the lad with their only rifle, of .22 calibre. They pursued a logical hunt down the Cherry Creek trail wending through Tewksbury headquarters, wished everybody a congenial good morning, and somehow inadvertently offended Edwin Tewksbury. Ed, without provocation, cursed John Gilleland, and punctuated his profanity with the contents of his revolver. The horsemen tried their best to flee. Only John Gilleland managed a few ineffectual shots in self-defense.[6]

Variations of such themes soon appeared in news columns of journals published in the nearest (yet decidedly distant) towns. Fair to assume, Stinson pressured the press of Phoenix and the Salt River Valley. Tewksbury backers had editorial friends in Globe. Newsmen, then as now, could be gulled by ruse and rumor. Among reports running through early 1883:[7]

Word reaches us from Tonto Basin that two herders of Mr. Stinson and the Tewksburg boys, herding for Mr. Stearns, had a row in which one of the former was killed and another dangerously wounded.

—*Arizona Gazette,* January 15

A serious shooting afray took place in Tonto Basin on the 16th ins., between the Tewkesbury boys and John Gillen and cousin. Gillen was wounded and his cousin, a boy, shot through the shoulder, the ball lodging in his lungs. The wound is mortal. The trouble was about cattle.

—*Phoenix Herald,* January 20

We learn that the shooting affray. . .is likely to lead to very serious trouble among the stock men, a number of whom are in pursuit of the Tewkesbury boys with the intention of taking summary vengeance upon them, and the Tewkesbury boys, have sworn that the matter should be settled without resort to the law, it is said, have decided that they will never be arrested. The probability is that there will be still more serious trouble.

—*Phoenix Herald,* January 22

THE TONTO AFFRAY.
The Statement Made by One of Mr. Stinson's Men.

In conversation with Epitacio Ruis, a Mexican, who has been in the employ of James Stinson, for the past nine years, we learn the following regarding the shooting affray which occurred between the Tewksberry boys and Stinson's men, in Pleasant Valley, some weeks since. Epitacio says that on the Friday on which the shooting occurred, he and John Gilleland, who is also employed by Mr. Stinson, accompanied by Elisha Gilleland, (a mere lad of sixteen years of age, who was visiting the place for the purpose of hunting turkeys) started down below to look after the stock. When they reached the Tewksberry's house they all stopped

and John Gilleland bade the boys good morning. Ed. Tewksberry, James Tewksberry, and one of their particular friends, Graham by name, were present. Instead
of answering the salutation, Ed. Tewksberry spoke up to John Gilleland, inter-
rogatively: "You are hunting somebody?" to which John replied, "I'm not; I've
lost no one." Simultaneously with this reply Ed. Tewksberry pulled his pistol,
and, remarking, "Well, I have, you thieving s— of a b——," began firing.
Thereat Ruis started to run, followed by the boy Elisha. John Gilleland, however,
pulled his pistol and twice returned the fire. Seeing his brother fall from the
horse, and being seated on a colt that was plunging and pitching, and also having
a painful wound in the left shoulder, he rapidly followed the Mexican. It is
claimed that ten or twelve shots were fired, and as John Gilleland only shot
twice, it is probable that Jim Tewksberry and Graham ran into the house, armed
themselves, and then participated in the affray. Young Gilleland had a rifle and
pistol, but never attempted to use either, being shot in the back while attempting
to get away. He is now hovering between life and death. A gentleman named
Rose, living at Stinson's, went down to Tewksberry's after the shooting, and they
helped bring the wounded boy home. It was rumored that the Tewksberrys
would resist arrest, and Constable Burch organized a posse of sixteen men and
went to their house. Jim and two other persons were arrested, but Ed. and Graham were reported as being in Prescott a few days ago, and it is very probable
that they are also under arrest now. What makes the affair look worse is that
there had been no previous quarrel between the parties. This version of the
story, it will be seen, differs essentially from that published in our issue of last
Saturday, by J.D. Tewksberry. The whole affair will shortly undergo official
examination, pending which, suspension of public judgment is asked.

(Adjoining column) James Stinson received a dispatch from Prescott to-day,
stating that Ed. Tewksberry was under arrest, and that the capture of Graham
was considered certain.

—*Arizona Gazette*, January 30

Mr. J. Stinson left on this morning's stage for Prescott, to attend the preliminary
examination of the parties concerned in the late shooting scrape in Tonto Basin.

—*Phoenix Herald*, February 8

In due course, testimony of participants and witnesses was taken
down, the grand jury in Prescott returned indictments against John Gilleland and Epitacio Ruiz, and a trial went forth in Prescott. Some records
likely were lost with their transfer to Phoenix, followed by a destructive
flood. The case ended in acquittal.

Never published was the full statement obtained by Justice Louthian
of Pine/Strawberry. Apparently, Louthian himself journeyed some
seventy-five miles back and forth in order to interview the wounded boy.
Preserved in the Yavapai County Courthouse in Prescott is Louthian's
labored handscript:

Tonto Creek Yavipai Co Arizona Feb 3 1883 the Statement of Mr. Elisha Gilleland Not being able to appear at Prescott on account of Wounds Recieved at

Plesant Valley do sweare this statement be the Truthe Borne in Texas Age 16 six-
teen years ocupation Farmer local Residence Tonto Basin on the 12 day of
January My Self and John Gilleland and and Potossio Went to Plesent Valley
Close to Tewks Bury house Ed Tewks Bury says you look as though you were
hunting some one John Gilleland said no Ed Tewksbury said if you Will get
down I Will hunt you very quick John Gilleland said I am not around hunting
Rows this morning Ed Tewks Bury said yess you are you Black harted son of a
Bitch and Began Pulling his Pistol then John Gilleland began Pulling his Also
John Gilleland got his out First and as he pulled it out his Horse Whirled and as
he Whirled Ed Tewks Bury shot at him then John gilleland shot at Ed Tewks
Bury then Ed shot at John gilleland twice and Wounded him dont know Which
shot struck him then John gilleland shot once more at Ed Tewks Bury then I was
shot onect I was about 30 thirty sepps from John gilleland to the left then my
Horse began Running then I Fell off my Horse I do not know Who Shot once
there was about 12 twelve shotts fired as near as I could tell there Was Present
Ed Tewks Bury James Tewks Bury and a man by the name of graham I think his
name is John graham I did not know any thing from the time I fell off my Horse
untill I Was taken to the House about an hour after I was shott
E D Gilleland
Taken before mee this 3 third day of February at Felons Ranch Tonto Creek
Yavipai Co Arizona 1883 a Justice of the Peace for Pine creek Precinct Yavipai Co
Arizona
Isaac Louthian, J P.

Elisha's perilous condition excused him from further deposition; not
so, the others. Arizona's 1883 February was the dead of winter. With a
hint of snobbery, the *Phoenix Herald* noted: "Prescott cold. Folks happy.
Thermometer failed to get below zero." Traveling, camping out, and putting up in town in such weather compounded the hardships of separation for all witnesses and defendants from work and family. The central
surviving fact: through these court proceedings the Grahams and Tewksburys were staunch pals; the relationship generated not a hint of
animosity. They presented a solid front opposing Gilleland and his boss,
James Stinson.

The summoning of Francis (Frank) Tewksbury especially rankled the
Tewksbury clan. This frail-of-health (tuberculosis?) teenager had sworn to
Justice Louthian he didn't see or know much about the Gilleland
shooting. Frank was driving a wagon some distance from the house. He
had gone to fetch some shake bolts a half mile from the house, and on
his way back, heard some shooting.[8] Requiring Frank to travel to Prescott in the winter was never forgiven by the Tewksbury family.[9]

On the stand in Prescott, John Graham told Justice Fleury he was
thirty-eight years old, had resided in Pleasant Valley four or five months,
and had been in Arizona Territory "a little over two years. I am a miner
by trade, got a few head of cattle now." With a hammer, he was
pounding lead into rivets with which to repair a knife scabbard. Jim

Tewksbury was pumping at the bellows of the forge.

"Edwin Tewksbury was standing there, had something in his hand." Epitacio and John Gilleland wore holstered pistols and Elisha carried a pistol on his belt, and bore a Winchester rifle. All had belts of cartridges.

The Gilleland party "rode up within fifteen or sixteen feet of us—we all spoke good morning—I mean Ed Tewksbury and Jim Tewksbury and myself John Graham. Mr. Edwin Tewksbury asked Mr. Gilleland who he was hunting. He said 'You, you-son-of-a-bitch,' and reached for his pistol, shot over Edwin Tewksbury's head, and fired again. I thought it was at me—the Pistol was pointed in my direction the ball going through my hat—cut the bellows handle off—close to James Tewksbury's head—the defendants Gilleland turned the horses, fired a shot over his left shoulder—Epitaso reached for his six shooter, the horse jumped and didn't get it out; they—Mr. Gilleland, Epitaso, and a young man I didn't know—run up the valley about two hundred yards; the young man fell off—I waited about two minutes, started up to the young man asked him if he was hurt bad—he said yes. I raised him up, took his six-shooter off. James Tewksbury came up, packed the young man to Mr. Tewksbury's . . . laid him on the bed. I started to get Mr. Rose and Mr. Epitaso to come down and help and carry the young man up to Stinson's stock ranch—I had taken my gun up with me—met Mr. Rose between Mr. Stinson's Ranch and Mr. Churche's—he had his gun and six-shooter with him—I asked him to come down and help pack the boy up—he refused to do it—we traveled up to Stinson's stock ranch together—I talked to him and coaxed him till I got him to—Mr. Rose, James Tewksbury, John Tewksbury, and Frank Tewksbury helped to pack him up to Stinson's ranch." *[punctuation added]*

Questioned further, John Graham said Gilleland drew first, and that his second shot "and Edwin Tewksbury shot—was about alike—you could not tell any distinction between the two shots—Edwin Tewksbury shot three or four times; I could not say." John Graham emphasized, "Tewksbury did not attempt to draw his pistol till Gilleland draw'd his'n."

Then, "You have said the ball from the second shot of Gilleland passed through your hat—have you that hat here." Answer, "Yes, sir," (showing).

John Graham's recollections were largely substantiated by his brother, Tom. Tom gave his age as twenty-eight: his residence, Pleasant Valley. Tom said he was standing inside the new house and could see between the unchinked logs. Brother John was pumping the bellows, and James Tewksbury had a pot of coffee in the fire. The Gilleland horsemen rode up to within a few feet of Ed Tewksbury, who said, "Good morning, fellows—and asked them who they were looking for—Mr. John Gilleland said, 'You, you son-of-a-bitch' and fired." Tom described Ed's pistol as a "bulldog pistol they call them, I believe." Gilleland's pistol was "large," and "nicle plated." Ruiz never got his pistol out of his holster. The boy had a "small-size Winchester rifle—he had a six-shooter on." A defense attorney raised doubts about the wound, and Tom stated he couldn't swear as to how the boy was wounded, or whether the wound was made by gun or knife.

Testimony of the other parties largely buttressed the opposing versions. The defendants were bound over for scrutiny by the Grand Jury, which returned a true bill of assault with intention to commit murder. In the spring of 1883 a jury, hearing virtually the same evidence, found both John Gilleland and Epitacio Ruiz innocent.

But for one twist of fate, the finding may have been acceptable. But stuck like a bone in the Tewksbury throat, the youngest boy of the family paid an awful price. Frank knew little of substance, but, dragged to the nearest justice in Strawberry, and forced by subpoena even farther to Prescott, Frank's vitality went into a decline. The *Phoenix Herald* of January 20, and other territorial newspapers, carried a single paragraph:

Frank Tewksbury died last week in Pleasant Valley, from measles contracted while en route home from Prescott, where he had been to attend the trial of Gilleland, et al.

Probably in the context of its time and place, the death of Frank Tewksbury was laid at the doorstep of enemies of the Tewksbury family. In time, blame may somehow have been transferred to the Grahams. Open to speculation: possibly it was in Prescott, during the Gilleland court actions, that Stinson approached the Graham brothers with an attractive business deal: a quick path to riches at the expense of the Tewksbury family. All it cost was a classic double-cross.

Frank was probably doomed anyway. And it was Gilleland who first fostered Stinson interests. No matter. As in both midsize and colossal wars, the progress of human volition and unavoidable act of God muddled into a mosaic of clan belief. As time went on, the death of Frank Tewksbury came to be considered the first casualty of "the little war of our own." The Tewksbury perception: the Grahams did it.

V. Forgery by Fire

For John Graham, the distance and difficulty of this journey were both cover and curse. At a price dear in time and discomfort, Graham could carry out his business with the desired degree of secrecy. And for the moment, John Graham did not want certain people in Pleasant Valley to know about his mission.

To reach Prescott, Graham had been obliged to ride a horse for most of a week, from the far eastern side of Yavapai County to Arizona's territorial capital and county seat. By straight-edge ruler placed on a map, the trek measured one hundred-eighty miles. But by horse, the trails may have covered that much again. Graham had to ford several chill, highland rivers in spring flood, and skirt the steep shoulders of a reach of land as raw as any remaining within America's maturing transmainland destiny. There simply existed no swifter access for Pleasant Valley residents to civil government.

One might loop northward by horse two days to Holbrook or Winslow, leaving still a long train- and stage-ride via Flagstaff. Or one might go southward three days by horse to Phoenix—there to join a bone-wrenching, twenty-four-hour, short-stop stage run up Black Canyon. Transportation

presented a continuing hardship for Arizona's seventy-five thousand settlers, many caretaking the territory's seven hundred thousand head of
cattle, or extracting eight million dollars worth of metal a year. Relatively
few had easy access to Arizona's sixty-five churches or thirty-three newspapers. Yavapai County, larger than New England, claimed thirteen
thousand whites, and grudgingly tolerated perhaps twice that number of
Indians, plenty unpacified.[1] To any industrious citizen of Pleasant Valley,
remoteness from Prescott exacted an extraordinary penalty for furthering
the smallest governmental procedure. Prescott's Whiskey Row offered
abundance for imbibers and sadists.[2] But these distractions scarcely compensated for the time and expense of responding to a subpoena or recording
a document.

And for John Graham, an appearance in Prescott invariably provoked
irritating moments. Scotland-born, reared in an immigrant family in well-
ordered Ohio and Iowa, John, with his younger brother, Tom, had ventured West in the 1870s. "Dude" was a term which especially offended
John. A burr in his speech, an inbred aloofness, a compactess of build,
set him apart. But wasn't everybody in the West from somewhere else?
Why, on the sidewalks of Phoenix there might pass by a Swiss clerk, an
Italian priest, a Greek miner, an Irish blacksmith, a Spanish merchant, an
English glassblower.[3] John and his brother were as daring and clever as
most westerners and more widely traveled than most. The Grahams had
risked and survived Alaska, Oregon, Mexico, and California, and had
proven themselves as miners, stock handlers, and proficient pistoleers.[4]
Yet even in a subnation of newcomers, the Graham brothers were considered somewhat peculiar. They had benefitted and escaped from the
regimen of Midwest farm toil.[5] Now they affected the best dress they
could afford and didn't hide their vaulting ambition. Through the man's
world of the American West, they cut a swashbuckling path: John the
more reserved bantamweight, Tom the heavyset glib one. They impressed strangers as being cocky and uppity. The Grahams sensed these social
slurs and resented them.[6]

John's business in Prescott involved livestock identification—not a
new need in animal husbandry, but only recently worth the trouble in
Yavapai County. An art of the ancients, branding was brought to the
New World in 1522 by Spaniards. Hernan Cortez's mark was "three
Christian crosses." Some twenty years later Coronado brought branded
cattle into Arizona, and native peoples along his routes began a robust
tradition: brands be damned and never eat your own beef!

Much American branding lore focuses on latter-day Texas. It was in
Texas that the term "maverick" was coined.[7] Pragmatic Texans favored
designs based on letters and numbers. Texans also advanced the technology for altering and blurring brands for unlawful purposes. Some legi-

timate branding might take place at any time of the year, not just at roundups. The tool for this work was the "running iron." The comment of an honest old-time cowman is preserved: "I can take an iron rod, bend one end into a half circle, and burn a damn sight better brand than I can draw on paper with a pencil."[8] But also it was just as easy for rustlers to convert a brand with a running iron or similar curved device. To those who discount brand doctoring as pulp fiction, Oren Arnold and John P. Hale, in their book, *Hot Irons,* responded, ". . .yesterday's cattle rustling *was* sensational. Brand changing *was* a studied art. The brand blotter or rewrite man *really* was a first-class villain with infinite bravado and ingenuity. . . . " In Arizona, livestock branding at first was voluntary, then required by law beginning in 1887. During the 1880s, hundreds of Arizona ranchers (in person or by proxy) recorded brands at county seats.

Thousands of head of cattle roaming eastern Yavapai County, primarily in Pleasant Valley, bore the unrecorded brand of James Stinson. In a wilderness where cattle joined coyotes, wolves, bears, and cougars in desperate combat, man-made ear crops, wattles, and other mutilations were only marginally useful for legal identification. From the mid-1870s, Stinson's large herds had prospered across virgin ranges in the vicinity of what today is Snowflake on Silver Creek, atop the Mogollon Rim. Colonizing Mormons offered Stinson a fortune for his water rights. Stinson, in turn, provided the Mormons with breeding stock. And in one of the largest cattle movements of territorial Arizona, Stinson, in three annual drives, stocked Pleasant Valley with some twelve hundred head of mother cows and their increase. Stinson's brand, an unembellished block letter, could be applied with two stamps of a hot iron bar. Only three inches wide and three inches tall, it was legal either on the left hip or left side. Its simplicity constituted an open invitation to rustlers.

Although larceny cannot be imputed more than a century later, numerous brands of suspicious shape were recorded in Yavapai and adjoining counties after Stinson's huge herds doubled and redoubled. Germane, too, was the location of the T brand on cattle anatomy. The possibilities: jaw, neck, shoulder, ribs, hip, thigh, side, right or left on any or all of the foregoing. Oldtimers preferred a placement to the rear, closer to a cow's flyswatting tail, thus reducing odds of infection. George Broker of Sycamore Creek, his left hip brand.[9]

Also for the left hip, John Collins of Williamson Valley recorded this mark.

F.G. and Arthur Fisher invented this brand for the left hip of their cattle roaming the Mogollons.

HT   Herbert Taylor of Baker Butte, a few days drive from
Pleasant Valley, recorded an H T for the left hip.

TR   For the left side of his beeves, Albert Rose
of Pleasant Valley put his mark into the brand book.

T   H.L. Strunkel, Upper Valley, created a stylish brand
for the left hip of his cows.

T   In the names of J.W. Bails and William McFadden, for application
upon the left hip this design was registered.

B   Men who signed as C. Soyer and F. Bissig
recorded their left hip brand.

TE Q   For one of his teenage girls, Jesse Ellison
established a herd bearing this trio on the left hip.

TC   Logically enough, Thomas Carroll, not far from Tonto Basin,
chose this unadorned pair for placement on the left hip.

L   To the north of Stinson's Pleasant Valley range the Aztec Land &
Cattle Company turned loose tens of thousands of drouth-stricken
Texas beeves upon railroad land grants. The Hashknife outfit took its
nickname from its brand, patterned after a familiar chuckwagon utensil.
In Texas, the Hashknife had been registered as a brand with the straight
handle down, and the curved blade up.

U   But when it entered the Yavapai brand registry, for unexplained
reasons the Hashknife was turned top to bottom, for placement
on *both* sides of its stock.[10]

Literally scores of other brands incorporating a T were legalized for
Pleasant Valley and adjoining spreads. They ranged from a TX to a block
T to a bow-and-arrow done with a T. In later years, Glenn Ellison drew
from memory such Gila County variations as the Lazy H, T Up and T
Down, T Swinging H, VT, ZT, T4E Connected, TJE Connected, T Lazy
T, and T Open A.

In the springtime of 1884, John Graham of Pleasant Valley had a
pocketful of this sort of legitimization. At 1:10 PM on March 25, he
appeared before the county recorder in behalf of his brother, Thomas H.
Graham, to attest:

Know all men by these Presents that I have adopted as my mark for Cattle a smooth crop off the left ear, and a crop and slit in right ear and my brand for livestock:

E

branded on the left hip of cattle. Stock ranges in Pleasant Valley Yavapai County Arizona[11]

It was common local knowledge that the TE Connected adorned Pleasant Valley Cattle co-owned by Tom (Graham) and Ed (Tewksbury). In recording this brand, John Graham made no note of Ed's equity. It scarcely could have been an innocent oversight. For, in following the elaborate procedure, the county recorder, in India ink, drew freehand or traced the face of the handcrafted iron. A scrap of hide, deeply scorched with the iron and inked for identification, was submitted for safekeeping in the recorder's archives. Perhaps of significance, no provision was made to legalize the TE Connected brand for use on horses.

Nor was John Graham finished. He recorded a second brand in the names of himself and brother Tom; the ear marks were identical to the old TE Connected. The JT Connected was made legal for horses; placement on cattle was indicated "on left hip."[12]

JT

Whether John Graham and James Stinson were traveling together is conjectural. Stinson was a politically connected and moneyed man, and although no linkage is hinted in the brand registrations, John Graham, three afternoons later and on an adjacent page, may have acted as Stinson's proxy in recording:

as my ear mark for cattle a smooth or close crop off the left ear and a wattle on the left jaw and as my Brand for Horses and Cattle

T

branded on the left-hip and on the left-ribs of Cattle and on the left-shoulder of horses.

Routine. Or so it seemed. But with three quick strokes, Ed Tewksbury effectively was denied ownership of any existing and future TE Connected stock. The Grahams created a logical family design containing a T for the left hip. And the lone letter T, on left hip or left side, became the official brand of James Stinson in Yavapai County.

Almost predictably, within three months (June 2, 1884) following the recordings of the Graham and Stinson brands, a brand was entered at Prescott in the name of Lydia Tewksbury. The docket page gives no clue as to whether she appeared in person or by proxy, but her brand was definitely for application upon the left hip of cattle of "stock range of Pleasant Valley":

LT

In the same week Edwin Tewksbury recorded the

JK

A bit more than a year later, on July 21, 1885, Lydia's husband and patriarch of the Tewksbury clan, James Dunning Tewksbury, at the request of his son, Edwin, sponsored a brand which, within a combination of the older man's initials, JDT—almost, *almost*—camouflaged the central letter. It was, of course, a T, and the brand was to be positioned upon the left hip:

JP

Other T brands proliferated throughout Apache, Maricopa, and Gila counties as these coexisting or newly formed entities established brand books.

According to William E. Simson of Phoenix, on the Lower Tonto E.F. Kellner used this brand.

EK

Simson said Andy Cooper with a running iron would alter this brand into one of his own.[13]

AC

According to Drusilla Hazelton, the James D. Tewksbury JDT Connected made into a Circle Cross burned over the JDT. "Mr. Tewksbury saddled up and rode to the county seat and checked the brands recorded and as no Circle Cross was recorded he promptly recorded the brand in his name, returned to Pleasant Valley and notified a certain settler, a man whom the Tewksburys felt sure was blotching the brands, to leave the valley in a specified time; the settler was gone in a fraction of the time allotted him."

Whether this was the same Circle Cross, or another perfectly legal, this advertisement for estrays published in the Prescott press evidences a feistiness of frontier character:

Another bit of cowboy lore involves the Lydia Tewksbury L T brand. While it may have been contrived to prey upon Stinson's T cattle, the L T itself was vulnerable. With nothing more than a redhot pothook, it could be "worked over into a pigpen, which belonged to some of the Grahams or their bunch":

LT   #

However the Hashknife (see page 54) might be extended from other brands such as the Stinson's T, the Hashknife was a difficult brand itself to edit. But many would try. "The Hashknife. . .was long-roped to death. . . .It was just too easy to eat in on an outfit like the Hashknife that was owned by a soul-less corporation and was spread out over several million acres of terrain. . .the Aztec Land & Cattle Company was generally regarded as fair game for anyone who could out-slick it."[14] "Sleepering" was the cow country term for penning up a maverick calf, or for ear-marking a calf in hopes it would thereby escape branding. In one cele-brated case, "the Hashknife brand was added onto until it looked like a cow drinking out of a trough. There were only a few animals found with this altered brand, but it was so absurd looking that it attracted immedi-ate attention at the spring round up. . . .

"It certainly did not seem possible to have altered a Hashknife to look like a cow's head, ears, eyes, and all. But the Hashknife foreman had such positive information on the alteration that he told the claimant he would kill and skin one of the animals. He promised that if the inside of the hide did not clearly show the older Hashknife brand he would double the value of the critter. The animal was shot and skinned in the presence of the cattle inspector and a crowd of witnesses, and, sure enough, the older Hashknife brand stood out clear and distinct on the inside of the hide. Even the thief had to admit it. 'I was jest a-funnin', 'he said. His 'funnin' ' cost him several years in the Yuma penitentiary. . . ."

More, much more, was at stake than uncounted thousands of valuable animals. Modern Americans take for granted the processes by which clear and lasting title to land is guaranteed. In Arizona, all land title derives from Indian and Spanish cessions, land grants, federal and state sales and exchanges, land scrip, preemptions, homesteads, desert land entries, and patented mining claims. Well and good, but in territorial Arizona before the turn of the century precious little land was surveyed—and even if a settler improved a piece of land in the hope of filing for a homestead, without surveys to authenticate the metes and bounds, possession remained nine-tenths of the law.[15]

For example, government surveys of the Adams-Blevins-Ramer meadowland along Canyon Creek were not perfected until 1910; at that time, a resident of twenty years was at last allowed to gain undisputed ownership through a government patent.[16] A pertinent memoir was left by L.J. Horton, in the first wave of American settlers of the Rim Country:

In the year of 1883 I located a ranch three miles north of Payson, built a log house in the west end and a fence all around the ranch. In May 1884 on the upper and east end which paralleled the Payson and Strawberry road, planted a patch of watermelons. After the melons got ripe a man by the name of Landing, who said he was a rustler, pitched his tent on the other side of my melon patch. I always made the rounds with a shotgun to keep the rabbits away. . . .He greeted me in a friendly manner. Will you have a watermelon?

"Yes," I said; and he climbed over my fence and brought me a fine watermelon. Then he pointed his rifle and said, "From now on I will keep all the rabbits away from this place." I thanked him for his assistance. While we were eating the melon he told me about the good shooting qualities of his gun; how he had just won a turkey at a turkey shoot. As I walked away he said: "I have jumped this ranch because you have too much land in your location. I will not charge you for that melon but the next time you will pay fifty cents for it."

Horton related that he and Landing exchanged hard words. Whereupon Landing cocked and aimed the rifle. Horton's impulse may have saved his life. A smoothbore rabbit piece is no match for a rifle at long range. So Horton charged Landing.

. . . to my surprise when he saw me coming toward him at full speed with both barrels cocked, he trembled and shook so badly that he could not hold the gun up. He banged away and kicked up the dust close to his feet, then he jumped behind his wife. She held up her petticoats to shield him, I thrust my shotgun around her, hunting for a vital place to discharge the gun, because it was a case of kill or be killed . . . the wife also saw from my looks that I was determined on getting a dead shot because she would say, "Don't you shoot. Don't you shoot!"

Just then a little boy about eight years old came running, and said: "Mister, please don't shoot my pa." I stopped, looked at him, and said, "I won't shoot your pa, but he'll give me that rifle." As I uttered those words the stock of the gun was shoved out from under his wife's petticoats and I grabbed it, saying, "Give me the belt of ammunition." This also was shoved out to me. I took the rifle and struck it on a nearby rock, bending it like a hoop."

. . . I said to the lady, "I would not kill a dirty, low-lifed claim jumper. He is not worth the powder to blow his worthless, cowardly carcass into the hot country. Now, my lady . . . if that treacherous cuss ever leaves one melon rind in front of this camp, I will settle with him in proper order."[17]

Horton's monograph states Landing fled the country within two days. But elsewhere in the Rim Country, for settlers neither foolhardy nor lucky, might made right. And where the land itself could not be branded properly with corner markers and chained boundaries, the brands sizzled into the hides of livestock took on a burden of legitimatizing real estate. When none of his branded animals remained, a rancher had little recourse than to give up everything. Within a few years, the selfsame Horton was rustled to ruin. He turned over his splendid homestead to Colonel Jesse Ellison in a gentleman's agreement by which Ellison would pay Horton for any remnants of a once-large herd. Ellison settled on Horton for eight dollars—for one old cow.

VI. Treaties of War

A document untended, like a child or calf or lamb, may stray. Destructive coyotes rove everywhere. Raptors of ruin—fire and mildew and acid and flood and radiation and inattention and pilferage—circle written knowledge in infinite patience. Faceless, faithful file clerks, not famous historians, are the shepherds of the past. And when an anonymous pastor of fact dozes on watch, a word or image may wander, allowing time's predators to pounce. Often, there is not even a small cry in the dark. Some precious fact voicelessly vanishes, likely forever.

For a century, one piece of intelligence of the Pleasant Valley War escaped detection. Why the war? What touched off the worst range feud of the American West? Could there endure indelible clues to the motives that escalated the neighborhood spats of Pleasant Valley to premeditated mankilling?

Over a century, the question piqued an odd lot of investigators:

• The War Correspondent. Joseph Fish[1] reached the peak of his repertorial powers at the height of the war. He lived in its midst. In 1896, he selflessly deposited his seven-hundred-page typescript with the State Historian.

• The Combatant. Like middle-aged Fish, Osmer D. Flake[2] was a Snowflake Mormon who professed neutrality. But before he was old enough to vote, rash Flake volunteered himself, his horse, and his gun as peacekeeper posseman. Bless him, he wrote down his memories.

• The Propagandizer. Neither Fish nor Flake ever laid hands on the written genesis of their war. Nor did sheepman James D. Houck, *gracias a Dios.* Given his genius at manipulating press and politics, Houck probably would have torn it up.

• The Negotiator. His Congressional Medal of Honor secure, Will C. Barnes marched to first rank in Arizona's historians. Casual though he was with fact, perhaps necessarily, in sanitizing records, he embraced the forester's creed: "The greatest good for the most people over the longest time." Thus, Barnes made better history than he preserved.

• The Commentator. Younger brother of the founder of the *Phoenix Herald,* James H. McClintock produced a watershed history, *Arizona,* which touched on Pleasant Valley, and his unpublished papers and clippings[3] bear insightful marginal notes and opinions. For years, McClintock was retained as correspondent for the *Los Angeles Times* and other journals. He was never able to get to the bottom of the feud.

• The Writer of First Book-length Nonfiction. Earle R. Forrest suspected the existence of agreements equal to treaties among participants in the Pleasant Valley War. He pored over court documents, but did not find the pacts. Arriving in Arizona after the turn of the century, Forrest interviewed the second generation, defined the order of battle, and crafted a useful necrology.[4]

• The Novelist. Zane Grey "utilized numerous sources in his quest for material, but what appears in his novel *To the Last Man* is a romance loosely twined around a factual framework, rather than a precise and accurate history."[5]

• The Aged Refugee Remembering. In 1922, L.J. Horton, a newly welcomed guest at the Arizona Pioneers Home, announced his plan to write from memory "a history of the warfare conducted by the settlers of Pleasant Valley against the Apaches, and also a story of the feud." He did. During the 1880s, he had been driven off a homestead near the creek bearing his name. Somewhat amiss in dates, Horton nevertheless called up convincing, significant detail. In his six-year Prescott research, he did not find James Stinson's signed commission of the Graham brothers as private police.[6]

• The Long-lived Veteran. William Colcord, early settler and able range hand for both sides, might have resolved many riddles, including the war's origin. He agreed to tell all to newspaper historian Roscoe G. Willson in 1951, and a lengthy series of articles resulted. Did he know of the treaties of war? Alas, he did not say. Regrettably, the articles contained scarcely *one* theretofore unknown fact. To the end, Bill Colcord could not bring himself to break the code of secrecy.

• The Loyal Son. Robert Voris, steeped as a boy in loyalist Tewksbury tales by his father, William Voris, in 1957 participated in question/answer sessions running to twenty-thousand transcribed words.[7] And not a word from Bob Voris of the official treaty of war.

• The Teller of the Other Side. An extraordinarily loyal and inspiring regional historian, Clara T. Woody devoted half her life to rationalizing Tewksbury points of view. But for all her digging for it, the phantom document eluded her. She might have sold a piece of her soul for it, she wanted it so much.[8]

The Pleasant Valley Compact was always so far, so near, for everybody. Apparently, the inked and recorded covenant among crated territorial papers was transferred for storage from Prescott to the basement of the State Capitol in Phoenix. Subsequently, many early Yavapai County files were destroyed in a Salt River flood.

Incredibly, a notarized copy of the original had been made, put away, and lost to history. This copy had been placed in the file for a perjury action emanating from the bench of Yavapai County's Third District Court. In effect, this Treaty of War had been preserved in a non-obvious niche for more than a century:

County of Yavapai

Territory of Arizona

This contract made and entered into on the 14 day of November 1883 between John Graham & Co., parties of the first part of Pleasant Valley Yavapai County A.T., and James Stinson of Maricopa County A.T., party of the second part, witnesseth.

The said party of the first part for and in consideration of the within named sums as follows.

The parties of the first part agree at any and all times to give evidence of any facts that may come within their knowledge or otherwise that may lead to the apprehension and conviction of any and all parties depredating upon the stock— consisting of cattle belonging to the party of the second part in any manner or form—shall receive for such services from the party of the second part—the number of Fifty (50) head of good American Cattle—consisting of Twenty-Five (25) Cows and Twenty-Five (25) Calves—or as otherwise may be agreed upon between said parties of the First and Second part, and both of said parties hereby mutually agree that they will act and cooperate together in the interest of Justice to secure the conviction of any and all parties who may trespass upon the rights of the party of the second part in said stock above mentioned.

Note—Upon the conviction of any party or parties depredating upon the stock of the party of the second part—then the delivery of the cattle shall take place as soon as practible immediately afterwards

Witness

Henry W. Fleury

Witness our hands and seals this 28 day of March 1884
Jas Stinson [seal]
John Graham [seal]
Territory of Arizona
County of Yavapai
I, Albert E. Foote, Clerk
District Court of the Third Judicial District of the Territory of Arizona in and
for the County of Yavapai do hereby certify the above and foregoing to be a full
true and correct copy of the contract between John Graham & Co. and Jas
Stinson, entered upon the 28th day of March 1884.
In witness whereof I have herewith put my hand and affixed the seal of the Court
on this 12th day of July AD. 1884.
Albert E. Foote
clerk

It is what was—by turn—sought, ignored, and by a few individuals, gratefully assumed gone forever. Yet this certified contract reposed unnoticed, unappreciated, and unpublished in a dossier of the Yavapai County (now Superior) Court. The document came into the hands of the author on January 14, 1986, during an intense, last-chance effort to find it. The Clerk of the Court, Barbara Boyle, graciously granted permission for a page-by-page scrutiny of surviving papers associated with court cases of the 1880s. There it was, likely on the orders of Judge Sumner Howard, an exhibit supporting a theory of Graham perjury. The treaty's self-contained timing raises as many questions as it answers.

Firstly, Stinson and John Graham stipulated that the contract— perhaps an oral agreement—had been in effect since November 14, 1883. Whether an earlier written contract existed (in Maricopa County?) must remain for others to determine. A fair supposition: the date so specified suggests the parties put their names to a piece of paper. But then, much serious business on the Arizona frontier was sealed with a handshake.[9] At any rate, sometime between the Gilleland skirmish and its resulting magistrate proceedings of early 1883, and the following autumn, the Tewksburys' staunch allies and exonerating witnesses, the Grahams, secretly hired out as range detectives for cattle baron James Stinson. "Graham & Company" presumably spent the winter, spring, and fall of 1883-1884 sleuthing about Pleasant Valley.

Secondly, on March 29, 1884 (the day following the recording of the treaty) in Prescott, District Attorney Charles B. Rush, in behalf of the Territory, accepted a felony complaint brought by John Graham against Edwin Tewksberry, John Tewksberry and James Tewksberry [charging] them with the crime of altering the brand upon neat cattle committed as follows: That heretofore, to wit: on or about the 24th day of October, A.D., 1883, at Tonto Basin the said defendants did then and there being, did unlawfully, wrongfully, wilfully and feloniously alter and change the brand upon about sixty-two head of neat cattle then and there being of the goods and chattel of James Stinson and John Graham with the intent then and there thereby unlawfully, wrongfully, wilfully and feloniously to steal the same contrary to the form of the statute in such cases made and provided, and against the peace and dignity of the Territory of Arizona. Wherefore, a warrant of arrest is prayed. . . .

That was just the beginning. The Grand Jury took up the accusation and expanded it. By May, in anticipation of the June term of District Court, the Grand Jury returned at least four separate indictments. Charged with grand larceny were not only the three Tewksbury brothers but three of their friends, George Blain[e], William Richards, and H.H. Bishop. According to the original true bill, witnesses examined by the Grand Jury were James Stinson, John Cole, Thomas H. Graham, John Graham, F.N. McCann, J.D. Adams, Edwin Tewksbury, and George Blaine.

The first indictment specified alteration of brands of ten of Stinson's beeves valued at twenty dollars apiece, and their theft. A second indictment accused the six defendants of altering brands of ten more Stinson animals valued at twenty-five dollars apiece. Both of these indictments alleged that all of the offenses occurred on November 21, 1883, at Tonto Basin. A third indictment named Edwin and James Tewksbury in the alleged January 4, 1884, theft of two head of Stinson stock. A fourth indictment accused James Tewksbury and William Richards. The crime: theft of one Stinson beef on April 7, 1884.

The indictments loosed a paper storm across the Rim Country. Bench warrants were issued, peaceable arrests made. Some (Edwin and James Tewksbury, for example) if not all the defendants were arraigned June ninth. Rush and Wells took the defense. Judge Sumner Howard set bonds at a stiff eight hundred dollars apiece. Preserved bonding instruments reveal that Albert Rose and Garret O. Sixby, two of Pleasant Valley's earliest pioneers, gave their personal assurance that John Tewksbury would appear for trial; Sam J. Houston and J.R. Walker, another pair of Yavapai oldtimers, went the bond of William Richards. It is a fair guess that the other defendants likewise gained freedom, but no other bonding data persist in the case files. Subpoenas for a veritable who's who of Pleasant Valley personalities went out for service as far as Globe.[10] All the defendants voluntarily traveled to Prescott and surrendered to Sheriff Jacob Hinkle, who placed them under arrest "now here in my custody before the Court, as I am within commanded." By all accounts, the defendants and their accusers put on their best behavior in Prescott, stabling horses at the OK corral, camping on vacant lots, and passing one another wordlessly on the boardwalks.[11]

Details of the trials in extant courthouse documents are limited to minutes and other procedural filings of the clerk. One entry notes that

Defendant William Richards was "discharged during progress of trial."
No explanation was given. Names of jurors in trial of indictment number
one, witnesses, times and dates of sessions, and final disposition are
blackly inked in the clean hand of W.W. Wilkerson, deputy clerk.[12] If
testimony was preserved, no transcript could be located. But if brevity
gives a clue, it must have been an open-and-shut case of acquittal. In a
typical trial, for the indictment against Edwin and James Tewksbury,
James Stinson and John Graham and Sheriff Hinkle were the only pros-
cecution witnesses. The Tewksbury brothers took the stand in their own
behalf, and testifying for them were William Richards, J.J. Vosburg [sic],
Andrew Pringle, J.L. Montgomery, and Albert Rose. The contract
between Stinson and Graham and Company as private investigators was
entered as a defense exhibit. An enduring if small mystery: also given as a
defense exhibit was a Statement of Account in name of Edwin Tewksbury, payable to George A. Newton, Globe jeweler and firearms retailer,
for October 1883-March 1884 showing cash draws, and charges mostly
for tobacco, hundreds of rounds of pistol and rifle ammunition, and for
the date January 30, 1884, fifty cents worth of pistol targets.[13]

In the action against James Tewksbury and William Richards, L.F.
Eggars and John A. Rush pressed the defense. Prosecutor Charles B.
Rush summoned witnesses James Stinson, John Cole, F.N. McCann,
John Graham. Witnesses for the defense were Joseph W. Watts, George
Blaine, Albert Rose, plus the defendants in their own behalf. The
"smoking gun" Stinson-Graham contract was read into evidence. For
some reason, the prosecution read a passage from the *Farmer's Almanac*.
Instructions requested by prosecution: "By a reasonable doubt is not
meant any fanciful, or possible doubt, but a doubt that is substantial in its
nature and comportable with reason; such a doubt as would influence an
ordinary man in his own most important affairs of life."[14] In only two
days of trials, juries found all defendants of the several indictments
innocent, and Judge Howard dismissed the cases. Without doubt, the
treaty, that is, the contract by which Stinson hired the Grahams as detectives, was decisive for the defense. With hardly time for a recess, perjury
charges were leveled against the Grahams by J.J. Vosburgh and Albert
Rose. The Grahams were released on bonds of two thousand dollars.
Specifically, the complaint alleged that the Grahams lied when they said
that Tewksbury, et al, drove ten head of Stinson cattle into the Middleton Corral, and changed brands and ear marks. The case was handed
over to the Grand Jury, Morris Goldwater, foreman. Bonds were
provided by James Stinson and Joseph R. Walker.

On the conclusion of the case at Prescott last week of the territory vs. James
Tewksbury et al, charged with grand larceny, Judge Howard, immediately after
the rendition of a verdict of not guilty by a jury, in a most scathing address, criti-

cized the testimony given by the prosecuting witnesses, Thomas Graham and John Graham, and directed District Attorney Rush to have warrants immediately issued for their arrest on a charge of perjury. That was done and the parties were taken into custody. The action of Judge Howard, though having an electrifying effect on the court officials and jurors in attendance, met with the general approbation of that part of the community cognizant with the case.[15]

The wrath, if not righteous indignation, of the Tewksbury circle, which was provoked by the Prescott trials, spilled over into news columns of that day:

Before leaving Prescott it is stated [George] Blaine. . .purchased at one of the leading stores in Prescott a supply of .45 calibre cartridges and while placing the same in his pistol belt remarked that he would use them to clean out some of the damn Stinson gang. . . .

What transpired over the next week is open to conjecture. The Tewksburys certainly must have been crowing. The Globe element, with Jerry Vosburgh and George Newton leading both defense and attack, had carried day in far-away Prescott. The Tewksbury transgressions, if any, were wiped clean. Jim Stinson and his lackeys, the Grahams, were repulsed and put under punitive bonds.

Yet the legal maneuverings, however successful, were costly also for the Tewksburys and their current allies. By one account, Jim Tewksbury, for the pittance of fifty dollars, was obliged to sell a lovely ranch meadow to Joseph Haigler to raise funds to pay court costs. Jim's debilitating tuberculosis may also have been a factor, but the Tewksbury clan by now was of a mood to blame all ills, including pulmonary, upon the Grahams. Both sides "pickled the pearl of compromise in the vinegar of retaliation." A court had found the Tewksburys wrongly accused of stealing. The Grahams surely felt abandoned and betrayed by material witnesses, who may have been intimidated. Stinson, meantime, was rapidly losing control of a considerable fortune on the hoof.

Injured pride. Vicious gossip. Galloping paranoia. Mischievous meddling. Neglect by neutral neighbors. Trouble built like a Tonto Basin cumulonimbus.

It was the July 23, 1884, edition of the *Herald* of Phoenix which broke the next sensational story:

ROW AMONG CATTLE MEN
Another Shooting Scrape
in Tonto Basin
Marion McCann Kills George Blain
and Wounds John Tewksbury, in a Fight

By a telegram from Fort McDowell to Mr. James Stinson, of this place, we learn of another serious shooting affray, in Pleasant Valley, Tonto Basin, which took place yesterday forenoon among the cattle men of that section, the Tewksbury men being engaged on one side, and Stinson's men on the other. Jeff Adams, one of Stinson's men, immediately came down to McDowell, arriving there this morning, and forwarded the following particulars concerning the fight, which occurred at Stinson's house, in Pleasant Valley, at about 10 o'clock yesterday forenoon.

The Tewksbury party came up and stationed themselves around Stinson's house and had some words with Stinson's men. Marion McCann, one of the employees of Mr. Stinson, said to them that he wanted nothing to do with them. George Blain, one of the Tewksbury party, then said to McCann, "You have run this country long enough, you d—d son of a —," and shot at McCann, but without the shot taking effect. McCann then returned the shot, his ball taking effect and passing through the jaw and out the back of the head. John Tewksbury then opened fire on McCann, firing several shots, but without anyone hitting McCann. McCann in the meantime was returning the fire of Tewsbury and one of his shots, it is thought took effect, as Tewksbury fell over his horse but was able to keep his seat and rode away.

George Blain was alive when Adams left but was insensible, and it was thought that he would live but a short time.

At this moment, George Blaine (which seemed his preferred spelling) was alive, suffering grievously, and fated to recover. In Phoenix, the opposition, Democratic *Gazette,* was left to rewrite the hated *Herald.* Eager to provide a choice morsel of background, the *Gazette* huffed and puffed:

ANOTHER KILLING IN TONTO

...the origin of the affair is supposed to be in the differences that have existed among the cattle men of Tonto Basin for some years past. McCann was in charge of Stinson's cattle, which were being gathered up for delivery to Reed & Murray. Bad blood has existed between Stinson's men and the Tewksberry boys for some time past, eighteen months ago the latter having killed one of Stinson's herders and wounded another severely. Blaine and Tewksbury were recently indicted by the Yavapai grand jury on a charge of stealing cattle, but on trial were acquitted. They have not been home to exceed ten days since their exoneration. Blaine, it is claimed, had a very bad reputation in Colorado before coming to this territory. On the other hand, Marion McCann, who is well known here, is a very quiet, peaceable and respectable man, but with a determined character, which was not likely to brook any intimidation.[16]

Now the Pleasant Valley War, heretofore limited in interest to Yavapai County and borderlands, gained the attention of the territory and beyond. In Tucson, the *Citizen* took notice, and in Globe, the *Silver Belt* printed, "We do not question the fact of the shooting, nor will we be surprised to learn in the near future, of further violance in that locality."[17] In turn, the *Phoenix Herald* borrowed a long paragraph from the *Globe Chronicle:*

Another Version. . . .The story of the shooting scrape at Pleasant Valley is as follows: John Tewksbury, George Blaine, Ed Rose, and William Richard went to

Stinson's to see about the "round-up." There is a feud of long standing between
the parties. After the Tewksbury party had transacted their business they left the
camp, and when about 30 feet away the Stinson party, eight or ten in number,
who were well fortified, opened fire upon them. John Tewksbury returned the
fire and the Stinson party scattered. Blaine was hit in the face, but the wound is
not considered necessarily fatal. None of the rest of the Tewksbury party were
hurt, and it is not yet known whether any of the Stinson men were hit in the
Tewksbury volley.[18]

The *Herald,* a few days later, interviewed a traveler who opined
"Blaine. . .was. . .not expected to live. John Tewksbury. . .is reported to
have been but slightly wounded." If true, the Tewksburys refused to give
their enemies the satisfaction of knowing through a formal complaint.[19]
The *Gazette,* growing desperate, ran a clip the next day from the *Prescott
Journal*: "A telegram has been received at Prescott from a resident of
Strawberry Valley. . .which states Blaine is doing well as could be
expected. A warrant was issued by Judge L.P. Nash, of Strawberry Valley,
for the arrest of John Tewksbury, who was one of the Blaine party at the
time of the shooting, Deputy Sheriff Morlan, from Strawberry Valley,
was sent to serve the warrant. Mr. [Ed?] Rose, of Pleasant Valley, who
was with the Blaine party at the time of the shooting, said that he was a
deputy sheriff, having been appointed by the judge in Prescott, and that
Morlan could not take Tewksbury. Morlan then returned to Strawberry
Valley, and was ordered to obtain a posse and return to arrest Tewksbury, and also to take Rose, dead or alive. It is not yet known whether
Rose and Tewksbury have been arrested. More trouble is anticipated."[20]

That night, a Saturday, who but Marion McCann arrived at Phoenix
to give the *Gazette* exclusive insights, but not much: "Mr. McCann said
he anticipated trouble when the party rode up to the house. . .his effort
was to avert it, and in a quiet manner he asked Blaine and Tewksbury to
move on about their business. . .Blaine opened fire. . .Tewksbury started
to run at this juncture, which, doubtless saved him from injury, as Mr.
McCann is a very true shot."[21]

The following Saturday, the daily edition of the *Herald* went with an
exchange item from the *Prescott Miner* and its source, an "unengaged
spectator," Charles H. Ryall, who in part was quoted, "The trouble was
virtually over the round-up of cattle, and the Tewksburys, with that end
in view, went over to Stinson's house in the hope of arriving at some
amicable understanding in determining an acceptable locality to both parties, and a convenient time for such purpose. In trying to settle the matter, when, without any warning, McCann of the Stinson party immediately commenced firing at John Tewksbury, who retreated at once to the
rear of a stone wall. In an instant the firing became general. . . . The next
day both parties signified their willingness to 'have it out' and forever

settle the long-existing bad feeling between them, but through friends, further trouble was prevented. Warrants were sworn out. . .but the law in that locality is looked upon as a dead letter and no action was taken to bring the guilty ones to justice."²² The "unengaged" disinterest of Charles H. Ryall could have been challenged, for he owned a full interest with W.A. Richards and Fred Platten in the 77 Brand of Pleasant Valley. Richards was a name regularly allied with Tewksbury interests. In fact, Bill Richards was "a member of the Blaine party." So much for impartiality.

And if indeed a warrant was outstanding for John Tewksbury, Yavapai authorities must have looked the other way, for the *Herald* reported the man vocally public, attending the Democratic convention in Prescott, in early September.²³

It is a matter of court record that Lafayette P. Nash, Green Valley (later Payson) precinct justice, on July 30 took exhaustive testimony from available and willing witnesses. Following the Blaine shooting, McCann promptly surrendered to Nash, but refused to make a statement. Justice Nash dutifully forwarded a hefty sheaf of depositions to Prescott for Grand Jury consideration. Apparently, no indictments resulted, although the sworn statements survive.²⁴

They were taken by Justice Nash in behalf of "the plaintiff," presumably the territory, with cross-examination led by Marion McCann, "defendant." All witnesses were Stinson hands and McCann underlings. And assuredly Stinson was present—one cowboy testifying "last night is the first time I have ever seen him to know him." The witnesses: John Cole, twenty-six; Ed Williams, forty; J.M. Adams, relationship if any to Cap Adams not given; Charles Cameron, twenty-one, Stinson herder six months; and J.W. Richards, eighteen, (no relation to W.A. Richards in the Tewksbury party) Stinson cowboy at the time of shooting, two days.

Through several pages of transcribed testimony, Cameron gave his recollection of July 22, 1884, events. Cameron was at Stinson's ranch, not doing much, when George Blaine, John Tewksbury, Ed Rose, and William Richards rode up. McCann spoke first, good naturedly, and asked all but Ed Rose to move on. With no provocation, said John Tewksbury and George Blaine, "You damned, fly-blowed son-of-a-bitch, I have been bulldozed by you long enough." With that Blaine called for McCann to come out fifty feet from the house. McCann obliged. Blaine snapped off a wild pistol shot in McCann's direction. McCann shot Blaine, who fell off his horse.

Cameron wound up his testimony with an account of Blaine's suffering, the wounded man's pleas for help, and resulting first aid. Not surprisingly—with Stinson hanging on every word—his cowboys gave the same story in nearly all detail. Teenager J.W. Richards confessed to cowering inside the house. Several of Stinson's cowhands alleged that

John Tewksbury joined the gunplay, and when things got hot, raced off on his horse.

Two of the cowboys told Justice Nash that John Tewksbury had abused them, and they took it, and that it was common knowledge that John Tewksbury sometime in 1884 had whipped John Graham in a fist fight. Nash's inquiry apparently was as far as the Blaine shooting case went officially. Five entrenched eyewitnesses swore that Blaine not only questioned McCann's courage, but also doubted aloud publicly, unsmilingly, the honor of McCann's mother—in the West, a gross insult even two decades before Wister's Virginian schooled his own enemy, Trampas, in rangeland etiquette. The price of Blaine's transgression was a gruesome facial scar. At that, he was lucky.

Undiluted hard feelings prevailed in Pleasant Valley during the remainder of 1884. Now the tortuous, boulder-strewn bed of Cherry Creek became the natural demarcation of feudal territory: Grahams to the west; Tewksburys to the east. Pockets of conflicting loyalties persisted behind the lines. . .people couldn't pick up their ranches and move them. So some ranches became hedgehogs. Hunting pieces and weapons unfired in anger since Indian conflicts were strapped on for protection during routine chores—horse-catching, wood-cutting, freighting. Women were wakened at night, required to prepare and dish up meals, and retire without seeing their tables of furtive guests.[25]

Gathering cattle for identification, treatment, and sale from unfenced rangeland inevitably presented westerners with a fundamental need to cooperate. At least once—and likely twice—a year a community roundup logically dealt with homogenous herds grazing unrestrained on unsubdivided public domain. In 1885, there existed no U.S. Forest Service. No Taylor Grazing Act. America's initial national park had been set aside only a decade or so before. America's "first bureaucrat" had run the theretofore unexplored Colorado River no earlier than 1869-71. The interrelated ways of the wilderness were imperfectly understood even by the people who derived a living from the land.

Ideally, all hands gathered all cattle they could, regardless of ownership. Some of these animals were in every sense wild. To one or more rodeo grounds such rank range creatures were driven, then held for counting, culling, branding, earmarking, castrating, dehorning, doctoring. The best of pasturages could not carry large concentrations of livestock infinitely. In the common interest, cooler heads among Pleasant Valley ranchers called for a general roundup concentrated at Spring Creek in May of 1885. And as usual, extra hands were welcome, not many questions asked.

Among casual help hired was a personable chap who said he was just drifting through, out of New Mexico. He had no local sponsor; in fact, he was a stranger in Pleasant Valley. He gave a common nickname, which met the unwritten code: it wasn't considered polite to inquire closely into a man's past. Only later would Pleasant Valley learn his real name: Robert Carr Blassingame.[26]

Regarding the Pleasant Valley country in 1885, nearly everybody in the livestock business was a neophyte. Plainsmen from Texas tripped over the vertical topography. Southerners never breathed such dry air under such blue sky. Midwestern farmers acquainted with the black bottoms of Ohio now dug their fingers into thin, unstable, granitic soils as fragile as spiderwebs. At a mile or more elevation, under phenomenal solar radiation, a seedling that made it through the last frost of May might wither in the drouth of mid-June. Precipitation patterns seemed malevolent and perverse. Lilies masqueraded as cactus, bunchgrass grew as tall as trees, toads grew horns, rabbits looked like donkeys, grapevines grew bigger than barns and made fruits smaller than peas. Some days in March were so wet, fire would balk at cotton soaked in coal oil; in August, the Indians would strike a spark to consume fifty thousand acres.[27] It seemed illogical that the carrying capacity of the range might be one cow per square mile; yet it was so, counting competition of deer, elk, antelope, javelina, feral horses, and other grazers and browsers. It was open season, no limit, on predators—eagles that might occasionally kill a lamb, and lions which infrequently acquired a taste for horseflesh. Losses over a season to grizzly bear, cougar, bog, disease, miscarriage, and accident were expected, but excessive shrinkage raised suspicions.

For Tom and John Graham, this would be their first roundup since their purchase of two hundred head of heifers from Flake. And against Graham expectations, the Graham herds were a hundred head short. It was a jolting initiation to the cattle business, Pleasant Valley, 1880s-style.

Immediately following the roundup, on May 20, 1885, the personable part-time cowboy authored a complaint alleging larceny. Three weeks later, the complaint was filed in far-off St. Johns, seat of Apache County. He signed his name, Robert Carre Blassingame. Witnesses listed in addition to Blassingame: James Tewksbury, W.S. Atchison, Oscar [Osmer] Flake, Marion McCann, Louis Parker, John Cole, and A.A. Ward.[28]

At the hearing, Blassingame led off testimony before William M. Rudd, county judge. Under oath Blassingame swore he was a stock raiser residing twenty miles south of St. Johns, a deputy sheriff of Yavapai County, and a hired detective for the Apache County Livestock Association. He had heard of strayed cattle belonging to W.S. Atchison. And why didn't Atchison go after his own cattle? "It was a pretty hard country, and a long way over there, rough roads more expense than they were really worth, and putting a particular friend of his in trouble for informing him they were there." Blassingame further stated that in early

May, he observed the Grahams closely herding two head of cows, one a red roan and another a red and white spotted, both four to six years old. Witnesses were James Tewksbury, Ed Rose, Bob Sixsby, Jim Tewksbury, Ed Tewksbury, O.C. Phelton [Felton], John Graham, "Mr." Parker. Blassingame had the animals roped and thrown down for closer inspection. The cattle bore on the right hip a disfigured: A.

And on the left hip "not straight enough to have been made with a made iron": JT Connected.

Under cross-examination, Blassingame at first evaded the defense attorney's questions as to how he knew the cows were in Pleasant Valley and that they were in the Grahams' possession. Wasn't Blassingame in fact tipped off by James Tewksbury?

A. Yes.

Q. Then Tewksbury informed you that the cattle were there?

A. Yes, he informed me that the cattle were there, and saw them stolen.

Q. Did he say that he was present when they were stolen?

A. Yes, was in their employ.

Q. The first information of these cattle being in Pleasant Valley was from what James Tewksbury told you was it?

A. Yes, that was the first information I had.

Osmer D. Flake testified that in October 1882, he had helped vent and deliver two hundred yearlings to the Grahams.[29]

I think the Tewksburys were there [Pleasant Valley] but the Grahams were miners over in the Globe country. They had a good claim, which they sold...they wanted to try the cattle business which I do not think they had much experience in. They liked Pleasant Valley; it was a beautiful country with grass everywhere. They went to Snowflake where they bought two hundred heifers from W.J. Flake, none over two years old. The Tewksburys were experienced cattlemen. The Grahams hired Jim Tewksbury to help them. We branded out the cattle to them near Snowflake and they started for the Valley. The following day, Mr. Flake sent one of his men, Chris Nielson, to follow them across the range and see that they did not take any stock that did not belong to them. When he caught up with them one of them told him:

"We have some of Flake's cows in the herd; they got in and when we cut them out they followed up. We thought we would take them to the corral on Park Wash, where we will camp tonight, and leave them in the corral in the morning. After our own stock got out of sight one of us would turn them out and start them back toward their range and of course they would drift back to their range."

They asked Nielson to camp with them, which he did; and in the morning, cut out the strays and started home. They drove across the Wash and on to the West but didn't go far. Nielson drove the cows (twelve or fourteen) about six miles toward home; it was quite a hot day and the cows would bush up under the trees; being alone he could not do much with them but knew the cows, close to their home range, would drift on when it got cooler in the evening. Being a long way from home, he left the cows and went home, getting there about dark. Little did he dream what was going on behind him. Two of the Graham bunch followed him, while the other herded their stock, and when Nielson left the cows, they gathered them up and drove them back to their bunch, taking them into the Valley. (We learned all this from Jim Tewksbury, a couple of years later.)

A lot of stock had been stolen. . .and a stock association was formed and they hired a cowpuncher. . .to work as a detective. . . . His name was Carr Blassingame. Blassingame went into the Valley and hired out as a cowhand in the Spring of 1885, found what he was sent for. . . .William S. Atchison of Springerville, stockraiser, said he had owned these two cows since January of 1880. His brand was a little A on the right hip. He helped the roundup when W.J. Flake sold two hundred heifers and steers to the Grahams. They asked Atchison if he wanted to throw his stock into the deal, and he declined. At the time his cattle were watering on Silver Creek, Show Low, and Phoenix Park.

At the St. Johns inquiry, Atchison was asked how he learned about his cattle being in Pleasant Valley.

A. Six weeks ago I had a letter from a friend from Flagstaff that the Grahams had two of my cows without a vent with a brand disfigured and my ear marks cut out.

Q. Where is that letter?

A. I cannot produce it today.

Q. Who was that letter from?

A. It was from James Stinson.

From James Stinson!

He who just the year before had signed the Treaty of War with the Grahams, registered brands with them, hired them as range detectives, joined them in bringing charges against the Tewksburys, and posted their bonds in the perjury matter, had by now so turned against the Grahams that he precipitated a charge against them in an alleged, three-year-old crime.

James Tewksbury declared he had known the Grahams nearly three years. He was employed by the Grahams when they bought a starter herd from W.J. Flake and Isaac Turley in early fall of 1882. Tewksbury helped drive the herd south from Snowflake toward Pleasant Valley. Tewksbury said some cattle of other owners were allowed to join the herd. Later, Tewksbury said that at his home corral he helped the Grahams brand the stolen stock. Questions for the defense:

Q. You told Blassingame all about this taking of these cows and branding them did you not?

A. Yes.

Q. Did you ever swear out a warrant against the Grahams here?

A. Yes but the warrant was not signed by the Justice of the Peace so it did no good.

Q. And you took a warrant over to Pleasant Valley to arrest the Grahams didn't you?

A. Yes, sir.

Q. What interested you in the matter to make you do all that?

A. Simply because he came over and paid me three dollars per day and my expenses and that it would have him there to come over here.

Q. Were you not making that much at home?

A. No sir.

Q. Now your idea was, Mr. Tewksbury, because you were the only one present with the Grahams when those two cows were taken by you and them that you had a dead moral cinch on them. That was your idea then was it? You were all in a little bottle together?

A. No sir, that was not it, if I was in a little bottle I could not ride over here for a warrant.

Q. Who was present when the Grahams branded those two cows with JT Connected at Pleasant Valley?

A. There were the two Grahams and myself and brother and John Gilleland and Ed Rose come there just after the cattle were branded and were looking at them. . . .

Q. Things have not been altogether pleasant in Pleasant Valley between you and the Grahams for some time have they?

A. No, they have not, there has been a great deal of trouble here lately, putting them under bond for perjury, lying.

Q. Had you in for something, didn't they?

A. That is what they did.

Q. What for Mr. Tewksbury?

A. For stealing cattle.

Q. Now you think what is sauce for the goose is sauce for the gander don't you?

Later in the questioning:

Q. Who had you arrested for taking cattle over there?

A. John Graham had swore out the complaint.

Q. When?

A. Last spring sometime 1884.

Q. You knew all about this two-cows transaction two years and a half ago didn't you?

A. I did sir.

Q. You never said anything about it until John Graham swore out the complaint against you did you?

A. No, sir, I did not.

Among other statements, Louis Parker, cousin to the Grahams, claimed the Quarter Circle A brand on the right hip to be his own. The Grahams gave him the cows as wages. He said he put the brands onto otherwise unbranded right hips himself with a straight bar, and that he had several witnesses, including John Cole. Yet John Cole, also under examination, said he didn't see the act of branding. . .merely saw the cows afterward.

John Graham stated he was thirty-two years of age, Scotland born, resident of Pleasant Valley since August, 1882. He said the Grahams did buy two hundred heifers from Flake, a few from Turley, one from Bagnall. All were driven to Pleasant Valley, to the corral of James Tewksbury. There they branded a calf which had been born at a sheep corral. They didn't make their first roundup until May 1885, and were a hundred head short of their expectations. In April 1884, the Grahams sold six head of cattle to Louis Parker.

Much same story was told by Tom Graham. He said he was born in Franklin County, Ohio, and had been a resident of Pleasant Valley since September 1882. Half the cattle purchased from the Mormons had been branded JT Connected, the other half, TE Connected.

Scrawled in ink on the reverse side of Tom Graham's transcribed testimony were the words:

"It appearing to me by the within depositions and statements that the offenses therein mentioned, that of grand larceny has been committed, and there is sufficient cause to believe the within named John Grayham and Thomas H. Grayham guilty, I order that they be held to answer the same, and that they be admitted to bail in the sum of one thousand dollars each this June 12, 1885. by William M. Rudd, judge of the county court."

Apparently the case went to the Grand Jury. On September 1, an information was filed by Apache County District Attorney C. L. Gutterson in St. Johns. John and Tom Graham were accused of cattle theft. A hearing, scheduled for October, was then continued to March 25, 1886. At the request of the district attorney, a motion of *nolle prosequi* was entered. The motion was granted, the defendants discharged from custody, bail exonerated, and a trial jury dismissed by John C. Shields, District Judge.[30]

Once again, the mounting difficulties of Pleasant Valley had reached the chambers of a court, only to be turned aside, unresolved. Osmer D. Flake noted that "...Pleasant Valley men traveled in two bunches and did not get into each other's way at all. After reaching the Valley, there was a tacit understanding just where the dividing line was between the two ranges, and they went heavily armed and gazed in each other's way for about eighteen months before fighting actually started. However, there was plenty going on. . . . "[31]

VII. Coming of the Hashknives

Not all ludicrous notions about exploiting western lands originated in the East, but in the last half of the nineteenth century, it certainly seemed that way. The ethic of restrained multiple use, the morality of management for future generations, and the science of soil conservation were decades away. "Hostile" was a term more likely associated with semiarid lands than "fragile." The worshipful prose about the desert by John C. Van Dyke would not appear until the turn of the century. Those who first set the rules for the opening of the West were not environmentalists. Nor were the first westerners.

Land rape and ruin during the 1880s and 1890s served as operating policy for the Hashknife outfit, and foredoomed the company's cattle experiment to humiliating failure. During those two eventful decades, the Hashknife cut gigantic enemies down to size, and whittled a way of life that translated directly into legend.

Those who implored the Territorial Legislature to set standards of behavior and business ethics might just as well have saved their breath:

The Thirteenth Territorial Legislature, which met in Prescott in 1885, was one of the most colorful in Arizona history. It was then known as the "bloody thir-

77

teenth" because of the lawmakers' propensity for settling their differences with fists or guns.

It also was known as the "thieving thirteenth" because of some rather remarkable overspending. Five Pima County legislators, for example, each claimed $330 in travel expenses at fifteen cents a mile. To reach Prescott they traveled by train from Tucson to Los Angeles and then through Needles, California, to Ash Fork [Arizona], where they caught the stage for Prescott

Encompassing two million acres, the Hashknife was not the West's largest ranch, equalling merely the area of Rhode Island and Delaware combined. No, the Hashknife was peculiar in that its holdings occurred in alternate, staggered checkerboard squares a *mile on a side*. The politicians who scribed those tidy lines on God's irregular map appreciated little about plateau nature, understood less about human spirit, and knew absolutely nothing about a cow.

The Hashknife's unnatural divisions derived from the post–Civil War hustle toward Manifest Destiny. To foster westering rail transport, Congress rewarded builders with grants of public land. The Atlantic and Pacific Railroad between New Mexico and California had call on most odd-numbered sections of lands extending twenty miles on either side of completed train tracks. If the odd sections already were sold or preempted, the railroaders could select sections located farther from the tracks. So in practice, the A&P's holdings became scattered for forty miles—or more—wide, and six hundred fifty miles long.

Investors, including some of the original rail tycoons, thought they saw a sure thing. Drouth and barbed wire crimped the cattle business in Middle America. Westward lay inexhaustible (so they thought) ranges of lush grass. The founders, incuding Edward Kinsley, Henry Kinsley, Frank Ames, James McCreery, and the New York banking firm of Seligman and Seligman, capitalized the Aztec Land & Cattle Company in New York. In Arizona's Yavapai and Apache counties, the company bought a million railroad acres (mostly south of the tracks) for fifty cents an acre, and acquired the brand and remnant of an old but struggling West Texas-New Mexico livestock enterprise. The Hashknife took its mark and name from a familiar chuck wagon chopping utensil. More important, the Hashknife brand was considered difficult to alter.

From the outset, decisions voted in Eastern boardrooms tended to be vetoed on the scene.

Trouble is brewing between the sheep raisers of Apache County and the Aztec. . . .The company recently made arrangements with the A&P Railroad for 200,000 acres of railroad land and the company thereupon drove the sheep off the land. As the land is not yet surveyed or patented the sheep men claim that this action was unjust and high handed. Trouble is likely to occur at any time . . . a very bitter feeling exists.[2]

Harsh notices were published prominently and frequently in cattle country journals, with the company objecting "most strenuously to entry upon its lands of any herds or droves which must necessarily occur when they cross from section to section." As for trespass,

The Aztec Land & Cattle Co. Ltd. are the owners in fee simple of all the odd numbered or railroad sections of Townships 14, 15, 16, 17, 18 and 19, in Ranges 9, 10 and 11, and pay taxes on the same in Yavapai County. All persons are forbidden to trespass upon said lands. All persons who have occupied and used any of said lands for their own benefit or to the damage of this company will be held accountable under the law. (Signed) Henry Warren, Vice President and General Manager.[3]

Aztec's expectation: it would freely graze its own 1,125,999 acres, plus the other million or so acres of public lands interspersed in the checkerboard. Where Aztec snapped up sections with cherished springs, resistance was especially strong. By hook or crook, entrenched sheep men, small-time horse breeders, hick town bankers, and Mormon and Mexican colonizers fought the takeover. The initial stocking of the Hashknife range filled four hundred rail cars from New Mexico and Texas to Holbrook. "The company . . . also bought up any brands which in any way resembled their own brand. . . . To handle their vast herds over their vast range, they hired many cowboys to live at remote watering holes and patrol a designated area. So widespread was this range that these men could absent themselves from their headquarters for considerable time without being missed."[4]

Before long, there were 33,000 Hashknife longhorns and a large remuda of horses contentedly grazing on the Aztec land. The range stretched from Mormon Lake to east of Holbrook, and from the Little Colorado River south to the Mogollon Rim. Ranch houses and camps were erected. Headquarters was an adobe building just south of Joseph City, but the offices were in Holbrook. E.J. Simpson was the local manager and John T. Jones the first foreman. The total investment had cost the Aztec Company $1,331,372.26, but it was going to cost them much more in worry and headaches.

Much of the country was rough and hard to work. Cattle got lost in deep canyons or roamed back up in the Mogollon Mountains, where they would stay four or five years and come out wild as deer. They often bogged down in Mormon irrigation ditches and canals. It took a lot of men to work that kind of terrain.[5]

Men of a hardbitten breed, in fact. Commonly Texans: more likely sons than daughters of beaten but unreconstructed civil disobeyors. Younger rather than older. Poorer rather than richer. Less rather than more formally educated. Comparatively well paid: twenty-five to thirty dollars a month and board for themselves and if married, for their families. Hashknife cowboys were given to action rather than deliberation. Good with a gun. Of a roping tradition. Not much to dwell on their past. After a century, historians are still trying to sort out the aliases and nicknames: Windy Bob, Poker Bill, Johnny-Come-Lately. Killers from other parts, such as Tom Pickett, sidekick of Billy the Kid, made a Hashknife hand; yet Burt Mossman's flinty honesty got himself promoted to first captain of the Arizona Rangers. Some authorities list a dozen or so Hashknife cowboys enlisted as part-time participants in the Pleasant Valley War.[6]

Good men or bad, Hashknife riders were overfilled with macabre humor. Once, Hook Larsen got drunk and his Hashknife bunkies boxed him up at Holbrook, and as a joke shipped him by train to Winslow.[7] Troops of Hashknife celebrants routinely terrorized brothels, shot up taverns, and raced down streets. When a Hashknife cowboy rode his horse into a Winslow saloon, the bartender shot him dead.[8]

A relatively few Hashknife hands were hired off local ranches—strong, cow smart, resolute Mormon youths in their late 'teens and twenties—but they generally lacked the outrageous vocabulary and value system of veteran Hashknife hands. As one Mormon 'puncher set down in his memoirs, the Hashknife:

... had some real fine men in their employ; they also had some of the worst men that ever left Texas. There lived along the foot of the mountain, from Show Low west to the Chevelon, a number of families all of whom had a few cattle and a small farm. There also sprung up a number of camps; some private individuals ... others kept by men working for the Hash Knife ... and their were so many thieves among the latter that they soon run most of the respectable people out of the country, largely by stealing everything they had loose.[9]

By some estimates, Hashknife herds rapidly increased to forty thousand (that was O.D. Flake's number) to sixty thousand (an educated guess of Earle Forrest). The bovine population explosion destabilized endeavors across a vast area desperately needful of every civilizing influence possible. Unfenced ranges were invaded. Common law water rights evaporated. Sweat equities in unsurveyed farms were appropriated without compensation. Corrupt officials nearly broke some local governments, as in the Apache County seat of St. Johns.[10] With superior forces of order distant and disinterested, natural conflicts ran their course: Mormon vs. Mexican, East vs. West, Salt Lake vs. Santa Fe, sheep grower vs. cattleman, capitalist vs. wage-earner, townsperson vs. trailblazer, Yank vs. Reb, white vs. Indian.

"Northern Arizona was still frontier," reminded longtime Little Colorado chronicler Joan Baéza. "Trade routes had bypassed the high plateau region for two reasons—Navajo and Apache. Even after treaties were signed and reservations established, bands of Navajos and Apaches carried on guerrilla warfare, raiding small ranches at night, ambushing stages and wagons for supplies. One group of Navajos bragged that they had killed three eastern gentlemen passing through Arizona just to get a closer look at the strange clothing and silk hats they wore."

To such a social flux were attracted outlaws eager to take advantage of any weakness; not surprisingly, when Tombstone's cops became too tough, the surviving, notorious Clantons transferred their shady businesses to the alpine-like uplands south of Springerville. Well into the twentieth century hideouts for outlaws, be they highwaymen or bootleggers, abounded in outback Arizona.

To one such enclave deep in Tewksbury country in the mid-1880s gravitated a star-crossed Texas family whose flesh and blood would consecrate a dozen battle and burial grounds of the Pleasant Valley War. The family name: Blevins.

Martin Blevins was the patriarch of the Arizona immigrants. Missouri-born about 1840, he had married a Texas lass, Mary Atkinson, a few years his junior. Mart's passion was fine horses, which he raised on properties in Llano and Mason counties northwest of Austin, Texas. His fortunes declined when some of his headstrong boys offended the law.[11] Andrew Arnold (Andy), the eldest, was a fugitive before he was old enough to vote— by some accounts, he had had shot the right man or stolen the wrong horse, and ever a jump ahead of a sheriff, drifted through the Southwest. In Oklahoma, Andy, in a characterisic short-cut,

... engaged in the profitable but dangerous business of peddling whisky to the red men in Indian Territory until government agents learned of his activities, and the vigilance of troops made this occupation too hazardous for a man's liberty. Finally, when a Texas sheriff noted for a quick gun hand set out on Andy's trail for a murder committed in the Lone-Star State, he fled to faraway Arizona frontier, which in the 1880s was a haven for killers. . . .[12]

In Andy's defense, he is remembered much differently by his family. Fiery-tempered and sticky-fingered, perhaps, but Blevins clan authority and confidant E.D. Tussey always doubted Andy killed anybody outside Arizona. Tussey told Forrest: "He was wanted for horse-stealing. Years later, Mrs. John Blevins said that she never knew a man more gentle around children or women, and that he had a very pleasing personality." An accomplished gun handler, Andy may have enjoyed a mixed acquaintanceship in Oklahoma or New Mexico with another young man proficient in arms, Commodore Perry Owens.[13] According to one family legend, recorded in the 1930s, Andy was in custody of Texas Rangers when he boldly escaped from a train "around the year 1880."[14]

As early as 1884 and no later than 1885, Andy Blevins, using his long-standing alias, Cooper, wandered into the plateau country north of Arizona's Tonto Rim. Almost from the beginning, to the Mormons colonizing on and under the rim, Andy Cooper proved a holy terror; family histories of pioneer Mormons bristle with accounts of his incessant, sadistic bullying. At first sight, Andy coveted a lush meadowland improved by Will and John Q. Adams along Canyon Creek.[15] The prior claimant presented no great problem . . . Andy leveled a gun and ordered the Adams family off the place, taking only what could be carried in a wagon. Andy appropriated their stout house, ranch buildings, and cleared and irrigated fields, while the Adamses had to start all over again in Wilford, a hamlet atop the rim.[16] A less malevolent version has the Adams homesteaders trekking to Utah for a temple visit. In their absence, Andy took possession of Canyon Creek, and settled the Adams claim with a cash payment.[17]

Yet it's difficult to turn up much mention of Andy's redeeming virtues. Among his other alleged crimes: pistol-whipping an unarmed herder, terrorizing Mormon homesteads, stealing Navajo ponies, and threatening to "blow to hell the guts" of various Mormon menfolk who by and large kept religious pacifist vows.

Relentlessly hazed by Cooper was Charles Edmund Richardson, whose family preserves a memoir:

Cooper raced to my father's door demanding Richardson, whose guts he was there to blast out. . . . His vocal holocaust of scorching threats, designed to wither his listeners, fanned his own temper into white heat. Fearing he might take vengeance upon my father, my mother and sisters hovered near to protect him.

As soon as Cooper was gone my father saddled his horse, took his gun and rode down the canyon where there was a very large rock at the side of the road. He hid his horse and got down behind the rock, in earnest prayed asking if it was the Lord's will that he should take Cooper's life to send him that way. He lay there all day with his finger on the trigger of his gun. In the evening he came back home to my mother and said, "The Lord doesn't want me to kill Cooper."[18]

Whether providential oversight was a factor or not, Cooper lived to cut a wide and free path from his Canyon Creek base camp which strategically skirted and and broached the Mogollon escarpment. In so many ways, Canyon Creek was ideal for a man on the run with no visible means of support. Whoever owned Canyon Creek largely controlled traffic north and south, yet had access to the no-man's-land of the casually defined Apache reservation to the east. Oldtimers were all but unanimous: Andy Cooper used Canyon Creek and other roosts to rustle, rebrand, and hold livestock as part of a traffic extending all the way from Colorado to Old Mexico. Cooper and other rustlers were suspected of fencing off access to Diamond Butte, where beeves and broncs were hidden and doctored for rebranding.[19]

Nor were Mormons Andy Cooper's only victims. From L. J. Horton's typescript:

A man named Converse who helped me construct my house and corral left my house for Flagstaff traveling on the Upper Trail under the Rim to where the trail connected to Strawberry, thence up on top of the Rim. There he fell in with a stranger who said he, too, was going to Flagstaff.

"We traveled along together," Converse told me later. "Presently we came to a sheep camp. The stranger . . . swapped horses with the sheep man getting ten dollars to boot. . . . We resumed our journey. In a little while the stranger said he had lost his note book and suggested that I ride on while he went back to find it. He came back shortly."

Converse told Horton that next day before breaking camp, the stranger pried off his horse's shoes and re-nailed them backwards. He bade Converse farewell and took another trail. Northward, three hours later, Converse was overtaken and arrested by officers who said they tracked him from the sheep camp, where the sheep man had been robbed and murdered. Believing Converse's protestations of innocence, the lawmen went after the stranger. And eventually they found him— inside a cabin seated with his guns in his lap.

. . . they rode up, dismounted, and knocked at the door. "Come in," said the stranger. They pushed open the door. "I am Cooper Blevins," said the stranger, "the man you officers have been looking for. Can I do anything for you?" The officers said, "We will see you later," and rode off.

Converse came back to my house as requested by the officers. Finally he resumed his journey to Flagstaff. Fresh horse tracks showed that we were watched. When he left he agreed to drop me a line . . .

I never heard from Converse or from the officers . . . I have always believed that that cold-blooded murderer, Cooper Blevins, first waylaid and killed the two officers, then watched around my house and killed Converse when he left the second time for Flagstaff. To cover up the last trace of evidence of the murder of the sheep man for thirty dollars.

True? That Andy Blevins killed four men for the amount of a month's wages? L.J. Horton was well into years when he dictated his recollections, and some of his dates and details are wrong, but this tale does typify the widespread willingness to believe the worst about Andy Blevins, aka. Cooper.

It is lost to memory when all the Blevinses reached Arizona, but it's certain that the third-born son, William Hampton, made no move before the spring of 1885. That was when, for reason of poor health (epilepsy), and upon petition of influential friends of Llano and Mason counties, Texas Governor John Ireland granted Hamp a pardon from the state penitentiary at Huntsville. Hamp had served nearly a year of a five-year sentence for stealing a horse. Petitioners for clemency declared that father Mart Blevins was still in Texas, and that Hamp, only sixteen years of age at the time of the theft, was "morally innocent of the charge," having been "over-persuaded by two other parties of more mature age."[20]

Promising letters through 1885 from Andy on the Arizona frontier encouraged the Blevinses to seek a fresh start farther West.[21] Mart rounded up his horses, Mary bundled up her brood, and the Blevinses headed for the Land of the Second Chance. In the end, it may have been Mart's fondness for his blooded horses that cost him and half his children their lives.

PHOTO ALBUM

"Good Luck" coin carried by all three Graham
brothers when they were killed.
    —Courtesy of Estella Graham Hill

Courtesy Ruth Blevins Simpson

Courtesy Arizona Historical Society

One of the early structures to figure in the Pleasant Valley War: the Middleton Cabin on Wilson Creek. Here, the Middleton family twice was beset by Apaches, and later, Tewksbury fighters fired the volleys that killed John Paine and *(above)* Hamp Blevins. In retaliation, the cabin was burned to the ground.

When Al Rose laid up one of the first homes in Pleasant Valley, he installed gun ports along the doorjambs and under the windowsills. And for good reason—hostile Apaches had not yet been pacified by government forces, such as this band of Indian scouts led by Al Sieber *(foreground)*. Identity of the white man in ceremonial garb is unknown.

Courtesy Arizona Historical Society

Courtesy Ed Delph

Courtesy Arizona Historical Society

Typical of many of the early humble abodes of the Rim Country was the headquarters of the Long Tom Ranch, established by Will C. Barnes following his service as an army telegrapher and Medal of Honor recipient. Above is an early panorama of the ranch on Canyon Creek appropriated by Andy (Blevins) Cooper. A century later, as the OW Ranch, Canyon Creek meadows sheltered cattle and horses.

Courtesy Arizona Historical Society

Courtesy Arizona Historical Society

Only a mile or two from the center of Pleasant Valley on Cherry Creek was the Tewksbury headquarters and center of a prosperous hog-raising operation. As a young man, Edwin Tewksbury helped build cabins, corrals, and shops. He made his home here during his early bachelor years.

Courtesy Arizona Photographic Associates

Far distant from Pleasant Valley were the pioneering communities of Phoenix (shown with a parade in progress), Flagstaff (complete with pack mules), and Prescott, the Yavapai County seat (with freight wagons lining Montezuma Street).

Tempe figured prominently through the most violent years of the Pleasant Valley War; the farming, commercial, and social center also featured a ferry service and railroad bridge across the fickle Salt River. Episodes of the war were reported faithfully by Tempe's *News*, which shared quarters with blacksmith and carpenter shops. Also not much for appearances, but still popular, was the city's Manila Saloon.

Courtesy John Hughes

Courtesy Estella Graham Hill

Courtesy Arizona Historical Society

Bonds of love and loyalty united the fiery-tempered Annie Melton, Thomas H. Graham, and Charley Duchet. Annie and Tom, secret lovers, were married in the autumn of 1887, and the veteran knife fighter, Duchet, became their bodyguard. His right arm withered by wounds, Duchet is pictured here in later life, with his physician.

Courtesy Arizona Historical Society

Courtesy Arizona Historical Society

Courtesy Arizona Historical Society

Conflicts between sheep and cattle interests indeed may have provided economic incentives for Pleasant Valley warriors. P. P. Daggs, by his own admission, spent $90,000 in the war, and as early as 1883, John Tewksbury as an accused robber pledged his home as collateral when the Daggs brothers posted his bond.

Players in the Pleasant Valley War made a varied cast. Close buddies were Hashknife cowboys Tom Tucker and Billy Wilson; Tucker was gravely wounded at the Middleton Ranch shootout, and Wilson was hanged by a mob. William Colcord served both sides, but by some accounts joined the citizens' committee to end the war. Braulia López, fiancee of Edwin Tewksbury, helped disguise him before Ed went to Tempe to kill Tom Graham. As a teenager and moneyed young man George Wilson of Globe was deeply involved in the war for more than a decade.

Courtesy Ruth Blevins Simpson

Courtesy Ruth Blevins Simpson

Courtesy Arizona Historical Society

Courtesy Ruth Blevins Simpson

Courtesy Roscoe Willson

At a tiny frame house in Holbrook, four of the Blevins clan were wounded, three fatally, in what may have been the West's bloodiest gunplay precipitated and ended by a lone lawman. In the house on September 4, 1887, were Andy (Blevins) Cooper, his brother, John, and *(pictured in later years)* John's wife, Eva. Doing most of the shooting was Sheriff Commodore Perry Owens. A century later, this structure is preserved as a historic shrine.

Author's collection

Courtesy Arizona Historical Society

Courtesy Arizona Historical Society

Courtesy Arizona Historical Society

Author's collection

Political forces eventually focused upon Pleasant Valley War activists, with devastating effect. At Perkins Store (the rock house stood as part of a home a century later) on the orders of *(left to right)* Governor Meyer Zulick, a posse led by Sheriff William Mulvenon surprised and slew John Graham. Graham is buried with his younger brother, William, in the windswept cemetery at Young, Arizona.

From one limb of this pine tree atop the Mogollon Rim, vigilantes hanged three men, including the well-educated and -financed New Englander, James Stott. The graves of Stott and his companions occupy a small glade in the Apache-Sitgreaves National Forest.

Unusual for the times, the prosecution commissioned a photographer to record Tom Graham's murder scene at Tempe on August 2, 1892; Double Buttes School is at left. Numerous tracks, perhaps of Graham's wagon and his mounted assassins, etch the earthen roadway, which in 1887 was one of Tempe's busiest new intersections, Priest and Broadway. In the background are buttes, which in modern times became the site of one of Arizona's premier luxury resorts.

Real-life dynasties were established by winners in the Pleasant Valley War. Jesse W. Ellison was patriarch of a family that rose to political prominence, symbolized by his daughter, Duette, who as wife of Governor George W. P. Hunt, became Arizona's first "first lady."

Courtesy Arizona Department of Library, Archives and Public Records

Top gun on the Tewksbury side, Jim Roberts, won lifelong honor as a lawman—his six-gun and star are prized possessions of the Arizona Historical Society. A. C. Baker was one of a dozen attorneys who parlayed their fame and fortune from Pleasant Valley lawsuits into public service as high as the Arizona Supreme Court.

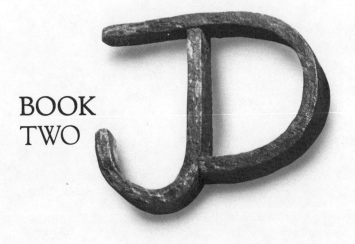

BOOK
TWO

The horse brand of James D. Tewksbury.
—Courtesy of Mrs. Walter Tewksbury

I. The Headless Shepherd

From afar, it must have resembled a soft, gray stratum of fog, slowly sliding toward a primordial edge of the Earth.

Silently, relentlessly, inanimately. The wooly cloud crept near the abrupt brow of a sheer drop of fifteen hundred feet. Yet, at closer range, individual puffs took form. Each one, distict and vibrant. Now they could be discerned as sheep in panic, compelled by instinct to flee perceived danger and follow herd leaders, even to an unseen doom. Streaming, drumming, bleating across the bogs through stark white stands of quaking aspen. Bug-eyed, winded, terror-stricken. Then plunging over the limestone precipice. Dropping into the very tops of towering ponderosa pines. Fleeces and flesh tearing down through branches of fir and spruce and juniper and oak. The exotic tinkle of Swiss bells accompanied pitious cries, as fluffy bodies tumbled in a living falls onto fields of boulders to stain the talus with their blood.

And atop the rim driving the laggards came men, horseback, shouting curses and brandishing pistols—shooting dogs, shooting burros, shooting goats. Three shepherds, held at gunpoint, helplessly witnessed the carnage. In a few minutes it was over.

Take the news to your bosses, their guards directed them. Tell them this will be the fate of all sheep threatening the cattle country called Pleasant Valley. Under cover of darkness the shepherds salvaged remnants of their savaged camp and hurried the news to their employers, the Tewksburys.[1]

Nearly every version of the Pleasant Valley War includes such an account. Here, campfire yarns. There, interviews at a pioneers' reunion. Letters to the editor. Diaries.[2] Scholarly history. Popular fiction. For casual analysts, most comfortable is the simplest conclusion: the Pleasant Valley War was *nothing* but a sheep-cattle dispute; or the diametric opposite—it was *never* a sheep-cattle conflict. Then between these tidy extremes, what of the more plausible universal human condition of mixed loyalties and misguided impulses? Of limited volition and infinite disinformation? Of irresistible foreign forces and scarcely any neighborhood control? War is not intellectual design. It is subjective muddle.

With self-righteous conviction, sheepmen of Arizona considered their pursuit not only honorable but ordained. Tenders of flocks were first in Arizona's semi-arid theaters so remindful of the Holy Land; they kept faith in an occupation as old as Abraham. Early to the New World by blessed Spanish ship came sheep and flockmasters. In 1540, Coronado, advised by priests, brought herds of *ganado menor* into Arizona-to-be. Two years later, his expedition a failure, he left sheep in the care of the padre at Pecos Pueblo in northern New Mexico. And if that church chattel did not persist, Juan de Oñate reintroduced blooded Merino sheep into New Mexico in 1598. Navajos kidnaped the king's sheep by the thousand and bred their own herds. At the same time Europeans were struggling to sustain colonies on America's Atlantic seaboard, puebloans of southwestern mesas clothed and fed themselves with Spanish sheep. Into the burgeoning economy of Northern Mexico, sheep drives totaling seventy-five thousand crossed Arizona from New Mexico to Sonora.

Sheep traversed Arizona to feed California's Forty-niners. "...Arizona furnished a trailway for sheep long before American flockmasters discovered its possibilities for production. Nearly two-thirds of a million ovine hooves beat their way through the Arizona dust en route from New Mexico to the gold fields, and more than a quarter of a million of them reversed direction from California again as the territory settled. Arizona's sheep trails eventually became wagon roads and railroads, while most of the highways within her borders today were known and long used by the shepherd and his flock long before the surveyor..."[3]

And as American military surveyors learned southwestern survival as well as topography, they brought along sheep for food.[4] It was by annihilating Navajo sheep that Kit Carson subjugated the Lords of the

Earth. Then, when Navajos were allowed in 1868 to return from exile to their sandstone canyons, the government issued two sheep to each Navajo man, woman, and child.

Off the Indian reservations in the West, sheep raising by Americanos and Hispanics generally was not so much a sideline (as on Eastern farms) as it was a big business. The first American sheep were raised for wool and later, as mutton sheep and market lambs. "Profit from a well-tended flock of sheep could be quite handsome. Profits of fifty per cent a year were not unusual, and some enterprising and fortunate men got their original investment back the first year. There was little expense in running the stock, as grazing was free on the public domain and sheepherders were paid only very nominal sums. During the 1880s wool prices were generally good, partly as a result of protective tariffs. Herds increased rapidly, and more and more men entered the business, many of them with no qualification other than the itch to make some money as rapidly as possible. By the end of the decade, all ranges were taken. . . ."[5] For all the slander circulated regarding the destructive effects of sheep grazing, it was in the fleece and on the feet of sheep that seeds of alfilaria—the nutritious cattle feed, "filaree," reached American ranges.

In a typical southwestern enterprise, animals were nominally divided into units of two thousand sheep, one ram for every fifty ewes. These flocks were tended on farflung, unfenced pasturages by a shepherd and perhaps a helper, day and night. If native-born, sheepherders and camptenders likely were Mexicans and plateau Indians, and if contracted from the Old Country, Spaniards and Basques. The latter, drawing upon wisdom older than writing, quickly adapted to a land of little water and much loco weed, five kinds of delicious quail and several species of lethal rattlesnakes, elusive rivers, and blinding dust storms. Basques clung to their unique ancient language, their trailfood customs, their fanatical work ethic. They knew to bell friendly goats and elderly wethers and habit-bound pack burros to mark and sooth their flocks.[6] More for posterity than themselves, they busied themselves in erecting everlasting stone monuments along sheep driveways hundreds of miles long. They trained their dogs and themselves to evade cholla cactus, outsmart coyotes, and thwart eagles. They intimately melded with "days of hell and nights of heaven," or as an Englishman would put it later, an outdoor Arizona that was "geology by day, and astrology by night."[7]

The romantic perception of the shepherd in his frontier time rivaled that of the cowboy himself. From the pen of a writer in 1884:

With his dog and gun, the shepherd follows his bands over the grassy plains and hillsides, and at evening they are bunched by the side of a stream or spring. The herder kindles a fire, and soon has ready his evening meal. After enjoying it, as only those can who have had their appetites sharpened by a tramp over the hills, blankets are spread on the greensward, pipes are lit, and after a recital of the day's events and a mapping of the route for the morrow, the tired shepherd enjoys the refreshing slumber which a clear conscience and good digestion bring. Myriads of brilliant stars flash in the blue canopy above him; the air is soft with the faint breezes of a summer night; around his camp the tired flock forms a wide semi-circle against the background of wooded hill and grassy plain. It is a beautiful picture of quiet and repose, and amply illustrates the shepherd's life in Arizona.[8]

Keener reporters included brutal losses to wolves and bears, hailstones the size of hen's eggs, sleepless nights, frozen dogs, and monotonous rations of mutton, beans, and flour. In the real frontier world, a shepherd's life was also a struggle—and an especially lonely one for foreign-speaking wanderers after sheep in the wilderness preempted by feisty cattlemen.

John Clark and William Ashurst were among the first Californians to look eastward, and see unclaimed grass blanketing the northern Arizona uplands. Hard on their heels came the Daggses with well-bred sheep from Long Beach and Los Angeles. J.F., W.A., and P.P. operated for fifteen years as Daggs Brothers & Company centered in Flagstaff and Winslow. The major stake of the Daggs Brothers is hinted in a cryptic remembrance penciled years later by P.P.:

... forty-eight years a desert rat and writing history. ...I know you would not be unkind enough to lure me into anything for which I would be captured and shot at sunrise. I have one consolation the enemy will not do it. They are all sleeping in premature graves with their "boots on." I ought to know something about the "Tonto War." It cost me enough. . .ninety thousand dollars. Gen. Sherman said war is hell. He was right. . . .[9]

Missouri-born of Virginia parentage, the three young Daggs entrepreneurs set out westward by train and horse in 1872. In Tulare County, California, they tried odd jobs, from school teaching to prison building, and made a stake fattening pork for a wealthy meat marketer. Plagued by malaria (perhaps originally contracted in Missouri) they sought health in retracing their steps—trekking springtime Desert Valley, trading with the Goldwaters on the Colorado River, doubling their money breeding horses at Snowflake atop the Mogollon Rim. Shrewd barterers, the Daggses brought in California sheep, sold meat to army forts, delivered saddle ponies to Navajos and cavalrymen, and earned rock-solid credit with rich banks from Santa Fe to the West Coast. When Mormon colonists coveted their Snowflake swap shop and pastures, the Daggs brothers took sheep as settlement for everything not nailed down. For some years thereafter, the Daggses had the Midas touch.[10]

By June 6, 1888, the *Tombstone Prospector* could report the "Daggs Brothers of Flagstaff are the largest wool shippers in [Arizona]." They were instrumental in forming and representing Coconino as separate Arizona county. They were founders and officers of the Arizona Sheep and Wool Association.[11] No commoners, then, Daggs men or Daggs sheep. Perhaps on recommendation of the highly regarded Jacobs men of Flagstaff, the Daggs firm listened favorably to a proposition presented to them by the Tewksbury clan in the spring of 1886: the Tewksburys would take at least two flocks on shares under the customary financial arrangement. They would broach the informal deadline along the Mogollon Rim and southward graze the flocks on prime ranges in competition with free-roaming beeves of the Grahams and their allies.

Not without risk—but what endeavor in the frontier West was a sure bet?—the Tewksburys were savvy livestockmen, proven fighters, and possessed of home base, manpower, water rights, and materiél. P.P. drew up the papers. "Maybe it was P.P. Dagg's scheme from the beginning, because, of the three brothers, he was the biggest dreamer. J.F. was the shrewd businesman, and W.A. was the superb range manager. More than once they had to pull P.P.'s chestnuts out of the fire."[12] If it worked, the Tewksbury incursion could open new pasturage all the way to the Salt River. Worth the candle on the other side of the bargain, "Tewksbury had in mind solely the profit from such a venture as dozens of others were succeeding."[13]

Be that as it may, fervent apologists for the Tewksburys have conceded that spite as well as profit sugared the sheep deal with the Daggses.[14] The forces accelerating toward collision were sufficient to test the purest of heart. Overall, the sheep industry boomed: not counting the flocks of Indians, Arizona in 1870 counted only 803 head of sheep; in 1876, 10,000; in 1880, 76,524; in 1890, 698,404. At peak of frontier days, Arizona annually sold five million pounds of fine wool at premium prices and shipped tens of thousands of animals for meat.[15] Yet in these very years, the last Indian resistance was quelled, and horizon-wide tracts were ceded to railroads. Shirt-tail ranchers squatted upon heretofore unencumbered creeks and springs. Absentee investors established cattle empires where sheepraising had flourished for nearly three centuries. Sparsely populated Pleasant Valley was up for grabs.

Arizona was an open range country in all that the term implies during the period from 1880 to 1890. Its mountains, mesas, uplands, and valleys were covered with a wealth of plants and grasses that seemed forever inexhaustible, all open and free to the cattleman, the sheepman, or whoever cared to use them. Except for the Indian reservations, one could go with his flocks where he would.

Without let or hindrance...sheep in the eighties could be driven from the slopes of the San Francisco, Mogollon, and White mountains where they fed in the summer months to the warm, lush valleys of the Salt and Gila rivers where the winters were passed. But it was not for long until the cattlemen, seeking a place in the sun for their herds, followed the sheepmen into the northern counties.[16]

Omens of change were abroad for all to sense. The Hashknife outfit employed enforcers like John Paine, who, when drunk, relished his role too much. To monopolize water and grass, Paine slashed defenseless sheepherders with his pistol barrel. Among the pious, teetotaling Mormons on the north slopes of the Mogollon, Paine was considered the incarnation of the anti-Christ. Historian Joseph Fish penned the Mormon point of view: "The company had hired Paine because he was a desperate character, for the purpose of keeping all sheep off the range that they claimed (in other words, all of it) . . ."[17]

A highly prized collie sheep dog was slain. Sheep men were haled into court for trespass. Cattlemen—Tom Graham among them—regaled their friends with boasts of black practical jokes: shooting into a shepherd's cooking fire to cover dinner with dirt and ashes; putting a perfectly placed bullet through a coffee pot just as a herder was pouring; "causing the visitor to forget his hunger and remember the details of the trail that had brought him there."[18]

While the sheep were in the Valley, the cabin of William Jacobs mysteriously burned to the ground. Jacobs, brother of sheepman F.B. Jacobs of Flagstaff, served as agent in the Tewksbury-Daggs grazing agreements. In the fall of 1886, a man named Gladden led a troop of cowboy toughs into the town of Payson. They announced they were looking for a half-breed sheepman, and called out local officials including Justice John V. Meadows.

. . . said, "I have killed two men, I had to do it. I will not be arrested by you or anyone else." While speaking he patted his gun in a significant manner. Then he insisted on treating the crowd.

After everyone had poured his drink Gladden leaned forward and looked down the line to Ed Tewksbury and said loudly, "Here's where I draw the line. I'll not drink with a black man." . . . Ed was quite dark. . . always well dressed. . . as Gladden spoke he walked down the line and slapped Gladden on both sides of his face, paused a moment, and repeated the punishment, saying contemptuously, "If you can't use both guns, draw one." Gladden made no attempt to draw. . . but rushed out of the saloon. . . across to his pack, crying, "Give me my rifle—give me my rifle."

. . . Ed Tewksbury said to Gladden, "Walk down the road to the right distance and place and we will shoot it out." But Gladden kept going neither stopping nor looking around. That was the last of Gladden. . . .[19]

A rumor rattled around the Rim country that James Stinson, prominent cattleman, was offering five hundred dollars for the head of any man who dared to push sheep south of the deadline. A century afterward, the truth of the rumor seems beyond grasp.[20]

What men believed, or did not believe, unsaid, may have rivaled in power truth itself. A crescendo of violence rolled along the Rim. Part of a buck herd, valued almost beyond price, was clubbed to death. The large herd of ewes was driven over a cliff, and the herders allowed to carry word to the Tewksburys. Another large herd of ewes was set upon. And in newspapers of February 1887, threat and portent and whisper distilled into indelible ink:

PLEASANT VALLEY WAR. SHEEP HERDER'S DEATH

The body of a sheep herder—a Ute Indian in charge of the Daggs buck herd— was found dead about ten days ago near his camp in Pleasant Valley, his body riddled with bullets. Some days previous to his death, some unknown person shot at the herder in his camp. He returned the shots. His gun missed fire at the second shot or he would have most certainly killed his assailant.[21]

It is fair to suppose that the source of the Globe news story was a Tewksbury sympathizer who additionally conceived a persistant local legend: the murderers' tracks led to the Graham stronghold. The news story also was published in the February 10, 1887 edition of Buckey O'Neill's livestock journal, *Hoof and Horn*, with one additional, inflammatory detail: The herder's head was completely severed from the body, presumably to make identification hard.[22]

True or false, the story was too compelling to forget. The Tewksburys embraced it as gospel.

II. "I Will Leave This Country"

Some souls appear destined to be *on hand*. Such a spirit was Will Barnes. Relegated to rural arenas most of his life, Barnes somehow managed front-row seats to historical drama in a vast and empty land. His middle name was Croft; it should have been Serendipity. And as often as not, Barnes took part in his opportune tableaux. Then he wrote about them.

An army telegrapher, Barnes in 1881 was stationed at Fort Apache when that remote outpost was besieged by hostile Indians. Barnes and a buddy volunteered to fetch help. The companion was killed, but Barnes slipped through enemy lines sixty miles southward to San Carlos and brought back a relief column of troops. For this deed, at age twenty-three, he was awarded the Congressional Medal of Honor. Barnes took an honorable discharge in 1883, made savvy buys of footsore cattle from westbound Texas trail herds, and expanded his sprawling ranch not far from St. Joseph, Arizona. He witnessed more than one famous western gun battle. He served in the territorial legislatures both of New Mexico and Arizona. He rose to high rank as federal conservationist and forester. He led efforts of save the longhorn breed of cattle from extinction. Of his tall shelf of published works, likely his classic *Arizona Place Names* will endure as his literary memorial. Fate arranged for Will Barnes to behold and record the decisive moment preceding the first raging fire-fight of the Pleasant Valley War.

Mart and Mary and their extended Blevins family occupied Canyon Creek in force by 1886. New light was cast on the Blevins move in a family letter heretofore only privately shared. Albert Charles (Charley) Blevins, in his letter to his Texas sister, Delila, not only confirms his summer 1886 residence at Canyon Creek, but indicates he had overwintered there, too. Beneath a thin veneer of rudimentary writing (and even more rudimentary punctuation), there lurked the gloom of a Hamlet:

Aug. 19th 1886
Miss Dellia Blevins i take the opportunity to drop you a fiew lines to let you no i am well. hope you the sam. well i havent got much to write. i would like to see you all. it seems like a lifetime since i saw you all. i would have come to see you all this winter if i had not had so much bad luck. i will come to see you all as soon as i can. Dellia i want you to kiss little sister for me. i never felt so down harted as i do now. i think if i could see you all it would hep me to bare misfortune sister. i want you to hold your head an be a lady. i hope that John and his wife gets a long all rite together. tell Huston i have not forgot him, that he might be a man before i see him, but i hope not. i had a horse for him if i had of com down this winter but my miss fortune held me back. well i hope if you marrie while i am gone you will not marrie some good for nothing fellow. i hope you all would marrie and settle down. as i never expect to share my troubles with any one. as i can't say my happiness as i would like to. Well sister i never expect to be hapy as i no i cant therefore i will say nothing more about my future. well i do hope when i see you all again you will be well and enjoying yourselves. And i hope the time want be long befor we can meet in happiness. nothing more. You need not answer my letter.
Your True loving Brother, Alb B

Some historians have not credited the Blevinses with much civility. Yet Hamp had the courtly grace to write into Duette Ellison's autograph book: "May your life be long and happy is the wish of your friend, C.H.Blevins." John was an accomplished fiddler who delighted country dances in his later years; Andy composed romantic poetry; and to embellish his letter to his sister, Charley included this drawing from Tonto Rim nature:

Mart, although younger than fifty, became known throughout Pleasant Valley and surrounding lands as "Old Man Blevins," differentiating him from his four sons. The first of a few of Mart's surviving letters from Canyon Creek exudes contentment. Daughter Delila was the sixteen-year-old bride of James McKelvey living near Llano, Texas.

to delila and jim
feb the 20 1887
well this leaves all well - hopping you all the same - well i am here in canion creek in arizona - wee have got a veary fine outfit here - wee have got all of Canion Creek except one place and that is not in our way - wee have got as fine timber and water and land and grass as eveary was seen in any country - we air rite under the foot of the muggaown mountain. hit snows some here. just a nuff to put a good season in the ground to make good grass and vegatabuls start in the spring - hit tis the finest country to raise vegatabuls that i eveary seen - our places has got 2 veary fine running creeks on thim. wee can irigate all of the land that we wants - horses will winter here fine - you can turn a pore horse looce here in the winter and he will get fat - air timber air mostly pine although wee have got a goodeal of oak some ash and some walnut and Boxelder and cottonwood and cherry. this is the timberd country i eveary seen - wee air on government land. hit has never bin surveyed. a man gets .160 achors By settling on hit - there is a good chanc for a pore man here - and this is a veary healthy country - well delila your [mother?] is in good health. she ses that she is dun with texas - she wants you and jim to come out here in the spring - well you wanted to no where andy and charley was. they air here - well jim if you here in the spring i think that hit wold Bee Better to come in a waggon. you must get a small one and hit must Bee a good one and load veary light - But you can come By rail - within 65 miles of here - well jim tell your paw that i thing he could do Better out here than he can do where he is for he can get a good home here for nothing - well i was on the road 67 days But I come 200 miles out of my way. i come the loar road. you must come the upper road until you get to holbrook station - then you will quit the raolroad and come to heber. from heber to wilford. 5 miles from wilford to canion creek .12. miles - well i will close. Mart Blevins. they was the finest garden onmy place that I eveary seen in all my lifetime. your maw is cooking cabbage for dinner now.[1]

Although the letter was dated two weeks after the murder and mutilation of the Daggs-Tewksbury sheepherder, no evidence of stress appeared in Mart's scribble. But now with a man dead, Pleasant Valley vibrated with false alarms and real worries. Much later, from the perspective of advanced age, Horton stated: "As soon as [Andy Cooper] got back to the valley, the Grahams sent him around with that infamous contract which read as follows: 'We, the stockmen of Pleasant Valley, who sign our names below, agree to pay Cooper Blevins fifty dollars for each and every one of the Tewksbury scalps.' They knew that he was safe in carrying out the above contract because anyone who lived there at the time knew that it was sure death for any man, unless he belonged to the Graham rustlers, to enter the

Valley." Horton said one rancher signed the contract under duress and fled. Another, George Haigler, refused to sign and was forced to leave. Horton and a few stubborn friends turned back at gunpoint badman Zack Booth, who was attempting to sieze ownership of a Pleasant Valley ranch. Booth later was hanged for another crime in Globe.[2]

Hardcases were not figments of Horton's imagination. Members of Tombstone's notorious Clanton gang, before and after the O K Corral fight, made a base in Globe and roamed the country northward to Springerville.[3] A boy, Peter, killed two vigilantes and in turn was shot to death near St. Johns in 1877.[4] The St. Johns newspaper carried a dateline "Springerville, June 17, 1886: Ike Clanton shot a Mexican, and an unknown person burned Johnsons Hotel and Saloon, also Pete Slaughter discharged all his bad men at once as soon as he arrived home from Texas, and there has been in that town such an unusual reign of peace for so long that the people are growing fidgety and unsettled." A year later, Ike was shot and killed by a mail-order detective while resisting arrest on upper Eagle Creek.[5] In September of 1887, Ike's brother Phineas was sent to Yuma prison for ten years for applying his brand to another's calves. A brother-in-law, Eben Stanley, in the same case was ordered to leave the territory within sixty days.[6]

Valid or not, gossip reached the Tewksburys that the Grahams, when in their cups in Holbrook, boasted that they were hiring strangers to exterminate their enemies. A Holbrook woman, of Indian blood, ostensibly passed the word to the half-Indian Tewksbury boys, with whom she was sympathetic. Another persistent tale had the Grahams entreating Chief John Dazen, of the occasionally peaceful White Mountain Apaches, to help "kill off the damned blacks," meaning Tewksburys. Chief Dazen is reputed to have said if his Apaches took sides, it would be "of the damned blacks."[7]

Another gent of bad repute, Marion Bagley, oversaw a suspected rustlers' stronghold on the southern fringes of the Pleasant Valley country. The August 6, 1887 *Arizona Sentinel* of Yuma carried the paragraph:

Marion Bagley, a noted horse thief in Maricopa County and surrounding counties, was shot and killed on upper Salt river by Deputy Sheriff Benbrook and posse on Monday last. Deputy [John] Benbrook notified Bagley who was resting on his cot at Gordon's ranch, that he had a warrant from Maricopa county for his arrest. Bagley immediately placed his hand on his six-shooter which was under the blanket when Benbrook and Bagley instantly fired. Benbrook received a slight flesh wound in the thumb of the left hand and Bagley fell forward and lived but two or three hours after the shooting.

The Gordon family, with whom Bagley was staying when shot, had tried to make a life under the Tonto Rim in what became known as Gordon Canyon, but cold years froze them out. They found warmer, lower altitude at Grapevine Springs on the upper Salt River. The Gordons may have been the unnamed but highly regarded benefactors of young Frederick Russell Burnham, whose incredible memoirs of these times include such passages, "In Arizona my every turn was enmeshing me more completely in a network of rustlers, smugglers and feudists. It was the twilight before the terrible night, wherein stalk murderers, bandits, and all the grim underworld which, once entered, grips a man in bonds that at first seem light as cobwebs, but later have the cruel strength of steel."[8]

Bagley's body was scarcely cold when on the far perimeter of Tonto Basin the *St. Johns Herald* published an unusual caution:

We have been requested to warn parties who own horses between St. Johns and El Tule on the Little Colorado to keep a sharp look out for them. There are several parties fixing to leave this part of the country, who are not above suspicion. It will do no harm to keep your eyes on your horses until they have left.

In these months, too, according to Horton, he and his neighbors, notably Jim Roberts, heard rumors their horses were to be stolen. Horton wrote, "They had stolen over a hundred head of cattle from me and I could not afford to lose my horses which were my main asset in my freighting business upon which I now depended entirely for a living."

Was this Canyon Creek? Horton did not say. A scrap of paper held safe by Blevins heirs for a hundred years captured the state of mind of Andy himself during the tensions of 1887:

Canon Creek
April 17 1887
Mrs. Dellia McKelvey
you Write in your last letter Jim was under a 75.00 doler Bond. you tell Jime I don't think he can but inheni case he had Better Jump his Bond and come to this countery for a man stands no chance in that countery.
Well they air plenty of snow hear now.
Wee air all well at present - But Hamp is getting all tired from his hury.
Well i will clos
A L Cooper

Whatever Mart Blevins' involvement in the area's troubles, he must have suffered the anxieties of the innocent father or guilty accomplice. Two of his sons already owned records of criminal behavior. Now Delila's new husband also was threatened with jail; and renegade Andy was advising him to jump bond. Soon afterward (May 26), Mart wrote his daughter that he didn't know what he would do—that he was considering selling his Canyon Creek "places."

well this leaves all well. hoppin you the same - well of the Boys is at home to day and me and houston will start t holbrook in the morning to Buy some provision. hit is 75 miles - well wee would all like to see you veary well - well i heard that alf hammonds is ded. let me no all about hit - well i may sell my places and if i do i cant tell just no what i will do. wee have got 4 fine places all on the same creek - our grass and water is veary fine - well hit is so fait to the office that we cant get our mail any more than eveary 2 or 3 weeks - well i will close.

Briefer and more businesslike, Mart was still optimistic. Yet his mood, as revealed in his last letter, had undergone a transparent change.

June the 20 1887

well this leaves all well hopping you are the same - well i got your letter that you rote to hamp. he is not at home But I think that he will Bee in a few days and then wee will send you some money - well what is the charges againsts jim - and how many - well you can tell john m.c.gee that i gave that Bill of sale to jim m.c.gee and for him to got to jim and get hit without fail - i give hit to jim while wee was on hinton creek - let me no where jim is - well i am trying to sell my ranches and if i do i will leave this country. But i will nevear go Back to texas - well there is a new mail line to start in .12. days from now and there will Bee a post office at my house - and then i can get my mail once a week and then i can rite when i wanto - But the hit has Ben i only get my mail once a month - well you can direct your next letter to holbrook and hit will Bee sent to mee - rite just as soon as you get this letter and let mee no what all of our people is doing - and let mee know who had jim indited and let mee no all a Bout what hit was for - did old lib rainbolt have any thing to with or not - well if jim cant Beet his cases i think you will do Better here than you can thair for wee air a doing well here and the Boys will send you money in a short time - well rite soon -

M. J. Blevins

well your maw is in good health - houston and measy wants to see you veary Bad - wee have got the prettys Baby in the world. he is .5. montht old.

That was May. In June, Andy Cooper and his brothers, Albert Charles (Charley) and William Hampton (Hamp), departed Canyon Creek for a brief trip to Holbrook for supplies.[9] According to the never-before published typescript of Robert Allison:

The horses[10] had been turned out to graze in the canyon the day before the boys rode into town. The morning they left, Old Mart went out to bring them in. He rode the whole length of the canyon without finding them, but he found indisputable evidence that they had been stolen.

Old Mart returned to the house and told Johnny that he was going on the trail of the thieves while it was still warm. Shortly after he left, he met a neighbor named Demint, who offered to go along and help Mart look for them. The two rode away together.

Four days later, Demint came back alone. He told Mrs. Blevins that Old Mart was still on the trail, but Mrs. Blevins, knowing that her husband had not gone equipped for so long a stay, was suspicious. [The Blevins boys] came in from Holbrook the next day. . . . They set out immediately on Old Mart's trail. They were gone two or three days, but returned without finding any trace of him. They decided to split up. . .Hamp was to go toward Pinedale, to the northeast. The others went in different directions. On the way, Hamp met four riders from the Hashknife. . . .[11]

The record of some intervening days is lost, but on an afternoon early in August 1887, Will Barnes (typically) was present for a historical happenstance. Barnes had thrown his wagon outfit in with the Hashknife for summer roundup. Sometime around the third of August at sunset, into the Hashknife camp at Big Dry Lake, thirty miles south of Holbrook, rode Hamp Blevins and a friend, Robert Carrington. They were accompanied by at least three Hashknife cowboys, John Paine, Tom Tucker, and Bob Glaspie. There may have been more in the Blevins party. Thomas Covington, alias Edward Clark, is named in two narratives. The men stated their intent to go to Pleasant Valley to press the search for Mart Blevins.

Between bites of his supper, Will Barnes warned, "There's a war going on down there."

Paine shot back, "Maybe we'll start a little old war of our own."[12]

By one version, Ed Rogers, the Hashknife wagon boss, also tried to dissuade the men from going to Pleasant Valley. But probably he no longer could boss these cowboys; several territorial newspapers later reported that J.E. Simpson, Hashknife manager, had assembled all his hands to demand their help in an anti-rustling campaign. Five Hashknife cowboys, including Paine, Tucker, and Glaspie, chose to draw their pay and quit.[13]

Barnes recalled, "That night all sorts of conferences and 'medicine talks' were going on around the camp."

Next morning, "After borrowing all the surplus ammunition in camp, they left. . . but without a pack horse or supplies of any kind, except those of war."[14]

In the heavily armed party, Paine bore the only reputation for a mean streak. Generally accepted was charge of cruelty growing from Paine's beating with his quirt an unarmed and helpless Pinedale Morman named Peterson. Arrested by Deputy Dave Savage, Paine escaped, and was on the lam when he fell in with Hamp Blevins.[15] Paine had a permanent camp for his wife and four children at Four Mile Spring.[16] Paine first was hired by sheep interests, and was so effective that Stinson journeyed in person to Paine's camp and induced him to switch loyalties.[17] Fish wrote that "Paine drove off several herds of sheep and whipped the herders. Not being satisfied with driving off the sheep men, he undertook to drive off the [smalltime] ranchers and everyone else. He whipped several persons who he found upon the range for no other offense than that they were riding on the range looking for their own stock and attending to their own business. Paine's camp soon became headquarters for horse thieves in this vicinity. Being in sympathy with them, opposed to sheep men, and anxious for a fight, he at once espoused the cause of his friends, the cattle and horse thieves."[18] Barnes' thumbnail of Paine: "feared nothing that walked and loved a fight. He was pretty bad, drank excessively and was always ready to make a six-shooter play."[19]

On the other hand, Barnes thought of Tucker as a "big, good-natured chap, not hunting for trouble of any kind." Glaspie (Barnes allowed) wasn't so evil as he was stupid, "a Texan of rather low mentality. To be led rather than a leader. He followed Tucker blindly and looked only for adventure—which they both secured in rather large measure."[20] Carrington left few tracks in ink; of Covington's life, even less got into print.

The whereabouts of the war party from August 4 over the next five days remains open to speculation. The Blevins' Canyon Creek ranch would have made a logical stopover. Strong opinion has held that the knot of riders at least doubled numbers in a swing by the Graham Cherry Creek headquarters.[21] Thus reinforced, the horsemen may have swept the ranges afresh for clues of missing Old Man Blevins.

In so doing, the war party also may have alerted the Tewksburys. For certain, at about noon on August 9, principal members of the reconnaissance troop approached the old Middleton Cabin on Wilson Creek east of Pleasant Valley. In the mounted group "were at least eight heavily armed men." If they had joined the horsemen, the Graham brothers held to the rear.

The Middleton cabin was the selfsame building where the Middletons desperately fought off Apaches five years before. Defeated in spirit, the Middletons withdrew to town, and the cabin now was used by Globe partners J.J. Vosburgh and George Newton, with Newton's young brother-in-law, George Wilson, as a dude ranch hand.

Precisely who was in or about the cabin that day remains a mystery. Many years later, Mary Ann Crigger Tewksbury Rhodes, in a letter to her descendants stated, "The Tewksbury bunch was over at Newton's ranch....They were lying around in the yard reading and telling lies without even there [sic] guns near them, when the Grahams appeared on the scene and opened fire three or four of the Grahams were hit and I think one or two of them died I don't know for sure...."[22]

Historians who would place Mary Ann at the cabin are left with that cryptic deposition, and not much more. A *Flagstaff Champion* news story (August 16,1887) stated that a woman in the cabin doorway first greeted the horsemen, but that account was so erroneous in other details that the entire story was suspect.[23] Yet from a variety of sources and by reasonable deduction, a roster of Tewksbury fighters present at the Middleton cabin should include at least George Wilson, Jim and Ed Tewksbury, and Jim Roberts; then possibly John Tewksbury, Joe Boyer, Jake Lauffer. A.E. Edmonson and Jim Roberts were placed at the Middleton in a murder complaint brought by Louis Parker in Payson; Justice John Meadows took testimony of witnesses and dismissed the charge.[24]

Whatever weaponry the Graham/Hashknife party carried, they

probably were not so heavily armed as the Tewksburys. Hazelton says, "Somewhere along the line someone said that at the offset of impending trouble, Daggs Brothers supplied and armed the Tewksburys[25] with the latest and finest firearms available, and so, with six Winchesters pouring hot lead from the doors, windows and loopholes of the cabin, with three, if not four, of the best rifle shots in the West behind those rifles, the Graham and Hashknife cowboys could only shoot and run for cover. . . .[26]" Another frontiersman averred "The guns they used was .45-90s. They were big guns; it was like shooting a cannon!"[27]

Armament of the Pleasant Valley warriors ranged from decrepit fowling pieces to the latest in rapid-firing rifles. The-weapon-so-terrible-it-would-end-all-wars was the Model 1886 Winchester, invented by John Browning just in time for Pleasant Valley. The hefty lever-action was strong enough for the .45-90 round, substantially more powerful than the army's standard .45-70 and "adequate for any North American big game at moderate ranges."[28]

Contradictory information began flowing almost immediately as to who was there, how the combat began, and what happened. Glaspie, long after the war was over, told his wife the man in the doorway was Jim Tewksbury. Others say Ed. In later years, Jim Roberts was quoted by his son as saying "Hamp Blevins started the fight by reaching for his gun."[29] Newspapers of the day rushed into print with error-marred bulletins which were snapped up in exchanges throughout the territory and beyond. At Globe, the *Silver Belt* of August 20 was closer to the mark (although not perfect) with:

A DEPLORABLE AFFAIR
Two Men Killed and Two Others Wounded
in a Fight Between Cattlemen

The tragedy enacted in Pleasant Valley, on the 9th instant, in which John Payne and H. Blivin [sic] were killed and Thomas Tucker and R.M. Gillespie [sic] wounded and Thomas Carrington [sic] escaped with his clothing perforated by a bullet, was of such a vigorous nature as to affright even those accustomed to scenes of violence. It occurred at the ranch of George A. Newton, sixty-five miles north of Globe.

The cause, if any, that culminated in this unwonted act is only known to those engaged in it. The participants who occupied the house, have not been seen, nor are we aware of their having been heard from since the tragic event, and therefore the community must possess itself in patience until those now regarded as the attacking of Newton party, give their version of the affray which now appears mysterious and without a cause.

The statement gleaned from Tucker, one of the wounded men, who after being shot through the lungs, reached Al Rose's ranch, a distance of about nine miles, in thirty-five or forty hours—is, in substance, as follows, and was related to one who had it from Tucker himself: His (Tucker's) party rode up the fence enclosing Newton's house, and asked if they could get some dinner, James Tewksbury appeared and said, "No sir. We do not keep a hotel here." Tucker then asked if Mr. Bernap [Belnap?] was in, and the reply was given,"No sir, he just rode off." Tucker said, "Well boys, we will go to Vosburg's ranch and can get some dinner there." Whereupon the party turned and were in the act of riding off when they were fired upon by parties in the house, with the fatal result before stated, in addition to which three horses were also killed. Tucker asserts positively that they were leaving the premises, and his wound is said to bear out this statement. Nothing has been heard of Gillespie since being wounded, and, consequently, the result of the wound is not known.

Hamp Blevins indeed was dead in an instant, his brains blown out by a large caliber rifle slug at short range. Paine died almost as quickly from a wound at point-blank range. Through his son, Jim Roberts' impression of Paine's death:

Quick as lightning, John Paine fired at Jim Tewksbury; but the latter dodged behind the door a fraction of a second before the bullet sped through the opening and buried itself in the opposite wall. The next instant, Paine's horse crashed down in the agony of death, pinning the rider's leg to the ground. . . .As the cowboy struggled to free himself, a slug from Jim Roberts' rifle, aimed at his brain, clipped off an ear just as he jerked himself from beneath the body of the dying horse. With blood running down the side of his face and neck he started to run for shelter, but before he had taken half a dozen steps, another bullet from that gun in Jim Tewksbury's hand cut him down; and he, too, lay sprawling in the dust beside Hampton Blevins. . . .[30]

Throughout his life, Tucker maintained that it was obvious to him and his friends that the Middleton place was occupied—even to chickens scratching the yards—that his intent was to obtain some food—and that as soon as the riders turned their backs, the guns from the cabins blazed. Pandemonium followed, with horses plunging and colliding, men shouting, spurring, drawing, snapping off return fire, screaming in pain when hit. In the papers of James H. McClintock, Phoenix Public Library, an undated *Silver Belt* clipping refers to Tucker's story as published above: "Another Version. In the above account it is suggested that men were shot in the back at the Newton ranch. After reading this story, a man who was *there* [likely young George Wilson] had the following comment to make: "I'll say Tucker, Gillespie and Carrington were getting out of there after Payne and Hank Blevins had been killed. Tucker wheeled his horse when Blevins went to the ground with a bullet between his eyes. A second bullet from the same gun that got Blevins caught Tucker under an arm pit, went through both lungs and out the other arm pit. That's how fast things happened. I happened to be there on the day they came to run everybody off, after giving ranchers a certain time to leave the country. It was not my fight. I was speechless and could not move my feet while it was going on."[31]

Tucker's actions were chronicled in another account as follows:

Jim Tewksbury shot at Payne after he began calling Jim names. Tucker ran down the flat and jumped off his horse on the right. Ed was trying to shoot Tucker but hated to shoot his horse. Tucker was trying to get his rifle from the saddle, reaching under the horse's neck. Ed was placing his shots well. He first got Tucker in the arm, then in the leg, and after that he shot the horse. When the horse was down he shot Tucker in the chest, bullet went clear through. Ed said Tucker turned the horse over in another attempt to get at his rifle. Failing- ...Tucker grabbed a horse running free... and rode out of range.[32]

Another version picked up the action:

Tucker was badly wounded, being shot in the right side just above the nipple. His horse carried him from the fight until he slipped from his saddle, exhausted from loss of blood and pain. He fell unconscious. How long he lay he never knew. He was roused in the night by a tremendous rainstorm followed by plenty of hail....The cold revived him. [Not unknown in Arizona uplands, even in August. Although no weather observatories were maintained in Pleasant Valley, *sleet* was reported in mid-August at army forts Verde and Apache.] In this condition, with an iron nerve he dragged himself alternately unconscious, and then able to move slowly, for an hour or two. He finally reached the ranch of Robert Sigsby, or Sixby, who took him in, dressed his wounds and cared for him as well as he could. Sigsby said afterwards that when Tucker came, his wound, which was wide open and uncovered, was fly-blown and maggoty, and the man was in a frightful condition....[33]

Poor Tucker. His flight to help was, he said later, complicated by an attack by a mother bear and two cubs, which he managed to fight off.[34]

A rifle slug tore through Glaspie's right leg. Another bullet killed his horse. A story in the August 28, 1953, *Arizona Republic* described his escape. "He managed to make his way across a seemingly endless open space to the shelter of a wooded area. After things quieted down he crawled painfully to his dead horse and dragged his saddle to a hiding place. Later he was to return with Ed Rogers, Hashknife wagon boss, and retrieve the saddle. It took him two nights and three days to reach the Blevins ranch...he had nothing to eat. He bound his wound with his underwear. He had a little chewing tobacco with him. That helped. When he finally reached the Blevins ranch, the cook, an old man, made him some coffee. Bob said that was the best coffee he ever had. The cook made a poultice out of lye, soap, and salt. This drew the black blood out of his wound. He made two poultices and afterwards applied some salve to the wound."[35]

As his stars would dictate, Will Barnes, who had seen the civilian cavalry ride into battle, was also standing by to witness the retreat. Barnes recalled that sometime in September, both Tucker and Glaspie once again passed through the Hashknife camp at Big Dry Lake. "Chastened and sobered warriors," Barnes remembered. Glaspie "was even then sitting sideways in his saddle from the effect of the wound. The bullet that struck him first went clear through the cantle of his saddle, then in and out of the fleshy part of his buttock.

"I was a leanin' down low over my horse's neck," he explained, "a ridin' for dear life an' a lammin' the old skate with my quirt; me aimin' to git out there just as fast as I could, when I gits this little souvenir."[36]

III. For the Love of Brothers

In Prescott, Sheriff William J. (Billy) Mulvenon perused a telegram he had anticipated, perhaps with mixed hope and dread. Who sent the wire? With James D. Houck a logical informant, the author well may have been Frank Wattron, Holbrook druggist addicted to his own patent nostrums and political concoctions. The language simply *hums* with Wattron's irony and idiom:

Three more men have been killed in Pleasant Valley on Tonto Basin and things are looking squally. McFadden and Gillespie, cowboys of the Aztec Cattle Co. and members of the Graham party, were first killed, the fight growing out of an old feud between the Graham party and the Tewksbury party. Six men have been killed in the feud before the recent killing of McFadden and Gillespie. A number of men have left Flagstaff for the scene of the killing and a bloody fight is anticipated. The determination on both sides can lead to little short of extermination of one party or the other. The most exciting news is momentarily expected.[1]

Of course, no telegrapher fond of his job could keep such a transmission—wrong name McFadden and wrong spelling Glaspie and all—from Editor John Marion. Either with or without Mulvenon's permission, the telegram appeared in the earliest possible edition of the *Miner*, and a day later, via Associated Press, grew into a regional sensation. Now the white man's law in the white man's territory had an affrontery worthy of the white sheriff's time: five white men shot, two of them fatally.

No doubt the particulars of the Middleton fight trickled into Mulvenon's office through other means of communication. From the governor down to Whiskey Row bums, Arizonans expected Mulvenon to act. This time, the sheriff couldn't hand the duty of dealing with a double murder off to a small-town magistrate and a couple of part-time constables. As soon as Mulvenon could pack for the trail, summon deputies, and obtain a handful of warrants, he made tracks eastward toward Pleasant Valley.

The immediate aftermath of the firefight—not at all unusual in bloody battle—was interrupted by an incident of comic relief and unsolved riddle. Echoes of the gunfire subsided; Hamp Blevins and John Paine sprawled in the dust. A dying horse weakly rolled to and fro out on the flat. Behind their log walls, the occupants of the Middleton cabin had no way of knowing if they were under surveillance by more armed horsemen. Prudence made them stay put for a little while at least. Yet avengers from the Graham stronghold might soon be on the way.

Some time passed. Jim Roberts and (Roberts said later) Joseph Boyer kept their rifles leveled while a few of their friends slipped out a rear portal to reconnoiter. And abruptly the scouts tumbled back into the cabin with alarming news:

"Up the hill! Behind the house! Men on horses! There must be thirty or forty of 'em, and they're ridin' in. . . ."

The cabin defenders groaned. They couldn't resist three dozen of the Graham bunch for long. Supplied with little food and less water, this weather-sprung stack of logs was no fort for holding off a determined siege by a superior force.

Slowly, the multiple ranks of mounted men wheeled off the ridgeline and minced toward the Middleton cabin. Drew close, peered about.

"They're Indians," hissed Roberts to his friends. "Apaches! And they're painted up for war! Now, what the hell are they doin' *here?*"

Roberts never would get an answer to his wonderment. When the band of braves reached the cabin clearing, they reined up and absorbed the chaotic battlefield still littered with human bodies, equipment, and dead horses.

"*Chin-de.*" Dark power of the dead, anathema to Athabascans.

Then the Indians perceived the barrels of Winchesters protruding from the cabin portholes. As one, the Apaches turned their horses and galloped for their lives.

"All you could see," Roberts laughingly told his son later, "were G-strings and horsetails."[2]

Almost as quickly, the occupants of the Middleton cabin saddled their own horses, abandoned the cabin, and retreated to a forest redoubt.

By sundown the next day, the Middleton cabin burned to the ground. Who torched it?[3] Understandably, the Tewksbury circle, notably including the owner, George Newton, briefly and philosophically assumed that the renegades had returned to ransack the place and set it afire. But soon, an even uglier report made the rounds: certain Pleasant Valley men burned the log cabin, milk house, and fences in retaliation. Existing Payson precinct records substantiate this belief. William Voris, age nineteen, cow rancher, resident of Pleasant Valley, testified he was present at the burial of Paine and Blevins at noon August tenth. He said, "I went there and buried these men and eat dinner and I believe that is about all that occurred on that day." He claimed he had no idea who burned the ranch.

And so it went, for a day of testimony in the justice court of John Meadows in Payson. Accused of arson in a complaint signed by George Newton were Al Rose, Billy Bonner, Louis Parker, Miguel Apodaca, John Doe, and Richard Roe. Besides Voris, witnesses were George Newton, "reside Globe, jeweler, my trade, also stockman, six miles east of Pleasant Valley, and place known as Middleton ranch"; Louis Naegelin, age 32, stock raiser; Ed Rose, Al's brother, "was called upon by Johnny Graham to burying some men that was killed at Newton's ranch;" and Charles Perkins, Pleasant Valley storekeeper. Not witnesses but in the burial party were Anton Besong, Dick Williams, Al Rose, John Graham, Miguel Apodaca, Thomas Carrington, Charley Blevins, and others that some witnesses could not identify.

Although the testimony resulted in no charge, electric loyalties and fears energized the statements.

More from Voris:

Q. Previous to the burning of the property did you hear Mr. Rose make any assertion that they would burn or destroy that property?
A. I don't remember.
Q. Did it appear to you that it was generally understood that they would destroy the property?
A. Yes sir.
Q. Did Mr. Rose act or sanction that?
A. He did just before we left there.
Voris was asked where Rose was when the house was on fire.
A. He was about one quarter of a mile away when the flames went out through the roof.
Q. How long after you seen Mr. Rose piling up the kindling did you notice the fire?
A. About five minutes after.
Q. Where was Mr. Rose when you saw this smoke?

A. Either on his horse or fixing to get on.

Under cross-examination Voris averred:

Q. Did you hear anybody other than Charles Blevins say that they would burn this house or property?

A. I heard them say they would fix the house before they left.

Voris' responses were generally supported by Louis Naegelin.

Al Rose made the statement, "After the graves had been dug, the men placed in the graves, there were some shakes brought to be placed over the bodies before we threw the dirt on the graves. Those shakes were not all used and after they had been covered and a fence built around the graves I picked up the rubbish shakes and packed them away from the graves and throwed them up against the corral. There was also some timber brought away from the corral and I packed them back to the corral. There being more than was used." Reasonable enough. But at the time Al Rose made this measured response, he had but twenty-three days of breath remaining before the noose.

War was ever a messy business. According to elitist, veteran gunners of the Arizona National Guard, whose genesis dates to companies of all-Pima Indian militia, it was the perfection of artillery "which lends dignity to what otherwise would become a vulgar brawl." Churchill noted that "War is little more than a catalogue of mistakes and misfortunes." War reportage rivals war's confusion, and often adds to it, as crucial episodes go unnoticed. In these regards, the Pleasant Valley War was normal.

Possibly the Middleton cabin battle was followed immediately by another skirmish which, overshadowed by accelerating events, went unreported. "According to one well-authenticated version," repulsed horsemen from the Middleton cabin fiasco gathered at the Graham headquarters to tally their casualties and plot the next move. Hot heads prevailed. They impulsively led a reactive force back to the Middleton shack, picked up the trail, and tracked the Tewksbury group to a stronghold in the mountains. The defensive position discouraged direct assault, but the Grahams ringed the rocky refuge and guarded the nearest spring of drinking water in an attempt to force the Tewksburys into the open. In the darkness, Jim Tewksbury slipped out to the spring and filled his thirsty friends' canteens. As he returned, he was detected; brother Edwin shouted a warning; Jim fired over his own shoulder; a Graham cowboy fell mortally wounded in the thigh. "The name of this man is not known today."[4]

The Tewksburys, with plenty of extralegal blood on their hands, would not necessarily want more credit; the Grahams, having lost two good men, might be reluctant to admit the death of one more. In a later, more dramatic age, he would come to be called the Unknown Soldier. His death may give reason to the way that Justice Wattron of Holbrook began his telegraphic advisory to Sheriff Mulvenon: "*Three more men have been killed in Pleasant Valley. . . .*"

The earliest effort toward a legal remedy in the Middleton cabin deaths was a complaint signed August 16 by Louis W. Parker in Payson before the overbusy justice, John V. Meadows. Accused of murder in the deaths of Paine and Blevins were J. Roberts and J.A. Edmonson.[5]

What led Parker to name Edmonson was not documented, or if so, the paperwork did not survive. Edmonson easily established an alibi. James Cody [he signed his name, Coady] swore that Edmonson was at Cody's place twenty miles from Newton's at noon and through the after-noon of the ninth, and thereafter through most of the tenth. Charles E. Thomas, forty-three, Pleasant Valley rancher, asserted that on August 9, Edmonson was at Thomas' ranch, twenty-three miles from Newton's. On the eighth of August, he and Edmonson had camped at Edmonson's ranch, about eight miles from Thomas' ranch. On the tenth of August, said Thomas, Edmonson was at Thomas' ranch on Spring Creek. Together the depositions exonerated Edmonson. But in the otherwise perfunctory interrogation there occurred a pregnant exchange:
Q. Mr. Thomas are you in the habit of keeping a diary of events?
A. I have since the eighth of August.

Suddenly, a lot of people were keeping track of days. Justice Meadows discharged Edmonson, "there was no reason to believe (him) guilty therof of the crime of murder."[6]

Moderns attempting to assess the decisions and actions of war-impacted people of a century before must ever bear in mind the realities of communication, distance, time, strength. For example, right after the Mid-dleton cabin killings, from out of the blue, appeared an honest-to-God fearless lawman, Deputy Sheriff Joe T. McKinney, hot on the track of a horse thief through Pleasant Valley. Al Rose flagged McKinney down, and thundered, "If you don't do something about those damned Tewksburys, we're gonna kill 'em all." Not my business, maintained McKinney. The Apache County deputy refused to investigate Yavapai County's trouble, and doggedly pursued his suspect to a successful arrest.[7]

Sheriff Mulvenon, the proper authority, first learned of the August 9 Middleton ranch deaths on August 16. For Mulvenon to acquire enough good information to justify service of murder warrants, and for him to muster a reconnaissance-in-force for a Prescott departure of August 19, was swift work indeed.

En route to Pleasant Valley, Mulvenon would have ridden across General Crook's military road, then southward through Strawberry and Pine to Payson. With Mulvenon from Prescott were Deputies M. J. (Mike) Hickey and E. M. Tackett. At or near Payson, Mulvenon was joined by deputies he had summoned by wire from Flagstaff: John W. Francis, E.F. Odell, John W. Weatherford, and Fletcher Fairchild.[8]

Justice Meadows of Payson by now held in hand a grab bag of murder complaints naming the Tewksburys et al. James Dunning Tewksbury (who possibly was far distant from the Valley at the time of the killings) was accused; so were Joseph Boyer and William Jacobs.[9] The Tewksbury brothers and Jim Roberts were named in complaints signed by Louis W. Parker.

In the nearest communities of size—Prescott, Flagstaff, Globe, Phoenix—elsewhere in the territory and the West, sensational news was expected, and shortly, received via the *Prescott Journal-Miner* of September 2, 1887:

SHERIFF MULVENON AND ALL HIS POSSE HAVE BEEN KILLED IN TONTO BASIN. We have wired Holbrook and Globe but get no reliable information from either.[10]

The alarm splashed not only in the Prescott press, but in rapid succession on front pages of Globe, Flagstaff, Los Angeles, and San Francisco papers. The *Herald* in Phoenix headed it, "SHERIFF W.J. MULVENON MURDERED, Eleven Men Killed and Seven Wounded, Posse Gone to Relief of Remaining Deputies." It was a hoax, origin unknown. But imagined widows went into mourning nonetheless, firebrands gained wider audiences, and newsmen spent days and even weeks in retracting the obituaries. At least one bewildered *Phoenix Herald* editor threw himself on the mercy of his readers:

No further information has been received from the Pleasant Valley troubles in Yavapai county. It would appear however from the *Journal-Miner* that there is a screw loose in the last report which came in Monday somewhere as that paper said that Sheriff Mulvennon [sic] and posse did not leave Prescott till Sunday and would reach Pleasant Valley today.[11]

Meanwhile, Mulvenon diligently went about the duties of his office. At Perkins Store in the middle of Pleasant Valley, Mulvenon emerged from his powwow with Meadows to meet with a livid knot of Graham riders, Andy Cooper the most outspoken. Mulvenon had no warrants for these people, he would explain later. "Graham told him that if he did not arrest the Tewksburys they, the Grahams, would take matters into their own hands and fight them into extermination," the September 3 edition of the *Champion* recorded. Most embarrassing, when Mulvenon and his posse went to saddle up, they learned all their horses were spirited away. His Irish up, Billy Mulvenon read the riot act to every Pleasant Valley male in earshot; his horses were swiftly returned.[12]

Cavalry again, Mulvenon's lawmen pressed southward to the Tewksbury compound. The September 3, 1887, *Prescott Courier* said that, "...They found no one home but Old Man Tewksbury and the wife of John Tewksbury. Neither of them would talk. They then went on to the Newton ranch."[13]

"There were two newly made graves near by and the bodies of two dead saddle horses not far off. . . . Mulvenon looked the place over carefully for some evidence that might lead to the detection of the crime but found nothing worth while."[14]

Then, "Before daylight the next morning, a man came to Mulvenon's camp and asked him and one man to come to a certain point to meet a man. Mulvenon went to the Newton ranch on this trip, and found it burned. Two dead horses lay in front of the ranch. Also there were the graves of two men. [George] Newton met him there, but what was said or agreed upon was never made public by Mulvenon.

"The two dead men were Paine and Blevins. Mulvenon, after this, came back to Prescott with his entire posse."[15] The impression prevailed that George Newton had pledged to Mulvenon that if he, the sheriff, would also obtain warrants for the Grahams, the Tewksburys would turn themselves in at Prescott. But the Tewksburys could not in good conscience abandon their families and herds to the mercy of the Grahams.[16]

In Phoenix, the *Arizona Gazette*, on August 28, scored a journalistic coup with information from its city marshal, F.D. Wells, by chance was on the scene at Prescott. Wells wired the *Gazette* regarding Mulvenon: "You can dispute any rumor as to his having killed any one connected with the warring factions as yet. The feeling here is that the Tewksberry [sic] boys can be arrested and brought to Prescott by postal card."[17]

Wells continued to provide the *Gazette* with solid, insightful copy:

That there has been some extensive killing done cannot be doubted, but that the killing has been murderously committed is not believed by the people of Yavapai County where the two contending factions are known. The Tewksberrys [sic] are the oldest settlers in the valley where they live, and have always been law-abiding citizens, though they have always been known to be ready at any and all times to defend themselves and their property when the occasion demanded. Mr. Wells says that in the difficulties a majority of the people up there believes that the Graham faction have been the aggressors and that the Tewksberrys have only acted on the defensive when they thought there was every reason to believe there was a well concocted plot laid to murder them. He further says that they can give bonds in any amount, and that the sheriff has no fears of trouble when he goes to arrest them. When asked how the people accounted for the disappearance of Old Man Blevins, Mr. Wells answered that they did not pretend to give any account of it, and as his body had never been found, they had serious doubts as to his having been killed by anyone. . . .[18]

Yet even as Wells and others minimized the troubles, action was outpacing reaction. On August 17 (two days before Mulvenon departed Prescott and eight days after the Middleton ranch battle) in some manner, a herd of saddle horses vanished from the Graham home corral. Impetuous youth, Billy Graham went to fetch them, and was ambushed. The mythology that, over the years, elaborated upon Billy's demise would fill its own book: He was returning from a dance; he was shot in the back, or chest; he tried to outdraw a sheriff and lost. Only weeks after his slaying, his body was exhumed for further examination; he was alone, and he had company; he was shot by mistake.[19]

Given so much inconsistency, history arrives at remarkable agreement vis-a-vis the dates. On the morning of the seventeenth, Billy rode north-westward on the Payson trail from Graham headquarters. Ohio-born, just past his majority, half-brother to Tom and John, Billy at age twelve had run away with them in 1878 to Alaska, to Oregon, to California. The favored baby in his brothers' eyes but no longer a child, Billy, with nine formative years on the frontier, qualified as a capable stock handler and man at arms. Nonetheless, he was no match for the talented and cal-culating executioner awaiting him.

James D. Houck knew mankilling. In common with many a fresh-starting westerner of the late nineteenth century, Houck was schooled by his own government in homicide. Another Ohio native, by family legend, fifteen-year-old Houck attached himself to a Union outfit heading for one of the bloodier battles of the Civil War: Shiloh in Tennessee.[20] Possibly so, but assuredly when old enough, he served as a private in a Wisconsin infantry unit afield in Kentucky. Honorably mustered out in 1865,[21] Houck followed western mining booms for a few years, then hired out as a civilian messenger for the army. "A hardy, self-reliant, reckless breed, the mail-riders rode alone through wild, unsettled country. . . . True to his adventuresome spirit, Houck signed up for one of the toughest, most dan-gerous routes of all—Fort Wingate, New Mexico, to Fort Whipple at Pres-cott, Arizona—a grueling ride over the Mogollon Rim and through the domain of the Tonto Apaches, the most-feared Indians in the territory. The Apaches had killed other riders on this route, but the young fron-tiersman, relying on the fastest horses he could find, safely galloped back and forth across the mountains for three years."[22]

In the process, he scouted his own special nook: an apparently barren but well-watered parcel of Navajoland on the proposed railroad route across northern Arizona. Houck dug in; the Navajos tried to dislodge him. He threatened to shoot any meddling Navajo, including the local chief. In time, Houck's camp became useful to the Indians as a trading post and rail stop. Houck and his New Mexican bride, Beatrice McCarty (called Bessie), prospered. They made enough in five years to finance cattle and sheep ranches along the Rim. A morbid pattern colored Houck's press notices. "James Houck, who keeps the station fifty miles east of Prescott, has been arrested by the authorities at St. Johns on a charge of complicity with a tramp, in the murder of a doctor from Cincinnatti, Ohio, a few days since at the station of said Houck. It is known that the doctor had, at the time he was killed, on his person, some three thousand dollars. A Mr. Crane, of Bacon Springs, New Mexico, has been subpoenaed as a witness."[23] By Houck's own account, while at his trading post, he helped form a citizen's committee that captured a wagon train bandit, took him to Prescott, and had him hanged.[24] Then, "April 24, 1885, popular judgment was executed five miles below Holbrook, when two murderers from the town, Lynn and Reed, were run into the rocks by a posse of citizens headed by Jas. D. Houck, and killed. The couple had killed a man named Garcia." This seems to have closed the matter.[25] That Houck persisted in vigilantism for decades seems clear. Yet in his time, such expediency often elected individuals to positions of law enforcement. Many an extralegal activist in the Pleasant Valley war went on to jobs with a badge.

Houck coveted Tonto Basin range, as confirmed in a St. Johns newspaper article:

STOCK TROUBLES IN TONTO BASIN

We learn that the J. D. H. [James D. Houck outfit?] which left the vicinity of Springerville for Tonto basin two weeks ago has been advised by the cattlemen in that country not to settle there unless they first secure water rights and their herd of cattle has been turned to another direction. Would it not be well for our cattlemen to take some action in regard this matter? We have previously spoken of the injustice in herds of cattle being turned loose on the already overstocked ranges and again we call attention to the fact that intruders should be informed that the usual courtesies will not be extended to them. It is an outrage for men to drive their cattle into a country without having prior to their coming secured a range with sufficient water for their stock. One determined effort by our stock men would settle this question forever.[26]

A rabid Republican, Houck represented Apache County in the legislature.[27] In the summer of 1887, he wore a deputy sheriff's star of Apache County. Houck never made any bones about his friendship with the Tewksburys and other sheep men. In these months Houck seemed to regress to his military courier business—carrying advices among the Tewksburys, delivering press releases to the outside, and generally skulking about in a county outside his jurisdiction. In fact, Houck considered himself to be *the* leader of the Tewksbury side.[28] The question begs an answer: could Houck have baited his trap with the Graham horses?

The Graham version of this episode was told years later:

The Bill Graham killing was a horrible tragedy....The bullet that struck his body was large and it opened his belly to allow his intestines to spill out. Bill said he would have died right there, if it hadn't occurred to him that the others would come for him, and be ambushed, too. So with his shirt he pushed his guts inside and tied them in, and somehow remounted his horse and rode the several miles back to the Graham ranch. The ride loosened the shirt bandage, and he arrived by some astounding effort at the ranch with his bowels hanging down nearly to touch the ground. He fell into his family's arms.

They were a hundred miles from a doctor, and had nothing but the roughest tools and materials. They washed the intestines and sewed up Billy with needle and thread. They built a big fire, but poor Bill died in indescribable agony.

The Grahams were profoundly affected. They swore oaths over Bill's grave. That was when my father went to war.[29]

Houck often took credit for Bill's slaying.[30] William MacLeod Raine quoted Houck as saying, "One day I was coming down from Holbrook and stopped at Hegler's [no doubt Haigler's]. I says, 'I guess I'll get supper and stop awhile.' He says, 'Get supper but don't stop.' I says, 'All right, I'll eat and go on. . . .' I knew John Graham would come along, and I had a warrant for him and was going to get him. Instead of John Graham, Bill Graham come, and I didn't have a warrant for him because he was one of the younger ones. I stepped out, and Bill drew a gun on me. I tried to stop him, but it was no use. As he pulled his gun I turned loose and shot him. His horse whirled, and I shot two-three times—knew it was the only thing to do, for he was pumping at me as fast as he could pull the trigger. He went away and died in two days."[31]

Volunteered when Houck was an old man, the explanation does not differ substantially from Houck's initial statement on September 29, 1887, to a newspaper reporter for the *St. Johns Herald*:

Hon. J.D. Houck arrived in St. Johns last Monday night fresh from the bloody acts and scenes in the Tonto Basin, and from he we gather the following account of the stirring events that have transpired in that hotbed of lawlessness since the fatal affray at Newton's ranch. . . .

On the 17th of August, Mr. Houck, who had been compelled to keep in the brush for some time by the Grahams, saw a man whom he took to be John Graham, riding along a trail. He waited until the horseman drew abreast of him, when he called, and the man looked up, at the same time drawing his pistol. Mr. Houck then discovered that it was Bill Graham, and told him to go on, that he did not want him. Instead of moving, however, he took a shot at Mr. Houck, which was returned by the latter with fatal effect. Graham succeeded in reaching his home. . . .[32]

Once, Houck told Will C. Barnes, "We both drew at the sight of one another, but I shot first and got him."[33] According to Osmer D. Flake, Houck, shortly after the shooting, was guiding a posse, and blurted, "I killed Bill Graham right over there. I was riding down a trail and just as I entered a little opening I saw who I thought was John Graham entering on the other side. I jumped off my mule and drew my gun. When I saw I was mistaken I shouted, 'Don't shoot. I was mistaken in my man.' He shouted, 'I'm not mistaken,' and fired at me, but the shot went wild and I killed him before he got off another shot."

Second-guessing Sheriff Mulvenon began immediately and lasted a century. Whether he was unsure of facts, overly or correctly concerned for the safety of his troop, nervous about civic support—his first invasion of Pleasant Valley accomplished little. Mulvenon confirmed the Middleton ranch deaths, gained firsthand knowledge of the killing of Billy Graham,[34] heard with his own ears threats against the peace and dignity of the territory, and failed to bring in one Tewksbury suspect. The sheriff remained in the Pleasant Valley neighborhood for a week or ten days[35] and withdrew. Most of the posse went back to Flagstaff; Mulvenon was in Prescott around the first of September.

Had Mulvenon remained on the scene?

History disagrees as to exactly who was keeping house and tending stock on September 2 at Old Man Tewksbury's cluster of ranch buildings on a flat on the east bank of Cherry Creek. By one account, James Dunning Tewksbury himself, his wife, Lydia, and sons Parker, six, and Walter, three, were temporarily residing in the Salt River Valley. Sons Edwin and Jim with sidekick Jim Roberts were avoiding the law in their "mountain hideaway."[36] But just as clear was the memory of a woman, Bertha Acton, who was a little girl present in the cabin that day. Besides herself, she said the elder Tewksbury, his wife and children, Mary Ann Tewksbury, and John Rhodes were at the Tewksbury headquarters; that John Tewksbury and Bill Jacobs as a precaution had camped out in the woods the night before.[37]

An overnight houseguest was a Mrs. Crouch, schoolteacher on the first leg of her trip to Phoenix.

Early in the morning, John Tewksbury and Jacobs went afoot with grain sacks and halters to fetch horses for themselves and Mrs. Crouch, eager to resume her journey. Sheriff Mulvenon had just completed his sweep of Pleasant Valley; a two-week truce in the feud had prevailed. Their horses in hand, Tewksbury and Jacobs led the animals off a hill west of the Tewksbury place, then picked their way along an unnamed tributary of Cherry Creek. As the men passed an especially large boulder, shots rang. Both Tewksbury and Jacobs were hit in the back.[38]

Jacobs, with three bullets buried in his backbone, ran about twenty feet, fell, quivered, and lay dead. Tewksbury was hit once at the back of his neck. He collapsed in a rage of pain so unbearable he grabbed and tore out fistfuls of hair from his head. One of the attackers walked to where Tewksbury writhed, and shot him three more times. Then the assailant lifted a great stone, and dashed it downward onto Tewksbury's head. The skull was crushed. Tewksbury died.[39]

Mary Ann, great with child, was preoccupied this early morning with canning fruit. From the cabin or near it, she heard the shooting and investigated. She and Mrs. Crouch discovered the bodies and were driven back by gunfire. Somehow, Mary Ann managed to summon Jim Roberts. She dispatched Roberts with the alarm to Payson and Meadows,

and from there to Prescott and Mulvenon. For three days, gunmen peppered the ground at Mary Ann's feet during her every daylight venture
toward the dead. Where the bodies lay near Cherry Creek the ground
formed a gridlock of rocks—most difficult for digging a grave. She could
only go at night to cover the corpses with bedclothes held down with
perimeters of stones.[40]

Half-wild hogs foraged Cherry Creek. The beasts frequently visited
the bodies, tore at them, half-devoured them.[41] In later life, Mary Ann
told her daughters that she begged Tom Graham to allow her to bury the
bodies. He refused her.[42] Repeatedly, Mary Ann tried to shield the
remains from further desecration. In a remarkably restrained letter years
later to the son she carried within her that summer, Mary Ann wrote: "It
wasn't a very pleasant memory."[43] Eleven days went by before the long-
suffering justice, John Meadows, arrived with a coroner's jury and burial
party that included William Voris, Louie Naegelin, and "a Dutchman."[44]
Charles Perkins, storekeeper of Pleasant Valley, also was there, and much
later he told Will C. Barnes:

It was not possible to move them. They were badly torn by the hogs, and decom-
position had gone so far that burying them was a most disagreeable task. All we
did was dig two very shallow graves and roll the swollen, mutilated bodies into
them with our shovels.[45]

Numerous comments eventually found print. Posseman John W.
Weatherford was under the belief that "the hogs partially ate the bodies
before Mrs. Tewksbury got to them."[46] Mary Ann allegedly tried to reason
with Tom Graham, and he said, "No, the hogs have got to eat them."[47]
Andy Cooper is said to have wanted to scalp the dead John Tewksbury,
but Tom Graham would not allow it.[48] Andy Cooper proposed to wait till
dark and burn out the surviving Tewksburys, but the Grahams vetoed the
scheme because of the presence of women and children.[49]

Abroad in the Pleasant Valley country that week on official business
was the flamboyant brother of John Meadows, Charley, of Payson. In a
recollection, Charley stated, "John as Justice of the Peace and coroner
buried John Tewksbury and Frank Jacobs. I do not think that any
Grahams prevented them from doing it but the men did not want to take
the chances which would have been suicide. The women covered the
bodies with blankets. I was there the day after the inquest serving bench
warrants for witnesses for Mulvenon."[50]

Yet another summary of facts was assembled from informants who
were children in the Tewksbury house:

Walter Tewksbury also spoke of the attack made on the Tewksbury house by a
group of gunmen—supposedly the Grahams and their henchmen. Walter stated
that his brother John and Bill Jacobs had gone out to find and bring in the horses

of Mrs. Crouch who had spent the night there, and both were shot in the back and killed from ambush.

Walter said the house was guarded for several days by snipers and when any-one stepped outside they immediately drew a hail of bullets. The men took wood and water into the house at night. A drove of range hogs coming to Cherry Creek for water discovered the bodies of the two men, and Walter further stated that the justice of the peace from Payson got there ten or eleven days after the killing and the men were buried. At that time there were no saw mills in Pleasant Valley and any lumber used had to be made with a whip saw and was a slow pro-cess, so under the circumstances the bodies of the two young men were buried in the most convenient thing at hand, an Arbuckle Coffee packing case, and buried in a single grave.[51]

The bizarre and protracted ordeal of Mary Ann Tewksbury would become grist for the next century's pulp magazine articles, western novels, popular and family historical publications, gross, unsubstantiated exaggeration, and idle gossip. In the story's more barbaric constructions, there could be no undoing of it. For many writers and readers, there were fusilades of musketry drumming against the cabin walls; starvation of tiny children and feeble old folks; murky villains and pure white heroes; a diabolic scheme to humiliate enemies even after death; a hero-ine in delicate condition defying her tormentors with shovel rampant; the grudgingly granted truce to allow her to bury her dead; then, finally, the miraculous overnight appearance of Justice Meadows to abort annihi-lation. The most contributory work of this sort of material regarding the Pleasant Valley War contains its own glossed-over caveat:

Few other events in the history of the old Arizona cow country hold as much tragic interest as the fight at the Tewksbury ranch that day. A halo of romance has been woven around the events of this battle by many campfire tales told these sixty-odd years, and by romances written around the feud. Just what actu-ally occurred that day will probably never be known. . . .[52]

For the *only* eyewitness record left to posterity was Mary Ann's late-in-life letter to her grown son. In that letter she could not, or motivated by honesty or propriety, would not, contribute more to the sensational shelf of published material inspired by her desperate moment, long ago.[53] Perhaps Mary Ann realized more than anyone that facts now were frac-turing through a prism of fury, and what she knew to be the truth didn't matter. What mattered was what people let themselves believe. The chauvinistic young lions now rallying to the Tewksbury ranch, oiling their weapons, conjuring strategies, needed to believe the worst.

"No damned man," Jim Tewksbury told Deputy Sheriff Joe McKinney in the September of that year, "can kill a brother of mine and stand guard over him for the hogs to eat him, and live within a mile and a half of me."[54]

IV. "I Fired through the House"

Worry weighing as much as a petrified tree stump knotted within Frank
Wattron when Sunday, September 4, 1887, dawned dry and dusty in the
one-street train stop named Holbrook. Town druggist, political manipu-
lator, community booster, self-styled lawman, sarcastic gossip, Wattron at
age twenty-six had all his personal ambition before him. Now human
energies he helped direct and to which he had tied his reputation were
pulsing with a purpose of their own.[1]

Holbrook drinkers were up and about early this Sabbath, soothing
their Saturday-night nerves. Only seven years past its origins as Horse-
head Crossing on the Little Colorado River, Holbrook, an Atlantic &
Pacific railroad town, scarcely filled one side of its only street. Aug-
menting a sparse scatter of company facilities were houses, some shops,
stables, a mercantile store, blacksmithing services, and emporiums
catering to masculine entertainment. There was no church.[2] As the war
in Pleasant Valley intensified with the death of a son and the disappearance of the father, the Blevins circle rented a small frame house on the
north side of the train tracks.

For some weeks it was common knowledge that the Blevins house was overcrowded with people, mostly women and children. During the forenoon, Wattron as usual was bellied up with his cohorts at Banta's and Herrick's when an electrifying aviso buzzed along the boardwalks. Andy Blevins was in town. Alias, Andy Cooper. Also known as Unadulterated Trouble.

What brought Cooper to Holbrook? Thirst, maybe. He had been on the trail, dogged by extreme stress for several weeks. . .searching for his father, burying friends, railing at the law, ambushing enemies. Presumably he had no way of knowing the firestorm being fanned by a far-off press. In particular, the *St. Johns Herald* of August 11 inflamed public opinion, charging Cooper with murder, rustling, and gangsterism. The editorial wound up with a strident call for Cooper's scalp, and the prediction that the "best citizens" would take up vigilante action.

Self-fulfilling as the prophecy would prove, the opinion was not at first unanimous. The *Critic* at Holbrook stated that Apache County Sheriff Commodore P. Owens, in front of bystanders, had assured one "Mr. Cooper" face-to-face that he had no knowledge of an outstanding warrant for Cooper's arrest. And the debate was on, with the *Herald* all but admitting that Owens publicly had led Andy into believing no warrant existed:

The *Critic* takes the press of Yavapai and this county to task for saying their is a gang of rustlers operating near the line, and committing depredations in both. Rather taking up the cudgel in defense of Andy Cooper, of whom the *Herald* gave a short account a few weeks since. It was one of the *Critic's* neighbors who was our informant and we have been told since that this same Andy Cooper knew before the gentleman got here, that he was coming, and his business in visiting the county seat. In fact, that the "rustlers," by some means, were made acquainted with every step taken, either by the legal authorities or by private citizens, for their capture or any efforts looking to that end. Hence the reluctance of private parties on informing on them, or doing anything to incur their ill will. Such attempts always bring swift and severe punishments on those so offending.

"Mr. Cooper," the man whom the *Critic* steps out of the way to defend, we are informed belongs to the family known in this section by the name of Blevins. The father—"old man Blevins"—recently was found dead, and we are told owned six hundred forty acres of as good land as can be found in Texas, on which he could have lived comfortably and made money. But such a life was not to his taste. He preferred one of excitement and adventure, so rented his farm, came to Arizona, and organized this band of rustlers about which so much has been said and written. He has some six or seven sons, and all are "chips off the old block." Andy Cooper, alias Blevins, however, appears to have taken the lead, and is more audacious than any of the others.

From all we can learn, this "Mr. Cooper" has killed in pure wantonness— without cause or provocation—more than one Navajo Indian. This "Mr. Cooper" was seen by more than one reliable witness, driving along the public highway, from seventy-five to one hundred head of horses he had stolen from the Navajos. From description this same "Mr. Cooper" is the same man who sold the horses in Phoenix, that James Flake, and some others from about Snowflake recovered a short time since. It was this same "Mr. Cooper" that told a gentleman of this county to his face that he had lain in wait for him for two or three weeks for the purpose of killing him. It is strongly suspected that a brother of this same "Mr. Cooper" is the murderer of Samuel S. Shull of Verde Valley, and a sheep herder, who was found dead some two or three months ago in Yavapai County.

Sheriff Owens may have stepped up to this "Mr. Cooper" and greeted him cordially, may have assured "Mr. Cooper and the bystanders that he had no warrant for his arrest, and if there was one in existence he was ignorant on the subject." The records, however, tell a different story. We find a warrant was issued for the arrest of the "Mr. Cooper" from the County Court of Apache on the twenty-fifth day of March, 1886, and that Mr. Owens received the warrant from his predecessor in office, and sent it to Taylor for the purpose of having it served.

How a newspaper can defend or apologize for such a man this "Mr. Cooper" is known to be, is more than we can make out. Our ideas of the objects and aims of all newspapers have been exactly the opposite. We have thought it their duty to decry and hold up to public scorn, all thieves and murderers.[3]

In just a few days, the editorial quarrel would be moot. For whether Andy was "Mr. Cooper" or "desperado," he soon would be begging anybody and everybody to please shoot him again to put him out of his misery.[4]

Midmorning, September 4, Cooper and Wattron met. Or so Wattron said. When, where, how? Events denied Andy a chance to rebut. Wattron said that in the morning he (a county deputy sheriff and town constable with broad authority) drew Cooper into a conversation. Wattron mentioned a horse-stealing case active against Cooper. According to Wattron, Cooper asserted "he would never give up to an officer having a warrant and that if he lived through his present trouble until the spring term of court, he would go to St. Johns and give himself up for trial but that he did not want any monkey business about it."[5]

Apparently Wattron did not press the issue. What Wattron knew, and when he knew it, has since fascinated four generations of analysts. It is likely that Andy Cooper participated in the slaying of John Tewksbury and William Jacobs in the early morning of September 2 in Pleasant Valley, some ninety miles southwest of Holbrook, up and down the Mogollon Rim. About midway between the Tewksbury cabin and Holbrook late in the night of September 3- 4, James E. Shelley was camped alone when he overheard a party of seemingly intoxicated horsemen riding close by in the cedars above Dry Lake. The riders were boasting and laughing about the killings.[6] Then, "On Sunday morning last, Cooper was on the streets of Holbrook and stated openly that he had killed one of the Tewksburys and another man whose name he did not know, on Friday. . . ."[7]

Wattron might well have known of Cooper's bragging about the

double ambush and could have easily received confirmation of the slayings from other sources. Which raises another unanswered question:
Could information of the double murder also have reached Apache
county's chief lawman, Sheriff Owens? The omnipresent Will C. Barnes,
later a respected legislator and historian, averred in his memoirs that he
himself was tending cattle ten miles from Holbrook when he got wind of
the impending climax. "When I was told that the sheriff was en route to
Holbrook to arrest Cooper, I went to the horse herd, changed horses,
and beat it down the road for town. I wanted to see how the little affair
would come off." As the drama unfolded, Barnes casually chose a spectator's seat on a bench on the railroad station's elevated platform overlooking the front of the Blevins house.[8]

Whatever. . .somewhat straining mere coincidence. . .a few hours after
Cooper's appearance in Holbrook, Sheriff Commodore Perry Owens
rode into town. And Wattron & Company descended upon Owens like
chickens pecking a June bug. According to Barnes, politically powerful
Navajo County livestockmen told Owens to arrest Cooper or they would
yank his badge.[9] Whether or not they questioned Owens's courage
outright, the answer was soon in coming.

Owens the man cultivated an air of mystery; his origins likewise were
obscure. A biographer commented, ". . .there was nothing remarkable
about his youth. He was born on a farm in East Tennessee, July 29, 1852
on the anniversary of Commodore Perry's victory on Lake Erie. As a
boy, he moved with his parents to Indiana. His father has been described
as an egotistical, abusive, violent man. His mother has not been described
at all." Other researchers placed Owens turning twenty-one at an
Oklahoma ranch, where he broke horses and played detective. "For at
least one season, he hunted buffalo on the prairies, perhaps for the railroad, which was on its way westward at the time." It was work to hone a
keen edge on a man's marksmanship.[10]

By the time Owens followed the rails to Apache County in 1881, he
cut a formidable figure. He hired on with several large cattle companies,
and guarded horses at Navajo springs for a stage line operating in the east
part of the county. By some accounts, the proven buffalo hunter considered Navajo Indians fair game. When he established his own place ten
miles south of Navajo Springs, his cash crop was blooded horseflesh.
Indians who attempted to kill him or drive him away came to consider
him a ghost—their bullets missed him, while his aim was unerring.

A man who camped there with him once told this tale: "Early one
morning, Commodore was engaged in the domestic business of baking
biscuits. Two Navajos persisted in shooting at the house, one from the
left, one from the right, in crossfire. Owens grunted, picked up his Winchester, walked out the door, shot one and then the other. Satisfied by a

long silence, he came back in and finished his baking."[11]

Just five feet, nine inches, with light blue eyes and a slight build, Owens often dressed like a dandy; he let his hair grow long in the style of a past generation of mountain men. When he posed for an oft-reproduced portrait (see photo, page 96), he affected fringed buckskin dress, grasped a single-shot Springfield rifle (which may have been a studio prop), and wore his pistol butt-forward on his left hip, leading his biographers to deduce he was adept at the cross-draw. Owens' postcard pose and other postures encouraged this sort of analysis: "If one can acquire an enigmatic expression, and at the same time remain reasonably silent, he is bound to inspire confidence in people who are generally willing to associate silence with depth."[12]

According to a St. Johns newspaper, by 1886 Owens had become a Apache County deputy. He accompanied Lew Lynch to bring in Pat Maher, who had just shot J.G. Berry near Emigrant Springs.[13] Through the middle 1880s, Apache County lurched along in civic chaos. It was New Mexican sheepraiser vs. Arizona cowman. Texas Hashknife vs. dirt-poor homesteader. Hispanic Catholics vs. Anglo Mormons. American Indians vs. greenhorn Easterners. All in their own ways full of pluck and vinegar. There was precious little law could or would do regarding shooting scrapes in a jurisdiction of twenty thousand square miles, larger than Vermont and New Hampshire combined. "In the whole murdering history of the county, only two men have ever been sentenced to death. They were just unlucky."[14] The tradition of vigilante law was quickly and solidly established.

When Owens ran for sheriff, newspapers in St. Johns and Holbrook supported him. A Holbrook paper's editorial:

Commodore Perry Owens, he who will add as much glory to the successful issue of the welfare for freedom from an infamous government of Apache County in 1886 as did the old commander of the Flagship Lawrence for American honor and American glory. . . .Commodore: you can be assured that the old ring will make the labor of your friends arduous, but they shall not prevail longer against the interest of Apache County. . .you must and will be elected to the responsible office of sheriff, and the enemies of the people will be driven into their holes and hiding places to stay till the day of their judgment shall come.

If possible, the St. Johns press was even more supportive: "The Commodore possesses all the traits of a good and efficient officer; temperate and discreet, yet at the same time fearless and conscientious. . . ."[15]

In the election of November 1886, Owens handily defeated the pioneer Indian trader, J.L. Hubbell, four hundred ninety nine votes to four hundred nineteen. New broom Owens literally cleaned house, beginning with the ramshackle jail. Springerville rowdies toed the line. Owens won praise for bringing the tax returns current. How much consideration should Owens have given the warrant for Cooper's arrest? The alleged theft was of Indian ponies. The case languished a year and a half, and suffered from a scarcity of witnesses. By his own admission, Owens did not carry the Cooper warrant on his person.[16]

"No one doubted the bravery of Owens," Barnes wrote in his memoirs, "but he and Cooper had been range pals and it was believed that he was avoiding the arrest, feeling sure that one or the other would be killed. Perhaps both, for each man was a dead shot. Owens almost always carried two revolvers, and could draw either with his right hand or his left with wonderful speed. Several times I had seen him stand twenty feet from an empty tomato can and keep it rolling and jumping with alternate shots from his two guns until it was torn to pieces. Cooper was a single-handed gun man, but very expert and quick on the draw."[17]

One version of the September 4 preliminaries:

Apparently it was shortly after Cooper's arrival in [Holbrook] that Sheriff Owens also rode in from the south. . . .

John Blevins, who was in the stable, noted the sheriff's arrival, and as inconspicuosly as possible, slipped out and went across the track to find Andy. . . .

Finding Andy talking with a friend, John drew him aside and asked him if he knew Owens was in town.

"Yes," replied Andy. "Get my horse out of the stable and take him over to the house."

"Are you going to the ranch?" (The Blevins headquarters on Canyon Creek).

"Yes, right away. Get the horse." . . . Shortly after John's departure Andy looked over toward the house and saw his horse tied to a wagon. He then crossed the track, entered the house, quickly came out again, and was in the act of saddling the horse when he saw Commodore Owens approaching. . . .[18]

Stableman Sam Brown later related that he also had braced Owens about capturing Cooper. Brown said he had spoken firmly to Owens, who, at the moment, was cleaning his pistol at a bench in the stable. Owens reassembled his six-shooter and made ready to leave.

"Where are you going?"

"To arrest the Blevins boys."

"I'll go with you."

"If they get me, it's all right. But I want you and everyone else to stay out of it."

Then deliberately, his Winchester rifle cradled in his right arm, Owens walked the hundred yards due east to the Blevins house.[19] Sam Brown paddled along behind Owens as far as a rock structure near the Blevins house.[20]

At about four o'clock in the afternoon, Wattron was standing in the door of his drug store when he saw Owens depart from Brown and Kinder's Livery; he could see Cooper fussing with the saddle of his horse, which was tied to a cottonwood tree. Wattron hustled down to the railroad station and took a seat next to Barnes, to watch the show.

The Blevins house, with its four small rooms, was (and still is) situated north of the railroad tracks, about a hundred yards from the post office, fronting Holbrook's old main street, now called North Central Avenue. Altered somewhat in the ensuing century, the rectangular house originally measured about twenty-eight feet wide at the front and was thirty-six feet long.[21]

Inside abided a remarkable assemblage of humans. There were three grown men—Andy Cooper, John Blevins, Mote[22] Roberts, and a boy, Sam Houston Blevins. Widow Mary Blevins. John's wife, Evelyn, nicknamed Eva. Their infant son. Artimesia Blevins, nine-year-old daughter of widow Mary. A thirty-two-year-old family friend, Amanda Gladden,[23] was breast-feeding her baby at a window. Mrs. Gladden's nine-year-old daughter, Beatrice, also may have been in the house.[24] Mote Roberts was seated and was writing a letter, either on a bed or at a table in the southeast corner of the front room. According to Blevins family accounts, neither Andy nor John had been downtown. The family and friends had just finished Sunday dinner and were resting. The men had removed their gunbelts.[25]

Several eye witnesses to the shooting say that Sheriff Owens went to the house armed with a Winchester rifle and six-shooter; knocked at the front door, whereupon Andy Cooper came to the door of the east front room, while John Blevins went to the door of the west front room. Cooper and Blevins saluted. Owens said, "I have a warrant for you, and I want you to come along with me." Cooper replied, "What warrant is it, Owens?" The sheriff answered, "The warrant for stealing horses." Cooper asked to think for a few moments and Owens said "are you ready," and was answered by Cooper: "in a few minutes." Owens said, "No! right away," then fired the ball from his Winchester, striking Cooper in the center of the abdomen, passing through the bowels and coming out near the spine; Cooper fell to the floor. That no injustice be done to the sheriff and in justification for shooting, we give Mr. Owens' statement in which he says Cooper refused to go and that he received in reply to his last request, the answer, "No, I won't go", coupled with a movement to raise his six-shooter, which Cooper held in his right hand.

Sheriff Owens then jumped back from the door, (at the time he shot he was about three feet from Cooper and the door), throwing another cartridge into his gun, at the same time turning as he did, so as to face the door of the west front room, and fired the second shot, which passed through the right shoulder of John Blevins, thence through the door, striking the partition wall opposite. At this time, the sheriff retreated diagonally back, to the corner of Armbruster's blacksmith shop, in doing so, he observed Andy Cooper lying near to and under the east front window of the east room of the house. The sheriff, thinking Cooper was not yet dead, fired the third shot, the same going through the house below said window, grazing Cooper's left arm.

At the time of the shooting of Cooper, Mote B. Roberts was sitting at a table in the southeast corner of east front room writing a letter. This table was opposite the door in which Cooper was standing when shot by Owens. On hearing the shot which killed Cooper, Roberts jumped up from the table and attempted to get away. He crossed the east front room (in which he was sitting when the first shot was fired), passing into a bedroom, adjoining the east front room—being the north-east corner room of the house. In this bedroom is a window facing east, and about five feet from front the north-east corner of the building.

Roberts, in trying to make his escape, jumped out this bedroom window, six-shooter in hand, and as he turned the north-east corner, Owens fired the fourth shot, which took effect in M.B. Roberts left shoulder; the ball entering from behind, passed through his left lung, carried away part of the left collar bone, and finally buried itself in a spoke of a wagon. Roberts passed on around corner of the house and re-entered at rear door into the kitchen, or rear north-west corner room, where he fell in a heap, and lay weltering in a pool of his own blood. After shooting Roberts, Sheriff Owens began filling the magazine of his rifle from cartridges in his belt; this done, he walked west from fifteen to twenty feet from corner of blacksmith shop, where he stood awaiting developments. At no time during the shooting was Sheriff Owens more than thirty-five feet from the house, while three shots (two by Owens and one from the house) were fired at a three or four feet range.

The sheriff had stood in his last position perhaps ten seconds, when Sam H. Blevins, (a youth of fifteen or sixteen years) rushed out, his mother after him, through the same door in which Andy Cooper was killed, with Cooper's six-shooter in his hand. The boy and his mother were about four feet from the door; seeing the sheriff, she screamed, grabbed hold of her son and rushed for the door, but too late to save the life of the foolish boy, as Owens' unerring rifle belched forth its fifth shot and the boy fell face downwards at his mother's feet, head and shoulders inside the door; the door through which he had stepped but a few moments before, but not a lifeless corpse—all within three minutes.

After firing his fifth and last shot, Sheriff Owens cooly threw his rifle across his left arm (muzzle pointing away from the belligerous house), and calmly walked past, at a distance therefrom of twenty-five feet, going to Brown & Kinder's livery stable, where he had left his saddle horse.[26]

Owens' own statement at the subsequent inquest stands as a model of economical, extemporaneous exposition. In its entirety and with original stenographer's punctuation, and parenthesis added by the *Apache Critic:*

TESTIMONY OF COMMODORE OWENS

I says to Cooper I want you. Cooper says what do you want with me, I says I have a warrant for you, Cooper says what warrant, I told him the same warrant that I spoke to him about some time ago that I left in Taylor for horse stealing. Cooper says wait I says Cooper no wait; Cooper says I won't go. I shot him. This brother of his to my left behind me jerked open the door and shot at me missing me and shot the horse which was standing side and a little behind me. I whirled my gun and shot him (hitting him in the shoulder and putting him out of combat) and then I ran out in the street where I could see all parts of the house. I could see Cooper through the window on his elbow with his head toward the window he disappeared to the right of the window I fired through the house expecting to hit him between the shoulders I stopped a few moments.

Some man (Mose Roberts) jumped out of the house on the house on the north east corner out of a door or window I can't say with a six-shooter in his right hand and his hat off. There was a wagon or buckboard between he and I. I jumped to one side of the wagon and I fired at him did not see him any more. . . . I stood there a few moments when there was a boy jumped out of the front of the house with a six-shooter in his hands I shot him (Sam Houston Blevins, a fifteen-year-old boy who died within a few moments) I stayed a few moments longer I see no other man so I left the house. When passing by the house I see no one but somebody's legs sticking out the door (the boy's) I then left and came up town.

Owens brushed by various townsmen, said little, saddled his horse, and rode out of town. The *Critic* added:

So soon as the firing ceased, several citizens went to the house, where a horrible sight met their gaze. Dead and wounded in every room, and the blood over the floors, doors and walls. One little child, seven years of age, was literally bespattered with clots of human gore. The agonizing groans of the wounded, the death rattle of the dying, mingled with the screams of the females made a sight that no one would care to see a second time.

Numerous people remembered seeing Andy's horse shot. Only five years old, Hugh Larson, whose mother had recently died, was playing in a wagon bed parked in his grandmother's yard across the street from the Blevinses'. The pony caught the slug square between the eyes, reared breaking its reins, galloped a hundred feet, and fell dead. Sam Brown was at the rock house with D.G. Harvey. "I see the boy run out of the house with a six-shooter in his hand and run about two feet around the corner his mother reached out and grabbed him and as she was pulling him back Comadore shot I saw another fellow looking at me from out of the window with blood on him and a pistol in his hand. I retreated after Comadore came to where I was. I asked him if he had got him he said he had got all of them. I mustered courage and again tackled the house looked up and saw another fellow with a six-shooter in his hand and waited until Mr. Harvey came up when I ventured into the house I then saw the boy laying in the door with a six-shooter alongside of him and apparently dying and afterwards saw him in the back room dead."

Q. Did you recognize the parties you saw appear in the doors with pistols and blood on them.
A. Yes sir I saw Roberts come in the kitchen door of the house with a pistol in his hand braced himself against the door, and fell in the house the other man I saw was after the shooting of the boy and was Johney Blevins he was standing in the east front room also with a pistol in his hand the same being the same one that I saw Mr. Harvey take from him.[27]

At Sam Houston Blevins's inquest, Wattron testified: "About this time Mr. Harvey came across the street and says to me go over and help Owens arrest those men. I went over with my shot gun and met Owens coming down the street from the house I says did you get them he says yes when ever I draw a bead I know I hav got them I says what did you say to Cooper when you went to arrest, he says I told him I had a warrant for him Cooper asked me what it was for and I told him for steeling Navajo Horses and that I wanted him Cooper says I wont go. and then I shot him."

Of one reality, all agreed. The *Critic* was not accused of exaggerating the horror:

SERVING A WARRANT.

Sheriff Owens Kill Andy Cooper and his Brother, and Wounds Two Other Men. The Coolness of the Sheriff, and his Unerring Sight. The Scene of the Tragedy, Clots of Ropy Gore, "Thick as Autumnal Leaves That Strow The Brooks in Vallombrosa."

For a day or so, Holbrook was famous; the *San Francisco Chronicle* commented: "In the discharge of his duty and his Winchester, Sheriff Owens of Arizona fatally rifled the vitals of four desperados of the Graham gang."

Most official inquiries were led by Justice of the Peace D.G. Harvey, himself an eyewitness.

At one of the proceedings (they tended to be repititious), Eva said she was sitting in back room in the doorway with her baby. She heard a shot, then another. She broke for her baby, shouting, "What is the matter?" No one answered, but she "saw a man walk around the fence corner with a gun in his hand and a pistol round him. . . ." Eva said she had heard three shots when Houston demanded John's gun, she "told him he had no use for it," and had no pistol when he left the bedroom where she was. She was busy with the scene of her husband John shot and needing help, and Roberts stumbling into house and collapsing in a pool of blood.

Many years later, in 1936, Eva told a different story to a most sympathetic listener, Robert Allison, then a budding journalist who went on to become the sports editor of the *Phoenix Gazette*. Allison's typescript written for the state historian was never published. Eva told Allison, "You may think I'm twisting it a bit because it was my family, but as God is my judge, that is the truth. The people that wrote about it never came to us. If they had we would have told them the truth. And if I ever told the truth in my life, I have told it to you today."

When I heard the knock on the door Mote was writing a letter. . . . Andy was in the back somewhere.

I went to answer the door with my eight-months-old baby Hamp in my arms. I opened it and Commodore Owens stood there. I didn't know who he was. He said, "Is Andy here?" I said, "Yes, of course," and called Andy. Andy came out of the back room. He wasn't wearing his gun, it was on the table. He stepped to the door, and I was still standing there when it happened.

Commodore Owens said, "I want you, Andy," and that's all in the world he ever said. He shot with his Winchester rifle almost before he quit speaking. He hit Andy in the stomach. As he fell, the blood saturated my baby and me.

When Roberts heard the shot and saw Andy fall, he dropped his letter and jumped out the window. I don't know why he did it—excited, maybe. Commodore Owens saw him jump out and ran to the corner of the house and shot him in the back. Roberts didn't have a gun. There were only three guns in the house—two pistols and a rifle.

Houston grabbed Andy's gun off the table and ran outside. Maybe Commodore Owens told him to stop but I didn't hear him. Mother Blevins ran after Houston and tried to hold him back, but Commodore Owens shot. . . .The shot went through and killed Andy's saddle horse standing by the house.

Commodore Owens had backed up about forty or fifty feet from the house. My husband came in and grabbed the rifle where it was standing in the corner. He jumped outside and fired at Commodore and missed him, and Owens shot him through the shoulder. My husband couldn't shoot any more and ran back in the house. Then a lot of people came. . . .

It all happened so quick. I was still standing by the front door, covered with blood, when everybody came in. At first they thought the baby had been shot because there was blood all over him and me.

Andy lived for about a day after that. He died in awful pain. Mote lived for about a week. He was shot through the stomach too. He was getting better and suddenly he died. We always thought they wanted him to die to get him out of the way. . . .

Houston was shot through the heart, and he never knew what hit him, I guess. Mother Blevins took his death awful hard.[28]

Amanda Gladden testified that from where she sat in the east front room window, nursing her baby, she saw Owens step onto porch. The only thing she heard was Owens asking if Cooper was ready. Mr. Cooper said he would be ready in a few moments. She never saw anybody of the Blevins party with a pistol in hand.

Poor M.B. (Mote) Roberts. A century of sifting evidence invariably arrives at the conclusion: Mote Roberts, if not entirely innocent, was a supremely unlucky man. He was not a member of the Blevins family and had no apparent business connection. He said he had once stayed five days at the Blevins ranch; a hand with horses, he well may have been involved in Cooper's alleged thievery. At any rate, at the time of the shooting, Roberts probably was seated in the east front room at a little table writing. The coroner's jury took pains to preserve his unfinished letter including its postdate:

Holbrook A T Sept 5th

Mr Shefling

Dear Sir I started to drive one of your horses to flagstaf and sell him when I took off Bomens horses and he give out the first day and I left him he is here on the range you can get some of the boys that works for Bowman to get

To Mote Roberts' scrawl, Owens added a final exclamation point. Hopelessly wounded, Mote lingered in extreme agony for eleven days. His death anticipated, he was privileged to testify at his own inquest. He swore he was unarmed, that he heard no words between Owens and Cooper, that his only inkling of trouble was Owens' first shot, that Owens never called to him [Mote] to surrender, that he dived out the window in an attempt to get away, and that the bullet hit him while he was still in the house. Roberts also stated he saw Owens kill the boy. Yet a preponderance of evidence has him bailing out the window, gun in hand, fleeing north away from Owens, stumbling dreadfully wounded into the back of the house, and with Eva the witness, pitching headlong into the cook room. Dr. T.P. Robinson both saw Roberts shot and later examined the wound. Excerpts from the doctor's observations:

I saw Mr. Owens shoot in a northernly direction toward the N.E. corner of the house and found in a wagon spoke a ball evidently from a winchester rifle attached to which was a piece of human bone The line of this shot would be such as to cause the shooting or hitting of a person in a position at the N.E. corner of the house and it is my believes that this ball is the one that killed Roberts. there was a small particle of flesh covering the bone and attached to it.

After examination. . .I find a gun shot wound on the left side which entered from the back through the spine of the Scapular and passed upwards and forwards and out between the first and second rib three and one half inches from the medium line of the Sternum. This wound caused death. . . .

Long after Owens was exonerated in the deaths of Andy and Houston, a separate coroner's jury under the authority of a different justice of the peace, Albert F. Banta, returned this finding: ". . .the evidence adduced before us, that the said Mote B. Roberts, was trying to make his escape at the time he was shot by the Sheriff; that said Roberts was shot from behind, the ball entering at the back."

Mecea [Artimesia] Blevins said she was "standing in the east front room when the shooting commenced. . .went out in the kitchen as soon as Andy was shot and stayed in there the shooting was all over and the Man was gone."

John Blevins: "I was standing in the door going into the cook room and saw Owens when he come up onto the poarch in front of the window then I walked on about four feet toward Owens and about that time I heard Owens say come on and saw him shoot then the next shot that was fired he shot me, then I did not see Owens any more until he went off."

John Blevins swore no shots were fired from inside the house. He himself definitely did not shoot. John said he did not see Owens shoot him. John admitted he was wearing his belt and pistol yet never drew the weapon; he explained the one spent shell: "Yesterday I shot it off once as I was coming in with Andy."

The responses of Mary Blevins were poignant and brief, extracted by an examiner who was obviously concerned about this woman, who, in the course of ten weeks, lost her husband in a mysterious disappearance, had three sons shot to death and one son seriously wounded. She steadfastly held that she was near Andy; he was not armed; did not resist; when mortally shot, staggered backwards whimpering, "Oh Commodore, don't do that." As for Houston, she testified that:

I Mary Blevins saw the Boy come out the middle door between the two front rooms and then went out on the poarch through the east front door, and when he got out on the poarch Owens was standing at the corner of the Blacksmith shop the front or southwest corner I went out also and he (the boy) says Oh Ma he has killed Andy, I stepped out after him. I took hold of him to pull him back and said dont go out there, and then I saw Mr. Owens shoot the shot that killed him I drug him back to the door and there he fall.

Q. Did the little boy have a pistol in his hands.
A. Not that I know of if he did I dont remember it.
Q. Did you see Andy shoot out of this door.
A. No sir he did not have his pistol on.
Q. Did you see any one in the house shoot.
A. I did not.
Q. How old is the Boy.
A. He was fifteen on the 12th day of July last.
Q. Are you the mother of Hueston Blevans.
A. I am.

Owens' testimony at Houston's inquest was even briefer:

The boy ran out during the fight with a sixshooter in his hand and the instant I saw him I fired at him he had his sixshooter raised his face toward me and as if about to shoot and made some remark which I did not understand just as he jumped off the poarch and throwed up his hand

Q. How did you come to shoot the boy
A. Because I thought he jumped out to kill me.
Q. What were you doing there.
A. I went there to arrest Andy Cooper
Q. Was there a warrant out for his arrest
A. There was not only one but three.

Justice D.G. Harvey made his statement:

Yesterday afternoon I came out of Bantas Saloon met Sam Brown at the door who said I am going home to cook my dinner I came across the track to the Livery stable a moment after we arrived there Comadore Owens rode up just then I came into Browns dining room remained but a moment or two and went back to the Livery Stable I heard Comadore Owens say as I went into the stable is Cooper in town? Brown or myself answered he was I says I am going to take him in people have talked enough about me being afraid to arrest men I expect I have a warrant at the Post Office for him which I ordered sent here from Taylor I says Comadore as an officer you dont need a warrant to arrest a man when you know a crime has been committed or is about to be committed. I have been shooting my pistol considerable to day he says I will clean it and then I will arrest cooper, he came or went into Browns dining Room in a few minutes I went in there also and saw Comadore putting his pistol together and which he reloaded and put it into his scabbard and then went into the stable when he got into the stable he says where is Coopers Horse I says Johney came and got it while you were cleaning your pistol, he stepped into the granery and picked up his winchestrer looked to see if it was loaded and stepped out doors and asked where does he live I says just beyond that adobe house and this side of the blacksmith shop. comadore went that way and passed out of my sight. . .I heard three shots fired and saw Comadore run out into the street I walked back to the barn and met Sam Brown and we started to go over to Coopers and saw Comadore standing at the corner of the blacksmith shop I walked out near the RRCrossing and saw a Boy come out of the door leading into the east front room of Coopers house he had a pistol in his hand partially raised just as he stepped off from the poarch comadore fired in that direction just at that instant a woman caught the boy and the boy fell on the poarch I started again to go to the house with Sam Brown when I saw a Man come to one of the Doors with a pistol in his hand I says lets not go over there and turned and walked back to the post office where I met Frank Wattron and says to him get your gun and go and help Comadore arrest those men; Wattron and myself with others went over to Coopers house where I found the boy lying in the East room front door I called some one and told him to help Me carry the boy into the bedroom and layed him down on a mattress where he died almost instantly. . . .

As I stepped into the house I met John Cooper or Blevans in the doorway between the two front rooms with a pistol in his hand I said Johney give me that pistol and he done so. . . ."

Judge Harvey said of three pistols he recovered from the house only one—John Blevins' revolver—contained a spent shell.

John Q. Adamson said he was sitting in Mr. Terrill's saloon reading when heard shots. He responded in time to see "this young boy come out with a pistol in his hand and the old lady followed him out just as he stepped off the poarch she caught him by the shoulder and started to pull him back into the house just then there was a shot fire from the corner of the blacksmith shop, saw a man there and recognized him to be the sheriff and I saw him fire the shot That is all until I went over except that the old lady pulled him or he fell back into the Door." A question was asked about the position of the pistol in the boy's hand, and Adamson replied, "It was up in the air in a position as if he was about to shoot."

Charles Banta was in the post office. Heard shots, dashed outside in time to see the sheriff in front of Blevins house at the time Owens fired through front wall. Saw Owens fire one shot between the Blevins house and the blacksmith shop. Banta reached the corner of Adamsons & Burbage store and saw the boy come out on the porch, "his mother was right behind him between him and the west front room she appeared to have hold of the boy she looked over toward Comadore Owens and as she saw Owens she screamed again and made a rush for the door appeared to be trying to get the boy along with her, she was about two feet from the boy when Owens fired a shot and as she rushed back she turned the boy partially around and at this time the sheriff fired and the boy fell on his face head and shoulders inside the door. I afterwards as I went over to the house stepped over the body of the boy he was then breathing his last. . . ."

Next witnesses. "If the boy had a pistol I did not see it," stated D.B Halcomb, who witnessed most of the gunfight. But Houston was armed, asserted O.P. Chaffee, Henry F. Banta, W.C. Yancy, B.M. Terrill, and William Adams, Jr., "dealer in chalcedony," who began, "I was lingering at Mr. Bantas Saloon engaged in the customary vocation incident to such a place when I heard three shots fired in rapid succession. . . ." Adams ran to see the boy "raising his pistol as he advanced and almost the instant and when only about one half his body was in sight of Owens like a flash he Owens droped his rifle on the visible part of the boy and snap shot him the boy fell back in the doorway." A somewhat different view by Frank Reed: "I came out on the railroad track here to see where the shooting was I saw Comadore Owens standing alongside the black-smith shop with a rifle in his hand saw at same time a commotion in Ble-vans house saw an old lady which I since have ascertained is Mrs. Blevans attempting to hold back a young boy or youth saw a boy come out of the house with a white handled revolver in his right hand this revolver was held in both hands as he backed out of the house the old lady pulled him so as to release his left hand from the pistol he dropped the revolver to his right side holding the same in his right hand The Old Lady gave him a push toward the house at the same time Comadore Owens fired and Boy fell in the doorway. . . ." T.P. Robinson, M.D., also testified that Houston held a pistol, but history has all but ignored one portion of Dr. Robinson's deposition. Matter-of-factly the doctor swore that Houston was shot *twice:* "I found two gun shot wounds one a slight abrasion on the point of the right shoulder this wound being in no wise fatal the other gun shot wound about one half inch above the iliums of the pelvis on the line with the fourth lumbar of the vertebra entering on the left side passing directly through the fourth lumbar vertebra and out at the same given point on the right side. This wound was sufficent to cause instantaneous death."[29]

On September 5, a coroner's jury exonerated Owens in the death of Sam Houston Blevins, and next day, in the death of Andy Cooper.

In due course, a warrant for Andy Cooper's arrest surfaced. The sheriff inked the front, "Party against whom this warrant was issued was killed while resisting arrest," and deposited the paper with the clerk of the county court.[30] The September 9 edition of the *St. Johns Herald* supported Owens: "Too much credit cannot be given Sheriff Owens in this lamentable affair. It required more than ordinary courage for a man to go single-handed and alone to a house where it was known there were four or five desperate men inside, and demand the surrender of one of them . . . outside of a few men, Owens is supported by every man, woman and child in town."[31]

To some, Providence seemed a factor, "That he should have gone single-handed, and succeeded in getting the best of four such desperate men, without being killed or injured himself, is almost miraculous."[32] More prescient was the outlook of the September 10 issue of the *Apache County Critic:* "All this is simply a chapter of the Tonto Basin history, and no man as yet can foretell the end."[33]

V. The Full Weight of the Law

Even without the bloodiest moment ever precipitated and concluded by a lone lawman in a Western American town, the Pleasant Valley War had become a national curiosity and regional embarrassment.

Gunfire along the Tonto punctuated speeches and editorials of eastern establishment politicians and opinion-makers who, for other less laudable reasons, opposed statehood for more western territories. To far-thinking nation builders, the obvious ultimate need was to grant Union membership to two future "Southern Tier" foundation blocks like Arizona and New Mexico. Those already franchised foresaw a range of threats from populist western movements to ethnic political power. But opponents, as often as not, debated issues of statehood not with reason but ridicule.[1] How could two seats in the United States Senate be offered to a populance who settled civic affairs with gunpowder?

"Not even a wolf could make a living there," Kit Carson had told the East about Arizona. As all mainstream America was supposed to know, Arizona was a part of the region that Daniel Webster once called "a barren region of prairie dogs, cactus, shifting sands and savage Indians; incapable of producing anything, and therefore not worth retaining."

General Sheridan was even more succinct: "We fought one war with Arizona to win Arizona; we ought to fight another war to make her take it back."

In Arizona, the Pleasant Valley War (or rather the negative publicity it generated) became a bone in the throat of the highest public officials. As for the private sector, the perception of lawlessness unsettled business leaders eager to picture Arizona as Utopia, not Bedlam. These boosters wanted to talk about water reclamation, freight rates, monetary policy, land entry—not to have to explain every week how and why enclaves of feudists hunted one another down like beasts with impunity. Rumors abounded that federal authorities were considering sending troops from Camp Verde to quell civil insurrection in Pleasant Valley.[2] The very thought of military intervention mortified Arizona promoters. Now that Geronimo was in exile, they yearned for bankers from Boston, not soldiers from Washington.

Still, published predictions were pessimistic for that paradoxical placename, Pleasant Valley. More wishful than stern was one *Phoenix Gazette* squib:

A MISNOMER

A *Gazette* reporter was informed yesterday by a gentleman who has been in the Tonto Basin country for several weeks that the Sheriff would not be able to bring about the capture of the remaining forces in Pleasant Valley, as they are always on the alert and provided with large field glasses and are conversant with all that transpires in the country. Both sides are fortied [fortified] in the mountains and will resist with all their lives. All attempts to capture them, the gentleman states the Grahams and the Tewksberrys still keep up the battle and it has now come down to Bushwacking in the hills and mountains. "Pleasant" Valley is indeed a misnomer for such a place, the *Gazette* is of the opinion that Sheriff Mullvenon Yavapai's brave Sheriff will yet succeed in bringing these people to justice.

A little later, the *Gazette* affected a more strident tone: "The Pleasant Valley quarrels are getting numerous and should be stopped, if it takes the whole civil force of Yavapai."[3] All around the great green circle of Tonto Basin, propagandists prevailed upon willing editors to present favorable views and facts. One historian concluded that the Grahams were far and away the better military publicists.[4] Comfortable as that bias might set with Tewksbury sympathizers, it ignored the effective, hustling press-agentry of James Dunning Tewksbury, eloquent in his own right and reinforced by his articulate English wife. Their party line was given top-of-front-page play in the *Phoenix Gazette:*

A LIE REFUTED
An Old Man Speaks and Denies the Base Allegations

Editor, *Gazette*: In the Issue of the *Daily Arizonan*. . .there appears an article purporting to be an interview between a "Scribe" of that paper and one Thomas H. Graham. . .in which the Tewksberry family are represented as having taking part in certain proceedings not entirely sactioned by the laws of this Territory.

As to their being any plot organized by, or participated in by the Tewksberry [sic] family, to murder families, it is most emphatically not the case. On the contrary they have no love for men who murder or steal horses.

Who is the man Thomas H. Graham? Is he not the man who, while testifying against the Tewksberry boys during their trials at Prescott, in this Territory—some years ago—and from which they were all acquitted by the jury which tried them? Was it not he that, was at the command of Judge Sumner Howard, then the Chief Justice of the Supreme Court of the Territory, ordered to be arrested and appear before the grand jury of that county, for having perjured himself at that trial?

Is not his house the rendezvous for horse thieves and murderers? Did not the two men that killed the herder, about two years ago, stop at his place? Is not he and his brothers mixed up in some way with the horse stealing in that neighborhood? Haven't they said they would "clean out the Tewksberrys?"

Have they not shot into flocks of sheep at different times among the herders? We would like to know who burnt Shield's house. Who burnt Jakerson's and Jacob's houses and corrals. Who burnt Joe Watts' house and corrals?

Who is the man Al Rose? Didn't he serve his time in the penitentiary in California?

If so, you had better drop him as I did.

I regret to have to call the attention of the public to these facts, but when I am assailed and my family brought into disrepute by statements from persons whose characters are as above pictured, I cannot but give some ideas as to who my accusers are.[5]

The tireless senior Tewksbury made such partisan statements to the press in Globe in late August.[6] He then went to Prescott and loudly surrendered to Mulvenon. As the *Prescott Courier* of September 6 reported, "The father of the Tonto Basin Tewksburys is in Prescott and has convinced all who have talked with him that his boys and their families are in the right."[7] Few would fault the Tewksbury patriarch for trumpeting his side, but to argue that he was not a participant is to say that propagandists in general play no wartime role. The omnipresent Houck apparently never avoided an opportunity to sway public belief, as in Phoenix: "The Hon. J.D. Houck who came in with a band of sheep from his range in Yavapai county a few days since via Tonto Basin and the Reno Hill road, paid the *Herald* office a pleasant call last evening. With regard to the trouble in Pleasant Valley Mr. Houck did not care to commit himself at present further than to say that he believes it is not ended yet by any means. The immediate cause of trouble of late, he thinks, has been the wholesale horse stealing that has been going on in that section, several bands having been driven from there into Colorado and Utah."[8]

Gallows humor did little to relieve the suspense: "Peace must be preserved in Pleasant Valley even if the [*Prescott*] *Courier* has to sacrifice all of its non-paying subscribers." The rival *Journal-Miner* countered with "One correspondent who takes a political view of the affair writes: 'Things are progressing finely in Pleasant Valley. Nine Democrats less that we know of, and good chances of the Democratic majority there being still further reduced.' " But for every fun-poker there were a dozen fire-fanners: ". . . nearly every citizen in Pleasant Valley and the valleys in the immediate vicinity have taken one side or the other and, unless arrests are made, further trouble will ensue."[9]

In such an atmosphere, the meeting in Prescott capital must have resembled very much a council of war. Conrad Meyer Zulick was a New Jersey lawyer and Tombstone investor appointed to govern during the stormiest years of the Pleasant Valley War. Zulick had commanded a black regiment with distinction during the Civil War; however, because of bad debts of some of his clients, attorney Zulick had had to be rescued from a Mexican jail in order to take his governor's oath.[10] His opponents alleged that Zulick drank excessively.[11] Mulvenon, Massachussets-born in 1851, had been a Prescottonian since he was twenty-four. His early and continuing interest was mining, although he worked as liveryman, bartender, and deputy sheriff. His ambition was not behind him when he was elected sheriff; eventually he served two terms in the territorial legislature.[12] J.C. Herndon, graduate of the University of Virginia school of law, was only thirty-seven and two years an Arizonan when he had to deal with civil insurrection in a fastness as foreign to him as the backside of the moon. Yet Herndon possessed sound credentials from one of the better law schools of the world, and a sense of personal destiny. He, also, would go on to serve in the legislature.[13]

Arizona learned about the meeting of these formidable players right away through a story telegraphed from Prescott in the September 7 *Journal-Miner*:

Governor Zulick, District Attorney Herndon and Sheriff Mulvenon held a conference this morning relative to the affairs in Tonto Basin. Just what conclusion will be arrived at cannot now be stated. Some vigorous steps will, however, be taken to put a stop to further acts of violence there. It has been proposed that the sheriffs, with a posse of ten each, from Yavapai, Apache, Gila and Maricopa counties, making forty men in all, go to the Basin and scour the country until every man for whom there is a warrant out is arrested. Many of the depredations from rustlers have been committed in the adjoining counties, who are equally interested with this in breaking up a gang of thieves that are preying on stock men. When the whole facts are brought to light, it will be found that an entirely different cause of trouble exists in that county than what has heretofore been represented.

For some months, the prospect of a multi-county police action was widely discussed. Maricopa County balked. Zulick bit the bullet. On September 10, Mulvenon departed Prescott a good deal better prepared than he had been in August. The sheriff took with him Deputies George Burton,[14] E.M. Tackett, and S.J. Sullivan. Mulvenon was to be met at Payson by Deputy John W. Francis and a Flagstaff half-dozen. Together with expected support of Payson locals, Mulvenon anticipated a posse of fifteen or sixteen men. And *this* time, "Sheriff Mulvenon left Prescott with extra animals and a pack animal so that they will not be so easily starved out this time as on the former trip. . . ."[15]

Mulvenon had been on the Apache frontier long enough to appreciate the all-but-intractable problems associated with guerrilla warfare. By now, the Pleasant Valley unpleasantness had progressed from confrontation to thuggery. A pattern of constrained dueling had been displaced by wanton murder. Among probable but thinly documented cases:

• Two boys, Tewksbury horse herders, were shot from ambush. Then, two more. This was a favorite anecdote of "Cole Railston. . .who in company with another youth of comparable age. . .went to work for James D. Tewksbury Sr. in Pleasant Valley herding the race horses of the Tewksburys, but upon learning that two previous herders had been killed while herding the horses not more than three miles from the Tewksbury ranch the boys decided the job was too dangerous and presently left the valley; the companion of Mr. Railston was killed before they got across the mountains and Railston himself was so severely wounded. . .for the remainder of his life he carried his head to one side as a result of the injury."[16] One prominent old-timer maintained that the Tewksbury herders were buried at the foot of Vosburgh Mountain.[17]

• The Burnham deputy. Two ambitious deputies attempted to attach the Gordon family cattle to settle a mercantile debt. One deputy dropped at the sound of a distant gunshot. ". . .the old man. . .had trailed the deputies, and, with his long rifle, had killed his man at an astounding range of eight hundred yards." The Gordons paid off the other deputy to cover up the killing of the officer.[18]

• The careless Swede. In this twice-told Tewksbury family story, a chap known only as Swede attached himself to the Tewksbury clan. But welcome as an extra fighter might have been, Swede was too dangerous to keep as an ally because, during a battle, he would run for his life, throw his gun over his shoulder, yank the trigger, and work the lever of his rifle. Once, in such a panic, he very nearly shot Ed Tewksbury. They told Swede the sheriff was after him. Swede ran toward Old Mexico and never came back.[19]

• Duchet's dozens. Considering the paucity of tracks he left, Charley Duchet profited more in notoriety from the Pleasant Valley War than any other participant. A man of mystery, sheepman Duchet changed loyalties to side with the Grahams. He lived into his eighties, and with every year, his adventure stories enlarged:

Dushay was ambushed by some of Tewksbury's hired gun-men, who fired and ran. He fell off his mule and they left him for dead. He was brot to Phx. Dr. H.A. Hughes treated him. "How many holes in me?" "Three." "Then go back and you'll find 3 sheepmen killers in the trail dead." Daggs—sheepman, political power and wealthy—encouraged the Tewksburys, figuring if he could get the cattlemen fighting he could get the range for his sheep. His money hired a lot of killers on that side.[20]

Alas, by the time Duchet died, his obituary credited him with thirty-two slayings, most off the record.[21]

• Walter, no coward. In the summer of 1887, Old Man Tewksbury's cabin came under intense fire from Grahams dug in atop a hill. Little Walter, age eight, was caught in the open. "Ed come to the door and hollered at Walter, 'Come in here, you want to get killed?' They said he just. . .took his time, he didn't run, and they was kickin' up the dust all around him. . . .When he got to the house Ed said to him, 'Why didn't you run? Walter said, 'I thought it would be a coward to run.' "[22]

• The Perkins six. According to Charles E. Perkins, storekeeper with the centrally located rock house in Pleasant Valley, his own tally of victims during the bushwhacking days of late 1887 and early 1888 numbered six. These were either ill-advised strangers passing through, or enterprising gunmen dispatched before they found work.

• The murdered mercy rider. "When the feud was at its peak, Glen Reynolds' baby son, George, became seriously ill and it was necessary for someone to ride to Globe for medicine. A rider was selected and mounted on a fast horse. The horse's feet were padded and the rider's spur rowels were tied in place to prevent jingling, but despite all these precautions he was detected and shot on the lonely trail and never returned with the medicine; the baby died. Reynolds became disgusted with the situation in Pleasant Valley and moved to Globe. . . ."[23]

• Billy Bacon's bacon. Heading home from a trail drive to Colorado, Billy Bacon, well known to James D. Tewksbury, chose a short-cut through Pleasant Valley. One evening, with his helper, Bacon rode into a Tewksbury camp. They were taken prisoner while the clan debated executing them as Graham gunmen. Bacon prevailed upon the Tewksburys to go get Old Man Tewksbury, who rode the fifteen miles to vouch for Bacon's identity and neutrality. Bacon was freed, and thereafter gave Pleasant Valley a wide berth.[24]

• Tom Horn, participant or liar? "Early in April of 1887, some of the boys came down from Pleasant Valley, where there was a big rustler war going on and the rustlers were getting the best of it. I was tired of the mine and willing to go, and so away we went ["we" generally is taken as "Tewksbury friends"]. Things were in a pretty bad condition. It was war to the knife between the cowboys and rustlers, and there was a battle every time the two outfits ran together. . . . I was the mediator."[25]

• Mrs. Bishop's dead husband, Elliot. Another casualty on Charles Perkins' roster had but one name, Elliot. The name (first or last?) was all Perkins had, together with the recollection that after Elliot was bushwhacked, his widow married a man named Bishop.[26]

By no means all of the tales of ambuscade in Pleasant Valley at the height of the feud, they provide the better-documented sampler of war stories current with their time. Uncounted more yarns no doubt were converted, varnished, and cut of whole cloth.

If Mulvenon's invasion in force needed further justification, it came while he was still on the road, en route to Pleasant Valley. In mid-September occurred the engagement called "The Ambush." At the time, scarcely any details were put into writing. No officers were present. No complaints were signed. No testimony taken. Yet bits and pieces of remembered fact and reasonable deduction formed an indelible if incomplete scenario of the desperate doings of September 17. That was the day of the only full-fledged cavalry charge of the war.

Freshly inked words on a far-away press recorded the first premonition. An Associated Press dispatch datelined Prescott, August 17, ". . .certain parties has recently shipped into that section a large number of Winchester rifles and a quantity of ammunition. The rumors have, however been discredited by the officers but this morning, Governor Zulick received a telegram confirming them all as facts and a later telegram was received by the Sheriff of this county as to the same effect." The *St. Johns Herald* reported that "the Tewksbury men are in Holbrook replenishing their ammunition and other supplies," and a latter-day historian chronicled that "the Tewksbury party was attacked in camp en route home from Holbrook."

The Graham side, for questionable reasons, stubbornly went to battle ahorse. A mounted gunman always suffers from a basic handicap: an unsteady firing position. Yet, in repeated failures from Gilleland to Paine, cowboys preferred to fight from the saddle.

Just before dawn of August 17, 1887, the core of Tewksbury fighters encamped not far from the Tewksbury Cherry Creek ranches. The place was described variously as "at the foot of a mesa," and "in a ravine." Most were asleep in their bedrolls. Of those present, the names of Jim and Ed Tewksbury and Jim Roberts were remembered, and George Newton may have been there.[27]

At false dawn, Jim Roberts quietly dressed, saddled the camp horse, and climbed a height to gather the rest of the horses, which had been hobbled to graze overnight.

... the Tewksburys were on their way back from Holbrook. They were in camp and the Grahams went down there and attacked them in camp. They [the Tewksburys] killed two or three there. ...at a place called Rock Springs and so the next morning, it is pretty early, Jim Roberts had got on a horse to go up to look for the horses to bring the horses in camp, and Jim Tewksbury was up but just got out of his blankets and didn't even have his pants on, when Jim Roberts saw a bunch of men crawling through the grass down on the Tewksbury camp. He said, "Look out down below boys!" and the Tewksburys jumped out and grabbed their guns and ran down under the creek behind pine trees and boy, when the smoke cleared away, there was only three or four of the Grahams left.[28]

In the stampede of Graham horsemen through the camp, Harry Middleton was severely wounded, possibly by a bullet that mangled his thigh. Joe Ellenwood[29] lost his seat, and scampered to cover behind a tree. The battle developed into a sniping match. The way Ed Tewksbury told it to a friend years later, Ellenwood patted his rump in a derisive gesture, and Ed obliged him by shooting him there. "He jumped ten feet," Ed chortled.[30]

They got behind low rocks and succeeded in driving off their attackers. . . worked their way up the hill toward their horses, pinning their attackers down. Finally the Graham party asked leave to bury their dead and Ed told them if they would come down and act peaceable they would help them do it.

The Tewksburys. . .permitted them to bury their dead. They (the Tewksburys) sat on the mesa and watched them throw bodies into a crevass, cover the bodies with rocks, and pitch in earth. Jim Roberts was sore about this. . .he wanted the Tewksburys to kill the whole gang right there. Ed would not allow it.

As for the burying, "there was a place on the side of the hill where there was a big crack. . .there was three or four of those strangers that nobody knew who they were. Anyway, they took them and . . . laid them down in the crack and they took a shovel that they used to cover the dutch ovens with, and covered them up."[31] Bennett may have been one dead man's name. The others were not known—likely hired guns, passing through. "The men in the Graham party were all strangers, showing again that Graham was using outsiders to do his dirty work."[32]

Certainly, Middleton and Ellenwood were hit. Middleton was taken to the Graham ranch, where he died. He was buried in the ranch graveyard next to Billy Graham. Storekeeper Charles E. Perkins thought that Harry Middleton was "a wandering Hashknife cowboy." But an old Hashknife contemporary countered, "He must have changed his name when he went over into the Basin looking for trouble, for as far as my recollection goes there was no man working for the Hashknife company at that time by that name."[33] Yet another sketch: "Harry was from Texas and worked for the Defiance Cattle Company with headquarters at Navajo Springs."[34] Perkins said he furnished a rough box, built of store merchandise packing crates, in which to bury Middleton. Funny thing, said Perkins. The thumb on Middleton's left hand was missing.

"Ellenwood, or Underwood as some call him, was evidently a roving cow person," and "Ellenwood, unhurt, dismounted and ran to the shelter of a nearby tree. There, gun in hand, he was attempting to get a pot shot. . . .The tree was rather small and he accidentally exposed one leg. This caught the eye of one of the concealed warriors, who promptly drew a bead on it, planting a calibre .45 rifle bullet below the knee. Suffering agonies, Ellenwood held his ground till dark. . . ."[35] Some weeks later Ellenwood was met, riding sidesaddle, on the trail to San Carlos, where he eventually found medical attention and a bench warrant.[36]

Press reports of the Ambush filtered in, often garbled:

The *Phoenix Herald*, September 23: "Under Sheriff Waddell has received word from Tonto Basin that a fight occurred on the 18th instant in which Thos. Graham, Joseph Ellingwood and a man named Middleton were killed on the Graham side and George Newton and James Tewksbury on the Tewksbury side."

On the next page, same paper: "A report reached town this morning from Tonto Basin by parties coming in that there had been another collision between the Tewksberry and Graham parties in Pleasant Valley on Tuesday last in which a man named Middleton of the Graham crowd had his thigh shattered by a ball and another named Elwood had been shot in the arm and that there were several members of the Graham crowd missing. How much fact there is in the report the *Herald* has, so far, been unable to determine, but it is probable that there has been another conflict of some kind."

The September 27 issue of the *Herald*: "Messrs. Abbott and Bagley, arrived on Sunday evening from the mouth of Wild Rye Creek, Tonto Basin with a pack train. They have heard the rumors from Pleasant Valley but know nothing more definite than has been heard, though they think more men have been killed than the people has ever heard about." And in the same edition: "The *Journal-Miner* says that four letters from as many different parties in Pleasant Valley have been received in Prescott all to the effect that the fight an account of which was received in our Saturday's dispatches had taken place but not exactly with the results there stated. The casualties on the Graham side were Thos. Graham, Joseph Ellingwood and Middleton wounded, the latter probably mortally, and on the Tewksberry side Geo. Newton and James Tewksberry were severely wounded by their wounds are not considered fatal. . . ."

The *Phoenix Gazette*, September 24: "Undersheriff Waddell has received word from Tonto Basin that a fight occurred on the 18th inst. in which Thomas Graham, Joseph Ellingswood and a man named Middleton were killed on the Graham side and George Norton and James Tewksbury on the Tewksbury side. The Graham party ambushed Newton at John Tewksbury's house and found James Tewksbury on guard.

When the Graham party was discovered, both commenced firing. . . ."

The *Gazette*, September 26: "Verde, Ariz. A Courier just in from Tonto Basin reports another conflict there in which two men were shot. A man named Ellingswood was shot in the hips and has died. Another man named Bennett was shot in the knee. The Courier says he saw Sheriff Mulvenon at Tomkin's ranch practicing at target with his posse. He was minus his horses but the Courier was unable to say whether they were stolen or got away from him. He also says that Mulvenon could find nothing of the Grahams or the Tewksburys. The Graham faction did the shooting." (This was signed by the telegraph operator.)

Mogollon weather intervened, perhaps delaying Mulvenon long enough to prevent the ambush from happening. Prescott measured nearly four inches of rain in September, and Fort McDowell, more than eight.[37] Mulvenon was obliged to wait several days at the Verde River crossing because of unusually high water. So not only did Phoenix learn from the courier, Mulvenon did also.

When Mulvenon reached Payson he conferred with Justice Meadows and mustered into his force a number of Tewksbury clansmen. Mulvenon allegedly recruited Jim Roberts outright as a gun, and accepted the volunteered help of George Newton and Ed Tewksbury. At Payson Mulvenon was also reinforced with a group from Flagstaff: the redoubtable Deputy Francis, Constable E.F. Odell, two sheepmen named Jacobs, and "some Payson residents who wanted to go along. Mulvenon had over twenty men when he left." Among the Payson possemen was William Burch. On his march toward Pleasant Valley, as a hardlearned security measure, Mulvenon simply took prisoner everybody he met, "so that news of their movements could not be given away."[38]

Several splendid firsthand accounts were written about the second Mulvenon invasion. One matured as a typescript edited by Levi S. Udall of the recollection of Osmer D. Flake, who, in 1887, was an impulsive, intelligent Mormon lad enlisted into the the posse from Apache County.

Although they began in the same squad, tactics in Pleasant Valley divided Flake from his leader, Deputy Sheriff Joe T. McKinney, who also penned a lengthy essay for the historical record. Thus they experienced happenings from different vantages, and commingled excerpts from their writings make points and counterpoints as this mission of frontier law was pursued to its bitter end.

From Flake:

On a Sunday, in the latter part of September, 1887, [Joe T.] McKinney with two men came into Snowflake about noon; said they were following three men who had robbed a train over at the water tank and wanted to get help as he did not have enough men to go into Pleasant Valley. I was always ready for a little adventure. I was nineteen years old. Father and Mother were both away so I got a horse from Locy Rogers, and with Joe Hirschey joined him and started west. . . .

When we were up near the old Baca ranch, Jim Houck rode up to join us. He was on his way to Apache County to get a posse to go join Mulvernon [sic] in the Valley. When he heard, at Heber, that we were on the trail ahead, he came after us. When we reached the Canon Creek ranch we. . .hunted for a note. . . McKinney dug in the ashes in the cook stove and found a note. It was partly in code but we made out that Charley Blevins had gone to the Valley. . . .We laid out in wet blankets during a slow rain, near where the road now strikes Cherry Creek, and in the morning went on west to Frank Hegler's [Haigler's] ranch. . . . There we slept until about three in the morning when Mulvernon took all the men but McKinney's crowd and went on foot to the Perkins' Store, which he took possession of, hiding the men inside the partly-built walls (about four feet high) of an addition being built onto the store. Just at break of day we mounted our horses and drove east, crossing Cherry Creek a couple of miles below Al Rose's ranch. The sun was up and we started along the trail toward the Valley, as if we had just come down the old road from the north, or in from the east, or south. All those trails joined a short distance below the Valley. When we got near the crossing just north of Rose's place, several armed men run down in the brush, evidently to see who we were, but as we were all strangers they did not learn much. As we went on toward the store we saw horsemen come down from the Rock House, and the men who had been watching us, meet. We rode on up to the store and spent perhaps fifteen minutes there, to make it appear we were just passing through the Valley.

From McKinney:

. . . Jim Houck came alone. He said he was just in from St. Johns and had warrants for all the outlaws in Pleasant Valley, that in all probability my train robbers had gone there any way and that I might get them by going there. He said that Mulvenon. . .would be there with a posse and that a general round-up would take place in the Valley.

I and my posse, which consisted of John Scarlett, Lou Hawes, of Navajo Springs and Joe Herschey and Osmer D. Flake of Snowflake and myself, went direct to Heggler's [sic] ranch, and then up above the ranch to a *cosy* little nook we found Mulvenon's camp. He was glad to see me. It was in the afternoon. We talked over plans and I told him that some one had seen me and my men that day and went toward Pleasant Valley in a hurry as far as I could see him, that I thought they would be on guard and looking for a posse. He replied: "Five or six men don't bother those fellows; I was in there a short time ago with that number of men with me and they came right into my camp and made their big talks of what they would do and what they wouldn't do and I saw that I had the worst of it and I denied having any warrants for them."

After talking things over we agreed to move into the Valley that night and his outfit would hide their horses back west of what was then Perkins' store. He and his men would secrete themselves in and about the store building. I was to take my outfit, starting about four o'clock the next morning and cross over the foothills on the south side of the Valley coming into the Valley three or four miles below, and ride up through the Valley in broad daylight avoiding any difficulty or if possible keep them guessing who I was. I was to ride up to the store, tie our horses and walk about there so that they could see that a posse was there. He said they could get their army together and come down and interview me and make me explain my business. That was what we hoped they would do but I waited there awhile when we concluded that they were not coming and Mulvenon put one of his men on my horse and six men rode away just as we had come.

From Flake:

McKinney stopped there and Mulvernon told me to go a mile west and meet four men (a rancher had just come in and told him of them). When we rode off we could see two men on horses about a half mile down the Valley and before going out of sight we saw they were starting toward the store. We met Glen Reynolds and four men, none of whom I had ever seen. They kept their guns up in front of them as we rode up, and when I told them the Sheriff had sent us out to round them up, they laughed, put their guns down, and wanted to know what came next. I learned they were from Globe. . . .

From McKinney:

It was not long until we saw two horsemen approaching from the East. They came up to within about four hundred yards of the store when they spurred their horses off to their right and they came all the way around the store and approached it from the south-east corner. We were lying down in the half built walls of the new store building. It was being built of stone and the highest part of it was about five feet, with places left in it for doors and windows. When they were within about ten or fifteen steps Mulvenon slipped out from behind the half built building and came around the southwest corner, saying, "Put up your hands, boys, I want you." The spurring and kicking of their steeds began. John Graham pulled his pistol but a charge of shot from Mulvenon's shotgun in his horse's neck brought his horse to the ground. He then turned on Charley Blevins and the next barrel of his shotgun took effect in Blevins' back. Blevins was drawing his Winchester and had it partly out of the scabbard and doubtless it dropped out before the horse went far.

From Flake:

I was told of the fight. . . . The two men rode up from the east; when near the store they turned and went around the north side, then to the west, getting nearer all the time until when they got in front of the store (east), they were not more than twenty yards off. Mulvernon stepped around a corner and ordered them to surrender. Both the men grabbed for their guns. The Sheriff shot Graham's horse in the neck, killing him instantly. John lit on his feet with his hand on his pistol. The other barrel of the Sheriff's gun tore most all the flesh off his right arm. About fourteen men from behind the walls were then shooting. A heavy ball passed through his body from side to side, just above his heart. Charley Blevins, the other man, whirled his horse and tried to draw his gun as he went toward a big cottonwood tree. Thirty shots must have been fired at him. When he neared the tree, some sixty yards away, he jumped toward it, lit on his feet and fell at the root of the tree dead; never moved a bit. Joe told me he got in three shots. Others said they shot twice. One man standing by, whose brother had been killed by the Graham gang, said, "I only shot once, and this is it", and he stuck his finger almost full length in a hole near the heart. Eight balls passed through his body. McKinney was mistaken . . . that they were made by buck shot from Mulvernon's gun.

From McKinney:

Jim Houck started for Blevins and as I was afraid he would shoot him if he was not already killed, I ran right at his elbow and when we reached Blevins I pulled Houck around and said, "Don't shoot him, Jim." He replied, "I wasn't going to unless he made a play." We turned him over on his back and the pallor of death could be seen on his face. We carried him to the shade of the big trees that were in front of the house. Nothing but the buck shot from Mulvenon's gun had hit Blevins. Graham was hit with a rifle ball. It hit his left arm a little above the elbow and went straight through his body. He lived for a while. I got him some water and gave him a drink. He said nothing that I heard. Mulvenon said to him, "Johnny, why didn't you put up your hands when I told you to; didn't you know me?" Graham shook his head. Mulvenon then said, "He knows he is a damn liar, he knew me." That was cruel, I didn't like that.

From Flake:

Reynolds and I left the others and went back to the store. Before reaching there, I said, "there has been a fight; see that dead horse with the saddle on." Just then five men walked out and looked at something and one took all the guns and the other four picked up a man and carried him to a shade near the house. We rode up and saw there were two men laying there; the Sheriff sat by one, talking to him. I recognized him as John Graham. I walked up to him and Mulvenon asked him if he knew me and he said "yes," and spoke to me. The Sheriff said to him, "Now, John, you can't live but a short time, and may go any time. You better tell me if Tom is in the Valley. If he is I will send a man for him, he can stay with you while you live, and then ride off, I will not arrest him." But John insisted that Tom was not in the Valley, so died an hour later, without a friend near him.

With the aid of glasses we could see them [Graham men] gathering horses from a small pasture and we knew they intended to try to get away. A man sat in a tree and watched them, and told us what they were doing. I went to the Sheriff and wanted him to send some men over and try to stop them but he would not; said he did not want any more men killed and it was no use to send a few men. I told him John Scarlett and I could get on the hill behind their house and keep them from leaving, until he could get their with the posse, but he would take no chances. In a little while the man up in the tree told us they were getting on their horses. I got up the tree and watched the three ride off. Later in the day we learned the three were Tom Graham, Louie Parker, and a man named Adams. They rode up a hollow to the northeast.

From McKinney:

Our men with our horses heard the shooting, and were soon there with our mounts. We went then to John Graham's house first and we put a line of men probably more than a hundred yards long, in front of the house. Presently a woman came toward us from the house with a babe in her arms and a little one holding to her dress. When she reached us she dropped down on the grass and Mulvenon advanced to where she was. She said, "I will tell you all that are in the house. My husband Joe Ellenwood is in there, and he is wounded and not able to get about. Miguel [Apodaca] is in there also. They are all that are in there."

Mulvenon told her to return to the home, that he wanted neither of the men. As we were approaching the ranch two men made their get away. They were Louie Parker and [William] Bonner. They were never seen in this country after that. . . .

From Flake:

. . . about twenty of us mounted and started for the Rock House of the Grahams. When we got on a hill just west of the house and the Sheriff called them to come out, no one but a woman showed up. She said there was no one there but Joe Ellenwood, who was wounded and in bed, a Mexican named Miguel, and her husband. The Sheriff left a small guard on the hill with orders to not let anyone leave the house, and we went on down to Al Rose's place. We could see several men walking around the place, and when we got within about a hundred yards from the house all stopped and the leader called Al Rose to come out, but he shouted, blusteringly, "if you want anything here come and get it." We thought that meant fight so turned our horses loose and got ready for action, but Ed Rose came running out from behind the house and hollered "don't shoot", and he came out and said "there would be no trouble, come right down to the house, Al was just trying one of his bluffs." We went down and stayed there about a half an hour. They made arrangements to bury the two men and we returned. John Graham was dead when we got back and Justice of the Peace Meadows, of Payson, had arrived. Mulvernon sent for him the day before, feeling quite sure he would be needed.

From McKinney:

After we had made our rounds to the different ranches we returned to the Perkins Store. John Graham had died during our absence. We then went to the Tewksbury ranch where we found all the Tewksbury party. Mulvenon had told me that the Tewksburys would be ready to surrender. We found there, Ed and Jim Tewksbury, Jim Roberts, George Newton, and Jake Lauffer. That was all that I can remember now. . . . After the work was finished in the Valley, and Mulvenon had his prisoners in hand, I started homeward. I was to wire the Sheriff's office in Prescott, on my arrival in Holbrook, of what had occurred. . . .

By yet another continuity of memory was saved a bittersweet scrap of dialogue. One speaker was Mary Ann Tewksbury, just one week past the horrid duty of guarding her dead husband's body, and just ten days before giving birth to his son. "Mel Vernon. . .came by John Tewksbury's house and Mrs. Tewksbury, his wife, was still there with the children and he told her, he said, 'You better get ready and let us take you out of this Valley until this trouble is over.'

"And she said 'No, this is the home my husband built for me and I intend to remain and there is nobody that is going to run me out!' "[39]

Some newspapers indicated in these same days that Sheriff Commodore P. Owens, accompanied by thirty possemen, tried to set a snare for Tom Graham and others on the run from Mulvenon, but trails evaporated in a labyrinth of rocky canyons, and Graham, at least, escaped to Phoenix.[40] Indicative of how close-mouthed some possemen behaved, one witness waited fifty-five years to go public in the March 1932 issue of *Arizona Highways* magazine:

I was pleased to note that you have in preparation the story on the Tonto Basin War. In the spring of 1886 I was employed by the Daggs Brothers Sheep Company and was stationed at their headquarters ranch forty miles south of Winslow. I had first hand information of the fracas. Later I accompanied Sheriff Billy Mulvennon [sic] and party into Pleasant Valley to arrest the parties. We were at the store in Pleasant Valley when John Graham and Charley Blevins rode up. When they saw us they started to run and drew their guns, but Billy beat them to the draw and both they and their horses were killed. . . .F.B. Jacobs, Mesa, Arizona.

Yet another spokesperson for the Mulvenon posse had to hustle a good one hundred-twenty miles in order to cause his own version of the shooting to be printed immediately in the September 29 *St. Johns Herald* by his editorial ally:

Hon. J.D. Houck arrived in Saint Johns last Monday night fresh from the bloody acts and scenes in the Tonto basin, and from him we gather the following interesting account of the stirring events . . .

On the twenty-first instant Sheriff Mulvenon and posse arrived at a store a short distance from the Grahams' ranch, between daybreak and sun-up, secreting themselves. The sheriff had detailed six men to take a circuitous route and approach the houses of Graham and Rose, with the intention of drawing the Graham's to the store, which partially succeeded. A short time after the decoy party had passed, a signal of two shots was fired from the house of Al Rose, which was immediately answered by three shots from the Graham house.

Two men were then seen to leave the house on horseback and come toward the store. They were too cautious to ride directly up to the house, but made a circuit of the building. Mulvenon and his men were inside the wall of a stone building which was unfinished, the wall being about five feet in height, and kept out of sight. They finally ventured up pretty close to the wall and raised themselves in their stirrups to look inside. As they did so, Mulvenon stepped out and called on them to throw up their hands. Paying no attention to his commands, they wheeled their horses and started to draw their Winchesters. The men secreted inside the walls then fired, killing them both. . . .Blevins had six or seven bullet holes in him, and Graham two.

Sheriff Mulvenon then arrested Al Rose, a Mexican called Miguel and Underwood; the Tewksburys came in voluntarily and surrendered, and the sheriff and posse started for Prescott.

In his final word on the subject, McKinney believed the slayings at Perkins Store "ended the war proper, but as one of the participants said: 'There will be a quiet assassination going on here for some time to come.' "

BOOK THREE

Possibly Tom Graham's six shooter with
Tewksbury bone handle.
  —Courtesy of Francis X. Gordon.

I. Judge, Juror, Executioner

Al Rose must have known his two remaining chances were slim, and none. Yet how could he run? To where? Quickly enough? He had perhaps had a brush with the law in California. Certainly, Rose behaved as if Pleasant Valley was his personal promised land. Here was his precisely adze-squared log cabin, his stone fireplace so plumb and tightly fitted that it has stood a century without mortar, his blacksmith shop, his water right, his gardens, his orchard, his well, his brother, his ranch headquarters, his friends. His children. His Liz.

Rose was accused of arson in August. Then, according to the October 1 *Silver Belt*, somebody took a pot shot at him—just missed—in September. The sheriff came to his door and made him endure a preliminary court hearing in October. As if he didn't have enough external turmoil, Rose constantly dwelt with another troublesome being: his own fiesty, bombastic personality. Rose was one of the early ones, and no doubt many a time he wished he could close the gate behind him. Born October 1, 1841, in Sweden, Albert Rose would have been in his twenties when the American Civil War drew him into a company of the 17th Illinois Infantry. A brother, Ed Rose, may have preceded Al to Pleasant

Valley. In the late 1870s, Ed constructed an unusual shelter: walls of juniper trunks set vertically in a rectangular trench ten by fifteen feet; pole beams burdened with six inches of clay; then all covered with split cedar shingles. A stone fireplace, gunports, and tamped earthen floor completed the decor.[1]

Al was his likely assistant in the project. The Albert Rose of Pleasant Valley, whether lawless or upstanding, was undeniably industrious. By 1881, he was freighting between Globe and Willcox. A Globe newsman noted in the *Arizona Silver Belt* of January 23, 1883, that, "Al Rose came in with a six-horse team yesterday and a wagon made by Wisdom and Clark at Willcox. The wagon cost $430 and the harness $330. The workmanship in the outfit is creditable to the makers and the enterprise displayed by Rose is altogether commendable."

When he had recovered his investment, Al, with a hand from brother Ed, laid up a more traditional "dog run" log house: a snug, one-room winter quarters joined by a breezeway to a like-size utility room. Two miles apart, the cabins of the Rose brothers perched on the west bank of Cherry Creek. Al's house was in sight of the Graham headquarters.

Beyond his bowers of cottonwoods and black walnuts, his hayfields and rangeland, Al Rose chanced upon another object of affection. Elizabeth Koehn was the stepdaughter of Sam Gilson, who peddled precious water from a dug well east of Globe. By all accounts, Liz became a stunning beauty and fiery spirit of Pleasant Valley. When she married Al Rose in 1883, Lizzie was just eighteen years of age. Soon, the Roses had two sons.[2]

Thanks to the central location of Al's ranch house and to Lizzie's skills as practical nurse, trouble often found their door. Hungry, half-tamed Apaches were the least bothersome of Liz's visitors; she simply fed them. She would walk six miles through snow to ease the delivery of a child. Scarier than Indians were the white-lipped constabularies rushing the roads past the Rose cabin, and reactionary forces which judged every non-friend a foe. The Roses—because they were there—were conscripted by the feudists as peacemakers, gravediggers, medics, orphanage keepers, quartermasters, and message bearers. If the Roses vowed neutrality, geography worked against them. And Al's penchant for outrageous sarcasm (he gruffly nicknamed himself "Shoot-'em-up Dick of Outlaw Valley") often rubbed already-ruffled fur the wrong way. When involved in the 1884 Blaine shooting, it was Ed Rose who resisted arrest and for a while was hunted, dead or alive. It was Al Rose who alleged that William Graham had been shot in the back, and demanded that Justice John Meadows exhume the body and conduct an inquest (finding: Graham was shot through the abdomen from the front).[3]

After John Paine and Hamp Blevins were slain, as many as twenty curiosity seekers and gossips from Pleasant Valley formed the burial party. Some of their tales named Al Rose as the burner of the Middleton cabin, owned by George Newton, who promptly brought criminal charges. Angry enough about the arson, Newton was doubly infuriated when Rose and Apodaca beat the case in Justice John Meadows' Payson justice court. Still, Rose couldn't leave well enough alone. His taunts ground even more salt into Newton's wounds. Rose had foolishly alienated himself from the law by bluffing resistance to arrest on the day Mulvenon's posse killed John Graham and Charley Blevins. A Pleasant Valley oldtimer expressed a judgment widely held through the years: "What got Al Rose killed was his tongue."[4]

From the pragmatic, taciturn, egocentric personage of Colonel Jesse W. Ellison, generations of latter-day analysts would draw a classic western character: reed-thin, habit-bound, hawk-faced, begrimed, ambitious, hardened, prolific, and convinced to the core that right was on his side. By such hungering human energy, unfettered in a free society, dynasties were driven.

As were several key figures in the Pleasant Valley feud, J.W. was predestined to be cannon fodder for the Civil War. He was born in Brazos County, Republic of Texas, September 22, 1841, just a week earlier than Al Rose. Jesse's father and mother were purebred Southerner Texicans who put their Q brand on hundreds of cows and their mark on eight children.

Ellison's mother was daughter and granddaughter of army officers. So naturally, before he was old enough to vote, Jesse gained appointment as a Texas Ranger, riding against marauding Kiowa and Comanche Indians. In the autumn of 1861, to serve what he considered a higher cause, he enlisted into the Sixth Texas Volunteer Cavalry. He saw combat throughout the South, and suffered the humiliating, protracted retreat from Sherman's scorched earth march through Georgia.[5]

Ellison had married Susan M. Smith on furlough; after Appomattox, they began civilian life anew with two items of value—one poor cow remaining from their scattered herd, and Ellison's amnesty grant, issued upon his declaration of loyalty to the Union. Privately, he fumed, and all his long life afterward he called himself an "unreconstructed rebel."[6] Instead of "mavericking"—branding someone else's unmarked animals as his own—he took herds on shares by which he legally could own every fourth calf born. For a decade, Ellison drove cattle up the Chisholm Trail to such rip-snorting Kansas railheads as Abilene and Fort Dodge. In Shackleford County, Jesse Ellison began to feel crowded; wire fences he threw around his legally leased state land were cut again and again by competitors. Drought and poor markets worsened. When an Arizona friend, Henry Thompson, invited Ellison to consider moving, the man was ready.[7]

A scouting trip to the Payson country clinched the decision. A circle of Ellison's Texas neighbors put their cattle in a pool, and in the summer of 1885, cowboys and warbags, mounts and tack, furniture and disassembled wagons, and the "colonel"[8] and his kids started west. Some of the family went ahead by wagon to a meadowland eighteen miles northeast of Payson; the menfolk and some of the older children followed with the livestock. In July, Ellison and two thousand head of fine cows, bulls, and saddle horses arrived at the railhead at Bowie Station, Arizona. The punchers opened doors to the cattle cars. By some oversight, only a few troughs were provided to water the stock. Crazed by thirst and unaccustomed heat, the beasts burst their pens and stampeded through one-street Bowie, knocking houses off foundations, shattering windows, carrying off clotheslines, and terrorizing women and children.

When "the damnedest melee ever"[9] was done, the hard-riding Texans managed to round up twelve hundred beeves; eight hundred had escaped into ravines and thickets.[10] In that first crew of drovers, Ellison counted men who later would strengthen their alliance through business partnership and marriage. Both Henry Thompson and Glenn Reynolds— double-cinched, hard-tie Texas ropers—would become celebrated Arizona county sheriffs; others were young William Voris, Bob Samuel, John Jacobs, Houston Kyle (who married Minnie Ellison), Bud Campbell (who married Rose Ellison), William F. (Old Man) McFadden who had a ranch up country, and a pair of Tonto Rim horse breeders, Harvey and Bill Colcord.[11] Bob Samuel probably was typical of Ellison's hands—he "used to brag all he came to Pleasant Valley with, was a wagon, a brown horse, a .44-40 rifle and a pistol that took the same ammunition, a bull whip, and a white shepherd dog."[12]

For himself, Ellison in his advanced years once explained to a newsman that, "When I left Texas, conditions there were just about as they are now. In 'eighty-five, when I left there, I bought yearlings for seven and eight dollars which I later sold here for twenty. Sold enough to pay expenses. Then cattle dropped to six dollars," and abruptly Ellison was insolvent.

"I was not only clean broke, but I owed $10,000, and I not only had to face it, but I had to make my family realize it, my wife and daughters who had everything that money could buy." Ellison said he chose to tell them out in the open forest, where he "spoke to them as man to man. I gave them my financial rating and then I charged them not to seek escape from hardship by marriage to a scalawag, and there were plenty of them as there are now.

"My girls said to me, 'We helped you spend it when you had it, and we'll stay with you until you have it again.' My girls stood by me." Old Jess bragged his frontier daughters could outperform modern cowboys at ranching chores.

"They were all good ropers and good shots and, believe me, they worked like Turks. They drove cattle instead of playing bridge and they lived on beans when we could get 'em, and sweets of any kind were unknown. For five years we did not have a bit of sugar in our coffee." Their nearest neighbors lived eight or ten miles away.[13]

Ellison and his fellow Texans didn't realize it, but the Tonto Basin already was severely overstocked with cattle. Native grasses heretofore lush and high as a horse's belly were receding from searing "living fire"—livestock in uncontrolled numbers turned loose by white men upon the fragile land. In earlier days, the heads of grama grasses touched the stirrups of a horseman. Tonto Creek from its source to its end formed timbered vales from bluff to bluff. Streams seeped and trickled through sloughs the year around. Beaver dams dotted Tonto Basin every-where. Mountain lions were plentiful, and deer populated every point. Coyotes were scarce, skunks unknown. The earliest settlers ran jack rab-bits with greyhounds. They mowed waist-high black grama, and cured it into hay. A man could drive a wagon anywhere. Bunch grass held back the brush. Steers on grass in three years fattened to thirteen hundred pounds, dressed. Better range yearlings dressed five hundred. Cows calved every year, and bred and raised calves until they were twenty years and older.[14]

By the time of Colonel Ellison's arrival, the Tonto was fully stocked. Gullies were cutting the swales. Rank, sour brush was infiltrating mesas where grass had flourished before. Hooves pounded the life out of loam, and exposed the earth's skin to erosion. Some men didn't see this—but some did. In fact, as the Ellison drovers pushed their new herds north, they were met by a delegation of armed settlers. Henry (Rim Rock) Thompson assured his concerned neighbors that Jesse Ellison indeed had purchased an existing grazing right, and that the Ellison stock would not further punish the wounded land. So the Ellison cattle were allowed to pass, first to winter on the Salt River bottoms upstream from the conflu-ence with Tonto Creek, and next spring to be taken northeast of Payson, under the rim.

The vanguard Ellisons camped a while in wagon boxes, and moved into ranch shelters as they were finished. In time, eight or nine single-story rooms were roofed. Situated as it was on the road between Payson and Pleasant Valley, the Ellison headquarters, called Apple Ranch for its bounteous three-thousand-tree orchard, became a natural stopover for travelers. Household goods hauled in from Texas included a square grand piano,[15] which most of the family could play.[16] Jess was a fiddling fool, and daughter Duette could make a guitar sing a waltz or chant a polka. The Ellison boys had attended dancing school in Texas, and they expertly called squares and reels. Duette's education included a stint in a convent in Waco—and never would she dress in trousers, or allow an uncouth male to wear spurs or chaps in her house.[17]

The Ellison enterprise had a shaky start. Cows in nutritious grass starved for a lack of salt; some died before learning to scratch through crusted snow to rich feed underneath, or to drift to a warmer elevation during winter. Not alone, Ellison applied prairie remedies to rim country range: for example, he annually set fire to mature pine bunch grass, expecting it to come back green; the shallow-rooted species did not come back; it died. Some years when beef prices collapsed, Ellison branded his calves and kept his old steers. He established brands and herds for all his children. As Slim Ellison recalled, "He kept two bronc busters busy from spring till winter breakin' young horses from three to eight years old."[18] Under rancher pressure, the territory offered a twenty-dollar bounty on cougars, whose natural prey was deer, not cattle. Freed somewhat from predation, deer populations exploded, putting even more pressure on the land.

The colonel wasn't the only contributor to catastrophe; his reflexive grab for more and more cattle for more and more range was typical. And if there wasn't enough feed to keep a shipment close-herded on a drive to the Holbrook railroad pens, Ellison built log corrals, large enough to hold two thousand head, each a day's drive from the other. Majestic Merriam's elk were shot to extinction, not so much for food or sport, but to eliminate a perceived range competitor. Bears provided Ellison and family and packs of hounds their favored sport.

The skins of some of Arizona's greatest trophy bears were tacked upon Ellison outbuildings, only to rot away and leave their awesome dimensions outlined in rusted nails.[19] Before the restraints of enlightened range management, Ellison, on one ranch, was grazing more livestock than someday would be allowed on the entire three million acres of the Tonto National Forest. Ultimately, the land fell back from the onslaught in the same way that Ellison had retreated from Sherman. By the vertical yard, the topsoil blew away, slid in sheets, opened cracks miles long, rushed downhill toward the sea, vanished forever.[20]

That would happen later. For the moment, there was a fortune to secure, economic power to accumulate, political influence to cultivate.[21] In some years, by their own estimates, the Ellisons put up four thousand overnight guests, and Miss Duette filled her memory book with autographs of her swains and soul sisters. At party times, Colonel Ellison enjoyed pulling on his jug of corn and cursing a blue streak. If his wife objected, he'd say, "Set down, Sue." And she sat. On such occasions

Ellison entertained his beholden admirers with a replay of how, during the War Between the States, he led cavalry charges against the dam-yankees. Once his mock attack strayed under a low tree limb, and the colonel was swept out of his saddle and dumped into the dust.

"Them Yankees are gettin' tougher, Pap," one of the boys hooted, and laughter (including Jesse's) echoed across the Apple Ranch.

From that kind of raw material was wrought an oft-heard rule of the Rim country. When things were going well, Colonel J.W. Ellison could be a wonderful host.[22]

In Boonsboro, Iowa, Samuel Graham scarcely knew what to think or do. Since his adventurous boys left home, he had learned not to be surprised by unusual news regarding them, from Alaska to Mexico. He did not altogether disapprove, remembering his own youthful itch to move: Ireland to Scotland to America, then Ohio to Iowa. When Samuel Graham took up a farm in Boonsboro, not more than a dozen families had preceded him. He tilled only forty acres, but his persistence paid off. He earned a reputation of "plodder," but he was one of the few farmers of Boone County who always had a bit of money put by to lend.[23]

Beginning about 1884, reports from his sons turned sour. They had invested their own prospecting profits in a ranch and their herds increased. But then the boys were involved in charges and counter-charges in the courts. They were quarreling with their neighbors—half-breed Indians no less!

Now, in late September, Samuel Graham received a cryptic, stunning telegram. The wire stated he had lost his sons and gained a fortune. A local newspaper the *Boone County Standard*, made a story of it:

A SAD MESSAGE

Mr. Samuel Graham well known as one of the old residents of this community, living a short distance west of Boone, received a dispatch from Arizona on Thursday afternoon, by way of Fort Worth, Texas, saying that his two sons, Thomas and John and a grandson were killed by the Apaches, which have recently gone on the war path again. Mr. Graham left on the night train for Kansas there to meet Mr. Wood Parker and probably they will proceed together to the scene of the massacre. There is valuable property left by the deceased to be looked after. Sitting quietly in our Iowa homes, and burying our dead in peace, we have much to be thankful for over those who are exposed to the villainies of these murderous red cutthroats.[24]

The errors quickly were siezed upon by another newspaper. A telegram "from a justice of the peace in Arizona territory, from the court in which his sons had a ranch" stated that one son was killed and one missing. "It was first circulated that an Indian uprising was the cause of the death, but the dispatches in the daily papers put another face on the matter."[25]

There followed some reprinted clippings, contradictory of fact and fulsome in interpretation: "Tucson, September 28: Second in importance to the Indian troubles in this territory have been the troubles arising from the Tewkesbury-Graham factions. No more bitter or deadly conflicts were ever waged between Scottish clans than those that during the last few months have been fought between the two rival families of Graham and Tewkesbury. Each family seemed bent on exterminating the other family or dying in the attempt." The Boone reporter regretted that he let Sam Graham get away without an interview, but the gentleman "started for Arizona immediately. . .he has not been heard from since. It is a long way out there and he has to do about two hundred miles of staging to reach the scene. The Graham boys. . .were running a large ranch and are reported to have accumulated considerable property, estimated to be over $50,000. This will be inherited by Sam Graham."

Not quite, for in Phoenix to meet them was unwounded son Tom.

Tom had much to tell his father and Wood Parker. Willie was indeed dead, and so was Sam's firstborn, John. Louis Parker was unhurt, and safely in hiding. Tom convinced Sam Graham that he and his brothers scarcely knew the Blevinses; that Willie was bushwhacked without cause; that John was murdered in cold blood, when, in good faith, Tom sent John to Perkins store to determine if Sheriff Mulvenon carried warrants for their arrest; that he, Tom, would have surrendered in Pleasant Valley but for the fear of similar assassination; and that in general the Grahams were the oppressed. To his close friend, Judge John A. McFarland of Boonsboro, Samuel Graham dashed off by the speediest mail a memo:

We arrived at this place this morning [October 4] and found some of the friends of the boys. They inform me that a lot of desperadoes and half-blood Indians undertook to clean out Pleasant Valley in order to get the range. Willie Graham went out to get up the horses and was killed. There were fourteen men in ambush. Johnny was killed the same way. The other two boys are here in the near vicinity, watching things, but have to keep out of sight. They have seven hundred head of cattle here and one of the finest ranges and water privileges in the valley.[26]

Tom managed another revelation to his father. The Pleasant Valley War, like all wars, had scrambled personal priorities. Tom had a young Salt River Valley maiden in a family way.

How far along? Six months. . . .Six months!

The seventy-year-old father and his thirty-three-year-old bachelor son had a great deal to talk about, and do. First things first. On October 8, 1887, in the Tempe home of her parents and with her father, Baptist Minister William Jasper Melton officiating, Thomas H. Graham and Anne Melton were married.

Then, second. Tom presented himself to the nearest office of the law.

And third, he made himself available to whatever friendly press he could find:

THE OTHER SIDE—TOM GRAHAM, THE ELDER OF THE GRAHAM BOYS, IN TOWN—HE MAKES SOME PLAIN STATEMENTS REGARDING THE PLEASANT VALLEY VENDETTA

Tom Graham of the somewhat notorious Graham family, if we accept newspaper reports, participating in the Pleasant valley fight, arrived in town today, and reported at the Sheriff's office. Sheriff Halbert having no warrant gave him the liberty of the town, and is now awaiting telegrams from Prescott, Yavapai County, and St. Johns, Apache County.

Tom Graham, instead of suffering any wound in the vendetta, is hale and hearty, and gives a story, truthful of belief, that does no credit to certain officials and people.

He was in Phoenix at the time of the fight at Newton's [Middleton] house, and none of his relatives were there. John Graham who accompanied the searching party, having gone over to Canyon creek with another man before Newton's place was approached. This party was hunting the whereabouts or remains of old man Blevins, who mysteriously disappeared a few days previously, while searching for horses stolen from him.

After the report reached Phoenix of this encounter, Tom Graham started home. Before reaching there, however, his younger brother William, was fired upon from ambush and one of the shots virtually disemboweled him. The poor boy rode ahead on his horse a short distance, then dismounted and laid under a tree, for some minutes, acting the part of the hero, in not crying out for assistance, knowing that his brother John, and friends at the ranch, would fall in the same trap. After a time, and with superhuman effort he mounted his horse, and reached home, reciting these facts before he died. This lad had never left home during the disturbance and was the victim of a murderous scheme previously concocted.

In the fight near Tewksbury's house, in which Henry Middleton and Joe Ellingwood was shot, Tom and John Graham were not present. Middleton was in search of two stolen horses that were hobbled below old man Tewksbury's and suffered death from his temerity.

Now, as to the killing of John Graham and Charley Blevins. When Sheriff Mulvenon first came into Pleasant Valley he was informed by Al. Rose that the Grahams were willing to submit to arrest, if he had warrants for them, and to come over to their house. He stated that he had no such warrants and was looking for the Tewksburys. On his second trip he and a posse passed the Graham ranch and went down to Perkin's store. Tom Graham who was shoeing a horse at that time, told his brother John to go down and see if there were any warrants against them, and if so to surrender, and if he (the sheriff) wanted assistance to arrest others, they would accompany them. Charley Blevins told John Graham to wait until he saddled his horse and he would go along. Both boys left on this peaceable mission to the store and were shot down. Charley was pierced by eight different bullets and John Graham was mortally wounded in two different places, and after he fell from his horse George Newton wanted to shoot him again.

This unvarnished tale is told by Thomas Graham, and he wishes the Arizonian to state that instead of being intimate friends of the Blevins family, he never met any of them till the old man came to his house searching for stock. They had not long resided on Canyon creek, some twenty or thirty miles distant, and outside of hearing the name the Graham boys knew nothing of them. Andy Cooper, who was a stepson or other kin to Blevins, had stopped at the Graham ranch two or three nights during the past two years, and never before.

If there was any way to check perjury, the public would doubtless form a different view as to the Pleasant Valley difficulty, and reach the conclusion that men of money were trying to obtain control of ranches located, for honest purpose, by hard working and honorable boys.[27]

Stories along much the same lines begat secondary and tertiary mentions in the Arizona press, and across the nation. Sheriff Mulvenon was not amused. His costs to invade Pleasant Valley twice now exceeded three thousand dollars,[28] and taxpayers were grumbling. Informed by Maricopa County that his most-wanted fugitive was free on the streets of Phoenix, Mulvenon caught the earliest possible stage. He amiably brushed off the press, saying only that John Graham and Charley Blevins had resisted arrest and "grasped their weapons, whereupon some of the Sheriff's posse fired with the result already known." On October 7, without incident, Mulvenon arrested Tom. The next day, the two went together to Prescott, where Tom was jailed.

In these days, too, justice was grinding in Payson. In mid-October, John Meadows examined Ed and James Tewksbury, Joe Boyer, Jim Roberts, George A. Newton, Jacob Lauffer, and George Wagner on the Middleton ranch fight, and ordered them held for the grand jury.[29] The jury was empaneled November 2 in Prescott. "There will be forty witnesses to dispose of,"[30] reported the *Prescott Daily Herald.* Within a month all seven Tewksbury partisans were indicted for murder by the grand jury in the death of Hampton Blevins. Thomas Graham, Louis Parker, "and others," likely including Miguel Apodaca, also were ordered to be tried during the June 1888 term. Presumably the crime was murder, but records are unclear. Witnesses failed to appear. The cases were continued to the November term, then postponed again until January 1889. For want of evidence, the prosecution apparently allowed the cases to drop.[31]

That Tom Graham during the autumn of 1887 was under considerable mental and physical stress goes almost without saying. He was held under the key of the sheriff who had cut down his brother. In Prescott, three years before, he had heard an intemperate judge blast him as a perjurer. Now he was driven from his home and dispossessed. Meantime, his enemies were abroad, making this sort of news: "Ed and Jim Tewksbury spent one day in town this week, replenishing their exhausted stock of ammunition."[32]

Unquestionably, the coordinated invasions of three sheriff's posses touched off general abandonment of the Graham cause. Bonafide Graham allies fled, as did suspected Graham sympathizers. Faulted by mixed-up dates, the transcript of L.J. Horton nonetheless testifies convincingly of the exodus: "All day long, four to six at a time who had committed lesser crimes with a swinging trot, winking, and blinking, at every bush, they passed by and before the sun went down, all had skipped the country except fifteen that were shot or hung, which completely annihilated the last one."[33] The flight of nervous men left tracks. A spate of train robberies, stagecoach holdups, and highway stickups occurred as people in need of quick cash fled. That was Colorado badman Billy Bonner's last resort and fatal mistake:

An Albuquerque dispatch says: News has been received here of the killing of William Bonner, a cowboy who belonged to the Graham faction in Tonto Basin, A.T. When the body was discovered it was covered with sagebrush. From the appearance of the body, it is evident he was ambushed and killed, probably by members of the Tewksbury gang as he belonged to the Graham faction. With Bonner's death ends a list of twenty men who have been shot and killed in that neighborhood in the past two months.

It is stated on good authority that Bonner was the party who recently held up the stage between Ft. Apache and St. Johns, securing quite a sum of money. He is said to be one of the parties who robbed the Atlantic and Pacific train at Navajo station a short time ago. He has participated in all manner of crimes that have stained the annals of Arizona, and there is no question that his death is a welcome one.[34]

In jail in Prescott, Tom Graham was allowed to receive mail, and at least one letter grated against his supersensitized and somewhat paranoid psyche. In an exquisite touch of irony, Tom somehow obtained a blank letterhead of a local butcher who operated the "Tragic Market." Upon this macabre stationery, Tom penned a rejoinder to his bride:

Prescott, Arizona 1887
Dear Annie
I have received a few lines from you you sed you Was quiet Well I am glad you ar Well and hope you always Will be but dont you think you Write terible short letters I gess you ar tired Writing Just say yes and no fooling this is the 3- letter I have Writen you your sympathy for me is not mentioned and am glad of it I have had lots of letters from strangers ho do suympathyse with me and ho try and say a Kind Word for me But you no that I ant looking for sympathy as I am able to stand it all alone if tare is eny letters for A.B. Graham in the post office take them out my case is at the present time Before the grand jurors- howar all the folks and every Won dont think hard of me for Writing this Way for I am mad yes and you are ashamed to sign your name you hadent better Write eny more yours as ever Thomas H. Graham
[*on reverse side*] I always have tried to be good to you so dont Write eny more to me if you are ashamed[35]

After languishing in a Prescott cell, Tom was released October 22 on three thousand dollars bond. He returned to the Salt River Valley. By letter he contracted with Bill Colcord [in hindsight, a curious choice] to look after his Pleasant Valley livestock. Tom went about the details of starting life afresh, as an irrigation farmer. (Gushing romantic fiction to the contrary notwithstanding, neither before nor during their marriage did Annie Graham ever visit Pleasant Valley. When, many years later, she made her one, swift trip to the Valley, she hated the place. She played no role as peacemaker.)[36]

Exactly when and by whose instigation was initiated the Committee of Fifty may never been known. Its origin may have been fashioned in a smoky room of Prescott or Globe, or in the barn of a Valley ranch. Certainly, by the summer of 1887, the committee was fully structured, although likely the membership never approached fifty. The committee may have been suggested by an invasion of Pleasant Valley by a body of men—"self-appointed vigilantes"—from Maricopa County led by Captain W.C. Watkins in early 1887. This prominent Lower Tonto rancher and storekeeper allegedly passed the word that if rustling did not cease, he would return to stop it.[37] No more insulting response could have been contrived than the brazen burglary of Cap Watkins' store less than a year later. Although the suspects eventually escaped, Watkins was able to muster a posse of "an officer and twenty-seven of the best citizens of the Valley" to take up the chase.[38] Of course, the committee could have been nurtured by a George Newton or a James Houck. But whatever its genesis and expansion, as early as the summer of 1887 it was taking its orders from Colonel J.W. Ellison, chairman.[39]

Of the diversity of details attending the demise of Albert Rose there are two points of agreement: Rose spent his last days rounding up some of his cattle at the old Houdon Ranch on Spring Creek, and on November 1, 1887, he was executed by a group of men.

The version of widest belief was sworn to a thousand times by Louis Naegelin. An early settler who professed his neutrality to a fault, Louie always insisted he simply tried to help his friends in any way he could. In such a role (he said) he accompanied Rose on a final roundup prior to Rose's intended removal of himself, his family, and a fraction of his material wealth from Pleasant Valley forever.

According to the memory of the youngest Rose son, he and his brother and Lizzie were at the Houdon Ranch the day Al Rose was killed.[40] That wasn't the way Louie Naegelin ever told it. And insofar as written record might show, Elizabeth Rose had no comment.

At any rate, it was widely held that Al Rose was a sub-chief in the Graham gang. As Mary Ann Rhodes wrote in her letter to her son, "Al Rose, thinking to save himself, went in with the Grahams and lost out." Naegelin's unswerving account for public consumption went about as follows:

With two companions, one of whom was Louis Naegelin, [Rose] had camped at the Houdon ranch; and while his comrades were busy getting breakfast the next morning he went out to look for their saddle horses that had been hobbled. . . . Scarcely had he disappeared when several shots startled the men in the cabin and when they rushed out to investigate they found Al Rose stretched out in the grass, dead with a bullet wound in his back. The tracks on the ground told a plain story. A shot from ambush had ended the career of another Graham fighting man, and his assassins had walked up to the body to make certain of his death. His comrades packed the corpse back to Graham's, slung across his saddle horse and lashed on with his lariat, and sadly buried all that was left of Al Rose in the little boot hill graveyard nearby. Now it held five victims of Tewksbury vengeance.[41]

Within seven days, the story found ink. The November 7 the edition of *Prescott Courier* had the bulletin, "An unsigned wire from Camp Verde to John Marion [editor] of Prescott says, 'A man came here today who says Al Rose was murdered by masked men. This man helped bury Rose.' "[42] An editorial in the same issue commented, "Mr. Sixby of Tonto Basin says that Louis Naeglin told him that Rose was killed at the Houdon ranch. Naeglin says he was present at the killing, having stopped over night with Rose. After the killing, the men left the ranch without any further attempts at shooting or trouble." The *Courier* had kind words for Rose: "Deceased is well spoken of by all who knew him. He was very hospitable. His death is a severe blow to his wife, children and friends. The *Courier* hopes that his slayers will suffer for their horrid crime. Rose was undoubtedly allied with the horse stealing gang but was trying to pull out."

One story had Rose shot through eleven times.[43] Years later, Ed Tewksbury ostensibly told Joe T. McKinney that Glenn Reynolds snuffed out Rose with a shotgun. Ed said a group of Tewksbury men staked out the Houdon ranch "looking for some parties," when Rose walked out of the cabin. Reynolds beckoned to Rose, and Rose made several tentative moves before sprinting toward the cabin. Reynolds pulled the trigger at a range at which he could not miss.[44] Over the years, Reynolds descendants vehemently disputed this allegation. Probably they were correct, in light of a plausible alternative made public ninety-five years after Rose died:

. . . these books claimed that he was shot; he wasn't, he was hung.

[Rose] was told to leave the country and he was over at the ol' Houdon Ranch on Spring Creek with Louie Naegelin. Ol' Louie Naegelin said they were masked, but the minute you would mention anything connected to the Pleasant Valley War where he had to call names, well ol' Louie Naegelin clammed up, he wouldn't say a word. The reason he said these men were masked was he didn't want to identify them. They weren't masked, they didn't wear masks. Ol' Louie said he was in the house cooking breakfast and ol' Al went out to feed the horses. . . .

. . . They took him out there and they tied a rope around ol' Louie; they was going to hang him, and he said, "Why are you hanging me for, I was neutral, I never took no hand in this fight. I haven't been stealing horses or anything like that?" They said, "We are going to hang you for being in bad company." Finally, they. . .told him, "All right, we are going to let you go, but don't you ever dare tell who any of us was or what took place." Good ol' Louie, they never did get anything out of him, they never did. When the time came to try to hold an inquest over the killing of Al Rose, well, ol' Louie said they was masked. He didn't know who they was.

They hung [Rose]. . . .Wherever they caught those guys they hung and left them hanging for several days. . . .My dad told me one time, he said he seen many men. . .hanging all up and down along Cherry Creek and all different places around that country. You would find them hanging down there for several days and the maggots were dropping out of them! Now, that is the words you use.

They were the same Vigilante group. They were the same ones. Colonel Ellison told me they hung Al Rose, he told me himself he hung him, and ol' Louie Naegelin told me they hung him.[45]

Another name of a committee member found its way into the archives:

Al Rose was NOT shot but was hung, so said Bill Colcord who was there, hanging was cheaper, shells cost money. Louis Naegelin, who was with Rose, was threatened too, but cleared with a promise he would betray no one, and tell a different story. His story was that Rose was shot as he came out to get wood to build a morning fire. No so, says Colcord, shortly before he [Colcord] died. Witnesses to his story, Dale King and Bob Voris.

While he was telling all to Dale King and Clara Woody, Bob Voris implicated his own father in an oral history transcribed for secret preservation for twenty-five years:

Now, I heard years ago, now this is confidential, remember that, I don't want this to go to print or to let anybody know for at least twenty-five years, I heard that a man made the statement that the Vigilante Committee, and my father was a member—now again this is personal—I heard that ol' man Ellison was the leader and that was when ol' man Ellison was alive; now don't you print this, you are not to print this at tall.[46]

Reluctance to talk. If it lingered into the 1950s, it surely was paralytic during and after the guns and nooses of 1887 and 1888. The court system went half-heartedly through the motions. Complaints, inquiries, recommendations to the Grand Jury, arrests, bonds, no true bills—the system lumbered along to nowhere. Eighteen months of concentrated establishment scrutiny eventually would be summed up in one paragraph news item in the June 1, 1889, *Silver Belt:*

Jim Tewksbury, Tom Graham, and Louis Parker and two others were turned loose by the Yavapai grand jury at Prescott. No bills were found against them. Nobody seemed anxious to testify either for or against them.[47]

How might posterity judge the futility of another century's legal process? Isn't it possible that vigilantism and hubris of activists, and apathy and cowardice of others, emasculated the courts? After all, in the early years, when the violence was escalating, no point of truth was too minute, no witness too humble, for consideration in the quest of legal remedy. Now, men had been butchered by the brace, and "no bills were found." Another interpretation of cause-and-effect might hold that the repeated helplessness of the courts led to and justified the appropriation of law enforcement by "responsible citizens." From her own additional and exhaustive research, Clara Woody came to believe that more than any other legal or extralegal force, the committee effectively wound down the war:

It was obvious that the courts had failed to end the feud. Not a single member of either faction had gone to prison.[48] The fruitless court hearings had precluded any chance for a real peace. Both sides emerged from those days of suspense and hope with intensified anger and vengeful spirit and the war of ambush and assassination resumed. The sharp lines that had been drawn between factions became blurred, however as a third group—the vigilantes—played the most significant role. This small group of prominent farmers and ranchers set about ridding the Valley of all bad men and rustlers. Their object was commendable—to reestablish law and order—but they believed that the way to do so was to eliminate all who were a threat to peace and to do it swiftly, vigorously and secretly. They had dispatched Al Rose swiftly and silently. . . .

As the attempt to rid the Valley of "undesirables" picked up momentum, the settlers began to be specifically distrustful of "intruders." Old timers recall that strangers passing through the Valley sometimes fell victim to suspicious vigilantes. If they were unable to explain their presence satisfactorily, they were unceremoniously hanged, though they may have been innocent of any crime.[49]

Supporting this line of logic is the remarkable document left by Robert Voris, the eighty-two page transcription of his 1957 oral history recorded within the Globe's Gila Pueblo in the presence of responsible historians. The recording was converted to typescript by a stenographer, edited lightly for clarity, wrapped in a paper marked *Confidential*, and locked away in the Arizona Historical Society for safekeeping for a specified twenty-five years.

Although in his oral statement Robert Voris does not mention a specific date, he provides enough clues to suggest that during the early 1930s,[50] nagging rumors regarding his father became unbearable to him. Voris needed to know—was his own deeply respected pioneer father a member of the Committee of Fifty? Many of the men who could answer that question by then were dead, of natural causes or feudal revenge. But one figure lived. . .Colonel Jesse W. Ellison. The Confederate true believer, the grizzly-bear fighter, the patriarch of a family of legends was crippled and sightless, prisoner in a despised city, but bright of mind. Under questioning, Robert Voris averted:

Ol' man Ellison was still alive. . .the time that he lived in Phoenix. I went to ol' man Ellison and said, "I want to know the truth about it, was that true?" and he wouldn't tell me nothing at first; he would just look at me and grin. "Well," he said, "I wouldn't worry my head about it."

I said, "Well, I am worried about it, I want to know the truth about it. Is that true or false?"

So he told me, "You come back this evening and. . .I'll tell you whether it is true or whether it is false." When I went back there that evening, there was nobody there but Miss Lena—this was after the old lady Ellison had died, and the old man was blind. . . . He said, "Don't you ever repeat anything I have ever told you or the names of anyone I tell you until everyone that is implicated is dead." I said, "All right," and I made him that promise. I told you this is strictly confidential. Ol' man Ellison was the leader, and the ones that was members of the Vigilante Committee was John Rhodes, Bill Voris, Bill Colcord, Harvey Colcord, and ol' man McFadden.

Q. McFadden was arrested?

A. No, McFadden was on the Vigilante Committee.

Q. I know, but he was arrested by the sheriff of Apache County and taken over there and one other man with him. The county attorney had them arrested but he didn't prove anything.

A. That Houck, what is that sheepman, he said in *Arizona's Dark and Bloody Ground,* that they thought he was the one had something to do with the hanging of those men up on the Rim. He also said that Glenn Reynolds. . . .

Q. Who was the member?

A. Neither one of them; neither one of them are members; They were not in that at all. There is one or two names, I wrack my brain trying to remember who else he told me, but there was about eight of them all together, now, how many of them did I name?

Q. The leader and Rhodes, and Colcords, both Harvey and Bill, McFadden, Voris. You have named six.

A. And Bud Campbell and Huse [Houston] Kyle that makes it! So, ol' man Ellison told me he said, "Mostly in any country, there always has got to be a cleaning up process. You could not put a horse in a barn and expect to get him the next morning." He said, "You might have a herd of cattle today and tomorrow you wouldn't have anything."

In mid-March 1888, Jake Lauffer charged James Stott and Tom Tucker with the theft of his horse. Although records later disappeared (as did many Pleasant Valley court documents), the case was heard in Globe before Justice of the Peace Job Atkins. As a defense exhibit James Stott offered a bill of sale. The *Arizona Silver Belt* faithfully provided the finding of the judge:

The court has carefully examined and weighed all the evidence in the case and is of the opinion that the horse in question, that is the iron gray horse, branded now with U Quarter Circle and Circle is the property of Mr. Jacob Lauffer, and also thinks that he could if he would replevin said horse in the proper manner prescribed by law, that he could undoubtedly recover him, but in all the testimony given in the case there is not a particle of evidence that either of the defendants were ever seen in Pleasant Valley last June, there is no doubt in the mind of the court but that these defendants, Stott and Tucker stole or had any hand in stealing him, there seems to be an entire lack of evidence to convict. Therefore, there being no sufficient cause to believe the within named James Stott and Thomas Tucker guilty of the offense mentioned, I order them to be discharged.[51]

The finding did not sit well with half the citizens between Globe and Holbrook. They presumed that the Arizona judiciary, staffed by "the best judges money can buy," had done it again. Stott's ranch was near the Aztec and he buddied with Hashknife cowhands. In many minds, such association equalled guilt. Five months later Stott automatically became the prime suspect in another attempted murder in Pleasant Valley.

In early August 1888, Jake Lauffer was standing in the doorway of his cabin on Lower Cherry Creek, when from the short range of a hundred feet a heavy rifle slug slammed into his arm, breaking the bone, and crippling him for life.[52] But Lauffer's agony was only another incident in what had become a reign of terror in Pleasant Valley.

On the thirty-first of July the people of Pleasant Valley and vicinity assembled at Perkins' store fearing an Indian raid, as they had been notified by some of John Dasin's Indians that a large party was out.

. . . two men were sent to Tonto to find out what they could about the Indians. On their return next day they passed by Lauffer's ranch and found that he had been shot from ambush that morning, while he and Charles Livingston were after their horses that were picketed just back of the house.

Lauffer had his left arm broken just below the shoulder, the weapon being a .45-90 Winchester, as shown by the shells found under the tree from where the shooting was done. In the afternoon of the same day two men, [George][53] Cody and Coleman, both quiet, inoffensive citizens, and in no way interested in the Graham-Tewksbury war, were shot at from ambush as they were riding along the trail just back of Mrs. Rose's ranch, in Pleasant Valley, and Cody's horse was killed.

The parties doing the shooting, two in number, then got their horses and rode down into and across the valley and straight to Ed Rose's ranch, where they went in, and no one being there, they helped themselves to a pair of field glasses and a picket rope, and then pulled out.

Parties went on their trail but soon lost it, owing to rain. Since then every ranch has been deserted and the people are camped together for mutual protection, between Perkins' store and Mrs. Rose's ranch, no man feeling safe in the prosecution of his own business. . . .[54]

Except for such scraps of newsprint, fragile as elder leaves, scarcely anything survived the frightful year of 1888—the year that people huddled together in tent communes in view of the homes where they dared not stay.[55] Men were afraid to go about their work; travel of any sort meant a traverse of no-man's land. Although unauthorized to meddle in civil matters, the U.S. Army, in the summer of 1888, used rumors of a fictitious Indian uprising to show the flag in Pleasant Valley: "When our informant left the Valley there were two companies of United States soldiers there. . . ."[56]

No shrinking violet himself, Will C. Barnes retained for a half century his flesh-creeping impressions of:

. . .those fateful days when men—the writer among them—rode the trails of the Tonto Basin country only at night; slept with one eye open and weapons within easy reach and never turned a corner of a canyon or trail without first wondering if beyond it lurked an enemy, weapon in hand, finger on trigger.

He recalls well one afternoon about sunset when riding down a canyon trail near the Tonto Rim. In the distance he saw a horseman coming up the canyon on the same trail. Both stopped a moment, then swung out of the trail and turned up the canyon's side. The writer's revolver swung handily at the saddle horn, his Winchester rested under his right leg. The other had his rifle lying comfortably before him on his lap, his right hand resting on the lock.

From each side of the canyon, suspiciously and warily, we eyed each other for all the world like two old tomcats in the back yard. Our ponies nickered a friendly greeting across the canyon. They were far more human than we.

Coming closer, the stranger proved to be my somewhat doubtful friend, one Jim Houck. He knew me instantly. Between us there had been no love lost for several years. Each rode silently back to the trail, eyes straight ahead, nor lost any time in getting out of sight. A rear-view mirror would have been a godsend about that time.[57]

II. Jamie

Midafternoon. August. Seven thousand feet above the sea. Thunderheads six miles tall rumbled and rolled around the dappled green transmontane vistas. Fitful zephyrs gave the shakes to copses of quaking aspens, and won some winks from acres of black-eyed susans. A lazy summer interlude upon the Mogollon Rim, and James E. Shelley was leading his horse, merely dreaming along, shuffling slowly, his eyes focused on the cattletracks crisply embossed into the moist forest floor. . .when, in an unnatural space, a familiar object dangling head-high knocked off his cowboy hat. . . .

Shelley forgot about his lost cows. He stared eye-level, unbelievingly, at two scruffed cowboy boots. Shelley's gaze rose skyward. The boots were attached to a man, and from a rope the man was hanging from a hefty horizontal limb of a ponderosa pine tree. Suspended from the same limb were the bodies of two other fully clothed, properly booted men. Their blood-purpled faces leered grotesquely atop their monstrously elongated necks. Stiffly, slowly the corpses twisted on taut lariats.[1]

For a moment, Shelley's mind crazed like shattered glass, and he reflexively stepped onto his horse and ran. Then overtaken by reason, he reined in—looked back. The gruesome silhouettes still darkened the horizon. Then, in the deliberate haste of a devout Latter-day Saint possessed of godawful news about gentiles, Jim Shelley hurried toward his home near Heber.

Maybe Shelley was not the first, or even second, to make the grisly discovery. It was said that another man, gravely ill with tuberculosis, chanced upon the lynching aftermath, and found breath to hurry afoot sixty miles to Holbrook.[2] Clearly, the triple hanging was intended to make an impression, and it did:

... with two of my men I was up on the mountain at our Long Tom ranch. Early one morning, one of the men rode out to wrangle the saddle horses. An hour later he came tearing down the trail towards camp as if the whole Apache tribe was after him.

So excited, he could scarcely talk, he managed to explain that he had found three men hanging to one pine tree a few miles from the ranch, close to the trail leading down to Andy Cooper's Canyon Creek ranch. "Did he know them?" "Sure, they were Jim Stott, Billy Wilson, and Jim Scott." Naturally, there was considerable excitement in camp. Every one of these men were well known to all.

The horse hunter explained his discovery of the bodies. "I couldn't find the horses, but did run onto a lot of fresh horse tracks in the road. Thinking they might be ours I followed them down for a couple of miles. The trail led through a very rocky bit of ground—the tracks were hard to see and I was leaning down from my saddle trying to make them out—suddenly old 'Pete' gave a snort and stopped dead still. When I raised my head, I found myself within ten feet of three bodies hanging from a big pine tree. Their faces were just about opposite mine, hands tied behind them, eyes looking up into the sky but seeing nothing. Me. . .I just whirled Pete, jabbed both my spurs into his ribs and drug it for the ranch."[3]

Whether from the evening, August 11, alarm of Shelley or the next morning declamation of the Long Tom cowhand, sketchy accounts stuttered onto the wires at Holbrook and flew to the top of front pages of whatever newsprint was about to run through a press:

ARIZONA LYNCHING
Three Men Lynched By a Mob of Outlaws.

Holbrook, August 15: Information has reached here of the lynching of James Stoll [Stott], James Scott and Jeff Wilson by outlaws in the southwestern part of this county. The affair grew out of the recent war in Tonto Basin between sheep and cattle raisers. Warrants were issued and arrests made by unauthorized persons, and the prisoners were taken across the mountains into Yavapai county, where they were met by a pre-arranged mob of outlaws and hanged.

That was all that most papers, Arizona, and the world had to go on for a little while. Much more would be published thereafter, but those first seventy-two words were about the truth of it.

In North Billerica, Massachussets, these few details devastated the disbelieving parents of James Stott. The confirming telegram from a Hashknife cowboy, J.P. Burdett, on August 16, contained even less information. Post-haste, the Stotts packed for Arizona. From the officious East Coast, the Stotts had a shock awaiting them in the freebooting West. Now, the Committee of Fifty was coursing the land.[4] Although not identifying all of them by name, G.W. Shute gave a thumbnail of the Committee:

Strangers entering the Pleasant Valley area disappeared completely. Horse thieves infested the whole country. A cattleman or farmer, when he turned his horses upon the range, never knew whether or not he would see them again. At last, a "Committee of Fifty" was organized to bring law and order. . . .

. . .probably never numbered more than thirty. Its operation consisted principally of aiding law enforcement officers, but when an occasion arose, they were indeed direct actionists. Fast, grim and deadly, they soon became feared in Pleasant Valley as no other body was feared.[5]

James Warren Stott, born September 13, 1863, was undeniably different in his hometown, where he grew up directly across the street from the house of Thomas Talbot, twice governor of Massachusetts. Hyperactivity would be described as an affliction by succeeding generations, but in post-Civil War New England, Jamie Stott was considered admirably rambunctious. "All boy" was the term. The positive pride of his father and mother, James and Hannah Stott, Jamie excelled in local schools and played trapeze artist atop the Talbot woolen mills superintended by his father. The elder Stott was not one to restrain him, for discreetly, vicariously, the boy made him whole again. The elder Stott, in a cruelly unique accident, had lost a hand and an arm, torn from its socket, in rescuing one of his workers caught in millworks machinery. Jamie's dexterous grasp for an active life compensated for ten thousand impulses beyond the father's diminished reach.[6] Jamie graduated from the Wilmot Academy in New Hampshire; then, when "a youthful indiscretion" caused him to leave Harvard in his third year,[7] the parents acquiesced to an alternative: Jamie wished to go West and buy a ranch. They gave him their blessings and a grubstake.

In February 1883, Jamie arrived in Texas and went right to work. By March, he could boast in a letter home that he was at least an average roper on a Castroville horse ranch. That November, he hired onto a ranch near Bartlett, owned by a brother of Thomas Talbot. Over the next two years, Jamie earned his spurs at several Texas ranches, taking horses as pay. In letters, he chronicled his westering wander from spring to autumn of 1885. He and a range pal drove Stott's mustangs across New Mexico via Fort Sumner, killing a buffalo here, resting horses there, in what must have been the time of their lives. In October, Stott was in Holbrook, making friends, particularly with F.A. Ames, another Eastern lad working for the Hashknife outfit. Stott's pockets were deep enough to purchase the homestead right of a settler at Bear Spring some forty miles south of Holbrook.[8]

By every evidence, Stott's horse ranch became a family enterprise. He frequently reported transactions and accounted expenditures. The mother and father sent money regularly. In the summer of 1887, mother Hannah and a sister spent a week on the Stott spread. By now the young man had two hundred horses. He got along with his neighbors. He enjoyed a reputation for hard work and honest dealings, except in one instance.

Somehow, Stott came into possession of a blotch-branded iron gray horse claimed by Jake Lauffer. But that case was tried in open court in Globe, the very capital of Tewksbury country, and Stott was cleared. That Stott kept current with the progress of the Pleasant Valley War is evidenced in a letter he wrote his sister, Hattie, dated October 2, 1887. Stott estimated fatalities at that point to be between fifteen and twenty-five men, and that a friend of his—perhaps Harry Middleton—was the last to die.[9] Stott complained to his cowboy chum, F.A. Ames, that Jim Houck was plotting to gain possession of Stott's ranch as a sheep station. Harassment of settlers by thugs had reached such a state that both the Mormon settlements of Wilmot and Heber were virtually deserted through 1887 and 1888.[10]

"Some people have judged me guilty without taking the trouble to investigate the charges or giving me a chance to defend myself," Stott allegedly told Ames. "These men are not friendly to me so I shall not take the trouble to change their opinion. If they desire to know the facts they would see me before forming an opinion. If I should abandon my ranch and stock, these people would think it an acknowledgment of guilt. I would lose all my property and also be doing just what the Tewksbury gang desire me to do. I have done nothing wrong and do not intend to be bulldozed or intimidated. No man will believe me guilty until he has received some reliable evidence of the fact; such as prefer to are welcome to their opinion."

Few incidents of the Pleasant Valley War underwent more revision of facts over the years by establishment historians than the lynching of James Stott and the other two men. Decades afterward, Will Barnes set down from memory and news clipping a version of what transpired. By then well along in years, Barnes, in his book *Apaches and Longhorns*, proclaimed Stott guilty, if not of theft, at least of incautious behavior.

In his draft manuscript, Barnes wrote of himself in the third person— "the Boy"—which then was edited to the first person, perhaps in recognition that in 1888, Barnes scarcely qualified as a child, being a decorated Indian war veteran thirty years of age." Barnes' manuscript with edits differs revealingly from that which was printed finally in *Apaches and Longhorns*. A manuscript excerpt:

Shortly after [nearly a year] the Cooper killing in Holbrook, fate in the shape of a vigilance [changed to "citizens"] committee overtook another bunch of individuals suspected to being connected with the gang of organized "horse borrowers" that was operating in the region of which Holbrook was the center.

Up in the mountains, close along the Northern boundary of the Apache Indian Reservation, a young chap had a horse ranch. He was a tall, handsome, red-headed lad, and a general favorite. He loved, however, to "flock by his lonesome," as one man put it and apparently had few confidants. His language and general habits indicated a man who had been well brought up. Events proved this to be the case.

...Like many young fellows who, in those years, drifted into the wild and woolly west, he had a foolish notion that when he had crossed the Rio Grande he had left behind his morals and ideas of right and wrong and that most anything would get by in Arizona. His name was James Stott.

Eventually detectives employed by the stock association obtained almost [changed to "what was thought to be"] conclusive proof that the young man's ranch was the headquarters for the thieves who were stealing horses [changed to, "was being used as headquarters for a well organized band of horse thieves."] There, the bunches of horses from the North were exchanged for others stolen from the South. The nearby uninhabited Indian reservation offered a fine place in which to hide them away while brands healed over and owners turned back for home after losing the trails.

In common with many others, I had a strong suspicion as to what was coming to this gang. I liked the young fellow from Boston and tried to warn him of the danger he was running into. But he would not listen. "He could take care of himself any day." (Patting the six shooter which always hung at his hip.) "He'd love to see the color of the man's hair who could get the drop on him, etc., etc." "Well, Jim, my boy, I've warned you" were my parting words to him as Jim rode away one morning after spending a night at my home in Holbrook.

How and on what legal pretext if any were Stott, Scott, and Wilson taken into custody? By whom? Were the trio of doomed men then kidnaped by lynchers? Who knew what when? Was there a coverup of prominent citizens? Over the longer term, as law and even statehood came to Arizona, was history recast and bowdlerized to bleach this stain from pioneer clans nominated for canonization? Beyond his gratuitous placement of himself on the very fringes of the happening, was Barnes himself more deeply involved? They were, and are, fair questions which might have been cleared up forthrightly. They were not.

One non-mystery served as a case in point. Confusion by innuendo, falsehood, and confusion almost immediately lay down a smokescreen around the role of James Houck, consummate sheepman and sometimes law officer. In the beginning, at least, Houck was openly credited with arresting Stott and his companions, and assuming responsibility for their safety. As the story expanded to Flagstaff and was reported in the August 18, 1888, edition of the *Flagstaff Champion*:

Jim Houck, who is from the Tonto Basin, says Jake Lauffer was shot at and his arm broken by ambushed assassins at this ranch about two weeks ago....Two other men, Cody and Coleman, on their way to Lauffer's ranch were shot at. This, says Mr. Houck, was done by Jeff Wilson, Jim Scott and Jim Stott who were arrested by Houck and his posse, on warrants sworn out for their capture. The persons, however, were taken from them by an armed mob of some forty masked men who hung them after taking them some distance down the road.

Then Houck again, in a story enterprised by the *Prescott Journal-Miner* on August 23, 1888:

In response to a telegram sent to Holbrook for further information concerning the lynching in Pleasant Valley, the *Journal-Miner* has received the following:

Holbrook, August 16—Reports from Pleasant Valley of the lynching by outlaws of James Stott, James Scott, and Jeff Wilson, near Stott's ranch, on the afternoon of the eleventh, received here up to date are as follows: The parties were arrested on alleged ficticious charges and were in the charge of Jas. D. Houck, and five others. They were en route to Pleasant Valley and when near the Canyon Creek trail were met by masked men who ordered Houck and his men to move on. The prisoners were found next morning hanging near the Verde road. Houck arrived in Holbrook on Monday August thirteenth and the latest intelligence from the scene was on Tuesday morning, when the bodies were reported as still hanging. From the best information today the county authorities are taking no action in the matter.

The most diligent inquiry among the parties acquainted in the Tonto Basin country fails to elicit any information as to the identity of James Scott, the only one of that name known being the sheep man, and ex-member of the Legislature, who was not likely to have been found in the company of two such notorious characters as Stott and Wilson are alleged to be. The general impression is that the lynching party were not composed of outlaws either, as the man Stott, although arrested several times, had always managed to secure an acquittal to the disgust and annoyance of the better class of citizens, who were cognizant of his place being a rendezvous for horse thieves and bad characters, and who, as stated before had ordered him to leave the country.

"Masked men" and forty strong? To those who recalled the demise of Al Rose, the yarn must have rung familiar. Joe T. McKinney, Apache County lawman, held a different opinion of cowboy James Scott (not to be confused with the sheepman former legislator mentioned in the Prescott dispatch). McKinney later wrote that in New Mexico he had known cowhand Scott: agreeable, industrious, honest, and principled Hashknife hand from Weatherford, Texas. Scott was small of build, about twenty-six, and distinguished by one blue eye and one brown one. Scott made Houck's hate list on the day the young Texan forced Houck to back down in a Holbrook argument. Scott had the bad luck of staying with Stott on the eve of the lynching. McKinney maintained that Houck took advantage of the situation to pay off the old grudge. McKinney grieved the loss of Scott as a dear friend.[12]

Wilson's luck was just as sorry. By some called Jeff, but by most known as Billy, Wilson was variously characterized as an itinerant minerals prospector en route from Durango, Colorado, to seek his fortune in the mines of Globe, Arizona. Or as others came to believe, the Arizona Billy Wilson was the selfsame former sidekick of Billy the Kid in New Mexico.[13] Whatever his true identity, in a time when westerners changed their names with the weather, this Billy Wilson, too, chanced to spend a night at Stott's ranch.

A dozen recitations of fact grew out of the triple hanging. Notably Forrest, Shute, Barnes, McKinney, Joseph Fish, Roscoe Willson, Clara Woody, L.J. Horton, Robert Voris, Hazelton, and research by the William Jordan Flake family, and investigations by Stott's family, and contemporary news stories, as well as the works of fiction writers, brought both clarity and controversy to the occurrence. A disinterested synthesis of the writings and voice recordings, from the perspective of nearly a century, supports this scenario, although the full story may never emerge.

In addition to the three to die, on the evening of August 10, 1888, a fourth man spent the night at the Stott ranch. One Motte Clymer, ostensibly a tubercular, won the sympathy of young Stott.[14] Seeking to regain his health, Clymer accepted Stott's invitation to stay a spell at the horse ranch. In modest payment, Clymer agreed to do some chores, and watch after stock during Stott's travels.

According to Sam Brown,[15] Clymer was an eyewitness to the abduction of Stott, Scott, and Wilson. A group of ten or twelve men arrived at the ranch at about daybreak. Stott knew some of the riders, called some by name, invited them to breakfast. They let Stott prepare the meal, partook, and directed the three victims to saddle up. Barnes derived a somewhat variant version "from different sources later on." Barnes wrote, "The men involved did not, of course, 'brag' or even talk much of their part in it. Naturally, as days passed and where half a dozen persons were concerned, bits of information came to the surface from time to time, which when pieced together made a fairly understandable story of what occurred on the day the execution took place. There were two stories current at the time or soon after. This is one of them:

[The following text is from the edited manuscript of *Apaches and Longhorns* with Barnes's second-thought edits in his own hand indicated within brackets.]

The whole plan was worked out carefully in advance. One party led by a well-known peace officer went over into the Tonto Basin country where Wilson and Scott were known to be hanging out with a nest of bad men. They were run down and arrested on an old warrant the men [changed to "posse"] had with them. Scott and Wilson made no especial protest against their arrest, feeling themselves innocent of the charges mentioned in the warrant. The party making the arrest started north with the men ostensibly for Holbrook. Before daylight, the same day, August 11, 1888, another party of three men went to Stott's "Circle Dot" ranch at Bear Springs.

Hiding themselves near the log cabin in which Stott lived, they waited for someone to come out. The first man proved to be Stott. He came out half-dressed, started to the wood pile for wood for the breakfast fire. As Stott stepped clear of the cabin door unaware of any thing wrong a voice at the right snapped out, "Hands Up Jim."

As he turned towards the voice a man, Winchester in hand, stepped around the corner of the cabin at his left. Turning quickly, Stott faced the muzzle of a rifle held in the hands of a man he knew only too well. His reluctant hands went into the air slowly—but as directed. Was it possible, he must have asked himself, that he was to be taken so easily?

Barnes in his manuscript relates that the trio of abductors found Clymer sound asleep inside the cabin. Stott explained that Clymer was a "lunger," a "tenderfoot," a stranger who could do no harm, and should be left unmolested. Stott did cook breakfast for the lot. Barnes's manuscript went on:

When that was over they took him outside and placed him on a horse. His feet were linked together with steel handcuffs the chain passed under the animals belly, while the chain of the pair on his wrists was slipped through the arch of the saddle in which he sat, making it utterly impossible for him to escape or ride away from them.

Then, as he and two of the party rode off from the cabin, one returned and told the stranger that his friend Stott would not likely return to the "Circle Dot" ranch for some time—if ever. They would leave a gentle horse in the corral. . . .

Barnes stated in his manuscript that Clymer was encouraged to leave pronto, ride east, and catch a stage at Snowflake for Holbrook. The Barnes monograph went on:

Then the three men with their manacled prisoner rode off down the Verde road to the west. What happened later nobody knows, exactly.

It was said that Scott pled for a chance—just a show for his life. He undoubtedly knew what was ahead of him. Eventually the party ["with Stott," struck out] arrived at the trail ["leading from," struck out] from the Tonto Basin and Pleasant Valley. Here they met the party from that section who had Wilson and Scott in charge. ["Again nobody can say just what happened" struck out.] From the little which subsequently leaked out it is believed that Scott and Wilson broke down—and begged for mercy when they found themselves sitting on their horses under a pine tree, faces uncovered, each with a noose of rope ["looped" struck out] around his neck, the other end tied hard and fast to the limb above them. But the vigilantes were hard-boiled. The chains [substituted for "hobbles"] that fastened the feet of the two beneath the belly of each horse were opened [substituted for "unlocked"]. Unconscious of the part they were to play the horses stood quietly. A man stood behind each animal. At a signal, each delivered a crashing blow with a rope on the hips of the horse in front of him. A wild plunge forward and the riders were left swinging in the air. Their faces twitched, their bodies turned round and round in the bright sunlight, their manacled hands dragged in vain at the steel shackles which held them securely behind them. Then the vigilantes turned to Stott. Unafraid and undaunted, he faced them all and dared them to do their worst. Turn him loose and he would fight them all single-handed and alone. He addressed each man by name and called down on their heads every curse and malediction his trembling lips could voice.

As he talked, the horse he was on jumped from under him and Stott too was swinging back and forth—back and forth, with his two comrades.

"Dancing a dead man's jig" it was called in those lively days.

Some who later examined the hanging tree noted a chilling bit of evidence: "W.J. Flake states that the limb from which Stott hung showed several grooves, indicating that he had been raised and lowered several times, probably in an effort to make him confess his activities and associations."[16]

Barnes does not strongly disagree with the narrative of Joseph Fish, "an accredited historian of that day," and Fish's largely unpublished manuscript does not differ radically from Barnes's, except that Fish has a vigilance committee relieving the abductors of their prey. Barnes:

According to Fish three officers went to the Stott ranch and arrested the three men, Stott, Wilson and Scott. Handcuffed and feet chained together under the belly of each horse, the posse took their prisoners down the Verde road to the west—where they met the large posse from Pleasant Valley—just why they did this is not understood unless one accepts as a truth that the whole thing was pre-arranged, i.e., the officers were to meet the large posse, the prisoners were to be taken from them by force of superior numbers and hung. At any rate Fish gives this story as well authenticated. Not only this but he gives the names of every man in both posses. Fish worked quietly but wisely. He undoubtedly got the facts. Nobody has ever yet disputed his statements.[17]

Perhaps. Fish's place in chronicling Arizona history is secure, and indeed he may have worked both quietly and wisely, but his manuscript history deviates from other accounts, and not all of the names he supplies are complete or accurate.

He said, "James D. Houck, W. Vorse, and 'another person'" arrested the doomed men. Then the suspects were handed over to "Glen Reynolds, J. W. Boyle, W. McFadden, P. Ellison, N. H. Coleman, Tom Horn, J. Tewksbury, H. A. Larson, Colcord, Varis, and some others . . ." Fish thought that "Houck acted in accordance with the plan to get the men into the power of the mob, and was implicated and even assisted in the hanging."

A century later the makeup of the roster may no longer matter—but why not? Historians, through other endeavors, gained a vested interest in posterity's ability to understand the early days. Men and a few women who fell heir to high government posts and church leadership understandably desired to distance themselves from the taint of a premeditated lynching. Religion, scholarship, political muscle, wealth, and moral honor intertwined with the doings that day atop the Mogollon Rim. Some vigilantes belatedly realized they had had the backbone but not the stomach for strangling men—in particular, the good-natured Irishman, William McFadden, who, years afterward, when in his cups, whined that he never thereafter lay down his head for a night's sleep but that Jamie Stott at the end of a lariat clawed and gasped and kicked McFadden's happy-go-lucky dreams into maddening nightmares.[18]

Incidentally, McFadden and Boyle were obliged to appear in St. Johns on an open murder charge—the names of the victims not stipulated— and lacking witnesses District Attorney A.F. Banta of Apache County failed to make a case. A semi-serious attempt also was made to charge some of the Tewksburys, but nothing came of it. Joseph Fish also hints as much in his unpublished "Autobiography."[19]

The omnipresent Will Barnes remained involved with the aftermath of the triple lynching for quite a while. He wrote that on the day his horse wrangler discovered the bodies, he and some of his men rode over to take a look. This could have been August 11 or 12, with Barnes stating, "Indications were that they had been hung not more than twenty-four hours before." And, "The bodies swung there in the bright sun for three full days. Bloated and swollen, they were in a terrible condition. A few hardy individuals visited the scene, but nobody had the nerve to cut the bodies down. Nor did any of [the visitors] linger round the spot. Their curiosity was quickly satisfied. One or two hasty looks. . . ."[20]

Three days later arrived A.F. Banta, Holbrook justice; Sam Brown, stable operator; Ben Burke, Holbrook carpenter; F.A. Ames, Hashknife cowboy and pal of Stott; and S.I. Frankenfield, a Long Tom puncher. The five men convened as a coroner's jury, dropped the bodies into canvas wagon sheeting, drove their hack to a little glade nearby, and dug three graves in the soft earth.[21]

In those years, Barnes seemed to be everywhere. To whom would fall the duty of looking after James and Hannah Stott as they sought to get to the bottom of the conspiracy? Barnes!

The day before their arrival, a telegram reached Holbrook from Albuquerque, New Mexico, addressed to the Master of the Masonic Lodge at Holbrook, requesting that official to meet Mr. James Stott on the arrival of the noon train from the east.

The Master was absent from the town that day and the message was duly delivered to me as the next official in rank. With my mother, I went to the station to meet the train.[22]

With few exceptions to prove the rule, history has ever depicted war as man's work and worry. But as always, women were affected, too, and their desperate reactions and poignant moments documented a dimension common to all wars: for both sexes there was enough struggle, horror, loss, and grief to go around. Hannah Stott was issued her full share.

Fate also may have given her another sad bit of wartime grief: the ill-chance of drawing Will Barnes as escort and advisor. A half-century later, when he wrote his autobiography to be edited by the distinguished Frank C. Lockwood, Barnes doggedly clung to his published belief:

The deed was done by no "Mob of murderers" as has been claimed. On the contrary, there was at the time little doubt that the work was done by men, most of them reputable citizens, who were determined to put an end to the reign of lawlessness that for some time had terrorized the entire region.

Every man in the party knew the three victims and ["their record," changed in ms. to "the charges against them all over that region."]

With such a mindset, Barnes, founder in 1887 and perennial director of the Arizona Livestock Board, whose main purpose was throwing the book at rustlers, may have possessed the most dubious credentials for comforting and counseling an Eastern mother whose precious son had just been strung up without so much as a drumhead trial by "reputable citizens, who were determined to put an end to the reign of lawlessness." Barnes made no bones about it, again quoting his manuscript with edits in his own hand for the typesetter:

...the aged parents of Stott demanded that the perpetrators of the deed be arrested and punished by authorities. ["Convinced finally, that such action would probably create a difficult situation in the region" was changed in the ms. to "Believing that by such action looking toward the punishment of the Vigilantes would probably create a difficult situation in the region"], one that might bring reprisals on the citizens who were willing to make an attempt to help them, the two sorrowing ones went back to their eastern home, convinced their only son had been murdered and that justice had been denied them.

Barnes indeed hurried through a busy season as arbitor. He relates that:

An uncle of Jim Scott...a prominent Pacific Coast lawyer, asked me soon after the affair to come to Los Angeles at his expense and advise him as to what (if any) steps he could take against the men concerned with the hangings. The victim was the son of his only sister, who lived in eastern Texas. She had asked her brother to do what he could....So I urged my Los Angeles friend to take no steps against the Vigilantes connected with the hangings. I felt certain no grand jury could be gotten together that would indict these men, nor could a trial jury be selected that would convict them, if brought to court. I believe sincerely this was sound advice. In my judgment any attempts to punish these men would have resulted only in more bloodshed and accomplished nothing.[23]

Barnes's theories fit closely with a tidy construction placed upon Stott's horse business by persecuted Mormon families. They were tired of being pistol-whipped and stolen blind. But a thread of frayed logic runs through the conventional reasoning offered by a foremost pioneer Mormon spokesman:

One of the amusing things about it was Stott kept a record of every animal with which he had anything to do, and when he was hanged, W.J. Flake bought his property and got possession of the books; they told of animals stolen from Mr. Flake and others, calves, and colts that he had separated from their mothers and put on his brand.[24]

Osmer D. Flake, son of W.J., goes on to dispute further an allegation that an innocent man, Stott, was hanged. Stott's father supposedly was allowed to study his son's books.

When he handed them back he said, "Mr. Flake, I will never again say that my boy was innocent." Father said, "I did not want to show you those books but I could not afford to let you leave here feeling as you did toward those people. If they had been innocent, more effort would have been made to convict the men who were responsible for the deed."

A century later, perhaps no opinion is more widely held along the still-Mormon Mogollon Rim than this one. But a century later, any fair-minded observer must question the term "amusing" for a sly thief to keep precise accounts of his crimes. Troublesome, too, that thirty years of diligent effort on the part of the author of this work has failed to uncover Stott's alleged account books (the author counting among his closest friends thrifty Flake descendants, who have never discarded so much as a broken hoe handle). One must frankly demand: where are Stott's allegedly incriminating tally books today?

Those books could indeed buttress the beliefs of the Flakes. Or they might give credence to a letter written October 10, 1888, by Holbrook Justice D.G. Harvey to Jamie Stott's father:

I am fully convinced, after a thorough inspection of James' books and papers, that he purchased and paid a good round price for every head of stock on his ranch. But I do think that he was imposed upon by designing parties and through his kindness he had to suffer; and I believe this opinion is concurred in by every law-abiding person in the country.[25]

As a good friend might, that also was the opinion expressed by Ames, in his own letter to the Stotts: "Never was there a particle of evidence produced which would have had the slightest weight with an unprejudiced man. There is not a man in Arizona knowing Jim who believed him guilty and all the people there look upon his death as a cowardly, brutal murder as was ever committed."

A succinct rejoinder is attributed to Colonel Jesse W. Ellison:

I asked old Man Ellison, I said, "Well, now it is said that Stott, whatever his name was and these two fellows that was hung up there near the—between the OWs [ranch] and Heber were innocent. They said it was two men and a boy."

He said, "It was no boy. We didn't hang no innocent men."[26]

III. The Dastard Sneaks

Few crimes of the American Southwest before or since—as calculated in community outrage and national scrutiny—rivaled the brazen sun-up assassination of Tom Graham out in front of a schoolhouse in the farm hamlet and bridgehead of Tempe, near Phoenix, Arizona, August 2, 1892.

True, many a travesty in the early days of the West was visited upon explorer, aborigine, fur trapper, Mexican, and prospector, but those sins usually went unnoticed and unredeemed during Arizona's first territorial decades. (There were exceptions, such as the 1870 publication by a Prescott newspaper of the names of four hundred people killed by Apaches in Arizona.)

On the trail to statehood, *right* lagged far behind *might*. As often as not, law straggled in last.

Towns in Arizona with professionally administered courts could be counted on a hand. Justices were grossly undercompensated. Payson's magistrate, John V. Meadows, who examined, remanded, and buried so many fighters of the Pleasant Valley War, was roundly scolded for dunning the county for his measly fees for wringing a measure of civic order from chaos.[1] On the Arizona frontier, informality and impulse reigned.

Close-by editorial critics gave judges hell. Even in the best of courts, comedy vied with tragedy, and some were themselves sorry jokes. Arizona was where a judge might ask the accused, "Are you the defendant, sir?" and have the prisoner respond, "No, sir, I'm the man that stole the horse!"[2] Arizona was where a prosecutor might tell another judge, "This trial has to stop right here—the defendant's alibi is established," and have the judge inquire, "Counselor, what is the penalty for an alibi?"[3]

But laughter rang hollow when too many good men died beyond legal remedy. Throughout the final years of the 1880s, the Pleasant Valley killings of 1887 and 1888 went unpunished in the Arizona courts. Tom Graham and Ed Tewksbury and several of their followers were arrested and soon let go for lack of accusers. Spokesmen for both sides continued publicly and vehemently to complain about the fecklessness of the law. If anybody believed that all of the Tonto feudal wounds were healing, they were wrong.[4]

But slowly, to secure their multiplying families and mounting possessions, Arizonans increasingly agitated for reasonable approximation of the ideal of codified justice. In the early 1880s, vigilante violence attracted high-level disfavor even in wide-open Tombstone; the barbaric strangulation of John Heath from a telegraph pole directly outside the Cochise County courthouse wired a woeful message to the outside world; freelance retribution increasingly embarrassed Arizona ambitions for maturity. The prevailing mood looked for peace everywhere in the territory, at almost any price. Certainly that sentiment was gaining in the huddling burgs strung up and down the Salt River from Phoenix. The capital city itself grew "from about 1800 to about 7000 or four hundred per cent" between 1882 and 1892.[5]

For some years, Phoenix had flocked to a variety of houses of worship. For the day and place, Phoenix provided adequate public schools. Fraternal organizations lobbied for civic betterment. From its beginning as a field of wild hay, Phoenix boasted of one mill capable of grinding one hundred thirty barrels of flour a day. Just north of the major intersection of Van Buren and Centre (later Central Avenue) streets, Phoenix splashed happily in its own community bath house. Boosters laid claim to "one of the healthiest climates in the world. . .snow never falls, and roses bloom in December."[6] In 1887 the monumental Arizona Canal was completed, vastly increasing the amount of land under more-or-less dependable irrigation. In 1892, the nearest mainline railroad still lay twenty-eight miles to the south, but the telephone company bragged of nearly a hundred paid subscribers.[7]

Nine miles upriver, Tempe was fulfilling the first impression of its founder, Charles Trumbull Hayden: "This is an empire, and sometime people will find it."[8] In 1892, his own son, Carl, was fifteen and looking forward to an education at Stanford University, and a career in politics that would reach leadership in the U.S. Senate. On the occasion of his death in 1972, *Time* magazine characterized Carl Hayden as "a last link between the New Frontier and the real one."[9] In 1892, Tempe offered several comfortable, multi-story hotels, a banking system, its own churches, two major grain mills, a daily newspaper of rich literary tradition, and a rail spur significantly closer to the mainline than Phoenix's. While Tucson had fiddled around doing not much with its University of Arizona, for six years, Tempe had made a going concern of its Territorial Normal School.[10] In June 1892, Misses Victoria Shaw and Lillian McAllister graduated at Tempe.[11]

In a word, Tempe typified the territory's rush to *respectability*. Clearly, Tempe was not a town to abide cold-blooded daylight murder.

To a casual observer, the Pleasant Valley War would seem ended. Nearly five years had passed since Tom Graham withdrew from his home ranch with the graves of his gunshot brothers and friends. He had assigned his Pleasant Valley livestock interests temporarily to William Colcord, then more formally to Silas W. Young, who was paid wages.

In 1888, the newlywed Grahams were dealt another sorrow. With Tom away on business, her mother out of town on a visit, Annie had to cope overnight with a desperately ill babe. Diarrhea took Arvilla's life before Annie could summon help. Arvilla was but one of many American infants who died of unexplained dehydration in the "good old days." (Copious purple passages to the contrary notwithstanding, as Tom's wife Annie *never* set foot in Pleasant Valley.[12])

Within a year at Tempe, Tom and Annie started over again. The birth of their second daughter, Estella, softened their sorrow. Entering a one hundred sixty-acre parcel three miles southwest of Tempe, Tom used knowledge gained from an Iowa boyhood. He fell to the endless chores of reclaiming ancient desert gardens.[13] First, he cut three hundred cords of mesquite. Then followed the prying of stumps, clearing brush, breaking ground, extending ditches, planting seeds, harvesting crops. At first, the little Graham family slept under trees, then camped for a while under stacks of roughsawn timbers and flooring while their adobe home was built. Annie channelled her energies into trying to keep things clean in a dirt house. Estella, a bright, dark-eyed beauty, proved hardier or luckier than her sister. She survived to win the unabashed affection of mankiller Charley Duchet, who made Tom's farm his base camp for far-flung mineral prospecting expeditions. Many years later, some of Estella's more vivid childhood memories would be of curmudgeonish, knife-mutilated Charley, cooing and clucking over her like a proud grand-pappy. She would sit between Tom and Charley at supper; Charley called her "the Old Girl."[14]

On the face of it, peace had broken out in the Pleasant Valley War. But to a careful observer then, and certainly in hindsight, dire omens abounded. Through monumental will-power, Tom barely contained his bomb of rage. In a never-before-published letter to a favorite sister in the Midwest, he revealed bitterness regarding his being driven, dispossessed, from Pleasant Valley. Most incredible, Tom in his own words stated that after dark on the day his brother, John, was shotgunned by the sheriff at Perkins Store, he doubled back upon the posse to his home for his and John's belongings.[15]

Tom's letter in its entirety:

Dear Sister and family I just have received your Letter and Will answer you right a Way I have ben Writing to mary and the letters have all come back I Will send it to you and you Can send it to hur she need not Wory so much about not hearing from Lewis [Parker] as he Dont Want to be Writing as some Won might get hold of his letters you ought to no that he dont Want to show up till after my trial Comes off do you understand I am purfectly Willing to take my Chances and if I Come out all Write Why then of Corse there Will be no more Chanses for him to take he is all Write I Just hurd from him in speaking of Keep sakes I am shure you Can have all of them that there is the night Johney Was Killed that after Knoon 3 of us Went down to the house to see if Johney had ben Killed and the folks at the house Was so Bad scared they dident no eny thing and Beged for us to leave the house as thare Was 75 armed men Watching the house We told the Woman to Keep her shurt on and When We got grub and my gold Watch We Would get a Way from the house and she had ben in the trunks and hid Both Watches and it Was 1/2 ower before she Could think Whare she had hid my Watch finley I told hur to get on hur thinking Cap and get my Watch finley she thought Whare she had hid it and that Was all she Could find so We had to pull out again I told hur to gather up every thing and put it in to my trunks and When ever I got around if thar was eny thing thare Why you Could have it I have never ben up thare yet But When the Wright times Comes I am going up thare and see What thare is that is of hisen you no he Was no great hand for eny nice things the Watch I let allen have With the understanding that he Would send it to father and at his death to go to you and then to mary Johney Wanted him to have the Watch and also a silver dollar and a ten cents in silver Bill had it in his pocket When he Was Killed and so did Johney have it in his pocket Mrs. Grewell had it But she has never give it to me yet you see how I am I cant tak till after my trial Johneys pin is all I shoult like get ahold of if I ever see it I Will no it some of them got a Way With it It is an old Keep sake from Bill Webster annie isent at home and the Baby she has gon to see hur mother Went on a Wagon I gess Will have a Belly full of Riding on a Wagon the gurles Was out in full Blast at the park, so I had a good Chance to skip the tralall loo as anniey Was gon Mag I am sory of Wone thing and that is you are tryin to purswaid your sun to voat for Cleaveland for godsake dont vote your sun to Work you to death and that is the demicrat party cheap labor and free traid Will drive many a poor family to the Wall I am a republican for 1000 differnt Reasons What did the demicrat ever do ask your husband and if he is the Right Kind of a man he Can tell you What the Republican party dun for you and me I hate the sight of a demicrat and take your sun By the hand on the 4 day of November and pray for him to Vote for Harison the demicrats never dun eny thing onley set Back in some old Cabin with sun flowers growing all round the house and a lot of Bull dogs to pump an old stake and rider of fence to Bight some nabor Whome he harley new I am a poor man and if I new Harison Would be elected I Would go and Work Wone year hard for his support I tell you the demicrat plat form Wont do I Would hate to see my Mother if she Was living hafto Work for Cheap labor Wouldent you of cours you Can eat Corn Bread that is Cheap living. But the Republican Wont do that he Will Work and have his Wheat Bread for his family so if you ever talk Bandana tak Harison it Would Be Worth 500 a year to me alone if Harison is elected the demicrats Never have eny thing doing or going on in the Cuntry Just Wate on the Cloud to roll By and it never rolls We Want Buisness in the Cuntry Not talk What ar Both dans doing I ant doing eny thing this summer. . . .

Not only did the loss of Graham's personal effects rankle Tom, he could not have been happy with reports trickling in from Pleasant Valley. Dividing the spoils of war apparently began while John Graham's corpse was still warm. But the booty amounted to more than a couple of pocket-watches and cowboy gear. The Grahams had put together several range operations valued in one instance as high as fifty thousand dollars, considered a fortune in its time.[16] The livestock operations of the three Graham brothers, which centered on Marsh, Spring, and Cherry creeks, assumed coveted water rights and surrounding forage. Buildings and equipment a hundred miles from a lumberyard were especially dear. Graham animals on the open range included "several thousand" beeves, at a conservative ten dollars per head, accounting for thirty thousand dollars in themselves. Each brother had had his own cabin, outbuildings, and corrals.[17] Especially galling for Tom must have been the tidbits from a postwar victory fiesta sponsored by the Tewksbury clan for themselves and their sympathizers. High stakes gambling, barbecue feasting, and competitive drinking was said to have lasted a week.[18] Tom must have suspected he was supplying the gold, beef, and whiskey for the revelers. No doubt he was.

Another open sore was the May 1888 burglary of the Watkins store on Tonto Creek:

A correspondent writing from Tonto, says: There is considerable excitement here and it looks as if a worse war will be started than last year. A week ago two men came and robbed Watkin's store of quite a large lot of merchandise. They were followed by Watkins and sons and pushed so closely they cached the goods and abandoned three horses. Watkins took the horses and saddles which proved to be the property of Tom Graham of Pleasant Valley. Watkins then got an officer and with twenty-seven of the best citizens in the Basin took the trail of the men, and it having rained just before the robbery, followed the trail direct to the Graham ranch. This party finally induced the insiders to surrender but not before the robbers had got away. The posse laid in wait some time and the two robbers thinking the coast clear came in for grub. But by an untimely noise the robbers again managed to escape. Watkins' party claim to know the robbers well, and named Waddell [Watley?] and Dickerson—the former being known as Tom Graham's foreman. The people here are aroused and determined to put a stop to such work.[19]

Exiled in far-off Tempe, Tom fought for his good name. Two weeks later on May 26, 1888, the same columns carried another theory, that of Tom Graham himself:

The following appeared in the Phoenix *Arizonian*: The reporter interviewed Tom Graham relative to the robbery of the store of Captain Watkins at Tonto Basin, recently, the account of which stated that the robbers were traced to Graham's ranch; that the horses and saddles abandoned by the burglars were the property of Graham, and that the guilty persons were known to be Waddell and Dickerson—the former being known as Graham's foreman. Mr. Graham stated to the scribe that, while not thoroughly acquainted with the facts, he believed this to be "a put up job," calculated to have its effect at the next term of the district court for Yavapai county, which convenes next month. He has but one man in his employ—John Watley. The latter wrote to Graham, under the date of April 25, stating that two horses and saddles had been stolen from him, and to look out for the criminals in Phoenix. It is only about twenty-five miles from Watkins' store to Graham's ranch and it is not reasonable, so Graham states, that Watley, if a participant in the robbery, would abandon his horses before returning home, even it it were necessary to throw away the plunder. Another significant fact in connection with his theory of the matter is that the articles taken consisted of provisions and horse shoes. Mr. Graham has kept his ranch well-provided in this line, and in the six weeks previous to the robbery, sent out two different lots of provisions. In response to a letter from Jim Watkins he mentioned these facts, and also stated that he did not uphold crime, and if Watley was guilty he would be glad to see him arrested and punished. Graham's view, however, is that enemies stole the horses and saddles and afterward robbed the store. Then, riding in the direction of the Graham ranch, the animals and stolen goods were purposely abandoned. . . .[20]

Apparently while the story was being set into type, Cap Watkins himself appeared in the Globe newspaper office, perused a galley proof, and insisted on extending the report a couple more columns. The dispute was never resolved.

Watkins stated that he and his men tracked the unhorsed robbers directly to Graham's. But again, a serious dispute dissolved in charges and countercharges, conspiracy plots and double dealings. When the acrimony boiled off, both Watkins and Graham were left with bellies full of bile. Both prideful men, they considered their reputations in their home communities soiled by slander.

Ever stubborn, through the next five years, Graham refused to quit title to his Pleasant Valley holdings. Certainly his ownership interest in the three ranches was endorsed by the tax assessor; to the day of his death he was recognized as rightful taxpayer, if not *de facto* occupant.[21]

However depressing the year 1888 was for Tom Graham, it ended with a turn of fate a more mean-minded man could celebrate.

Jim Tewksbury died.

By some accounts,[22] the deadliest gun of the Pleasant Valley War, tubercular James Tewksbury could be compared to his similarly doomed contemporary, Doc Holliday. Hopelessly diseased, denied the customary male roles by frailty, Holliday was said to commit to battle with the fatalism of a man with nothing to lose.[23] Jim Tewksbury was haunted by the shade of his younger brother, Frank, who had died of tuberculosis. Jim, by himself, may have begun and ended the firefight at the Middleton cabin in 1887.[24] He never married; press notices emphasized not his powers, but rather, the pitiful price he paid in the least of efforts, such as responding to subpoena.

Most of the accused and witnesses numbering thirty to thirty-six were to have met at Haigler's on the 12th inst. [June, 1888] intending to start in a body on that day for Prescott and doubtless made the fruitless journey as no notice of a continuance of the cases had been received in Pleasant Valley up to the 11th, and therefore through the culpable neglect of the district attorney these people were subjected to the hardship of leaving the range in the midst of their roundup and compelled to make an uneccesary journey of 150 miles entailing a loss of at least ten or twelve days in time and to many their wages during the interval. The cost of the trip to each cannot be less than $50 and may greatly exceed that sum and in the case of many of those subpoenaed who are poor men this is a serious exaction and which are unable to meet and therefore are compelled to deny themselves the necessary food and shelter in order to comply with the court's mandate.

Mrs. Rose, widow of the late Al Rose, a victim of the Pleasant Valley fight, is one of the witnesses and she is required to travel 150 miles, 110 by trail, on horseback over a very rough country, leaving her two young children behind in the care of a lady. . . .

James Tewksbury, one of the defendants, is in a precarious condition suffering from quick consumption but although not able to stand the fatigue of such a journey he never the less essayed to go and after a great effort he reached Haigler's ranch twelve miles from his own place and in going that distance he was forced to stop and rest several times. It was thought doubtful if he could proceed further. . . .[25]

In August, the Prescott court continued Jim's case to the following November. For Jim, Prescott was beyond reach. He somehow mustered strength for one last trek—ironically, to Tempe. There, a higher authority intervened.

At 5:30 yesterday afternoon, James Tewksbury, who was at the time visiting Jake Starrar and had suddenly taken sick, succumbed to that dread disease—quick consumption. He contracted the malady in Tonto Basin during the Tonto war. Up to that time, he had been a healthy and vigorous man, but the exposure entailed by lying out without shelter in rain and snow brought on his lung troubles. His sister, Mrs. Henry Slosser, was with him in his last hours, and many sorrowing friends followed his remains to their last resting place this afternoon.[26]

Starrar's house was a mile south of Tempe. The most likely route of the funeral procession to the cemetery would wend westward, passing in front of the Double Butte school. Members of the Tewksbury clan unswervingly counted Jim a war casualty, and as the cortege crossed Priest Road, mourners could glance southward to the columns of smoke rising from brush fires signaling the beginning of a new Tom Graham agricultural empire.

What Tom Graham felt toward his fallen foe? His nature would have tempered his public face. By contrast, Duchet's could not contain the gloating glee with which he greeted every misfortune experienced by his personally populated menagerie of enemies. Duchet recognized but two shades of correctness—dead black and pure white. According to his most loyal biographer, Estella:

Charley Duchet was Irish-French, and he had come when young with his family to Visalia, California As a boy he was obliged to use his step-father's name, Ingram, but when grown he reclaimed his original family name. He had little education. There he fell in love with a stunning Spanish maiden. Her bullfighter boyfriend challenged Charley to a duel, and he accepted. The two men were locked inside a low, windowless adobe hut. While the fickle señorita was yelling, "Kill him, señor, I will pray for you!" Time passed. A knock from inside. Seconds flung the door open. The walls of the room were painted red. The bullfighter sprawled stabbed to death. Charley blinked at the daylight, staggered, and fell back. Everybody thought he was dead, too, but he pulled through, to be crippled for life. The Mexicans called him *El Diablo*. He had to kill two more Mexicans, escaped custody near San Francisco, and killed a sheriff's man. Disfigured and limited to the use of his left arm, Charley turned to highway robbery based in Mendicino County. He knocked off one stage for $80,000, and Wells, Fargo posted a big reward. It was in Mendicino that Charley became acquainted with the Tewksburys, who eventually were run out of there for stealing. They pulled out for Nevada, on the run.

In time, the Tewksburys asked Charley to come to Arizona and herd sheep for them and the Daggs Brothers. He took over a band near Baker Butte on top of the Rim. That's where Tom Graham chanced to visit him one day, and the men immediately became friends.

The Tewksburys tried to hire Charley to kill the Grahams. Old Lady Daggs in Globe was supposed to have made the proposition. She offered to winter and shear his sheep, and give him one thousand dollars per man killed. At the time you could hire killers for seven dollars a day. But Charley's sympathy was with Tom Graham. It actually was as a warning to Charley that a young Indian sheepherder, Daisy, was shot off his horse. But Charley took the alarm to Tom, and the Grahams gathered for a big powwow at the Houdon Ranch in the summer of 1887. Charley was at Tom's side throughout the war. He was utterly fearless.

Also, he could not disguise hard feelings. The moment he saw someone he hated, he wanted to kill, and many a time, he did.[27]

The Graham homestead at Tempe became a safe house for several Pleasant Valley refugees. Joe Ellenwood, presumably with his wife and family, stayed a year recuperating from his Pleasant Valley leg wound. At the Graham farm, Duchet prowled the shadows as Tom's bodyguard; in Tempe and Phoenix, Charley made much of his opportunities to taunt suspected Tewksbury sympathizers. Duchet often cautioned Tom about real or imaginary conspiracies and impending dangers. While the man correctly had foreseen threats in Pleasant Valley, Tom tended to discount his cries of wolf in Tempe. Tewksbury parties generally assumed Duchet guilty of terrorism by post; menacing letters from Tempe and Phoenix were addressed to people that Duchet openly despised. If indeed Charley was involved, he must have had help. He could neither read nor write, more than his signature, X.

Whatever, Duchet and Graham automatically were nominated as prime suspects in the mysterious disappearance of George Newton, Globe jeweler, Pleasant Valley rancher, Ed Tewksbury mentor, and rich woman's husband, in April 1892. Seventy-five miles up the Salt from Tempe, Newton vanished, leaving clues and scenarios to pique a century of speculation. From the April 19, 1892, *Silver Belt:*

Two horses were discovered at Salt River last Friday [the 15th] near the mouth of Coon Creek, one a pack horse with pack, dead, lodged on a riffle in the river and the other saddled and bridled grazing on the bank near by. The horses were identified as belonging to Geo. A. Newton of Globe who left there Monday last for his ranch in Pleasant Valley expecting to reach Pringle's [on Cherry Creek] that night but where he failed to appear. All the circumstances point that Mr. Newton was drowned for at last accounts he had not been seen or heard from.

From the May 19, 1892, *Silver Belt:*

NO TRACE OF NEWTON

George Wilson and companions returned from Salt river Wednesday, without having secured any trace of George A. Newton's body, further than finding his pistol and belt partially covered by sand on a bar in the river about seventy-five yards below the ford. It is believed that by some that Mr. Newton's remains were covered by the shifting sand, and there is talk of examining the bars near the scene of the tragedy.

Newton's role in the war was to undergo historical revision following his death; his wealthy, influential friends oversaw the rewrite.[28] But Newton's unflagging financial support and personal participation were manifest. He left documentary tracks plainer than a cow on the front porch. Newton shared Massachusetts origin with Old Man Tewksbury; Newton owned the Middleton ranch where cowboys Payne and Blevins were slain in 1887. Newton and Jerry Vosburgh expanded their Pleasant Valley holdings as other men lost life and nerve. Newton bankrolled George Wilson, his younger brother-in-law, who remained a lifelong Tewksbury ally. In numerous instances, Newton went hundreds of miles to stand by the Tewksburys in court. Records prove that Ed Tewksbury could draw supplies, ammunition, and cash from Newton in Globe. The parallel preoccupation of Newton and Ed Tewksbury toward fast horses was enough to bond a friendship.[29]

As details of the disappearance drifted home, the people of Globe expressed shock and anger. Newton had departed that place with two animals, a smallish brown saddle horse, and an oversize, overage race horse named Chub. On the trail to Redman's Crossing, Newton met several travelers and residents who cautioned him about the flooding Salt River. In Pleasant Valley, Ed Tewksbury became concerned when Newton failed to keep a date. Ed scouted the river, found one horse alive on a sand bar, and the other horse (legend has it) shot through the eye. Mrs. Newton offered a five hundred dollar reward for the recovery of her husband's body; it was never found. With Tewksbury, H.H. Pratt spent days diving the river's pools.[30] Also in the news at this time were allegations that both Newton and Ed Tewksbury had received threatening letters postmarked Tempe. From whatever source—perhaps a crafty meddler— in the mood of the times, Ed Tewksbury inferred afresh that he and his family faced unacceptable risk.

Even before Newton's April evanescence, Tewksbury and Company sensed that Tom Graham's economic sun was rising again. And that shadows were reaching toward the Tewksburys. By now, of seven thousand acres under irrigation on the Salt River's south bank, Tom was farming three hundred. Tom was listed along with the Tude Brothers, L.L. Harmon, J.W. Wolff, H. Jepheson, and Neils Petersen as most prominent southside growers. Tom's place was brilliantly selected, practically next door to the sixty-five hundred dollar mansion rising on Petersen's farm. Tom profited from the backing of his older brother, Allen, one of the wealthier real estate tycoons of New Tacoma, Washington. Through the spring of 1892, Tonto Basin ranges were lush, cattle fat, and Tom made no bones about his continuing interests in Pleasant Valley. Silas W. Young, a Tempe cobbler with two young daughters, had moved to Pleasant Valley as an operating partner especially to look after Tom's cattle. In fact, Pleasant Valley was rejected as the name of the community's first post office (an office of that identity already operated near Flagstaff); the name Young was approved, and Miss Ola Young was appointed postmaster, a position she filled for fifty years.[31]

Now Tom Graham's letters to his Iowa sister Maggie evolved into newfound optimism:

. . .this is a new Cuntry but at the present time it is offle dull I havent made $5.00

in 5 years still hoping it Will be better I am going prospecting in a fiew Weeks and see if I Cant strike a mine Will leave Annie With hur folks silver is up and so is Copper and now is the time to Russle

... thare is no friends of the grahams Can say But What Tom Graham stayed With his friends dont ever go back on a friend if it Costs your life Wone good friend let it be a stranger is better than all on earth I had friends that died for me and I Could not go back on the living so that is What got me in debt so bad but by next summer meby I will be on my feet a gain. . . .

A year later to the day Tom again wrote Maggie:

. . .if you Can get a Way from home Would Like to have you Come out here and stay all Winter Cant you Bring dannil a long and you Wouldent hafto go Back then Mag I am a purty good Russler if I have a Chance I havent Writen very much for a long time as I have ben so busy I have a nice little girl and she sings about hur aunt mag annie is canning fruit and I am geting Redy to putt in a Crop have just got through hauling Grain I had 2,000 sks of Barley. . . .[32]

"For five years Tom Graham had lived the peaceful life of a small farmer and rancher. . .near Tempe. He had made many new friends and his enemies had not molested him. To all appearances the vendetta was finished. In reality, however, the feuding families were as bitter and vengeful as ever."[33]

Spring, 1892. Tom Graham approached Lon Harmon, a prominent Salt River cattle feeder. Would Harmon purchase Graham's Pleasant Valley beeves? Harmon assented, but only if the herd was delivered to Tempe. Graham struck the deal, and in so doing, bragged more than Harmon considered prudent. The Tewksburys were afraid of him, Tom told Harmon. Harmon, who later served as mayor of Phoenix and forewent a good chance at the governorship, thought at the time that Tom Graham, reverting to his old cockiness, was begging trouble. For his part, Charley Duchet never needed much encouragement to walk proud.[34] In June, Tom and Charley saddled up for Pleasant Valley. Charley later told how it went: "The boys from around there rode out to meet us, and stopped about two hundred yards away and appeared to be holding a consultation. Finally Wm. Concord [Colcord] rode out from the crowd and came up to us and said, 'Well, boys, is it war or peace?' Tommy said, 'It is peace. We do not care for war. All that we want is our rights, any man will stand for his rights, and I have too much invested here to be bluffed. I think this matter has gone far enough, and should prefer peace if it is possible.' Concord [Colcord] shook hands with Tommy and I and the rest of the gang rode past us and all seemed to be cordial. . . ."[35]

And then, Graham Shot! The June 21, 1892, *Gazette*:

It was rumored in Phoenix yesterday that trouble had commenced in Pleasant Valley and that Tom Graham, who is up there gathering his cattle, preparatory to moving them out, had been shot, but nothing could be found out about it, and it may be only a rumor.

Two days later in its weekly edition, the *Gazette* followed with a story titled, "Graham Is All Right." Robert Morgan told the paper that Tom and Duchet would arrive safe soon.

Pausing but a day to pasture the stock and reassure Annie, Graham and Duchet made themselves available on June 25 to the press in Phoenix.

. . . When asked by a *Gazette* reporter if he had been killed, Mr. Graham said he didn't know for sure, but he thought not, though he had heard it reported that he had. He pinched himself and said he felt alive, at any rate he supposed the report must have been false.

He said that when he arrived in Tonto in company with Mr. Duchet, the rodeo (roundup) was in progress, and when they arrived on the ground all the people were there who supposed to have been on the opposite side, and the two leaders immediately absented themselves, while the others of the party met the visitors with a friendly handshake and treated the two in a very hospitable manner during their stay. Graham said he had business there and was not looking for any trouble and he doesn't think the others wanted any.

In his last month of life, could Tom have taken precautions to save himself? Likely not—his determined assassin possessed every advantage—but foreboding beclouded his days. Well into July, newspapers around the nation continued to reprint as fact Graham's premature Associated Press obituary. The *Gazette* grumped, "Outside papers are still re-publishing the item of the confirmation of the killing of Tom Graham in Tonto Basin. Everybody who reads the *Gazette* knows that Graham was not killed, and that reporter knew it at the time he sent that mis-leading dispatch to the *San Francisco Chronicle*." And a few weeks later, "The Phoenix reporter for the Associated Press is doing Arizona more damage than all the floods, drouths and Apache raids that could come, with his stretching of the truth in his messages."[36]

Another thrill engaged Salt River residents when Hiram Yost, a Graham hand in Pleasant Valley, was rumored killed. The erroneous bulletin took weeks to set right, when he appeared in the flesh before a newsman. From the eight hundred Pleasant Valley cattle still wearing Graham's brand, Yost brought in one hundred fifty steers and a band of horses. He said Tom and Charlet Duchet were tipped off regarding an ambush awaiting them on the trail back to Tempe, and they extricated themselves from Pleasant Valley only by employing "extraordinary precautions."[37]

The *Los Angeles Times* reinterested itself not only in the Tonto Basin feud, but the quality of wire reportage.

The Associated Press correspondent at Phoenix has been receiving a "turning over" at the hands of the papers there, for reckless and untruthful statements sent out and of course printed broadcast. A press correspondent with sense can be the means of doing his locality good, but in the hands of an ass, a press commission proves a boomerang. . . .[38]

Sensing trouble, through July newsmen made Tom's simple daily trips around the Salt River Valley into one-line blurbs and chatty paragraphs.

Perhaps coincidentally, perhaps oddly, figures prominent in the Pleasant Valley War shared news space in Phoenix and environs during these midsummer weeks. John Gilliland. James Stinson. W.A. Daggs. There was even printed a filler line speculation that Wyatt Earp might visit Phoenix.

No fresh recruit, but a veteran fighter, Tom Graham must have felt the darkness closing in on his flanks, and a rush of swift wings at his back, wherever he traveled around Phoenix and Tempe. Yet he brushed aside Duchet's advice to go armed. Most ominously, the *Herald* of July 1 tried to untrack an anticipated tragedy:

There is no attack can be made on a man so cowardly as a sneaking, secret attack, and no man can make such an attack unless he be that sometimes combination of a coward and a villain. The one thing about such beings, they are not men, is that they in fancied security overreach themselves and the object of their malicious attempts simply observes their futile attemps to injure him in some way in quiet amusement. Men with the manhood of men make open attacks or none at all. The dastard sneaks.

IV. Murdered

With one word atop a front page single column, *The Arizona Republican* took possession of the most sensational crime story of its two years of publication. Locked in a desperate struggle for survival as one of three daily newspapers in a Phoenix of four thousand residents, The *Republican* persisted with little cash money, a meager budget of wire service news, fickle advertisers, and a small but enterprising staff of professional writers. Directed by Editor T.H. Wolfley, *Republican* reporters from the outset recognized the greater impact of the daylight slaughter of Tom Graham. The *Republican* kept the story on page one for eleven days, and lavished the first illustrations it ever commissioned for a local news event.[1]

Under the subhead, "A Culmination of the Bloodiest and Most Savage Feud That Ever Cursed the Territory," the *Republican* of Wednesday morning, August 3, 1892, informed its three hundred subscribers:

Tom Graham died yesterday afternoon by a coward's bullet, and as to the principals the bloody Graham-Tewksbury feud it at last ended, though many more are likely to fall in the quarrels which will grow out of it.

The murdered man was the last of the Grahams, and his slayer, Ed Tewksbury, was the last of the Tewksburys. The murder was committed about 7 o'clock yesterday morning two and one-half miles southwest of Tempe and about midway between the ranches of Bud Cummings and Dr. Gregg. Mrs. Gregg was milking not far from the roadside. She heard the report of a gun and looking up saw a man reeling backward on a load of grain and another near him in the act of putting a gun into a holster. The man with the gun mounted a horse and rode rapidly away. Hurrying to the wagon it was found that the murdered man was Tom Graham. He was carried into Cumming's house and a daughter of Mrs. Gregg rode to Phoenix [more likely, Tempe] and notified the officials that a murder had been committed.

Word was at once sent to Phoenix and Sheriff Montgomery, accompanied by Hy McDonald, District Attorney Crenshaw and Jack Hickey, left at once for Cumming's ranch. In the mean time Dr. Hart of Tempe, had been summoned. When he arrived Graham was still alive and had recovered consciousness, which had at first deserted him, but his case was pronounced hopeless. Dr. Helm was sent for and arrived at the ranch about noon. He at once saw from the fact that the entire body was paralyzed that the ball had cut the spinal cord.

For some time it was not known who the assassin was but when it was learned that Ed Tewksbury had staid at the Arlington hotel, at Tempe, the night before, there was no longer any doubt.

This was confirmed by Graham whose dying statement was taken. He said that when he reached the point where the shooting occurred he was attracted by a noise at the roadside and slightly behind him. He had just time to see two men with guns leveled on him and the next instant both fired. One of these men was Ed Tewksbury and the other John Rhodes, who had married John Tewksbury's widow. The wounded man said he was perfectly helpless and his only thought was a fear that his horses would run away and hurt him.

This statement was made in due form before Justice Forsee and on the strength of it Rhodes, who came into Tempe unconcernedly, was put under arrest. After an attempt to give straw bond, which was prevented by indignant citizens, his case was taken before Justice Roberts who bound him over.

In the meantime Tewksbury, who was splendidly mounted, rode past Tempe toward Mesa. A telephone message was sent there and reached the town five minutes after Tewksbury had past through it. A posse made up of about thirty of the most determined men about Tempe, headed by Charley McFarland, were on the trail of the desperado, who had headed for his stronghold in Pleasant Valley. He was taking a straight course for the Superstition mountains. After having ridden several hours they discovered that Tewksbury's thoroughbred was constantly widening the distance and that the chase was hopeless. At last McFarland's horse fell and the pursuit was abandoned. The pursuers also believed that as Tewksbury was nearing his own country that he was provided with relays of horses.

Graham had been put under the influence of opiates and died about 4 o'clock afternoon. An autopsy was held which fully confirmed Dr. Helm's opinion of the character of the wound. The ball of a 44 caliber had entered to the left of the cervical vertebra, had passed inward and forward and came out just at the right of the larynx, passing through the spinal cord.

As soon as Graham was dead arrangements were at once made for the funeral. The body will be brought to Phoenix at 9:10 this morning and will be conveyed directly to the cemetery.

The murdered man was 38 years of age and a native of Ohio. He leaves a wife and one child in fair circumstances. He was a member of the A.O.U.W [Ancient Order of United Workmen], in which he had his life insured for $2,000. Graham was highly respected in his community and has left a host of friends. He was regarded as the most peaceable member of the Graham family and even when the feud was bitterest it was softened greatly by his influence. He was unarmed at the time of the shooting and it was a well known fact that, notwithstanding his life as continually threatened, he never carried a gun except when he went into the neighborhood of Tonto Basin. He believed that the feud was at an end. Night before last his bosom friend, Charley Duchet, one of the leading members of the Graham faction, saw Tewksbury riding in the bushes near Graham's house. He warned Graham but the latter replied that the hatchet was buried and that there was nothing to fear unless he visited the Basin.

Duchet, who has assisted in the killing of several of the Tewksbury crowd, threatens vengeance and swears that he will yet overtake Graham's murderer.

Rhodes was brought into the city last night by Sheriff Montgomery and Tom Elder. A couple of guards rode before. The feeling was so intense at Tempe that it was feared that a lynching would be attempted. No demonstration however was made and when the party reached the jail Rhodes jumped jauntily out of the carriage and ran up the steps into the corridor. He laughed and joked with acquaintances after he was locked up. He made some inquiries about attorneys whom he wished to see this morning. He refused to say anything about the affair which concerns him most deeply.

So ends one of the deadliest feuds that has ever cursed Arizona, and perhaps the most extensive one that ever existed in the country. It is said that forty-eight persons have been killed and that Graham is the twenty-seventh victim on his side. [There followed a dozen sentences of feud history.]

. . . officials do not believe that Ed Tewksbury will ever be captured. The fastnesses of Pleasant valley alone would furnish an asylum to an outlaw and unaided by numerous and desperate friends. The region is exceedingly difficult of access, so that officers of the law could hardly enter without making their presence known. John See, the wife murderer, is believed there at this time.

No murder ever committed in Arizona has ever aroused so much excitement as this one. The bloody record of five years in which the murdered man and his slayer were important actors is apparently closed, the fierce determination of Tewksbury which impelled him to ride more than 100 miles to kill his last family enemy; the cowardly manner in which his determination was carried out and his splendid escape invest the bloody affair with a peculiar interest.

With the perspective of nearly a century, the report was commendably accurate and prescient. It also sizzled with gross, libelous, inflamatory assumption, but no more so than accounts in competitive papers. The rival *Herald*, under greater deadline pressure the evening before, had Mrs. Gregg from her milk stool positively identifying Tewksbury as an assailant, although she never would so swear later under oath.[2]

Nor, for that matter, would Charley Duchet testify in court that he had indeed seen Ed Tewksbury skulking about Tom's ranch on assassination eve. Whether these attributions were invented or distorted by the press, or on reflection disavowed by Duchet and Mrs. Gregg, may never be resolved. The *Herald* noted "people have been looking for a report of this kind, though, for some time, so it is not much of a surprise." While the *Herald* staunchly defended the sheriff and possemen, their failure to apprehend the east-fleeing suspect, the opposition *Gazette* flatly pronounced, "Ed Tewksbury and John Rhodes were the assassins." And, "A telephone message had acquainted the Mesa officials with the circumstances and they were gathering on Main Street, organizing for pursuit when Tewksbury rode by. Justice Newell, with a double barrelled shot gun, was only a few feet from the fugitive, but allowed him to pursue his way unchallenged. . . ." Then further, "One of the weakest efforts to capture a criminal ever made by a Maricopa county sheriff, was that of the Republican sheriff yesterday in the Graham-Tewksbury affair. Mr. Montgomery is as good man to run a farm but he is not a success as a sheriff."[3] The *Herald* countered:

MONTGOMERY VINDICATED

The alleged inaction of Sheriff Montgomery in the Tewsberry affair, as given by a morning paper, is radically wrong and is entirely without cause.

Those who were on the ground say that the Sheriff and his deputies did all that could be done when they got there.

In this connection, Charles Roberts, the Justice of the Peace at Tempe, writes to the *Herald* this morning. His letter will explain the situation. . . .

Editor *Herald*—When anyone censured John Montgomery for not capturing Ed Tewksberry an injustice is being done him and his deputies. As soon as I heard of the affair, I had more warrants than enough and in place of running out to the man that was wounded I tried to catch the perpetrators. Ed Tewksberry has blooded horses and lots of them in this vicinity and his horse will go 100 miles where our alfalfa fed horses will not go 25. As far as Tewksberry is concerned he will be here for trial.[4]

In the same edition, the *Herald* again lectured the Associated Press: "Sensational newspaper work is largely responsible for the murder of Tom Graham. The sensational stuff sent out some weeks since by totally irresponsible newspaper hyenas who are without a cent's worth of interest in the community. . . ."

Tom Graham died hard. His town, Tempe, suffered with him. August days on Arizona's desert dawn hot and humid, and radiation rapidly intensifies. Like a sledge of light, the pulsing sun forges sodden Mexican zephyrs into lightning bolts and sand storms. Before evaporative cooling and air conditioning, people slept outside, worked early and late, and retreated to midday shade. For his own desperate final labor, Tom was lifted off his wagon and placed under the cover of the Cummings porch. Among those profoundly affected for a lifetime were the several Cummings children.[5]

The slowly dying Tom provided ample opportunity for adult involvement, too. Literally dozens of official, professional, and idly curious Salt River Valley personages found time to drop by to serve or observe. Rumors thick and prolific as hatchling flies buzzed around the Cummings veranda where Tom was stretched out, half sitting. Except for sympathy and drugs, the man was beyond medical help, giving gossip full attention. Someone recalled a now pertinent incident: a Mexican farm hand had quit the Grahams without cause a few days ago; then, what of the mysterious footprints discovered one recent morn outside a Graham window?[6]

The Daggses were now Tempe businessmen-bankers-sportsmen, and was it not true their fastest trotting horse was named "Jim T."?[7] Now the tales of Graham sympathizers receiving farewell letters embellished with skull-and-crossbones acquired believers.[8] Hiram Yost, a Graham cowboy, was still missing, was he not?[9] Maybe Tempe's Charlie Dobie wasn't killed as suspected by the Apache Kid, after all.[10] Another distinguished Tempe citizen, once a Graham sponsor, now estranged, was Jim Stinson.[11] Charley Duchet had been pestering Tom in recent weeks to go everywhere armed.[12] And what to make of the one-line notices that "Jno. Gilliland" from east Verde and "J.B. Ellyson" from his ranch and "W.T. Bonner" from El Paso were Valley visitors?[13]

In a hoarse whisper, Tom Graham during his last hours engaged in a remarkable amount of communication. He was paralyzed, yet he repeatedly shared with his physicians, relatives, and neighbors his impressions of the ambush. Tom also filled in the press. He first noticed Ed Tewksbury and John Rhodes just a few wagon lengths behind him. Rhodes was in the lead, leveling a rifle. Graham said two shots were fired. One missed.[14]

The circumstances of the killing are clearer than usual in the case and there appears to be no dispute as to the facts.

Tom Graham for several years has been living quietly in a quarter of a section of land south of the river, about six miles southeasterly of Phoenix. He has prospered and had this season good crops. Yesterday morning, he loaded some barley upon his wagon and started it for Tempe. He had arrived at a point opposite the school house of the Double Buttes district, when, hearing a noise of horses' feet behind him, he turned to see his mortal foes, Ed Tewksbury and John Rhodes in the act of leveling their rifles upon him. Graham, who was unarmed, at once started to jump from the grain sacks, upon which he was seated, but was too late. Two shots rang out in almost perfect unison and he fell from his wagon onto the road with a mortal wound in his body. The murderers cooly rode up. Rhodes handed his Winchester rifle to Tewksbury, who, thrusting one of the weapons into a saddle scabbard, rode over to the prostrate man, and once more leveled his gun with the evident intention of finishing him. He apparently was satisfied, however, that the wound already inflicted was a mortal one. . . .[15]

Charley Duchet, forty-six years of age—like a crippled lion, doubly dangerous—nervously paced the Cummings porch. Duchet had botched his business: professional bodyguard. This morning, he was busy with chores at a far corner of the Graham farm and did not hear of the shooting until forty-five minutes after it happened. He cursed himself for not accompanying Tom to the mill. Now the puffing, weeping, darkling wound in Tom's neck cancelled five years of Duchet's perfect wardship. Emotions of pity and revenge were but ashes and alum to Duchet the defender.[16]

Others were attempting to track the killers, Duchet knew, but perhaps as busywork, Charley picked up the cold trail. He went to the Double Buttes school, scrutinized the maze of wagon tire tracks and animal and human footprints. He saw where the killers smoked "tailormade" [machine-rolled] cigarets. He determined where Graham's four-horse team was plodding at the moment of the shooting.

Here was the wagon where Graham was killed, and the tracks come right up to the wagon, and one of the tracks went around the wagon on this other side. One of the horses had a round foot and the other had a long foot. This is where the horse with the round foot and the horse with the long foot come up here, back of the wagon and turned square around and you could see the other had come around on the right hand side of the wagon, and went up south of the wagon and went down this road east.

...The round track turned right here and came back and crossed this bridge right here and went right along the edge of the road after it crossed the bridge, and came to the school house here, but the brush was too thick, and it turned square around here and it started up this road. Came back here, and then made another turn again and went back and tried to cross through and couldn't and then comes back into this road....He passed right here. Here he tried to go through the brush and couldn't do it, and comes back a piece and tries and couldn't, and came back into the road again, and went the road for probably three hundred yards going north, and then he turned again, right back here, and he run kind of zigzag through there because there was a place he had to, he couldn't get through. ...

Duchet elected to follow the horse with the long foot. The footprints drew him eastward across the railroad tracks. And there the tracks of the horse commingled with those of a large herd of cattle. Later, incredulous lawyers questioned Duchet regarding his ability to stay with one set of tracks. In great detail, Duchet explained that he could stay on one track through a herd of fifty.

And on cross-examination, Charley Duchet provided an insight into skills that, for most in America's succeeding motorized generations, would be lost:

Q. I will put the proposition . . ... I ride a horse along this road this morning at eight or nine o'clock, and I take that horse to you and I show you that identical horse at two o'clock during the same day. Can you go in that road and pick out that horse's track?

A. Yes, sir; I can go with you and see that horse's track and pick it out of fifty head of horses shod with the same shoe: I can track it through the band. . . . Every horse don't set his foot down the same. There is something about it that I can follow that track clear out. And every man don't set his foot down alike. [17]

Some small segments of time passed before Annie Graham was notified; she had a child to gather up, then she had a couple of miles to travel. She arrived, grief-stricken, at Cummings'. Annie was twenty-four; trending stout; twice a mother; emotionally battered. She consulted with doctors in attendance, who told her there was no hope. She went to Tom.

She: Tom, the numbness will pass after the shock is over with. You can get well.
He: No. I can't get well. I can't live.
She: Who shot you?
He: John Rhodes and Ed Tewksbury shot me. I looked over my shoulder and saw them coming about twenty-five feet behind. John Rhodes was in the lead, and they both leveled their guns and fired.[18]

Both Annie and four-year-old Estella spent the day in and around the Cummings house. To the scarred, senior knife-fighter Duchet, Estella may have symbolized the cruelist twist of life's blade. To him, she was his "Old Gal," who would not enjoy her supper without him seated at the table beside her, who taught her to ride, who filled a grandfatherly role. Tom Graham asked Duchet to hold up Estella to his waxen face.

"I grow cold, Stella. I am a goner. Kiss me goodbye."[19]

Several times more through the day, Graham implored his daughter to kiss him farewell. Seven decades later she would remember it as if yesterday. Before noon, Graham was so rational that he asked that a tracker of high reputation, John J. Hickey, be summoned from Phoenix. Hickey, a thirty-year-old livestockman, arrived about eleven o'clock and mustered a band of similarly expert citizens. They scrutinized the shooting scene. Of the horse tracks left by the murderers, Hickey (as did Duchet) differentiated one mount with round hooves, the other more oblong. He judged the tracks were made earlier that day. P.H. Coyle, at forty-two a pioneer Phoenix freighter, joined Hickey in cataloguing peculiarities: type and conditions of horse shoes; size as measured with sticks; clues to behavior (one horse seemed to shy where a gun was fired). The men spent hours at the task.[20]

Certainly unusual if not unique, the district attorney's office engaged a photographer to obtain at least two photographs amounting to a panorama of the murder scene. The living Tom Graham filed a complaint of murder against John Rhodes and Ed Tewksbury. Lon Forsee, a thirty-five-year-old merchant and magistrate of Tempe, committed Tom's statement to paper. "The first thing when I got there, I asked him who shot him. I says, 'Tom, who shot you?' He says, 'John Rhodes and Ed Tewksbury.' "[21]

Despite his perilous passages in Arizona, Graham apparently had no will. As he lingered at the Cummings house, he dictated a simple last testament, leaving his all to his widow-to-be. Opportunity was such that when John Rhodes was arrested in midmorning without incident by Constable Manuel Gallardo in Tempe, the development was reported back to Tom Graham.[22] Small comfort, the victim knew at least one of his assailants was in custody and likely to hang. Meantime, to news reporters, Rhodes professed ignorance of the attack on Graham. One of the Phoenix papers blithely promoted Rhodes to chairmanship of the Committee of Fifty:

This very young man, John Rhodes, was the leader of the lynching party who hanged three members of the Graham party, Stott, Scott, and Wilson upon the Rim. He did not serve in the ranks all through the war, but was active near its close, cementing his alliance by marrying the widow of John Tewksbury.

At or around 4 p.m., Tom died.

Time also had allowed for the man's funeral services and interrment to be arranged before his death. The *Herald* of August 3 printed a dignified notice:

LAID TO REST

The body of Tom Graham was brought to this city today for burial, accompanied by his sorrowing wife and little daughter, Stella, Mr. and Mrs. Melton, father and mother of Mrs. Graham, Mr. Del Shay [Duchet], his partner, Mrs. Arthur and Rev. Hitchcock.

The body was met at the depot by the A.O.U.W. lodge of this city, of which the deceased was a member in good standing, and taken charge of by that body.

A short service was held at Tempe and also at the grave. The Phoenix friends of the dead man turned out to pay their last tribute to him.

Not important perhaps, but for Tom Graham, not even burial would be complete without a quirk of controversy:

There was a mistake in the grave in which the remains of Tom Graham were interred, and the body was moved to the family plot later in the day.[23]

V. Rhodes, "Not the Killer Type"

With one bird presumed lost in the bush, the irate establishment deemed John Rhodes securely in hand twice as dear. Public inquisition, outrage, and retribution in multiple measure focused upon him. "John Rhodes is still the object of curiosity," purred an editorial writer, "and the sheriff's office could derive quite a goodly revenue by charging a small admission fee."[1]

Even before the Graham assassination, Rhodes's comings and goings were chronicled in discrete detail. Furtively or openly, people eking out colorless existences along the Salt River embroidered their days with warp of insinuation and woof of rumor. To rival the mythical Grecian vale for which it was named, Tempe had a ways to go. The village itself huddled under Tempe Butte between the Maricopa and Phoenix depot on the west and Goldman's store under a hillock much later to be named Piker's Peak.[2] Only a half dozen structures, including the Normal School's four-room, single-story instruction building, rose south of Eighth Street. Hayden's mill and adobe hacienda anchored the north end of Mill Avenue not far from the only bridge, the triple trusses of the railroad. Between the Normal School and Hayden's thrived such enterprises as Hilge's bakery and the Coon Burtis & Coon tin-shop. Presently the town limits gave way to green and brown squares of millet, clover, melons, raisin grapes, cotton, tobacco, fruit orchards including plums, and nut trees, notably pecans.[3] Prosperity prevailed at the whim of the schizophrenic Salt River, which one day might withdraw to tepid, brackish puddles out of reach of the irrigation network, and the next, slosh silty snowmelt across the sills of Tempe shelters. No dams of note yet tamed the wild river, which willfully savaged bridges, levees, edifices. In the year just past, the Salt River ran eight miles wide at Phoenix. Before the days of guaranteed federal loans, Phoenix raised nine thousand dollars for flood relief, largely from saloons and brothels.[4]

Provided similarly thin social material, many an Arizona community struck deals with Bacchus. But under the influence of New England schoolteacher Charles T. Hayden, Tempe cast its lot with propriety, culture, conservative commerce, and the Lord. Thus Rhodes, in 1892, provided Tempe with an extraordinary subject: Texas-born, California-reared, unrivaled cowboy roper who sometimes snared calves at the very end of his hundred-foot lariat, ruthless guerrilla fighter, John Tewksbury's widow's son's stepfather, jolly story-teller, convivial drinker, and charter member of the vigilante Committee of Fifty. John Rhodes was gent worth watching anywhere. For Tempe, he amounted to an entire carnival.

Rhodes was not exactly new to Tempe. For years he had worked for Robert Bowen, who parlayed cattle interests in Pleasant Valley into feedlots supplying meat to much of the Salt River Valley. Bowen also was proprietor of a Mill Avenue hotel and bar where Rhodes slept, ate, and drank. In fact, Rhodes had been a regular resident of the Bowen's hotel for most of the summer of 1892.

Understandably, Rhodes's family and friends early overdrew him as a peaceable, deliberate sort. Historian Will C. Barnes, in a 1931 essay, detoured far from the narrow road of reporter to embellish the image: "Rhodes was not the killer type of man, but a good-natured, genial sort of a fellow who was never looking for trouble, but always doing his best to keep out of it."[5] To the contrary, Rhodes deservedly bore a mirror reputation: in his cups, he was known as a mercurial, dreadful force. Rhodes had hanged Stott in 1888. Four years before Tom Graham was bushwhacked, Rhodes well might have been credited with another killing:

SALT RIVER SHOOTING SCRAPE

Dave Freeman arrived in haste from Salt River on Saturday evening last, to announce a serious shooting affray which occurred that afternoon at the saloon of William Beard, in which the participants, Bob Pringle, Cap. Adams and John Rhodes were wounded. Adams was the most seriously hurt of the three, being shot through the right lung, the ball coming out at the back, below the shoulder blade, and the same shot is supposed to have been the one that struck Pringle just below the left corner of the mouth, making an ugly but not dangerous wound.

Dr. Stark went to the river to attend Adams, and after dressing the wound returned on Sunday. He pronounced Adams' injury dangerous, but not necessarily fatal. Reports received from the river during the past few days were that Adams is doing as well as can be expected and is likely to recover.

Rhodes, who fired the shot that did such execution, is said to be wounded in the hand from a shot fired by Adams. The two shots must have been fired simultaneously, as persons present and in the vicinity were under the impression that only one shot had been fired. Ed. Tewksbury is said to have been present and witnessed the affair, and Frank Montgomery, who was tending bar at the time, was near at the time but, we are informed, claims that he did not witness the row. In fact, no clear statement of the cause of the difficulty can be obtained. Rhodes gave his pistol up to Tewksbury and announced his willingness to go with him to Globe and give himself up. Upon reaching Wheatfields, however, he apparently changed his mind; reaching over he took his pistol from Tewksbury's belt and shortly afterwards disappeared. Deputy Sheriff Frank Hampton went as far as the scene of the shooting, in quest of Rhodes, but failed to find him.[6]

Beyond which, deponents said not much; if filed, charges were apparently dropped. Yet the facts of this fracas argued against a boyish, benign, behaved Rhodes. That said, whether by luck, collusion, or magic, Rhodes earned a historical asterisk by relieving Ed Tewksbury of a firearm. No buffoon, John Rhodes.

On the morning Graham was mortally shot, Rhodes was spirited off to jail in Phoenix under arrest, to the dismay of Charles Duchet. Soon after Rhodes was detained, Duchet tried to kill him with a pistol. Charley actually set out for Phoenix with a rifle, but was "persuaded to desist."[7]

Meantime, in his Phoenix cell, Rhodes was exhibited like a zoo creature. To most of the populace, his guilt was manifest. The victim had named him. Rhodes's horse's tracks were perceived at the shooting scene. When arrested, he shook with uncontrollable nervousness. By marriage, he was related to the Tewksburys. Rhodes's vaunted good nature cracked under the strain. He snapped at a reporter, "Young man, I haven't got a God damn thing to say regarding this affair!"[8]

Indicative of overheated public opinion, on August 4 officers "watched their chance" during the midmorning to hustle Rhodes to the courtroom of Justice W.O. Huson. With defense and prosecution attorneys present, the magistrate set a preliminary hearing for the following Monday. Before a vengeful Phoenix could learn of it, Rhodes was whisked back to jail. Nor was Rhodes's the only life in jeopardy:

WILL "STAY WITH IT"

A Tempe man requested to leave.

It seems there are several Tempe citizens who have been "spotted" by the Tewksbury crowd. From present indications there may be more trouble. Yesterday a citizen of Tempe received a card politely informing him that "his room was more desireable than his company," and that if he knew when he was well off he would disappear for a while.

In conversation with a *Herald* reporter, the gentleman who received the warning, said: "I think the matter is only a bluff, but in any case, I shall stay with it." He is going to stay in Tempe and look out for "breakers," and if any one makes a bad break the crimson tide will be very apt to flow.[9]

Charley Duchet? Perhaps. He was but one of sixty witnesses, reinforced by a large delegation from Tempe. As Rhodes's examination began, Duchet and the prisoner exchanged hard looks. Annie Graham, dressed in black and pale from grieving, brought four-year-old Estella to court, accompanied by her parents. Annie was allowed a seat inside the railing. Promptly at 10 a.m. Justice Huson called court to order, with the defense engineered by A.C. Baker and Joseph Campbell, two of Arizona's more expensive trial lawyers. Their service engendered open gossip—where did Rhodes, a working man, find that kind of money? And assumption pointed toward those pioneer sheepmen, the Daggs brothers, now, by coincidence, operating a Tempe bank. District Attorney Frank Cox cut short his West Coast vacation to represent the Territory, assisted by his assistant, J.W. Crenshaw and special counsel, Webster Street. As usual, the perception of the individuals involved depended upon which newspaper one read. One reporter inferred, "As Chas. Duchet, one of the witnesses for the prosecution, passed the prisoner's stand the prisoner cast a look of suspicion and fear upon him and paled visibly. Mrs. Graham came forward and took her seat *inside* the railing. She was dressed entirely in black and shows by her pale face how greatly she feels her bereavement. She was accompanied by her daughter, Estella, four years old."[10] Yet another newsman described Rhodes: ". . .a tall, swarthy man, apparently with a trace of Cherokee blood in his veins. The sharpness of his features is accentuated by a prominent Roman nose. His hair is black, somewhat tinged with gray, and a heavy mustache overhangs a rather hard mouth. He was very nervous, and watched the motions of several of the prosecuting witnesses in a way that indicated a fear of swift vengeance."[11]

Scarcely any of the opening testimony bore directly on Rhodes. First prosecution witness: Mollie Cummings. An hour before Graham was shot, a stranger rode past her father's farm. She said this man bore a resemblance to the man she saw at the scene of the crime.[12] Grace Griffith, now wan and jumpy, brought to the witness stand a note to attorneys from her doctor: "Very nervous owing to a long spell of fever. Try to excite her as little as possible." She corroborated Mollie's testimony. In the afternoon session, Cummings hired man M.A. Cravath told how he sprinted from his field work to assist the wounded man. Conscious at the time, Graham voiced the names of two men who had attacked him; on objections of the defense, Cravath was not permitted by Judge Huson to repeat the names in court.[13]

Bettie Gregg related her impressions of the suspect she saw. He was not Rhodes, but was dark with a dark mustache, something black around his neck, light felt hat with a scarlet ribbon, rifle right side of saddle. At the behest of Mrs. Cummings, Bettie hurried to Tempe to fetch a doctor and Justice Lon Forsee. Together, near the scene of the crime, Bettie and the judge recovered two hats—a stiff black one that seemed to have been folded tightly, and a light gray one flecked with blood.[14]

In all, the opening amounted to a boring day in the furnace-hot courtroom. But outside, sensational rumors circulated: A gang of mountaineers might rescue Rhodes; a lynching committee was forming. Ed Tewksbury was returning; somebody saw him on a Phoenix street; somebody else placed him in Globe; another said Casa Grande. The Maricopa County board of supervisors announced a "Proclamation of Reward. Notice is hereby given that a reward of $500 will be paid. . .for the arrest and conviction of the party or parties now at large, who killed Thomas H. Graham. . . . Frank J. Peck, Clerk."[15]

At last, an enterprising reporter milked Rhodes for a quote: "I think Tewksbury is a fool to come down here now. If he comes at all he ought to wait until the Grand Jury meets again. If he comes now he will have a hot time in this hole."[16]

Assuming that opening proceedings were prophetic of a continuing procession of bland witnesses and quarrelsome lawyers, some observers shunned the second day. They thereby missed "one of the most sensational and exciting scenes ever witnessed in an American court of justice."[17] For once, an Arizona territorial newspapaper may have resorted to understatement. For, in an action beyond belief in a work of fiction, Annie Graham assumed the role of avenger. She had tended to Tom through his death throes, had boosted up their beloved Estella for a final kiss, had heard her husband repeatedly name John Rhodes as an assailant, had protested the gagging of the witness, Cravath, and had heard in the street that his (Rhodes's) cronies would provide him an iron-clad alibi. She concluded that unless she took the law into her hands, Tom's murderer would go free.

Annie hid her intentions well from the public, but not entirely from her friends and family. Animated, even smiling at acquaintances, this distraught woman, only twenty-five years of age, asserted without challenge her right to be seated at the front of the courtroom within a few feet of Rhodes. Early on the second day, at her farm home in Tempe, she had made certain that Tom's six-shooter was loaded. How thoroughly she managed the loading has been debated ever since. Frontier child, six years lover and wife of a feud leader, with spunk to horsewhip a man in a paternity spat,[18] Annie likely possessed the knowledge and verve to handle a pistol. This one was a single-action army model Colt, commonly nicknamed Peacemaker, predominantly chambered in .45 caliber.[19] If

Annie inherited Tom's handgun as he left it, possibly the chamber beneath the hammer held no cartridge, but rather a rolled-up banknote. If, in her homicidal resolve, Annie herself loaded Tom's pistol, it is likely that she knew how.

Child of impulse, Annie gave signs of her scheme. She had blurted her intentions to her father, and he later stated he thought he had talked her out of it. Neither Annie's mother nor daughter accompanied her to court the second day; Mrs. Melton remained, loudly sobbing, in her hotel room. At any rate, following a morning recess requested by the prosecution to brief newly arrived District Attorney Cox and Judge Barrett, Annie smuggled Tom's pistol into court. She hid it inside an accessory variously described as a shawl, reticule, or small cloth grip. Annie had thrown back her heavy crepe veil, "exposing her handsome face," a reporter opined, "and her eyes glittered with a deadly purpose. She took a seat near the entrance to the bar and soon after she seemed to give way to grief and her sighs were heard throughout the front of the court room."[20] In reflection, the press later noted that when the first of the afternoon's witnesses, Mrs. E.M. Rumberg, completed her testimony, she took the seat nearest the entrance to the bar, thereby shoving everybody else, including Annie, down the row. Annie leaned over, whispered to Mrs. Rumberg, and they exchanged seats. Another witness was testifying at the blackboard and nearly all eyes were there, when Annie asked for a drink of water. A glass was brought. Annie stood to drink it, glared hotly at Rhodes, and:

All at once a black shadow shot from where the woman sat to the side of the prisoner. There was a terror-stricken cry and all was confusion and excitement. For a moment only a few of the spectators knew what had happened. They only saw a rush in the direction of the prisoner and there was a general belief that an attack had been made upon him by some persons, they didn't know who. One man stood with a chair raised high in the air; another held a revolver in his hand, and there was an impression that the old Graham-Tewksbury feud had suddenly been transferred from Tonto Basin to the court room.

Those nearest the doorway hastily left the room and as they passed down the stairs they wondered why the firing had not commenced, for the Graham and Tewksbury factions were not given to delay.

Meanwhile, those within the bar saw what had occurred. The Nemesis in black had reached Rhodes's side and placed the muzzle of the revolver against his back. She had concealed the weapon, a Colt .45 caliber, in a small cloth grip. It was already cocked and was withdrawn within the instant she crossed from her chair to where Rhodes sat. Just as she placed the muzzle against his back she pulled the trigger but the hammer caught the top of the sack in which she had concealed the revolver and wedged it tightly against the cartridge. The intervention of the cloth saved Rhodes's life. The prisoner sprang to his feet. With one hand he grasped Mrs. Graham's arm and with the other a chair. In the meantime

Sheriff Montgomery had seized the frantic woman and with the assistance of several persons, tried to take the revolver away from her. She held the weapon between her knees and it was more than a minute before the sheriff and his assistants succeeded in disarming her.

While the struggle was going on she screamed, "Oh, My God! Let me shoot! Oh, do let me shoot! Oh, God, let me shoot! Oh, God, he killed my husband! Oh, God, let me shoot! Oh, Jesus, let me shoot! Oh, God, he killed my husband! I have no one! They ain't doing anything! Oh, somebody help me!"

As she was taken out she cried, "Bring him out!" and this exclamation was nearly as dangerous as her attempt to shoot. There had already been a strong sympathy created and it was feared that this last appeal would precipitate a riot.[21]

Local press accounts differed in detail. The wire service reporter dispatched: "She placed the pistol against Rhodes's breast and pulled the trigger which caught in a handkerchief she was carrying and wedged so tight she could not cock it again. A mad rush from the court room followed, and lawyers and reporters were under the table. Mrs. Graham was removed from the court room; it took three men to disarm her."[22] I was not frightened," went an old cavalry smile, "but several troopers I overtook were scared to death." Joke became reality for Phoenix: "The courtroom was crowded before Mrs. Graham made the attempt to kill Rhodes. Three seconds after, it was almost empty. As soon as the woman's intent was clear, the crowd made a wild rush for the door, in a manner that attested illy for Arizona bravery. One man tried to climb through a window and a peace officer led the vanguard of the retreating multitude down stairs." This reporter also preserved a description of the firearm: ". . .revolver, which is now in the custody of the sheriff, in an old rubber-handled .45 caliber Colt's revolver, frontier pattern. In the cylinder were only three cartridges, but the hammer was resting above one of them."[23]

To the theatrics of thwarted avengement, the day's evidence took second billing. Yet before and after Annie's dauntless deed, the prosecution fashioned its circumstantial case. The above-mentioned Mrs. Rumberg deserved center stage, for at her home near the Normal School, she had exchanged greetings with a familiar, heavily armed acquaintance, Ed Tewksbury, as he rode into Tempe at five o'clock the morning of the murder. Two-and-a-half hours later, she had again seen Tewksbury, this time galloping his lathered bay gelding eastward out of town; she saw Rhodes, also astride a sweating horse, go by her place about six minutes after Tewksbury loped past. Mrs. Rumberg would not be shaken in her identifications . . . she had known Ed Tewksbury since he was a boy, and off and on, had seen John Rhodes around Tempe for two weeks.

E.G. Frankenberg saw Rhodes alone and horseback that morning south of Tempe. Boone Lewis and John La Barge methodically explained how they studied and measured tracks of the horses of two suspects at the murder scene. The print made by the left forefoot of one horse was identical to the track made by the same foot of Rhodes's horse. Further, the track of the alleged assassin's horse exhibited a peculiarity—a shoe was too short, and the rear of the hoof imprinted the ground. Rhodes's horse had an undersized shoe, and the rear of the hoof pressed the earth. It *had* to be the same horse, Lewis and La Barge insisted. Their beliefs were buttressed by a parade of witnesses, including John Bunch, A.J. Halbert, F.W. Buttler, J.H. Pritt.

"...F.D. Adams took the stand. Adams was an excellent witness, straightforward and loud-voiced and the defense handled him lightly. He gave his residence as 'Tempe and wherever he happened to spread out his blankets.' Saw Rhodes at 6:30 a.m. on August 2. Defendant was leaving town with Robert Bowen, mounted on a bay horse. Saw him return to Jones' corral at about 9 o'clock. Exchanged a few words with him, telling him that Tom Graham had been killed. Saw that Rhodes had a revolver in the band of his trousers and asked him 'if he was on the war path?' He seemed very nervous; got off his horse and tried to uncinch him. This Rhodes seemed unable to do, his fingers trembled so. Defendant then got a cup of water from the hydrant, but after drinking nervously, turned the water on still more instead of off."[24]

Dr. N.J. Hart was first to attend Graham, while the man lay on the wagon. "The sacks on the wagon were saturated with blood as were also his clothing. On examination of his pulse, I found it to be very weak. I gave attention to the wounds. There were two. One, on the left side of the spinal column a little below the level of the shoulder, and the other on the right side of the neck. I stayed with him two hours. Graham talked all that his strength would allow. He talked with the doctors, with his wife, Charles Duchet, Justice Forsee, and was perfectly conscious and answered all questions asked...Graham was sure he had received his death wound. Some friends told him that if he would be brave he would get well. He shook his head and said no. He was able to talk in a whisper and at other times quite loud and at other times weaker."[25] Dr. M.W. Brack of Tempe corroborated the diagnosis of Dr. Hart—likely part of the spinal cord was severed; death was certain; the patient held no hope; he was perfectly conscious until two hours before death.[26]

Next day, the eleventh, the Rhodes hearing momentarily gave way to yet another Tewksbury tale, but this one seemingly of substance: "Tewkesbery Coming. Has surrendered himself to the law."

Another record insisting to be set straight was Deputy Sheriff Sam Finley's. To his embarrassment, certain individuals and newspapers had cast him as a Tewksbury sympathizer—else how could he go alone into the redoubt and bring in Ed? "This is incorrect," went his press release. "I am a friend of no faction, but simply did my duty as an officer, and a man friendly to good Government. . . . Anyone who makes the statement that I am a friend of any faction is mistaken, to put it into language fit for publication." His own grump would be the nearest Sam would ever come to public honor.[27]

By far more serious, Arizona's ambitions for admission to the Union once again were beset by the cruelest of civic criticism, external ridicule. "If Arizona should have a few more feuds like that out in Tonto Basin it would be difficult to get enough people together there ever to admit her as a state," sniffed the *Los Angeles Times*. The *Phoenix Herald* conceded: "The *Times* has hit the nail on the head in this matter. As well might Arizona to expect water to flow uphill as to expect decent people and capital to locate itself in a region of country where life is subject to the bullet of the assassin at any moment and property is liable to be destroyed without regard to ownership by warring factions, in deadly, vindictive strife."[28]

Through the fourth day of the Rhodes hearing, prosecutors wove a tight web of incriminating circumstantial evidence and exquisite spectator sympathy. Or so they thought. The popular doctor, Scott Helm, blurted to the dying Graham, "They have got you this time, Tom." And Tom replied, "Yes, I am done for." The vignette honed the senses for the swearing-in of Annie Graham. Not one ear or eye in the audience ignored this dramatic woman,[29] and Annie knew well her pitiful place: "Only we two are left, myself and the baby."[30]

She was very pale and was evidently making a great effort to be composed. She testified that Mr. Graham left home about six or half past six. . .the next time she saw him was about nine o'clock sitting in a chair at the Cummings place with a bullet hole through his body. She went up to him and kissed him; his lips were cold; she sprang back and screamed. Dr. Brack told her not to excite him as there was a bare possibility of his recovery. Graham overheard this and shook his head and said: "No."

They had a talk in regard to his leaving his family. He bade his wife farewell. They held his baby up for him to kiss. He asked his wife to hold the baby up once more. He kissed his wife and said: "I am gone."[31]

Annie said Tom asked her to rub his stomach. She did, with all her might. Harder, he begged. Then he said, "I cannot feel it; there is no hope." Annie recalled Charley Duchet's arrival, "Cheer up, Tommy; there is yet hope," to which Graham responded, "No, Charley, I am a bleeding inside; I am a gone goose." The point was emphasized by a train of prosecution witnesses: W.T. Cummings, John Hickey, Reverend E.G. Roberts, Della Cummings, J.D. Grosse.[32] Upon which, the prosecution rested.

There was never a doubt regarding the defense. Rhodes had a perfect alibi. He was somewhere else. Mrs. M.K. Bailey placed Rhodes two and a half miles south of Tempe in the company of Robert Bowen and a

Mexican at about 7:40 A.M., August second. So did Jennie and William Lewis. In cross-examination, witnesses allowed that Tempe scarcely went by any standard time. Mrs. Bailey, for example, could not resolve discrepancies between "railroad time" downtown and the "sun time" on which her household ran.[33]

Star defense witness was Bowen. He was, after all, a prominent presence in the establishment that wanted Rhodes to hang. Hotelman and cattle feeder, Bowen claimed Rhodes as his range foreman and tender of several Tempe pastures.

On August 2, he saw Rhodes come downstairs from his room at the Tempe Hotel, at about 5:40 A.M. He got up shortly thereafter himself and, at 7:30 local time, suggested to Rhodes that they go to Bill Lewis's, where some steers had broken out. To this Rhodes assented and getting their horses from Jones' stable, they started off forthwith. They passed Adams and Tom Gardiner on Mill Avenue about two miles south of Tempe, afterward turning off eastward to Lewis's. Near there they found some loose stock which they drove through the break in the fence at the southeast corner of Lewis's ranch, assisted by Robert Michels and by Rafael Lopez, an employee of Bossen's, who at this time came up. It was just after this was done that they met Mrs. Baily. . .Had no feelings against Graham.

Judge Street [special prosecutor] in cross examination, pressed the witness closely as to his expressing any opinions as to Graham. Witness answered evasively. The prosecution then pointedly asked if at the time of the reported killing of Graham a few days ago, a man had not told him that he had good news for him, that Graham was dead, and if he did not then express himself a bad opinion of Graham.[34]

Rhodes's alibi was corroborated by the advance guard of what the press correctly assumed would comprise an army of witnesses. But in the long line of defense, Bowen counted most: he was Rhodes's boss, and he personally vouched for his time continuously from before six to about eight-twenty A.M.[35] William Bunch rode with Bowen's party for half a mile. Tom Goodwin saw them. Roland Nichols helped the men put cattle in a pasture. Raphael Lopez, cowboy for Bowen, swore he was there, too, with Rhodes. Frank Jones, who slept at his brother's stable, asserted that Rhodes's horse was not taken out during the night. Ed Jones fed Rhodes's horse at five and when he next saw the horse between eight and nine, the horse showed no signs of hard riding. P.F. Dillard said the same about the horse. S.W. Imley, bartender, averred he slept on a cot all night only four feet from Rhodes. George Reynolds filled another gap of time. John Harris said he saw Rhodes in the hotel bar from between five and six o'clock, until breakfast about seven. Stacy Penn overheard Bowen give Rhodes orders to help round up loose beeves. Miss Betty Sholein, hotel resident, saw Rhodes take a drink in the back ·yard at five-fifteen, and eat breakfast at six-ten. R.A. Smith saw Rhodes, unarmed, at breakfast.[36]

By mid-morning, August 15, some sixty witnesses had been examined before John Rhodes himself took the stand. He said he spent all of the first hours of August 2 at the hotel, sleeping on a balcony cot within four feet of Sam Finley. He and Finley arose at five and took breakfast together. He had worked for Bowen six years, and on this morning went directly to help gather loose stock. He saw a lot of people; they saw him. He didn't even own a Winchester rifle, and did not know the exact location of the Tom Graham farm.[37]

The cross examination, conducted by District Attorney Cox, was a vigorous one, under which the prisoner grew rather angry. He intimated that the next time he went into the hills he should take a private secretary along to record his words, in anticipation of future trials. Despite objections from his counsel, he was interrogated a long period of time regarding his relations with Tewksberry and Tewksberry's location at different dates during the past few months.[38]

Dispirited, it seemed, the prosecution's delaying tactics toward the end. The attorneys asked for time to produce witnesses who never materialized. Those few who testified added little or nothing. By and large, the defense stood pat. On Thursday, August 19, final arguments took most of the day. The summation of Joseph Campbell: "An eloquent argument, closing only at the noonday hour." And of District Attorney Cox: "The argument of Mr. Cox was one of which our district attorney has a good cause to be proud. He spoke for two and one-half hours in his most effective, yet rapid style, and showed that into the case he had thrown his best energies and talents." Mainly, said Cox, Rhodes had thirty or forty minutes of free time. He could have done it. And who were those providing the alibi? ". . .Rhodes's friends, as prejudiced and open to suspicion."[39]

But the Rhodes alibi held up. Late in the afternoon, Justice Huson delivered his finding, as recounted in the next day's *Phoenix Gazette:*

Upon the conclusion of the District Attorney's argument, there was hardly a pause before Justice Huson rendered his decision. He said in a rather indistinct voice, "I have listened carefully to all the testimony in this case and, although I was at first inclined to believe the defendant guilty of the murder, the defense has so conclusively proved their alibi that I must release the prisoner."

A look of disgust and amazement spread over the uplifted faces of his hearers. There is not doubt but that the decision pleased very few. Knots of men gathered all over the streets and discussed, somewhat angrily, the situation.

A number of wild propositions were made, the most popular being to hang the judge in effigy. But a milder reaction followed and none of the foolish schemes were carried out.

Still in fear of his life, Rhodes elected to spend night of August 19 in the protection of the jail. Next day, escorted by a troop of heavily armed friends, Rhodes left town.

Rhodes's release was decried by most of the Arizona press. Typical was the editorial reaction of the *Tucson Star* for August 20: "It appears that Rhodes did not have a hand in the killing of Graham. So Justice Huson of Tempe [Huson was of Phoenix] thinks, if he is honest in his decision which turns Rhodes loose on the community. If the Phoenix press reported the evidence correctly, and we have no good reason to believe otherwise, we cannot conceive upon what grounds the defendant was discharged. Why go to the useless expense of an examination which is but a travesty upon law and justice?"

In Phoenix, the *Herald* of August 19 turned the screw tighter: ". . . sufficient to alarm every good citizen and property owner in the county. When dangerous men are turned loose with evidence almost sufficient to hang them, against them, and a moral certainty that their freedom means additional murder or assassination, it is time the people of this county to begin to consider the kind of men they choose to preside over their justice's courts and the influences that are brought to bear on those courts to defeat the end of justice and destroy the protection of law and government generally. . ."[40] The *Gazette* of August 21 reported: "The following notice was found posted up on the street corner yesterday: 'Anny partes I am owing, call at my office, as I got money now, after Rhodes' trial. Willis O. Huson, J.P.' "

Elsewhere, sarcasm vied with indignation:

The conflicting testimony at the examination of Rhodes. . .leads to the belief that Graham committed suicide. He evidently dismounted from his load of grain, went behind the bushes, took deliberate aim and shot himself. He then rode away. If this theory proves incorrect, the lawyers in the case may succeed in proving that Tom Graham was not shot all—that he died of typhoid fever.[41]

Salt River Valley citizens likewise were furious; on August 27, forty-five of them called a mass meeting. Tempe leaders of the caliber of C.O. Austin, C.J. Ulmer, R.W. Mattison, A.W. Cosner, Mons Ellingson, C.N. Taylor, M.M. Hitchcock, Professor J.M. Emmert, A.H. Root, C.W. McFarland, and Dr. F.J. Hart agreed the Graham slaying "cast a dark stain" upon the reputation of the town.[42] A committee appointed at the meeting drafted the following resolution:

Resolved: That the action of one W.O. Huson, justice of the peace at the City of Phoenix, in relegating to himself the powers of judge and jury in the recent preliminary examination of John Rhodes, accused of the murder of Tom Graham, is hereby condemned as an unwarranted assumption of power. That it is the opinion of the meeting that the evidence presented at said examination was in the minds of all honest men sufficient to bind the accused over to await the action of the grand jury.[43]

Such were the sentiments of the day. Rhodes had cheated the gallows. But in the same editions, the other story was breaking. Ed Tewksbury was in custody, and coming to Phoenix for trial.

For what it is worth (hearsay of hearsay, lawyers might complain), Joe T. McKinney, decades later, acquired a statement from Rhodes and put it into the *Arizona Historical Review:*[44] "John Rhodes and I were talking over the affair and he told me as follows, 'I moved down to the Salt River Valley and went to work taking care of some cattle and I wanted to live in peace. I left off my pistol and didn't carry any gun at all. Everything went along all right for a while and people got to telling me that Tom Graham had sent for a man to kill me. I refused to be disturbed by such reports and went along about my work . . . until one day I saw Tom Graham pointing me out to old Duchet.' He immediately wrote to Ed Tewksbury to 'come at once very important.' Ed came and he told Ed what had to be done at once. He told Ed he could kill him or he, John Rhodes, would kill him. The fact is, Ed Tewksbury killed Tom Graham, but Rhodes was right there with him when it was done."[45]

VI. The Tewksbury Trials

If ever an Arizona suspect was pronounced guilty prematurely, it was Edwin Tewksbury in the murder of Thomas H. Graham.

Over and again, in his deathbed utterances, Tom named Ed as one of his assassins. These statements were elicited in the presence of leading Salt River Valley professionals and officials, who passed along the opinion as gospel. Tom was a highly respected farmer in the peace-loving agricultural and educational center of Tempe, nine miles up river from Phoenix.[1] Tempe's aspiration to culture centered around a tangible shrine—seven years before the Graham murder, the establishment of the Territorial Normal School gave Tempe the only institution of higher learning between the West Coast and Austin, Texas.[2] Under oath, Tom dictated his dying declaration to a judge, and although paralyzed, signed with an X a complaint charging Ed Tewksbury with inflicting the wound presumed by everyone—including Tom himself—to be fatal.[3] The allegation was supported by eyewitnesses.

These details were given the most sensational coverage in the territorial, regional, and national press.[4] Yet other facts never came to light—for example, at the time of the Graham killing, Ed Tewksbury was the duly elected constable of Globe.[5] Ed was highly regarded wherever he lived, and he also had lost virtually all of his close blood relations.[6] Yet no literary effort was spared to stir up sympathy for Tom's pretty young widow and four-year-old daughter. The words "murderer" and "Tewksbury" appeared together and interchangeably.

Tom Graham died yesterday afternoon by a coward's bullet, and as to the principals the bloody Graham Tewksbury feud it at last ended, though many more are likely to fall in the quarrels which will grow out of it.

The murdered man was the last of the Grahams, and his slayer, Ed Tewksbury, was the last of the Tewksburys. The murder was committed. . . .[7]

Not that the *Arizona Republican* was alone in affixing guilt. Under a half-dozen decked headlines topped with "Assassinated!" the rival *Gazette* printed:

Another chapter in the bloody Pleasant Valley war is to be written—it is hoped the last one.

Thomas H. Graham, was ambushed yesterday morning, near Tempe, and mortally wounded. The crime was a cowardly one, directly traceable to a past feud. Ed Tewksbury and John Rhodes were the assassins. . . .

Not to be outdone in conclusive leaps, the *Arizona Daily Star* at Tucson went with its wire report, "Shot Him Dead," flatly stating that "Tom Graham was shot and killed today by Ed. Tewksbury. Both are well-known citizens here, Graham being a cattle raiser and Tewksbury a sheep man. The shooting occurred. . . ."[8]

Unrestrained criticism was heaped upon Maricopa County Sheriff John Britt Montgomery and other officers for allowing the slaying to occur in the first place, and then permitting a suspect to escape. The Democratic *Phoenix Gazette* groused, "One of the weakest efforts to capture a criminal ever made by a Maricopa county sheriff, was that of the Republican sheriff yesterday in the Graham-Tewksbury affair. Mr. Montgomery is a good man to run a farm but he is not a success as a sheriff." Then, oozing sarcasm was the make-believe interview:

"I done sent Ed a postal card telling him he'd better give hisself up or there'd be trouble," said Sheriff Montgomery yesterday. "Ed has always been a pretty good friend of mine and he will sure show up."[9]

Newspaper reporters smelled out Judge Howell, and may or may not have put words into his mouth, and in so doing gave Howell sober second thoughts, for Howell, residing in Tonto Basin, considerably backpeddled from this story when he later was put under oath (he said he couldn't say for certain who the rider was).

A.J. Howell, superintendent of the Cross Seven cattle company, came in from the company's ranch, in Tonto Basin, last evening and met Tewksbury about four o'clock Wednesday evening at the sand wash near Sugar Loaf, eight miles beyond Jeff Adams' ranch. He was riding a bay horse, answering the description of the one he rode when he shot Graham. . . .[10]

Ed Tewksberry was seen about half past four o'clock day before yesterday at the Granite Wash, east of Jeff Adams' place, traveling leisurely along the road en route to his home. He evidently knows the strength of his name and has no fear of pursuit.[11]

The same newspaper editorialized:

It is a pretty state of affairs when a man can ride into the valley, shoot down a citizen and ride leisurely away. It speaks well for the efficiency of our peace officers.[12]

When Tom Graham's frustrated bodyguard, Charley Duchet, took a pistol shot at Tewksbury's alleged partner, John Rhodes, the bullet missed, but the resulting round of libel hit Ed Tewksbury dead center. And if the coroner's inquest into Graham's death exceeded its mandate, the press enveighed not, but rather joined the rush to judgment:

TEWKSBURY AND RHODES ARE RESPONSIBLE

The coroner's jury, after deliberations yesterday, brought in the verdict, that Graham came to his death by guns in the hands of Rhodes and Tewksbury. The verdict was given in accordance with the best evidence available, the facts of the case fully justified the rendering of such a verdict. None are disappointed and none are surprised at the report.[13]

The August 27 mass meeting in Tempe was more a cry for Tewksbury's gizzard than a protest of Rhodes' release. Sheriff Montgomery served as sergeant-at-arms, and anted two hundred dollars of reward money. Judge Huson, in his hesitant, mousy delivery of his finding, had magnified press criticism and public dismay. Now somebody, *anybody*, by God, would have to pay for this brutal outrage, and Ed Tewksbury met the qualifications.

Had Ed realized how thoroughly the press was poisoning public opinion (heightened, of course, with his self-knowledge of guilt), perhaps he would not have surrendered so willingly. At it was, he and his escort, Deputy Sheriff Tom Elder, were faced with problem enough—how to run Ed safely to a Phoenix jail cell through a gauntlet of eager, amateur, incited hangmen. Here is how they did it:

Finley arrived at the Newton ranch in Pleasant Valley on the afternoon of the fifth. There he met George Wilson, foreman for the cattle range of the George Newton estate, under whom Tewksbury had been employed as a cowboy. Finley told Wilson of his errand, that Ed was wanted in connection with the death of Tom Graham. Wilson said that he had several days before sent Ed to the home ranch, twelve miles distant, and at once sent a rider to inform Ed of Deputy Finley's presence at the ranch. Ed came without delay and quietly surrendered himself to the deputy.

The next morning they were on the road early for Globe for Ed to deliver himself to Sheriff [J.H.] Thompson, and accompanied by Dick Williams, a cowboy, whom Finley had hired as a guard. They went by the Apache Trail, to the east of the Sierra Anchas, down Cherry Creek, arriving in Globe on the second day.

At Globe, Mr. Finley said, there was nothing but sympathy and good wishes.

He said the town appeared as one in the belief that Tewksbury was innocent. A large number of volunteers offered their services in seeing the party safely to Tucson. Globe had been a Tewksbury stronghold since the beginning of the war.

Finley, Williams and Tewksbury set out across the country from Globe on the Silver King and Pinal City trail on the ninth. At Globe Finley notified Deputy Tom Elder of Maricopa County of their progress and and was met at Hardenburg's Desert Wells, eighteen miles east of Mesa, by Elder where he received the prisoner.

So it was off from Hardenburg's Wells at dusk to Casa Grande for Elder and Tewksbury to catch the train for Tucson due in there the next day.[14]

The appearance of such a celebrated figure in the Old Pueblo could scarcely be kept a secret:

Tewksbury arrived here yesterday in charge of Deputy Sheriff Tom Elder of Maricopa County, after a trip of over 300 miles on horseback. He was arrested by Sheriff Findlay of Pima county [Finley was deputized in Maricopa] on August 5, for the murder of Tom Graham.

Mr. Tewksbury is reported to be here for his health.[15]

In its next edition, the *Tucson Daily Star*, just ten days after Graham's demise and only a week after Ed's surrender, gained an audience with Edwin.

Tewksbury looks as if he had Indian blood in his veins but declares he has none. He is very bitter against what he called the persecution of himself and John Rhodes, and hinted that those at the head of it were not all they might be themselves. When the proper time comes he was sure he could get plenty of witnesses to prove an alibi.

"All I came here for," he continued, "was to get protection. Rhodes surely would have got it down there if the deputies had not saved him from the crowd." Tewksbury went on to say that he was at Desert Wells on the twenty-sixth and twenty-seventh, and started back for his ranch that day. He was looking for some lost horses. On the fifth of August, Wilson, his employer, told him Sheriff Findlay was looking for him. Wilson also told him Graham had been killed on the second and that he, Tewksbury, was wanted for the crime. This he said, was the first he knew of the killing. "When I heard Sheriff Findlay was at the ranch," he said, "I went and gave myself up."[16]

"Charley Duchet," he said, "is the prime mover against me. His real name is English.[17] Any one knows he would do or say anything to injure me. This is all I care to say now." These witnesses, he added, "will all swear they saw me when I was miles away on the third."

How Tewksbury was transferred secretly from Tucson to Phoenix in itself made a postscript for the *Tempe News* of August 20:

Henry DeNure, who went to Tucson for Ed Tewksbury, waited till late Monday evening before telling the Pima county officers of his errand so it could not get out and be wired ahead to Phoenix. The two men. . .left Tucson at four o'clock on the early morning train.

At Maricopa the engineer of the Phoenix train was asked to watch for signals about six miles south of Kyrene and to slow up for them but not to stop the train. The train slowed down and Tewksbury dropped from it. DeNure followed him. Henry Garfias was waiting with two saddle horses. The men mounted and rode off. Outside of Phoenix Tewksbury got off his horse and walked to the Court House with Garfias. They met Deputy Sheriff Barry and Tewksbury was soon safely locked up.[18]

Despite these uneventful—yet correctly cataloged—precautions, a web of romance soon was spun around the Tewksbury surrender. The succeeding generation's recapitulations portrayed Ed belligerently shouldering into Phoenix "armed to the teeth. Two six-shooters, a long rifle, bowie knife and everything. When the Sheriff approached, Tewksbury threw down on him with his rifle and threatened to shoot if he came a foot closer. Tewksbury, gun in hand, then kept the officer at bay slowly backing down the street, up a flight of stairs and clear into the law offices of Campbell and Baker, his attorneys. Here on their advice he finally surrendered. A fine bit of wild and woolly newspaper writing. Read the story in the *Phoenix Gazette* of August 1, 1916. It's a thriller and no mistake. But there wasn't a word of truth in it all. Fiction pure and simple."[19]

From some lost source, historian Joseph Fish may have given credence to the fable. "Fish says Ed came to Phoenix armed to the teeth. Was arrested on Washington Street by Sheriff Montgomery without a fight or any trouble. His friends threatened to rescue him. Montgomery placed armed men in the court house tower where night and day they watched for an attack. None came."[20] Model citizen that he strove to emulate, Tewksbury did not have long to wait for preliminary examination.[21]

On August 29, before Justice Harry L. Wharton, a procession of witnesses placed Ed with a rifle in his hands at the scene of the slaying earlier in the month. The preliminary examination in Phoenix lasted until September 8. Many witnesses from the Rhodes hearing were called and substantially testified as before. Some witnesses, of course, brought information pertinent mainly to the Tewksbury case.

There follow quite selective exerpts from the day-by-day court transcript, interspersed with commentary from the press, contemporary commentators, and historians.[22] (For good cause, many a reader may quarrel with the author's gross abridgment of the Tewksbury transcript. That document, however, makes a stack of paper in legal format about seven inches thick, or about 350,000 words.)

ED TEWKSBURY IN COURT

His Examination Begins Before Judge Wharton. One Witness Positively Identifies Tewksbury. Ed Tewksbury walked into Judge Wharton's court this morning at 10:10 behind Deputy Sheriff Barry, with five or six bailiffs bringing up the rear. The court room was well filled with an interesting throng, all men. It was expected that Justice Huson would sit in judgment, but after all arrangements were made the papers in the case were turned over to Justice Wharton.

Tewksbury bears all indications of having mixed blood. The high cheek bones, black hair, sallow color and piercing black eyes are those of an Indian. He is of medium height, and very powerfully put up. He took his seat without nervousness and appeared interested in the crowd, who stared back at him with compound interest.

Other observors noted that Tewksbury was characteristically neat and clean, gotten up handsomely in dark clothing. He affected a luxurious black mustache. He seemed overly sensitive about his hands (he habitually wore gloves afield), and he hypnotized onlookers with his piercing, intelligent eyes.[23] By one estimate, a thousand spectators stared back. As fate would have it, Annie Graham was not one of them; her fourteen-year-old brother had suffered a broken leg in a horse accident the day before.[24]

The prosecution pitched into its case. Drs. Scott Helm and M.W. Brack testified about Tom's wound, condition, and dying declarations. Mrs. E.M. Rumberg would not be shaken from two damaging points: she knew Ed Tewksbury for fifteen years; and just before sunrise on August 2 she saw him in Tempe. M.A. Cravath told of his rush to help Tom on the wagon. Neighbors Neils Petersen,[25] Grace Griffith, and F.W. Butler filled in details. But it was Mollie Cummings who transfixed the afternoon crowd:

...she heard shots on August 2 as she was driving out from the house to the road. She met the horses of Tom Graham and then drove up toward the wagon. A man was behind the wagon, with a gun raised when she first saw him. Miss Griffith was with her in the buggy, and the man with the gun rode by them.

Miss Cummings was told to look over the court room and reached Tewksbury, pointing at him and saying, "That is the man."[26]

Such high drama welcomed the comic relief of Dr. W.J. White, "now in the cattle business."

He looked at the defendant, and stated he saw "him or his duplicate," on the morning of August 2 at the Tempe Hotel. Witness had slept on the grass behind the beer garden, got up between four and five o'clock and went into the hotel bar to get a cocktail. The bartender mixed it and started to wait on others, when Tewksbury came in, took up the witness's cocktail and drank it. Witness kicked and said he was in a hurry and that it was rather impertinent to drink another man's cocktail. Tewksbury said he was in a hurry, too, and went off without paying for the cocktail. To the best of witness's belief the defendant is the man who took his cocktail. John Rhodes was in the bar room at the time.[27]

Whereas the first day's attendance was reported as "all men," the second day enjoyed "the presence of several ladies. Tewksbury sat and twirled his mustache..."[28] Dr. Fenn J. Hart took the stand to say Graham was rational, and convinced he could not recover. W.T. (Bud) Cummings heard Tom say as much. Troops of animal trackers—Charley Duchet, Hi McDonald, P.H. Coyle, John J. Hickey, James H. Pritt, Rev. E.G. Roberts, and Boone Lewis among them—had to admit that they could not tie the hoofprints at the murder scene to Tewksbury. They had no horse for comparison. But other eastside residents said they saw the murderer. Betty Gregg saw his face, and under oath identified Tewksbury as the man. Robert White, Orley Stapely, W.C. Parks, Michael McGrew, Frederick Fogle, E.G. Frankenburg thought they saw the murderer, too, and with varying degrees of confidence, named Tewskbury.

In the afternoon's proceedings Sheriff William A. Kimball of Mesa City, found a measure of courage he may have misplaced the morning of August 2:

He was at his place. . . .He had received a telegram from the sheriff telling of Graham's shooting, and giving a description of the supposed murderers. He went to saddle his horse, coming onto the porch again saw a man ride by. The man looked hard at him and turned in his saddle and watched him for perhaps fifty yards.

"Would you know that face again?" asked the prosecuting attorney. "Yes, sir." "Now, I'll ask you to look at Ed Tewksbury there and say if he is the man?" "Yes, sir, he is the man."[29]

It was on this day that A.J. Howell back-pedalled on the identification attributed to him on the day of the crime. Now Judge Howell swore that he indeed met a heavily armed rider thirty-five miles east of Phoenix on August 2, but identification was blurred when the horseman wiped his face with a red bandanna.[30] And poor George Green, Tempe bootblack; he sowed a little wind and reaped a defense dust devil:

He told how Tewksbury, or man much like him, came to his stand early in the morning of August 2, had his boots blacked and then went off toward Thalheimer's saloon. The defense came down heavily upon the witness, regarding his travels in late years and his intimacy with jails of this county and elsewhere. Green grew wrathy, admitting to serving several petty sentences for drunkenness, but held strongly to his story of the tall dark man, whom he recognized again in the person of the defendant.[31]

Understandably so, after her sensational pistoleering at the examination of John Rhodes, the appearance of Annie Graham was anticlimactic. She really didn't know much—other than hearing her husband repeatedly name Tewksbury an assailant. Defense counsel A.C. Baker saved his tough cross-examination for John J. Hickey, and met his match. Turning to the judge, Hickey delivered a sermon on abuse of witnesses. Said Hickey: "He'll have *me* guilty of killing Graham, the first thing I know!" Lon Forsee, himself a Tempe justice, explained how he took the dying Graham's accusations down on paper.[32]

On September 1, the territory rested. And after a few loose legal ends, the defense marched to the bar forty-three witnesses to be sworn en masse. Attorney Baker tipped his hand: in absentia, he would put John Rhodes again on trial, proving Rhodes was not at the murder scene, and provide Edwin Tewksbury with an unimpeachable alibi. Justice Wharton cautioned Baker that Rhodes had nothing to do with the case before him. Baker ignored the admonition. Wharton relented. So, for some two days, two dozen witnesses removed Rhodes from the crime; reportage turned boring as the defense attempted to show Tom Graham in error in naming Rhodes, and by inference, Tewksbury, too. Then, at last: "Now Comes the Alibi."[33] Beginning the clock about July 25, Thomas Buchanan of Silver King averred that Tewksbury was at his place perhaps seventy-five miles east of Tempe. Wiley Holman saw Tewksbury on the twenty-sixth not far from Silver King. Frank Babcock swore Tewksbury spent the night of the twenty-sixth at Desert Wells, twenty miles east of Tempe. Joseph Boyer picked up the account: Ed acquired some fresh fruit August 1 "and went east" from Boyer's Ranch sixteen miles west of Pleasant Valley. Charles E. Thomas, acquainted for eight or ten years with Tewksbury, saw Ed at Bouquet's ranch about 2 p.m. on August 1. Jake Lauffer, his arm mutilated by a heavy rifle slug from ambush five years before, testified:

. . .he had known Tewksbury ten years. He was at home on August 1 and Tewksbury came that evening and stayed all night. His place is fifteen miles northeast of Bouquet's [in all, about a hundred miles from Tempe to Lauffer's]. On August 2 Tewksbury went on east, toward home.[34]

J.W. (Bill)[35] Voris, stout Tewksbury ally for a decade:

. . .testified that about noon on August 2 he saw Ed Tewksbury at old man Tewksbury's ranch on Cherry Creek. The ranch is over one hundred miles from Tempe. He is a partner of Ed Tewksbury in the horse and cattle business. On cross-examination Mr. Cox asked if he was interested in this case? "Yes, sir, I am interested in every case where I know the prisoner is an innocent man."[36]

Then George E. Wilson of Pleasant Valley:

. . .said he was at the Newton ranch on August 2, and Ed Tewksbury came their about four o'clock on that day. Mr. Wilson has charge of the Newton ranch, representing his sister, and sent Tewksbury over to the horse ranch, ten miles away. The next day, the 3rd, Tewksbury came back, stayed all night and all the next day. The day after, the 5th, Tewksbury went to the horse ranch again, and the next day, when Sam Finley came after Tewksbury, witness went out to horse ranch and brought him in to Newton ranch. Witness has known Tewksbury nine years, and is not a partisan of either the Tewksbury or Graham faction. He came here without being subpoenaed, merely to see that Tewksbury got fair play.[37]

The final witness of the day was R.W. Williams, another fervent Tewksbury friend. He said he saw Tewksbury at 8 p.m. on August 3 at the Newton ranch. And that was the alibi, to be debated, denigrated, and decorated for years and decades to come. How far could a determined westerner with one super mountain horse or a relay of mounts travel in

a given period of time? And the question as old as friendship—were witnesses telling the truth? Long-winded, impassioned closing arguments
centered around those questions. On the evening of September 6, Judge
Wharton announced that Tewksbury would be bound over to the Grand
Jury. Two days later the justice entered his formal finding:

The Court: Our statute says that even in a felony case where a man may be punished
by capital punishment, unless the proof of his guilt is evident or the presumption
great, he is entitled to bail. Now, the question is, as to what that means.

I have examined closely the authorities cited, both by the prosecution and the
defence, and I have taken this to be the true rule: That a court or judge will deny
bail in all cases wherein the evidence as presented by the witnesses on the stand,
would sustain the verdict of a jury convicting the defendant of a capital offense. In
other words, if the evidence is clear, and strong, leaving a well founded belief after
a dispassionate judgment, that the accused is guilty, and that he would probably be
punished capitally if the law was administered, that bail must be denied.

And Judge Wharton found the alibi seriously flawed. Witnesses in
the alibi were confused about dates. Timepieces were scarce. Ranchers
didn't keep diaries; few bunkhouse walls held calendars. Not uncom-
monly, country people paid small heed to days of a week. Not even the
postal courier who served Pleasant Valley could always be certain of
dates. Yet thirteen witnesses placed Tewksbury in Tempe at or around
the time of the shooting. Although fraught with opinion and circumstance, prosecution witnesses made a convincing case. ". . .I cannot in
this case see any cause to admit the defendant to bail."

The story broke to emphasize alarming rumors of more death on the
wing. In Arizona, at least, this week the Sullivan-Corbett boxing match
took second billing. A boy employed as a cattle herder on September 6
had chanced upon a masked, armed horseman hiding along the road to
be used by Charley Duchet and Annie Graham. "Duchet and Mrs. Graham, who were warned by the herder before they had left Phoenix, are
of the opinion that the masked man was none other than an enemy who
was lying in wait to assassinate Charley Duchet on the same mode utilized in the case of Tom Graham."[38] Deputy Sam Finley, who had delivered Tewksbury to jail, was so incensed at Duchet he challenged him
"out to the sand hills where we will shoot it out."[39] When Joe Boyer and
Duchet joined in animated quarreling on a Phoenix sidewalk, they drew a
crowd worthy of a news story.[40] A dozen of Tewksbury's sidekicks hung
around town fueling fears of a jailbreak, but cooler heads prevailed.
Maybe Sheriff Montgomery *did* station a squad of marksmen atop the
courthouse. When bail was denied, the Tonto Basin men went home.[41]

No stoppage appeared in the flow of funds to the defense. Attorneys
Joseph Campbell and A.C. Baker, who would attain first rank in the
territorial and state judiciary, were not cheap. They loosed a storm of
writs. Nonetheless, Tewksbury, after examination by the Grand Jury, was

arraigned on a charge of murder on December 5. Literally scores of witnesses took sides in the venue question before another prominent Arizona jurist, R.E. Sloan (he eventually would rise to the Supreme Court). Of course, the court was told:

That one John Rhodes was jointly charged with the affiant with the killing of said Graham, and at his preliminary examination in open court, the widow of said Graham attempted to kill said Rhodes by shooting him in the back, and only failed in so doing because of the entanglement of the hammer of the pistol in the cloth with which it was wrapped.[42]

On July 10, 1893, Judge Sloan moved the Tewksbury case to Tucson. The trial opened December 14 before District Judge J.D. Bethune. In retrospect, Drusilla Hazelton would conclude that the first Tewksbury trial would convene "a battery of lawyers, the finest array of legal talent ever seen at any one trial in the West, and no other criminal trial ever attracted more attention than did this one." Assisting the defense was "Silver-tongued" Tom Fitch, equally famous and enriched for his work on West Coast cases.

Maricopa County's ardor for justice was tested as expenses of transporting, housing, and feeding witnesses mounted into the multiple thousands of tax dollars. Costs for the defense also must have been staggering; the money source never disclosed. "It is only an assumption that Daggs Brothers financed the Tewksburys throughout the Pleasant Valley War, and it is also a guess that it was they who stood by the vendetta chieftain to the very end."[43] Another educated guess by Voris: "I have rumors that a lot of cowmen around Gila County is the ones who financed his trial. Old man Ellison."[44]

Virtually the same testimony of the preliminary examination was heard at the trial. If anything, Tewksbury tried to strengthen his alibi with more cronies. The scheme failed. The jury received the case on December 21. Two days of deliberation resulted in: "We, the jury, duly impanelled in the above titled cause, upon our oaths, do find the defendant guilty of murder and recommend him to the mercy of the court. (signed) M. McKenna, Foreman."[45]

Tewksbury took the matter cooly and seemed to consider that he had a good fighting chance for his life.[46]

That he did. His attorneys held a secret ace. They apparently knew all along that they might not win, but they couldn't lose. Before sentence could be passed, they announced to the court that their client had never been asked to plead the matter of his guilt. A frantic scramble by clerks did not uncover a record of a plea. The prosecutor's nightmare was described in the *Gazette* of December 29, 1893:

District Attorney Frank Hereford has received word from Phoenix that there really is no plea of Tewksbury on record, although the district attorney of Maricopa County is pretty positive that the plea was made, as a change of venue could hardly have been granted before that formality had been attended to. It looks now as if the clerk of the court neglected to make the entry at the time.[47]

Thus, "Ed Tewksbury was yesterday granted a new trial on a plea of abatement."[48] The case was tried again in January 1895. Again Tewksbury's high-powered legal staff shored up his alibi. Now the deep pockets of Tewksbury's financiers provided yet another Supreme Court justice-to-be, Thomas D. Satterwhite. The defense mustered more than forty souls now, including a surprise witness: A.J. Stencel, a cowboy from Winslow, swore that on the day of the murder he met Tewksbury on the Reno Trail far from the scene of the crime. This time around, the territory lacked one psychologically crucial witness. Annie Graham had remarried and moved to California. Although invited, the woman who was once moved to homicide, did not appear. Clearly, the mood was shifting to Ed. He had been in custody going on three years. He stood mute, requiring the judge to enter a plea of not guilty in his behalf. The familiar march of a hundred witnesses tramped through the Tucson court. The jury slept on cots in the court room, leaving only under chaperone for restaurant meals.[49]

Judge Bethune's charge to the jury included these points:
- In the charge of murder, all accessories are principals.
- Premeditation of a crime may occur almost at the instant of the time.
- The declining of the defendant to testify should be regarded neither for nor against him.
- The feud between the Tewksburys and the Grahams was not to be regarded as evidence, except as tending to establish the credibility of witnesses.
- Dying statements, though not sworn to, were to be regarded as an oath, in view of approaching death. Dying statements were not, however, to be regarded as superior testimony.
- The burden of the testimony was on the Territory to prove the guilt of the accused, and if a reasonable doubt was entertained as to the guilt of the prisoner, he was entitled to the benefit of that doubt.[50]

After protracted deliberation, the jury at the second trial could not agree, deadlocked seven to five for acquittal. Everybody had grown weary of the case. Maricopa County officials had to suspect they were throwing good money after bad, inasmuch as:

A query has arisen, growing out of the possible complications in this case, that the lawmakers of the United States Congress and the Territorial Legislature have, evidently, not forseen. It requires three judges to constitute a quorum in the Supreme Court of the Territory. The Court at present constituted is composed of one judge, who will be incapacitated from acting on the case in the Supreme Court by reason of his having been Tewksbury's attorney, namely, Chief Justice Baker. Judge Bethune will be incapacitated from sitting by reason of the fact that the case will be tried before him in the lower court.

This leaves but two judges of the Supreme Court with the right to act on the case upon appeal. The query is, if Tewksbury is convicted can the Supreme Court of the Territory consider his case? If not, what will become of it.[51]

The Tewksbury trials therefore could be credited with influencing the Arizona court system. By statehood, provision was made for filling the seats of disqualified supreme justices from lower courts.

The case was again set for trial at Tucson but before the date arrived, the district attorney for Maricopa county, after consulting with other county officers, decided the county could not afford the expense of another trial. It had already cost the county over twenty thousand dollars. Another trial would probably result either in a disagreement or, due to the time that had elapsed and the building-up of a strong alibi for Tewksbury, in his discharge from custody, a free man. During the time between his surrender at Phoenix and the decision to drop the case, Ed Tewksbury had been in jail, bond being refused him.

Affidavit, filed January 11, 1895:

Ed. Tewksbury being duly sworn on oath states; that he is the defendant in the above title action; that as soon as he was informed by public rumors in Tonto Basin, Gila County, Arizona, that he was charged with the offense for which he has been indicted he went to the officer, riding many miles and gave himself up to the officer on either the 5th or 6th of August, A.D., 1892. He states that since that time he has been in custody upon said charge; that he has been held in jail at Phoenix and in the jail at Tucson; that during the time he was in jail at Phoenix on two occasions he had opportunities to escape from said jail and did not do so; that on other occasions three prisoners in the jail with him sought to induce him to endeavor to escape with them and in every case he declined; that during the time he was in jail at Tucson he was approached by prisoners who were planning to escape and he declined to take part with them, but informed officers of the fact. . . .

The motion was, for a while, denied. But on February 6, 1895, Judge Bethune set bond at ten thousand dollars. Within a matter of days, bail was posted. Ed quickly returned to Globe, where his admiring public thereafter employed him in several roles of lawman. It was a foregone conclusion that the case eventually would be dismissed, and on March 12, 1896, it was, at the behest of the prosecution.

Three years, eight months, after Braulia López had tied her lucky apron string around his sombrero, Ed Tewksbury was free and clear. They soon married.

For them, the little war of their own was over.[52]

Afterword

No fighting man named Graham survived the Pleasant Valley War. Cousin Louis Parker laid low around the West, keeping in guarded touch with Tom Graham[1] and by one report "died years later in Las Cruces, New Mexico."[2] Tom's widow, Annie, remained in the Salt River Valley through the protracted settlement of her husband's estate. To represent her continuing interests in some six hundred head of Graham cattle ranging in Pleasant Valley,[3] Annie hired a highly regarded Texas cowboy, Horace B. Philley, twenty-three.[4] Annie spent $17.55 outfitting Philley,[5] and directed him to assist Silas W. Young during the Pleasant Valley fall roundup. On September 6, 1894, a traveler encountered "a mass of flesh" about a mile and a half west of Moore's Ranch on the Reno Road. Philley had been shot in the back; his body was mutilated when his saddle horse and pack string stampeded.

The Graham improvements and cattle in Pleasant Valley in 1895 were sold to J.R. Haigler for thirty-one hundred dollars, and the farm in Tempe the following year was turned over to Niels Petersen for twenty-five hundred dollars cash and assumption of a five hundred dollar note.[6] Annie remarried a man named Hagen, a cattleman and shipper, and from their home in Los Angeles, the Hagens traveled the world. Maybe affected by the war's trauma, Annie in later years imagined threatening bogiemen and serpents, against which she permanently drew her curtains. She spent many years in a mental institution. As a tourist in the 1930s, she made her only journey to Pleasant Valley and put up at the old Perkins store, then run as a rude hotel; expecting the verdant Eden described to her by Tom, she was reportedly disappointed by the Valley's dusty, brown condition during the dry season.[7] On May 31, 1961, age ninety-four, Annie died in Phoenix.[8]

Brought up in California, Annie's daughter, Estella, married C. E. (Ed) Converse, a wealthy Pittsburgh steelman who relocated to California. When Converse, fascinated by western history, learned of Estella's connection to Charley Duchet, he insisted that she engage a detective to track the old knife fighter to his grubby minerals claim near Aguila, Arizona. The Converses sent train fare. Charley arrived in California filthy and disheveled, but days of sartorial attention and a spiffy new wardrobe at the Converse Santa Paula estate transformed Charley into a fragrant dandy. For several years, he had the run of the place—Estella lavishing affection and treats—Converse pouring drinks, and peeling off banknotes for Charley from his inexhaustible roll of bills. But in time the soft life paled for Charley, and he pleaded to return to his burros and beans. Charley Duchet, irascible and foolhardy to the end, allowed pioneer Phoenix doctor H.A. Hughes to treat an infected toe, but later impulsively unbandaged his foot and died of blood poisoning on St. Patrick's Day 1925.[9] In his final days, he dictated to Dr. Hughes's stenographer a rambling statement of scrambled fact and fancy. Duchet's obituary was printed widely; the St. Louis Post Dispatch credited him with thirty-two killings.

Recovered from his gunshot through the lungs, Hashknife cowboy Tom Tucker risked his hide twice again in New Mexico feuds.[10] He served as a Santa Fe undersheriff, killing "several men who disputed his ability to arrest them," and died of natural causes in Texas in 1929.[11] Bob Glaspie (his own spelling), wounded with Tucker at the Middleton cabin, mended well; he tended livestock in New Mexico, and in Arizona's Cochise and Graham counties. On June 29, 1946, at age eighty-six, he died of natural causes at Coolidge.[12] Out of habit if nothing else, historians devoted much space to Tom Pickett, Billy the Kid crony and activist in New Mexico's Lincoln County War, as feudist in Pleasant Valley. He may have been an Arizona fighter, but I can find scarcely any primary documentation of Pleasant Valley involvement for Pickett, and none at all for George Smith, Buck Lancaster, Roxy, Peck, McNeal, and Jeff La Force, all counted as combatants by Earle Forrest and others.[13]

James Stinson, he of the much-coveted T-brand cattle, derived a good living from ranching and farming in the Salt River Valley, and, during his later years, near Kline, Colorado, where he died, at age ninety-four, on January 8, 1932.[14]

From the first weeks and long after Martin Blevins vanished, several caches of bones found along Cherry and Canyon creeks were, at least by assumption, attributed to him. The *Journal-Miner* of September 10, 1887, reported that "a body stripped of flesh supposed to be that of Old Man Blevins was found in the brush in Pleasant Valley."[15] And, "Three years after his disappearance a skeleton with a spike driven through the skull was found not far from the ranch."[16] Adding to the confusion, well-preserved and not particularly old aboriginal remains abound in Tonto Basin. Will Barnes related that in 1894, J.F. Ketcherside, Flying V ranch foreman, found a human skull in a hollow tree about five miles due west of the Rock House in Rock House Canyon. A rusty rifle leaning against another tree was thought to be Blevins's.[17]

John Black Blevins never fully recovered from the shoulder wound inflicted September 4, 1887, in Holbrook by Sheriff Owens. Convicted of assault, John Blevins was pardoned by Governor Zulick as Owens was taking him by train to the Yuma prison. Blevins and his wife, Eva, lived in and around Holbrook, eventually proving up a homestead southeast of Heber atop the Mogollon Rim. Blevins died in an Arizona automobile accident May 23, 1929.[18]

By 1987, the historic Blevins cottage had come into the ownership of the City of Holbrook for immediate service as a senior citizens center and possible future use as a museum. The last century's violence is not the only historic qualification of the little frame house. On January 6, 1975, Bruce Babbitt chose the porch of the Blevins house as the setting for taking his oath of office as attorney general. Through succession and election, Babbitt later served nine years as the governor of Arizona.

The press considered it a newsworthy coincidence that on the same day (May 31, 1961) that Annie Graham died, so did Ella E. Tewksbury, sixty-four, only daughter of Edwin Tewksbury.[19] She was survived by her mother, Braulia, who, at age ninety-two, expired November 26, 1962, in Gila County Hospital.[20] Ed's firstborn son, Edwin Jr., lost his life at age fifty-six, September 18, 1956, while taking a bath in Cherry Creek. Investigating officers discerned no foul play, attributing death to a head injury sustained in an accidental fall. Both Ella and Braulia died embittered toward Pleasant Valley storytellers—in particular Amelia Bean, whose distorted "historical" novel incredibly incorporating the names of real people in imaginary situations, appeared in 1960 as a serial in the *Saturday Evening Post,* in which Ed Tewskbury was portrayed as a wanton killer. It may have been the sorriest moment of Ben Franklin's old journal. The Tewksburys thought to sue but did not; the *Post*, more interested in profit than propriety, generally ignored Tewksbury protests.

James Dunning Tewksbury died of natural causes March 17, 1891, on his ranch at Crouch and Cherry creeks. Three of Old Man Tewksbury's sons had predeceased him.[21] The senior Tewksbury left an estate valued at $5,150, including squatter's rights to his ranch, livestock, and a $3,000 claim against the United States for property destroyed by rampaging Apaches.[22]

Edwin Tewksbury and Braulia López were married March 12, 1897, near Dudleyville, Arizona. In the next four years, they had a child a year. Ed, at all ages, wherever he went, commanded attention. "His friends remembered him, and his enemies never forgot," goes an old western saying, which especially applied to Ed. His sympathetic biographer, Drusilla Hazelton, commented, "Had this man with his intelligence, personality and talents directed his thoughts and ambitions in the right direction he might have made something of his life, other than just a reputation as a warrior." Unquestionably, the man was bright. Scarcely able to write his name when, as a young man, he first went to Pleasant Valley, Ed absorbed the teachings of his stepmother, Lydia, and further educated himself through his long years in confinement. Not many of his papers exist, so that his letter (now part of the Tewksbury collection held by Prescott's Sharlot Hall Museum), mailed from Chicago dated May 21, 1903, must bear the burden of volumes:[23]

My Dear Wife:

I rec'd your letter this morning and was glad to hear that you and the children were well. I have rec'd the papers all right and the news are of great interest to me. I have begun my regerlar treatment and am feeling better every day. I can use my arm much better and can raise it up to my head. I enclose you a card of the new Drs. You will see that I am in the hands of one of the greatest Drs. in the whole world. The other Dr. is also one of the best. In regard to your going home for awhile if you want to go I have no objections, as it will be three or four weeks yet before I can come. If you want to bring your sister back she will be company for you if you should return before I get home. If you go you had better leave the key with someone and let me know in your next letter where it is so if I should come home before you get back I'd know where to get it. If that money should come let me know so that if I should need any more I'll know how to get it. I have been to a big expense but feel so much better that I don't begrudge it. I don't want you to worry any about Crawford and don't sign anything he brings you. When I get back I'll settle anything I owe him. I suppose you rec'd the postal I wrote the day I rec'd the $200.00. The office here had to write back to Mr. [Dan] Williamson for identification as I couldn't get the orders cashed without it. It will be all right as soon as the Express office here gets word from the office there.

I am getting anxious to see you and the children and hope it wont be long before I can be with you again feeling well enough to go to work. If I keep on improving as I have it will only be a short time. With love to you and the children I remain

Your Affectionate Husband
Ed Tewksbury

His hopes died with him in Globe, "of quick consumption," on April 4, 1904.[24]

George Wilson, teenager in the Middleton cabin when the Hashknife bunch was riddled, and surviving brother-in-law of jeweler George Newton, in time came to own much of Pleasant Valley including the old Ellison Q Ranch east of Cherry Creek. Later a prominent Globe banker, Wilson died in the 1930s.[25]

John Rhodes served a hitch as an Arizona Ranger. He worked ranches in Gila and Pinal counties. He and John Tewksbury's widow, Mary Ann, married and had seven children of their own.[26] Another remarkably long-lived pioneer, Mary Ann was eighty-nine years of age when she died on Christmas Eve, 1950, at a daughter's home in Florence.[27] Many considered Rhodes, even in his senior years, to be Arizona's premier steer team roper in small-town and big-time rodeo. Rhodes died in 1918.[28] His stepson (John Rhodes, née Tewksbury) was world's champion roper in 1936 and 1938; he tied steers as a team with his son, Tommy.[29]

John Gilleland, one of the first men wounded in Pleasant Valley action, was another to serve as a deputy sheriff, he in Gila County. Never far from an Arizona cattle deal, Gilleland homesteaded near Buckeye. He died January 3, 1936.[30] Epitacio (Potash) Ruiz was thought to have served as a U.S. deputy marshal in southern Arizona, and later as a guard at the Arizona State Prison at Florence.[31] Another of Jim Stinson's gun-toting foremen, Robert McCann, was the target of an assassination attempt in the autumn of 1907. Also a deputy sheriff, McCann was unhurt by gunshots directed at him through a window of his Phoenix home. McCann returned the fire, then tracked a bloody trail to where his assailant apparently was carried off in a vehicle.[32]

Jim Roberts, often described as the surest gun on the Tewksbury side, was yet another who graduated to the right side of the law. Sheriff William O. (Buckey) O'Neill commissioned Roberts as deputy in late 1889 to keep the peace in the booming Jerome mining district. He remained a lawman to the day of his death (of heart failure) January 8, 1934.[33] Forrest flatly states that at the turn of the century, as marshal of Jerome, Roberts "had to kill several bad men." Be that as it may, by 1928, "Uncle Jim" Roberts had become something of a curiosity as a special officer for mining interests in Clarkdale. As an old man, Roberts's prowess with a pistol was reinforced in view of Clarkdale teenagers. On June 21, Willard J. Forrester and Earl Nelson, employing an automobile equipped with an arsenal of weapons, kegs of roofing nails, and cans of cayenne pepper to ward off pursuing people, cars, and dogs, stuck up the Bank of Arizona for forty thousand dollars in cash. In their getaway dash, they made one large mistake. They took a farewell potshot at Jim Roberts. Jim fetched his six-shooter from his coat pocket, drew a bead on the speeding vehicle, and placed a fatal slug in Forrester's head. The car crashed into the Clarkdale High School, and youngsters from the windows watched Uncle Jim snap the cuffs on the surviving bandit.

In the vicinity of the Perkins Store at the time of the slaying of John Graham and Charley Blevins had been a Gila posse led by Sheriff Glenn Reynolds.[34] Two years later, Reynolds was escorting nine convicts, including the Apache Kid, between Globe and Florence when the prisoners seized control. They murdered Reynolds and his deputy, William H. (Hunkeydory) Holmes, and left stage driver Eugene Middleton for dead. Sentiments sixty-six years later were so strong that Reynolds family members successfully sued for damages and enjoined the Naylor (publishing) Company of San Antonio from distributing a book already printed and bound, *Ghost Riders of the Mogollon,* authored by Ivan Lee Kuykendall. Glenn Reynolds had helped Jesse W. Ellison stock his Arizona ranch in 1885, and still-powerful third-generation Ellisons rallied to suppress the book. The Texas judgment, which today stands uncontested, found that Kuykendall had libeled Reynolds, a "brave, honorable, and Christian gentleman."

What to make of Tom Horn? Friendship with Ed Tewksbury was alleged. "Known to have been associated with the Tewksburys, but his part in the vendetta has never been clearly established," had to satisfy Forrest,[35] and perhaps posterity. Accomplished rodeo roper, documented army packer, functionary in the Geronimo surrender, professed range detective, Horn claimed he was a deputy under three Arizona sheriffs and "the mediator" who eventually pacified Pleasant Valley. These assertions were put forth in an autobiography Horn generated under sentence of death in Wyoming.[36] The book was more a literary than legal success; Horn was hanged November 20, 1903, in Cheyenne for the murder of a fourteen-year-old boy.

James D. Houck had things his way most of his life. The admitted slayer of Billy Graham and shadowy lawman prevailed also in death. With great vision, Houck left the high country to exploit lucrative winter sheep pasturage north of Phoenix. (Irreparable damage from livestock overgrazing continues to plague modern developers and municipalities.) Houck is credited with killing yet another man (Houck pleaded self-defense) in the Phoenix stockyards.[37] He built a prosperous roadhouse, shearing station, and stage line at Cave Creek, only to experience business decline and family disappointment in his last years. The press, which in his prime Houck had so artfully manipulated, took notice of his final flourish as recorded in the *Arizona Republic* of March 31, 1921:

James D. Houck, aged Arizona pioneer, prominent sheep man, committed suicide yesterday at his home in Cave Creek by taking strychnine. He gave as his motive . . .that he was tired of living. According to members of his family, Mr. Houck came into the house after feeding the chickens about 10 o'clock yesterday morning and stated he had just taken strychnine. He lay down upon a bed and requested that his shoes be removed as he did not care to die with them on.[38]

Colonel Ellison's progeny populated several Arizona sagas. One son-in-law, R.L. (Bud) Campbell, was fatally shot from ambush while riding the range six miles south of the Q Ranch July 5, 1896.[39] "A white man killed him but the Apaches got the blame."[40] In the style and spirit of Will James, a grandson of the colonel, Glenn R. (Cibicue Slim) Ellison, committed his cow country "words and windies" to regionally popular and highly readable books. Another of the colonel's sons-in-law, George W.P. Hunt, was elected to seven two-year terms as Arizona state governor, and served as ambassador to Siam. His wife, Helen Duette Ellison, never felt comfortable in public life. In 1915, Colonel Ellison retired, turned over the Q Ranch to non-family owners and moved to the Hunt compound on East McDowell Road in Phoenix. Five years after the death of his wife, and two years after the death of Duette, Colonel Ellison died at age ninety-two with his boots off, January 21, 1934.[41] Hunt, Ellison, and many members of the families are entombed in a white pyramid perched on a hillock in Papago Park between Phoenix and Tempe.

During the governances of Hunt (himself a Progressive of Wisconsin-Lafollette leanings) the Arizona legislative establishment came to be controlled by ranching and other rural business interests, a regime not broken until the exploding populations of Phoenix and Tucson gained representation through one-person, one-vote court rulings.

Following statehood, as true tales of the Old West rapidly receded behind rosy lenses, Arizona newspapers quickly converted their legitimate, original heritage of fair and factual reportage. The remarkable-enough Pleasant Valley War was only one story recolored into lurid "historical" reflectives and exported Sunday supplement features. What a shame! Revisionist error mated with greed to beget marketable fantasy. As escape from solitude, oldtimers gained attention with their thrilling recollections at pioneers' reunions; rather regularly through the first half of the twentieth century, obituaries duly noted the passing of one "last man" of the feud after another. Latter-day journalists gave extraordinary prominence to run-of-the-mill car accidents, fistfights, and civil difficulties of survivors and descendants—particularly those named Blevins and Tewksbury, to the anguish of the families. Pulp western magazines, novels, and advertised history books ensured the immortality of fabricated legend, including wartime atrocities. Some people believe what they want to believe; so be it. But even when William Colcord ("the last man" again) ostensibly agreed to tell all to Roscoe G. Willson in the 1950s,

Colcord revealed not much—and emphatically forewent a chance to confirm himself and his brother Harvey as members of the Committee of Fifty. William C. Colcord cloaked his secrets with death, age ninety-four, May 16, 1961. His family remained convinced of his neutrality.[42]

The freewheeling Daggs brothers—A.J., P.P., and W.A.—bought into the Bank of Tempe in the 1890s. For a decade, they were in and out of court while the fortunes of the bank wavered. In 1897, the bank failed spectacularly and the Daggses fought off criminal charges; they all lived several decades into the twentieth century.[43]

In the long run, the greater costs incurred by Pleasant Valley War activists and neutrals were to be borne by following generations; and their loss, by the land itself. At zenith, Colonel Ellison's Q Ranch was running more cattle than are permitted today to graze the entire rangelands of the sprawling Tonto National Forest.[44] In hindsight—however the practices of Ellison and hundreds of others might be characterized: greed? survival? frontiersmanship?—the consequences of their rapacious practices changed the face of Arizona forever.[45]

It took only about ten years. In 1895, a decade or so after Ellison *et al* stocked Tonto Basin, and the Hashknife and other outfits beset plateaus north of the Rim, Will Barnes lamented:

There must be ten thousand head of wild horses loose in northern Arizona. Over in our country, south of Holbrook, they are the worst nuisance that can be imagined. It has got to the point that we can't turn out a riding horse. We have to keep our saddle animals and round-up horses stabled all winter or bring them down to Phoenix to pasture. The wild stock not only eat up the feed that ought to go to the cattle, but they run cattle off the range. They have chased off all the cattle from the west end of the Hash Knife range, one of the best grass districts in the northeastern part of the territory.

. . . since old Lot Smith passed over the divide his boys have let their horses run without attention till there must be three thousand of them, mainly without a brand. On the Puerco in central Apache County, there must be five thousand head of loose bronchos and perhaps the same number are on the Navajo reservation, the property of the Indians, who don't seem to know what to do with them. One way the Indians are getting a little revenue from them is to sell them when they are fat to a Holbrook butcher who is fattening hogs on them. The butcher pays $3 a head for them. That seems to be the ruling price for wild stock. . .[46]

Mercilessly stripped of its vegetation by horses, cows, sheep, goats—as well as wild browsers such as elk, deer, and antelope—the unstable plateau topsoil shed precipitation northward like a rain slicker. Waters that for eons had percolated underground to vast aquifers now raced to the sea. The seven "great rivers, some as wide as forty feet" which in the old days gushed southward from deep within the Tonto escarpment, pinched down to now-and-again trickles.[47] Beneath the Rim, besieged granitic soils let go; nature's scar tissue—chaparral and cedar—invaded ruined climax grasslands and denuded swales. Semi-scientific, pioneering foresters like Fred Croxon who went afield under the direction of trailblazing ecologists such as Gifford Pinchot must have felt mighty lonely in a realm of horizon-wide autonomy.

Nature wept. In 1891 the Tonto Creek/Salt River drainage gathered up its droplets and voted in the capital city of Phoenix with a flood eleven miles wide.

... it had rained steadily for twelve days and nights. At this time the country was fully stocked, the ground had been trampled hard, much of the grass was short, or gone, gullies had started and the water came rushing down. This flood took a great deal of the agricultural land from the ranches along [Tonto Creek] and was so high that it filled the gorge where it entered the Salt River at the present site of the Roosevelt Dam and backed a house up the Salt River about a mile.[48]

Ranger Croxon reflected in 1926 that "the drought of 1904, the worst since the coming of white men to these parts, at which time it failed to rain for eighteen months, hit the range country, and cattle on the overstocked and depleted ranges died in bunches. Since that time there has never been nearly as many cattle as there were prior to that time—and there never will be. To quote Florance Packard when he finished telling me of old time conditions—'The range is not overstocked at present, it is just worn out and gone.' And such is the case. White man, the most destructive of animals, brought his herds to a virgin range only fifty short years ago, and abused it in every way he could. We see the result today. Much of it is worthless, ruined beyond recovery, some will never come back."

In the end, not even the biggest of outfits could continue unrestrained:

The youth of the old Hashknife had been stormy, wasteful, and fascinating. Its old age was barren and sad. The faults of the outfit were not exclusive to them. They were the faults of almost every big cattle company in America at that time. The present success of ranching had to be built on its past failures. The old Hashknife died appropriately with the birth of the twentieth century.[49]

Along with increasing public concern and participation in the environmental movement of the 1960s, '70s, and '80s, there has arisen a childlike belief that the natural world possesses an inherent and infinite capacity to regenerate—if only we love the outdoors enough, support nature causes, stash trash, and tune in to television wildlife programs. Well and good, but some injuries from land molestation are permanent. Period.

People see Arizona as it appears today and think it always has looked this way. Sad to say, they accept the abused, overgrazed landscapes as a natural condition. But it wasn't like this once. Way back, Arizona was a land of milk and honey when grass ... was up to your beltline. Of course, that was B.C. (Before Cows).[50]

To this day the U.S. Forest Service is belittled as The Department of

Aggravation by some whose very livelihood depends upon enlightened range management. And I should hasten to add that some of the West's more progressive and effective partners with Mother Nature today are ranchers and other forest users who are attempting to ameliorate the sins of their forebears through modern multiple use/sustained yield management of fragile natural resources.

In the century since the bloody summer of 1887, the tiny farmtown of Phoenix has become the ninth-largest city in America; the grave of Tom Graham is all but forgotten in a dusty pioneer cemetery. The once-empty crossroads where he was shot has become a major Tempe intersection surrounded by freeways, homes, businesses, and resorts. Prescott, Flagstaff, and Tucson protect smallish reminders of the Pleasant Valley feud. The Blevins house at Holbrook may hold the best hope for preservation of a historic site. Taken together, the physical remainders of the struggle are not nearly as extensive as the words and images kept safe in archives. Great promise is seen in the citing by an Act of Congress of the home of the Northern Gila County Historical Society at the old forest ranger station on Main Street in Payson, only a few steps from where Ed Tewksbury humiliated the bully, Gladden, and where Arizona Charley Meadows announced his wedding gift of unbranded calves.

At this writing, Pleasant Valley presents one of Arizona's more peaceful retreats, a bowl of pines and pastures about a hundred miles as the eagle flies northeast of Phoenix. Pleasant Valley remains a remote upland retreat for ranchers, retirees, and recreationists. For some sixty miles from Roosevelt Dam to Kohls Ranch, no vehicular bridge spans Tonto Creek, so that access is restricted to unpaved country roads either off or under the Rim, or by way of the Apache Trail. When I first interviewed Ola Young, she was completing her half-century as the valley's first postmaster. Electric power did not reach Pleasant Valley until the 1960s. Only a smattering of public facilities provide fuel, grub, and lodging—although expansion likely is on the way. Ominously, the gnawing fingers of erosion pick away at the meadowland, and a perceptive visitor senses the disappearance of streambeds deeper than a man is tall. Once-murmuring Cherry Creek jumped its banks and changed its channel in 1916, threatening the John Tewksbury cabin. Soon afterward, the new owners numbered the logs, dismantled them, skidded them less than a mile downstream, and reassembled them into what is today a ranch house owned by Frank L. Chapman Jr.

Today, in autumn, the barren, fretful west wind scurries unhindered through empty, century-old cabins. Gone are the feudists, all. Soot is scattered over the plank floor that eighteen-year-old Lizzie Rose used to scrub, and whitewash is flaking from her mantle. Coyotes harvest the gnarled apples that drop from Tom Graham's unpruned trees, and his log house sinks another fraction of an inch, year by year. The winch has collapsed into the stone-lined dug well at the Flying V. In an expensive coffin he cursed, wrestled, and packed from Globe over the Sierra Ancha wilderness, Bud Campbell sleeps in the graveyard of the Qs. On Spring Creek, the back is broken in the breezeway of the Texas Dog Run cabin where the Committee of Fifty strung up Al Rose. Calves of Future Farmers of America gambol under the frost-blackened sycamores and among the shedding walnuts once the pride of Father Tewksbury. Floppy, paperish thistlepoppies thrust from the courtyard enriched by the blood of a Blevins boy and by the blood of a Graham boy. And where the sheriff jerked the triggers of his shotgun, a stone wall witches the gravity of a hundred winters.

Square gray boxes. . .hand-forged lantern hooks driven into ponderosa beams. . .collapsed chimneys. . .rock corrals. . .gunports guarding doorless jambs and windowless sills. . .segments of irrigation flume . . .meatboards anchored in tree trunks. . .stickery unpruned patches of floribunda roses. . .cedar fence posts delineating meaningless boundaries. . .a red scar named Jumpoff where wagons descended dragging a log behind. . .spooky, sparse cemetery where headstones editorialize, "Victim of the Pleasant Valley War." Skunks patrol a blacksmith shop, crows outrage the sunny goldenweed in Jim Roberts' horse pasture, busy Abert's squirrels scurry at the threshold where Mary Ann Tewksbury hesitated in horror before going to shield her slain husband.

Now they are gone, all gone. Some of the homes once held dearer than life stand untended, unvisited, unwanted. The west wind bangs a weathered door and hums across a tilted handsplit shingle, and no one hears. Somewhere else reposes the brittle, browning scrap of newsprint from the October 15, 1887, *Prescott Courier* bearing the conclusion, too little, too late:

. . . if the quiet, level-headed citizens of Pleasant Valley and vicinity had exerted themselves to talk sense into the Graham and Tewksbury factions previous to the outbreak, differences would have been amicably settled, much suffering and many lives saved, also loss of property and money. One thing is certain, peacemakers did not appear to have been plenty in the afflicted neighborhood.[51]

Notes

Abbreviations are employed for frequently cited works. Except for periodicals, additional data are included in the bibliography.

Allison: In the mid-1930s, Robert Allison, competent history buff who would become sports editor of *The Phoenix Gazette*, sought out surviving Blevinses, notably Mrs. Evelyn Blevins, who had survived gory September 4, 1887, when Sheriff Owens decimated the Blevins bunch at Holbrook. Allison's typescript first went to the State Historian—now is generally available in many Arizona history collections.

ADBG: *Arizona's Dark and Bloody Ground*, book by Earle R. Forrest.

Barnes, AHR: "The Pleasant Valley War of 1887," by Will Croft Barnes, published in two parts, *The Arizona Historical Review*, 1931 and 1932.

Barnes papers: At the research library of the Arizona Historical Society, Tucson, the papers of Will C. Barnes fill some thirty linear feet of shelves.

Braulia Tewksbury: On June 6, 1957, the widow of Edwin Tewksbury, and their daughter, Ella, assisted in the production of a document "to be confidential for twenty-five years." This statement from a loving wife and loyal daughter names Edwin as the slayer of Tom Graham. The document was quoted in the *Globe, Arizona*, book. In various modes, the document, now in public domain, can be found at the Arizona Historical Society, Tucson.

Champion: The Arizona Champion newspaper was established at Flagstaff in 1882, and kept that name through the war, providing Flagstaff and northern Arizona insights.

Fish: In his monumental typescript, circa 1896, Joseph Fish deals in some length with the Pleasant Valley War. A copy reposes at the State Capitol, Arizona Department of Library, Archives and Public Records.

Flake: Osmer D. Flake, who as a teenager participated as cowboy and posseman in the war, in later life set down, "Some Reminiscenses of the Pleasant Valley War and Causes that Led Up to It." Edited by Arizona's distinguished jurist, Levi S. Udall, a copy is held at the State Capitol, Arizona Department of Library, Archives and Public Records.

Gazette: Founded in 1880, *The Arizona Gazette* as daily and weekly thrived during the war years.

Globe, AZ: *Globe, Arizona*, book by Clara T. Woody and Milton L. Schwartz.

Haught: Typescript copy of Samuel A. Haught's beliefs, recorded and provided to the author by Haught descendants of Payson, Arizona.

Hazelton: A copy of the excellent but unpublished typescript, "Tonto Basin's Early Settlers," by Drusilla Hazelton, is held by the Arizona Historical Society, Tucson.

Herald: *The Salt River Herald*, as Phoenix's first newspaper, was established in 1878 and was published both daily and weekly as the *Phoenix Herald* from 1879 until the turn of the century when it merged with *The Arizona Republican*. Not to be confused with the *St. Johns Herald*, cited as such where appropriate.

Horton: The Pleasant Valley War typescript by L.J. Horton, in the possession of Sharlot Hall Historical Society, Prescott, Arizona. Born January 20, 1846, he arrived in Arizona in 1883. He dictated his memoirs during the 1920s while a guest at the Arizona Pioneers Home, and died in 1928.

McClintock papers: Some ten drawers of files plus scrapbooks of James T. McClintock, pioneer Phoenix newsman, are preserved at Phoenix Public Library.

McKinney, AHR: Combining a lawman's direct action and a minstrel's subtle inference, Joe T. McKinney left classic, major articles of "Reminiscenses" in two 1932 issues of *The Arizona Historical Review*.

Prescott Courier: Established in 1882 as a daily and weekly, it continued through the Pleasant Valley War years under several name changes, always including the word Courier.

Prescott JM: Since 1864, almost from territorial beginning, a newspaper under a dozen or more variations of the name, *Miner*, was published at Prescott. During many of the Pleasant Valley War years, the name was *Prescott Journal-Miner*.

Silver Belt: *The Arizona Silver Belt* newspaper was established at Globe, Arizona, 1878.

Tewksbury examination: Court reporter William Weed's exact and indexed transcript of a Phoenix magistrate's 1892 examination of Edwin Tewksbury in the murder of Thomas H. Graham.

Voris: Typescript of 1957 interview, Robert Voris, Clara T. Woody, and Dale S. King, on deposit at the Arizona Historical Society, Tucson. The information deals largely with stories told Voris by his father, Tewksbury clansman J.W. Voris.

Woody papers: Unprocessed notes, clippings, and writings amounting to some twenty-five thousand sheets at the Arizona Historical Society, Tucson, Arizona.

Introduction

1. Horton; Woody papers; *Globe, AZ*.
2. Chroniclers of the celebrated Hatfield-McCoy feud of Kentucky-West Virginia are hard put to document as many as ten deaths (*History Illustrated Magazine*, June 1966). The same can be said of New Mexico's Lincoln County War, counting even the slaying of Billy the Kid. The Johnson County "war" of Wyoming was over almost before it started, and the infamous Earp-Clanton feud of Tombstone flamed out in a matter of seconds. Haught accepts a count of forty fatalities for Pleasant Valley.
3. Barnes, AHR.
4. John Myers Myers, *Print in a Wild Land*.

5. *Jerome Chronicle*, 1895 (no date), Jerome Historical Society.

6. John Myers Myers, *Print in a Wild Land.*

7. *Silver Belt*, March 7, 1879.

8. John Myers Myers, *Print in a Wild Land.*

9. Roscoe G. Willson, *The Arizona Republic*, March 10, 1974.

10. *The Apache Chief*, April 11, 1884.

11. Dispatch from Vietnam, S.L.A. Marshall, 1966.

12. On September 6, 1987, the Blevins family and the City of Holbrook sponsored a day-long centennial, including the staging of the gunfight by the Hashknife Sheriff's Posse.

13. Robin W. Winks, *The Historian as Detective.*

14. The author's research of the Pleasant Valley War is to be placed in the Arizona Historical Foundation, Hayden Library, Arizona State University, at the gracious request of Mrs. Kathryn K. Gammage, with appropriate selected copies to be placed in the Northern Gila County Historical Museum in Payson, as study space permits.

BOOK I
Chapter I

1. Sunrise by "local railroad time" in Tempe, Arizona, occurred at 5:41 a.m. on August 2, 1892, and according to U.S. Weather Bureau Meteorologist Louis R. Jurwitz, equated with modern Mountain Standard Time. That said, the prosecution of the assassins of Tom Graham had difficulty establishing precise scenarios for a population lacking wireless signals so useful to succeeding generations. Conversations with author, 1962.

2. J.P. Brooks, letter to author from the Arizona Pioneers Home, January 30, 1962.

3. Mrs. Mollie Cummings McTaggert of Tempe, interviews, 1962.

4. Tewksbury examination.

5. Mrs. Bettie Gregg Adams of Tempe, interviews, 1962.

6. Tewksbury examination.

7. Mrs. Emma Sears Foreman in a letter to the author of October 11, 1961, belatedly detailed what she saw of Graham's killer. About age eighteen, she observed the passage of the horseback suspect, then met her brother-in-law, J.H. Harris. "He told me to go into the house and not say a word to anyone because they might make me go to court and tell what I had seen."

8. Tewksbury examination.

9. Ibid.

10. Ibid.

11. Ibid.

12. *Gazette*, August 3, 1892.

13. *Gazette*, August 7, 1892.

14. Hazelton, unattributed newspaper clipping, probably August or September, 1892.

Chapter II

1. Braulia Tewksbury.

2. Tewksbury examination. William Passey of Mesa, in a 1962 interview, attributed substantially the same anecdote to Mesa oldtimers, including his grandfather.

3. Woody papers. "The Rhodes family say Ed rode John Rhodes's horse out of the Salt River Valley, that Sockwad was part of the relay, and Ed rode into the valley on Jack, which resembled Sockwad." Mrs. Woody considered herself a confidant of many Rhodes descendants.

4. Glenn R. Ellison, *Cowboys Under the Tonto Rim.*

5. American Quarter Horse Association, *Ride a Quarter Horse.*

6. Woody papers. Over three or more decades, Mrs. Woody was converted by her research from the belief Ed Tewksbury was uninvolved in the killing of Tom Graham.

7. Ibid.

8. Ibid.

9. Ben K. Green, *The Color of Horses.*

10. Braulia Tewksbury.

11. Hazelton.

12. Edward H. Peplow Jr., "Fort McDowell," *Phoenix Magazine*, October 1973.

13. Mary Ann Rhodes, widow of both John Tewksbury and John Rhodes, in a letter written in November 13, 1924, states that Ed killed Tom Graham to keep John Rhodes from doing it. Facsimiles of this letter are kept at the Arizona Historical Society, Tucson; the Hazelton typescript; and the author's papers.

14. In the late 1890s, Judge Howell's disregard for sheep and sheepmen frequently found ink in the Phoenix press. Author's collection.

15. The road over which Ed Tewksbury was riding had been built by soldiers from as far away as Brooklyn and Benicia, whose task it was to construct a wagon road that would connect Reno with the outside world. For almost a year, the deterined troopers pushed the wagon-wide trail across low-land fords and brush-choked plains; they clawed with pick and fingernail up granite canyons and across tilted ridges for forty miles, all the while bedeviled by the most effective warriors America has ever known—the Apache. It was assumed that the wagon road, hung on hillsides with rock walls and cedar stumps, would make Reno relatively secure. For more information, see U.S. War Department, Fort McDowell post returns, National Archives (courtesy of Fred Eldean).

16. Braulia Tewksbury.

17. Woody papers.

18. Jeremy Decker, "Drinkers of the Wind," *Continental Airlines Magazine*, April 1986.

19. Horton.

20. *Silver Belt*, June 7, 1890.

21. Woody papers. Memoir of H.H. (Bert) Pratt. Jess G. Hayes, for the February 2, 1968, edition of *The Arizona Republic*, exhibited a .38 calibre Colt's single action army pistol. Hayes said he obtained the handgun from Mrs. Nellie Cameron, who had discovered it in the effects of her deceased father, Gus Bohse. The oft-told family tale was that Bohse took the gun in trade from Ed for a horse. Tewksbury was to have told Bohse that he packed the weapon throughout the war, and that he carried it the day Tom Graham was shot. The seven notches on the black bone [rubber?] grips, Tewksbury said, were for seven men he killed during the war. Who? "My father said. . .he never asked," confided Mrs. Cameron.

Chapter III

1. *Elliott's History of Arizona, 1884*. This standard reference was reissued in a splendid Northland Press facsimile edition in 1964.

2. Some late-eighteenth century Arizonans must have wondered about the bedrock stability of their new world. On May 3, 1887, a monster earthquake (now rated 7.2 on the Richter Scale) rumbled through northern Mexico, killing fifty-one, "rocked [Phoenix] like a cradle," opened geysers of mud and steam, knocked down people and livestock, triggered landslides which ignited forest fires, stopped clocks, and left a fault scar thirty-one miles long. In time since, the 1887 tembler proved to be Arizona's biggest—so far! See *The Arizona Republic*, May 3, 1987.

3. Claude Cline, in a series of letters to author, 1962.

4. John G. Burke, *An Apache Campaign.*

5. Ibid.

6. Will C. Barnes, *Arizona Place Names.*

7. U.S. Department of the Army, "Trail of an Indian Scout from Ft. McDowell, A.T.," September 27 to October 6, 1866," National Archives, courtesy Dr. Ben Sacks. This would not be Arizona's first or last garbled placename. "Coanville," in honor of the Coan family, was misconstrued by postal authorities as "Cornville," and Cornville it is.

8. U.S. Department of the Army, reports of Brigadier General Nelson A. Miles.

9. Dan Thrapp, *The Conquest of Apacheria; Globe, AZ*; Clara T. Woody, "Globe's Colorful Pioneer Days," *The Arizona Record* newspaper, April 26, and May 3 and 24, 1956.

10. Tewksbury correspondence file, Sharlot Hall Historical Society; Woody papers. A Tewksbury claim amounting to several thousand dollars dragged on for decades, became an item in the James D. Tewksbury estate, and eventually was settled in favor of the family.

11. Charley Meadows, in an interview in the (Yuma) *Arizona Sentinel*, December 13, 1931.

12. Thomas E. Way, *Ten Years on the Trail of the Redskins*.

13. The site of Fort McDonald eventually became a prime neighborhood of homes overlooking the Payson golf course. Stone fortifications remain.

14. Horton.

15. Hazelton.

16. James E. Cook, "Battle of Big Dry Wash," in three parts, *The Arizona Republic*, July 12, 14 and 16, 1987.

17. Will C. Barnes, *Arizona Historical Review*, January 1930.

18. The chronology of settlement of Tonto Basin and surroundings fueled verbal family feuds. As time passed, memories of some seniors betrayed them, resulting in contradiction and confusion of dates and happenings. By dint of diligent sleuthing, a dozen family histories of the rim country were assembled by Drusilla Hazelton, Ira Murphy, Frank V. Gillette, Jayne Peace, Clara Woody (see *Globe, AZ*), Fred Croxon, L.J. Horton, and a legion of writers who reported from annual pioneers' reunions such as those sponsored by the towns of Pine, Snowflake, and Payson, and by *The Arizona Republic* at Phoenix.

19. "Colonel W.R. Colcord of Hutcheson, Kansas, arrived in Flagstaff on Wednesday with three carloads of blooded cattle, consisting of Herefords, Shorthorns and Polled Angus, as fine a lot of cattle as has ever been brought to this territory. . . ." *Flagstaff Champion*, July 1, 1886. The Colcords originally were from Louisiana, where William Clay was born January 14, 1867. From Flagstaff, the Colcords drove stock to an area later named Colcord Mountain. The colonel returned to Kansas, leaving nineteen-year-old Bill in charge, with brother Harvey, sixteen, making a hand. W.C. Colcord died in Gila General Hospital on May 16, 1961.

20. *The Arizona Republic*, April 15, 1936.

21. *Silver Belt*, August 16, 1890.

22. Fred Eldean, conversations with author, 1986.

23. Barnes papers.

24. Fifty years later, the next sunset migration would fashion a familiar motto: "No good Okie ever made it to California in just one trip!"

25. Hazelton.

26. Braulia Tewksbury.

27. Barnes, AHR.

28. Horton.

29. James Dunning Tewksbury folder, Sharlot Hall Historical Society, Prescott.

30. Horton.

31. Tewksbury examination.

32. Woody papers.

33. Marriage license, Sacks Collection, Arizona Historical Foundation, Arizona State University, Tempe.

34. Woody papers; Voris; a David Shultes is listed as justice of the peace at Sunflower, 1877-1878.

35. *Territorial Expositor*, November 7, 1879.

36. Mrs. Frank Chapman, interview at Young, Arizona, 1963. The author succeeded in propagating cuttings from Lydia's roses in 1987.

37. Hazelton.

38. Bertha Tewksbury Acton, interview with the author, Phoenix, Arizona, 1962.

39. G.W. Shute, *Arizona Cattlelog*, April 1956.

40. Mary Ann Rhodes, in a letter to her son, November 13, 1924.

Chapter IV

1. Woody papers.

2. Frank Chapman interviews at Young, Arizona, 1962, 1987. The John Tewksbury cabin, which he came to own, was pulled down and reassembled when Cherry Creek flooded. Frank said cowboys stood on the banks, roped mature peach trees floating by, replanted them, and they continued to thrive in 1987.

3. Gilleland obituary, *The Arizona Republic*, January 1, 1936.

4. Proceedings, justice court, Prescott, February 1883.

5. Woody papers.

6. Proceedings, justice court, Prescott, February 1883.

7. Both the *Herald* and *Gazette* in Phoenix extensively covered the Gilleland shooting through January 1883.

8. Proceedings, justice court, Prescott, February 1883.

9. Woody papers.

Chapter V

1. *Elliott's History of Arizona Territory, 1884.*

2. Prescott's Whiskey Row was first strung along Granite Creek, but the "sight of water made the customers sick," so the sinful strip was moved to Montezuma Street. In the summer of 1884, a woman was kicked to death in the Palace Saloon.

3. U.S. census records.

4. Estella Converse Hill, interviews with author, 1962.

5. Boone County *Democrat* (Iowa), September 3, 1897.

6. Hill, loc. cit.

7. The term "maverick," at first meaning an unbranded calf and later including wayward humans, originated with the rustling of the Texas calves of Samuel A. Maverick. His yearlings were considered "loose ten-dollar bills on the hoof."

8. Oren Arnold and John P. Hale, *Hot Irons*.

9. Books of marks and brands, recorder's office, Yavapai County, Prescott.

10. Bob Carlock, 1987 owner of the Hashknife brand, in conversations with the author, said he doubts foul play; the pioneer county recorder merely drew the brand upside down in error.

11. Yavapai County, Book II, marks and brands.

12. Ibid.

13. William E. Simpson, letters to author, 1963.

14. Roscoe G. Willson, *The Arizona Republic*, April 5, 1964.

15. Fred Eldean, conversations with the author, 1986.

16. Horton; Ed Delph, conversations with the author, 1987.

17. Horton.

Chapter VI

1. Fish.

2. Flake. "This was not a sheep and cattle war, the trouble started years before Mr. Jacobs brought the Daggs sheep into [Pleasant] Valley. James Stinson moved about six hundred head of cattle, from the vicinity of Snowflake, late in the year 1881. He received four hundred fifty head of cattle from my father, W.J. Flake, in three payments of a hundred fifty each year, 1878, 1879, and 1880, and moved them with the increase to Pleasant Valley. [The Grahams] went to Snowflake where they bought two hundred heifers from W.J. Flake. . . ."

Osmer Flake in his memoir contends at length that on their way home, the Grahams siezed the opportunity to rustle more Flake beeves.

3. McClintock papers.

4. ADBG.

5. Candace Kant, *Zane Grey's Arizona.*

6. Horton.

7. Voris.

8. Woody papers.

9. William J. Flake, family publication. Apparently James Stinson and W.J. Flake, despite differing religious and economic motivations, forged trust and friendship on no more than handshake deals. When Flake made his final livestock delivery, he demanded Stinson's cherished saddle mule to boot. Stinson begged off, and offered fortunes in cattle to keep the mule. Flake said no, and took the mule, then delivered a speech praising Stinson, ending ". . . for a long time I have wondered what I could give you to show my appreciation for the many things you have done for my people, and I am now glad to present the mule to you, one of the squarest men I have ever met. . . ." Flake, founder of seven towns, died in 1932, leaving three hundred fifty descendants (*Arizona Republic*, August 11, 1932.)

10. Subpoenas were issued for William Birch [Burch?], Isaac Louthian, Edward Cole, James Johnson, Sam Houston, William Houston, Andrew Houston, George Newton, John Bauer, Sam Hill, Andrew Pringle, Tom Cline, Jim Watson, J.F. Montgomery, Joseph Watts, John Meadows, Albert Rose, Manuel Soto, Edward Rose, O.C. Felton, Jim Watkins, Christian Jerkison—all apparently for the defense.

11. The Prescott truce was confirmed by Lester (Budge) Ruffner, whose pioneer forebear, Sheriff George Ruffner, said the contesting parties camped peacefully together on the grounds of the O K Corral on West Gurley Street, in modern times the site of an automobile agency.

12. Yavapai court records list jurors for Indictment No. 1 as L.W. Vaughn, B.H. Smith, H.M. Hughes, G.M. Dallas, J.W. Harlow, J.L. Taylor, H.J. Wurzburg, C.J. Dyer, W.F. Holden, J.B. Ellmore, and D. Levy.

13. Ibid. Trial jurors were A. Zimmerman, J.F. Dillon, Wash French, G.A. Hammond, J.B. Ellmore, E. Puntney, Howard Nash, Sam Bright, O.W. Stull, A.S. Haskell, E.B. Taylor, and A.G. Dillon.

14. Ibid. Jurors who heard these instructions were H.M. Hughes, Chas. Allen, G.M. Dallas, J.W. Harlow, J.W. Hitt, E. Poe, J.M. Wilson, A.P. Williams, L.W. Vaughn, Ney Strickland, John Ricketts, and Norman Marlow.

15. Judge Sumner Howard had taken his oath May 20, 1884. Woody papers make much of the judge's sensational outburst from the bench. Mention is given in *The Phoenix Gazette*, "Forty Years Ago," July 15, 1924, an item likely borrowed from the *Prescott Miner*. Pertinent original examples of this paper are missing from the files at the Arizona Department of Library, Archives and Public Records.

16. *Prescott JM*, July 25, 1884.

17. *Silver Belt*, July 26, 1884.

18. *Herald*, July 28, 1884.

19. *Herald*, August 1, 1884.

20. *Gazette*, August 2, 1884.

21. *Gazette*, August 4, 1884.

22. *Herald*, August 9, 1884.

23. *Herald*, September 4, 1884.

24. Yavapai court records, August–September, 1884.

25. Horton; Voris.

26. Mrs. Ellen B. Burrows of Mesa, Arizona, in 1961, 1962 letters to author: Blassingame

was her father, born August 18, 1862, in Palo Pinto County, west of Fort Worth, Texas. He married Oasis A. Greer in St. Johns in 1884. Ellen was their only child. Livestockman in his own right, Blassingame often hired out as undercover agent. In that capacity he was sent to Tonto Basin to investigate, and "he returned to St. Johns with two suspects."

27. Arizona's awe-inspiring summertime skies both entertained and astounded new arrivals, especially easterners. An Arizona day could dawn mild as milk. By noon a puff of vapor as big as a man's hand might boil seven miles tall. Abruptly an arid climate would surrender to psychedelic flashes, rolling bombinations, drenching downpours. Cowboy James G. Bell, driving the first big herd of Texas beeves to California in 1853, described a lighting bolt: "Made a report like the explosion of a thousand cannon." Killed a bunch of cows, too. Electricity overtook Will C. Barnes and his men in the 1880s as they drove cattle through Pleasant Valley—"lightning dancing off the tips of the longhorns, when it flashed they'd look up and bat their eyes." The *Herald* of a summer day in 1887 reported "Lightning in a frolicsome mood entered the Globe telegraph office. . . ." Computers and satellites a century later would confirm what oldtimers suspected: Arizona attracts lightning—as many as 217,000 strikes statewide in August, with as many as twenty-two thousand in one day, according to the Bureau of Land Management.

28. Apache County court records.

29. Flake.

30. The disappearance over time of county records from the St. Johns courthouse has frustrated many an investigator into the Pleasant Valley War. Some history is not lost; it is stolen.

31. Flake.

Chapter VII

1. *Gazette,* February 27, 1987.
2. *Champion,* July 4, 1884.
3. *Champion,* June 18, 1885.
4. Woody papers.
5. Jo Johnson, "The Hashknife Outfit," *Arizona Highways Magazine,* June 1956.
6. ADBG.
7. Roscoe G. Willson, *Pioneer Cattlemen of Arizona.* From a hell-for-leather beginning, Hugo A. (Hook) Larson attained later-life respectability. He was a shadowy figure in the war. Born in Denmark in 1859, he grew up in Utah, and surfaced in Arizona in the '80s as a cowboy, freighter, and railroader. Willson: "In 1887 he was a member of the sheriff's [Owens's?] posse that tried to break up the Graham-Tewksbury feud. . .and was with the party that found the bodies of Stott, Scott, and Wilson who had been hanged as horsethieves. It was said he was the only one in the party who would approach and cut down the bodies."
8. Johnson, loc. sit.
9. Flake.
10. Johnson, loc. sit.
11. Blevins family research is hampered by the loss of most records in the blaze that destroyed the Llano County (Texas) courthouse. Blevins descendants, notably, Mrs. Ruth Blevins Simpson, have overcome this difficulty in remarkable detail, which they have generously opened to the public.
12. ADBG.
13. Ibid.
14. Allison.
15. W.J. Flake, family history; also see Annie Johnson, et al, *Charles Edmund Richardson;* Woody papers.

16. Woody papers.
17. Annie Johnson, loc. sit. Today, Canyon Creek is one of Arizona's premier dry fly trout streams.
18. Ibid.
19. Horton; Voris; Haught; Woody papers; *Globe, AZ*
20. Texas State Archives.
21. Allison. In his notes, he indicates that in 1884, the Graham and Tewksbury boys established a ranch in Chino Valley not far from Prescott for the express purpose of holding stock rustled in partnership. Allison in his typescript dates the arrival of Martin and Mary, four sons and *two* daughters, as November 10, 1866. Modern Blevinses believe one daughter, Delila, remained in Texas. The youngest daughter was Artimesia—and spellings since have included Messa, Missy, Messy, Macia, and Mecia.

BOOK II
Chapter I
1. Woody papers; ADBG.
2. Haught. The typescript contains two comments about sheep: "There was never a sheep in Pleasant Valley until just before the war. The Hashknives were at war with the sheepmen, and so from them and from [Billy?] Wilson's horsethieves, the Grahams were able to get most of their warriors." And, "Cause of Jim Houck coming into the war, he was sitting on his horse herding sheep in the Mogollon Mountains when two men came and shot his horse out from under him. Houck fell off backwards. . .and shot one of the men through the body. This man came to Marsh Creek and recovered. Afterwards he went back to Texas."
3. Edward Norris Wentworth, *America's Sheep Trails.*
4. Lieutenant Ives did not bring sheep, and had to eat his mules. Army surveyors who followed Ives brought sheep.
5. Bert Haskett, *Arizona Historical Review*, October 1935 and July 1936.
6. A large body of written work about the Arizona sheep industry exists. Aside from the superlative works of Bert Haskett, worthy of attention are those of Joan Baéza, Wink Blair, Platt Cline, Francis Raymond Line, and Sue Peterson.
7. Line, op. cit., quoting J.B. Priestly.
8. Dwight Watkins, *Arizona Highways Magazine*, October 1949.
9. P.P. Daggs, in response to an invitation to send his memoirs to the Arizona [Pioneers] Historical Society, letter, May 19, 1926.
10. Miss Jennie Daggs of Tempe, interviews and correspondence with author, 1962.
11. *Coconino Sun*, October 10, 1866.
12. Daggs, op. cit.; further, an even earlier relationship between the Tewksburys and the Daggses has been documented by attorney Richard E. Erwin of Carpinteria, California. Erwin maintains that on May 29, 1883, his great-grandfather, Joseph Fish, while tending store at Woodruff, was robbed by two armed men he later identified as Jim Tewksbury and George Blaine. The suspects were indicted by an Apache County grand jury on February 8, 1884, and a bond for $3,500 was posted by W. A. Daggs and Andrew Pringle on July 5, 1884. On the same day, John Tewksbury's Cherry Creek ranch was signed over as collateral; in the event of forfeiture, P. P. Daggs would get the ranch. This happened on August 6, when Tewksbury and Blaine failed to appear; in the end, they were cleared because Fish, in turn, failed to appear for their trial—Fish, a polygamist, had legal troubles of his own.
13. Jennie Daggs, letter to Clara T. Woody, May 31, 1960, Woody papers.
14. Woody papers
15. Haskett, op. cit.

16. Ibid.

17. William McLeod Raine, *Famous Sheriffs and Western Outlaws*; see also, Fish; Woody papers; and *Champion*, July 17, 1886.

18. Barnes, AHR.

19. Horton.

20. Barnes, AHR.

21. *Silver Belt*, February 12, 1887.

22. *Hoof and Horn*, February 10, 1887. Aside from coverage by W.O. O'Neill's influential Prescott weekly, the headless shepherd atrocity was circulated by a number of southwestern journals including *The Phoenix Gazette* and *Prescott Courier*.

Chapter II

1. Mrs. Ruth Blevins Simpson of Apache Junction and Show Low (both Arizona) kindly supplied the author with copies of the letters reproduced in this chapter.

2. Horton.

3. *Globe, AZ*; Woody papers.

4. Philip J. Rasch, "Farewell to the Clantons" typescript, Arizona Historical Society, Tucson.

5. *Gazette*, September 22, 1887.

6. *Herald*, September 22, 1887.

7. Woody papers.

8. Frederick Russell Burnham, *Scouting on Two Continents*. Clara Woody apparently frowned upon Major Burnham's fullblown autobiographical prose; in fact, she left in her papers her scrawl across this passage, "This is what drugs do to anyone using them."

9. Simpson, op. cit.

10. Mrs. Victoria Fredonia Gilliland, age eighty-nine, in a Phoenix interview, told the author that her father, name of Shults, took Blevins land in Texas in exchange for a band of fine horses. These were the horses Mart was seeking in Arizona when he disappeared. Incidentally, Mrs. Gilliland said that as an eleven-year-old, she met Sam Bass in Texas. The famous outlaw was enough of a dentist to be able to pull a painful tooth. He clamped her offending cuspid in a bullet mold, yanked, and held her when she cried.

11. Allison; Haught asserted: "When Old Man Blevins was missing, Tom Graham hired six men from the Hashknives to kill the Tewksburys. He agreed to give them a thousand dollars apiece. Old Man Ketcham...sent a runner [to] the Middleton ranch to warn them." More Haught: "Old Man Blevins was killed in the north corner of the Flying V horse pasture." In her papers, Woody states, "In the Frank Chapman firearms collection is a .44 calibre Model 1873 Winchester carbine, SN 570967B. Found in Valentine Canyon. Believed to be Old Man Blevins's rifle. It was cocked, unfired cartridge in chamber. Wood was weatherworn, had lain hidden in underbrush. A burnover had scarred the wood, and it was declared by men who should have known that it was the Blevins rifle. A few bones were found nearby. Forest men building a trail through the brush found it."

12. Barnes; Fish; ADBG; *Globe, AZ*; Woody papers, et al. Roberta Flake Clayton, whose typescript duplicate, "Pleasant Valley War," is in the author's collection, stated that one of the Hashknife riders was "Thomas Covington, whose real name was Eugene Clark."

13. *St. Johns Herald*, August 18, 1887. "It appears they put their liberty to use and enjoyed it but a short time."

14. Barnes, AHR.

15. Flake.

16. ADBG; Barnes, AHR: "I recall we took up a collection around the Hashknife wagon on the roundup to send his family back to Texas after he was killed."

17. Voris.

18. Fish.

19. Barnes, AHR.
20. Ibid.
21. Woody papers; Globe, AZ; Hazelton.
22. Mary Ann (Crigger Tewksbury) Rhodes, letter to her son, November 13, 1924, from copy at Arizona Historical Society, Tucson.
23. *Champion*, August 16, 1887.
24. Proceedings, Payson justice court.
25. Haught: "Daggs Brothers gave the Tewksburys Winchester rifles and a thousand rounds of ammunition and said they would back them with money, but after getting the Tewksburys in it, they never put up anything else."
26. Hazelton.
27. Voris.
28. Frank C. Barnes, *Cartridges of the World*.
29. ADBG; Voris; Woody papers; et al. Jess G. Hayes, in his biography of John Wentworth, states, "A number [of combatants] jumped into the fight just for the thrill, while others held personal animosities. Neither were all cattlemen on the side of the Grahams, nor were all parties' interest in sheep on the side of the Tewksburys. This was a complex, bloody affair." The Morris Belnap mentioned by the Hashknife party maintained a low profile, but Dan Williamson flatly stated that Belnap was a sidekick of Ed Tewksbury, indeed, his "right-hand man." See the *Silver Belt*, August 27, 1928. Samuel A. Haught says simply, "Cause of Jim Roberts coming to Pleasant Valley, Grahams stole his horses."
30. ADBG.
31. McClintock papers.
32. Woody papers.
33. Barnes, AHR.
34. Woody papers.
35. William R. Ridgway, *The Arizona Republic*, August 28, 1953.
36. Barnes, AHR.

Chapter III
1. Prescott JM, August 16, 1887. Also Barnes AHR: "There is no signature to this but it probably was sent by Frank Wattron, justice of the peace at Holbrook. It sounds like him, anyhow."
2. ADBG.
3. Ruth Blevins Simpson told the author that the Blevins family assumed Charley burned the place to avenge his brother, Hamp. Jess G. Hayes, biographer of John Wentworth, was another who was willing to accept that "a verdict of 'not guilty' in a case of arson was worth sixty dollars in gold. Wentworth had no alternative but to pay this amount (a connivance that he reported at least fifty years later, in his memoirs)."
4. ADBG.
5. Proceedings of Payson precinct court.
6. Ibid.
7. McKinney, AHR.
8. Barnes, AHR; also, *The Prescott Courier* of September 3, 1887, says there were six Flagstaff possemen, but does not name them.
9. ADBG. "Information was supplied from court records furnished by Mr. F.C. Bauer, of Prescott, Arizona."
10. *Prescott JM*, September 2, 1887.
11. *Herald*, August 24, 1887.
12. *Silver Belt*, September 3, 1887.
13. *Prescott Courier*, September 3, 1887.
14. Barnes, AHR.

15. *Champion*, September 3, 1887.
16. ADBG. Forrest quotes a letter from John W. Weatherford, posseman.
17. *Gazette*, August 28, 1887.
18. *Gazette*, August 31, 1887.
19. ADBG; Horton; Barnes, AHR; McKinney quoting Houck. Houck's pretense of at first mistaking Billy for John Graham doesn't wash. Billy was big and fleshy like his brother Tom, Tom's daughter told the author; John was smallish. And many in the ranks of the feud were very well acquainted. The September 30, 1886, *Silver Belt* lists delegates to a Winslow political convention: Glenn Reynolds, Will C. Barnes, A.F. Banta, William (Billy) Graham, James Houck, and A.J. Cooper.
20. Martha Houck Lee, letter to the editor, *The Arizona Republic*, n.d., ca. 1962.
21. U.S. Army pension records, in possession of State Historian, Arizona Capitol.
22. Frances C. Carlson, "James D. Houck . . .," *The Journal of Arizona History*, September 1960.
23. *Prescott JM*, April 9, 1880. The outcome of this case could not be determined by the author.
24. Martha Houck, typescript dated March 1916, Arizona Historical Foundation.
25. McClintock papers.
26. *Apache Chief* clipping, n.d., possessed by Estella Converse Hill. She guessed the time of publication to be about 1885-1887. Houck was active in the Springerville area at this time as a sheep, cattle, and horse dealer.
27. Carlson, op. cit. Houck was a member of the "Thieving Thirteenth."
28. Houck often was unseen, but he left tracks: he was expected at the Middleton cabin; he frequently alleged he had a pocketful of warrants for somebody or other; he claimed outright leadership of the Tewksbury clan in the Martha Houck typescript, 1916, Arizona Historical Foundation.
29. Estella Converse Hill, interviews with author, 1962.
30. Woody papers. "Seems Houck told this to a lot of people when he was drinking."
31. ADBG. William MacLeod Raine is quoted.
32. *St. Johns Herald*, September 29, 1887.
33. Barnes, AHJ.
34. *Herald*, August 29, 1887, perhaps via telegraph from the operator at Camp Verde, alerted by courier.
35. ADBG. Posseman Weatherford to Forrest.
36. Woody papers; *Globe, AZ*.
37. Mrs. Bertha Tewksbury Acton, conversations with author, 1962. Another list of alleged occupants would have filled that tiny cabin to the rafters—Bill Colcord was quoted by Roscoe G. Willson in *The Arizona Republic*, March 18, 1951, that inside were Ed, Jim, and John Tewksbury, father James and stepmother Lydia, John's wife Mary Ann, some children, Joe Boyer, Jim Roberts, and "possibly one or two others." Both Voris and Woody accepted that a Mrs. Crouch, schoolteacher, was an overnight guest.
38. Voris; Woody papers. From that summer on, the tributary went by the name "Graveyard Canyon."
39. Ibid.
40. Ibid.
41. McKinney, AHR.
42. Woody papers.
43. Mrs. Mary Ann Rhodes, letter to son, November 13, 1924, Arizona Historical Society.
44. Voris; Woody papers.
45. Barnes, AHR.
46. ADBG.

47. McKinney, AHR, quoting Mrs. John Tewksbury.

48. Estella Converse Hill, interviews with author, 1962.

49. Hazelton.

50. Horton, his letter from Charley Meadows, June 15, 1922.

51. Hazelton, as related in 1929 by Walter Tewksbury to Mrs. Buckner M. (Nora) McKinney.

52. ADBG.

53. Mrs. Rhodes, letter to son, op. cit.

54. McKinney, AHR.

Chapter IV

1. Missouri-born February 5, 1861, Wattron hit Holbrook with a five-dollar bill and a deck of cards. An early backer was James D. Houck. Wattron eventually melded his knowledge of drugs and skill as a politician to lead Navajo County as businessman and sheriff. He brought indelible, international notoriety to Holbrook in the final weeks of the nineteenth century with his flippant "wierd invitation" to his legal hanging of George Smalley, murderer. Wattron died of an overdose of laudanum in 1905.

2. Indeed, there would not be a church in Holbrook until 1913, then only thanks to the efforts of Mr. and Mrs. Sidney Sapp. She nagged her attorney husband into a building campaign. Local writer Jo Jeffers sketched Holbrook as "no place for the faint of heart. It consisted of a dozen or so frame shacks, most of them along Main Street, which ran between the river and the railroad tracks. There were about two hundred fifty residents, a Chinese restaurant run by Louey Ghuey, a livery stable, the Adamson-Burbage store, Nathan Barth's store, and five or six saloons including the euphoric Bucket of Blood, rendezvous of cowboys, sheepherders, railroaders, Indian traders, fancy ladies, professional gamblers and other socially elite of the area."

3. *St. Johns Herald*, September 1, 1887.

4. Roberta Flake Clayton, *Life of J.A. Hunt.*

5. Several Holbrook news stories quote Wattron to this effect.

6. Leland Shelley, interviews with author, 1960.

7. *Champion*, September 10, 1887.

8. Barnes, AHR. His *Apaches and Longhorns*, written many decades afterward, has been severely criticized in that he used records to refresh or embellish his memory. Posterity may wonder why Barnes, in the face of mountainous evidence to the contrary, vehemently maintained throughout his life that Owens's action had "absolutely nothing" to do with the Pleasant Valley War.

9. Will Croft Barnes, *Apaches and Longhorns*. Also, Flake. Owens habitually made the ranch home of James M. Flake his safe house. Owens told James Flake on or about September 1 that one or two of his bondsmen had withdrawn support, and other bondsmen had threatened the same. This would have cost Owens his job.

10. Jo Johnson, "Commodore Perry Owens," *Arizona Highways Magazine*, October 1960. Also see ADBG; Woody papers.

11. Johnson, ibid.

12. Ibid.

13. Ibid.

14. Ibid.

15. *St. Johns Herald*, October 21, 1886.

16. Flake.

17. Barnes, *Apaches and Longhorns*.

18. Roscoe G. Willson, *The Arizona Republic*, June 17, 1961.

19. Clayton, op. cit.

20. Inquest proceedings, Holbrook precinct court.

21. A Blevins in-law, Jim Simpson, in 1987 took these measurements for the creation of a scale model, donated to the City of Holbrook for exhibit at the Blevins house.

22. The name is variously spelled Mode, Mose, and Moze. The choice here is the one used at his inquest. Haught: "Mode Roberts had the Houston Basin full of stolen horses. Sheriff Mulvenon went in there but Roberts was foxy and had already gotten them out."

23. Woody papers. She interviewed William C. Colcord, quoted: "Mrs. Amanda Gladden was a housekeeper at the Blevins ranch." She may have been a relative or widow of the bully named Gladden, who was run out of Payson by Ed Tewksbury.

24. ADBG.

25. Allison.

26. *Apache Critic*, September 10, 1887.

27. Inquest, op. cit.

28. Allison. In 1962, he told the author, "The account of the killings in Holbrook is verbatim as Mrs. John (Evelyn) gave it to me. . . ." Allison in his manusript: "The grand jury found an indictment against Andy Cooper, but it was weak and defective, and found more for a legal score than for any other purpose. Owens was advised not to make an arrest on it, since it was not strong enough to warrant legal action. Thus it remains unexplained why Commodore Owens was in Holbrook, avowedly looking for Andy Cooper. . . .It would seem that if Owens's only interest had been in acting within the limits of the law, things would have gone differently that day." Allison's conclusion would not have been tolerated in 1887. Holbrook townsman Frank Reed tried to raise a lynching of Owens, and according to widely printed news items, he was told "to cheese his racket." Reed shut up.

29. Anybody who has been in combat may appreciate that when young Houston was blooded by a bullet grazing his shoulder, survival as much as revenge could have propelled him out the door into the path of the next slug, this one fatal.

30. Hazelton.

31. *St. Johns Herald*, September 9, 1887.

32. *Coconino Sun*, September 10, 1887.

33. *Apache Critic*, September 10, 1887.

Chapter V

1. Odie B. Faulk, *Land of Many Frontiers*.

2. *Silver Belt*, n.d., ca. early September 1887; McClintock papers.

3. *Gazette*, September 25, 1887.

4. Woody papers.

5. *Gazette*, August 13, 1887.

6. *Silver Belt*, August 27, 1887.

7. *Prescott JM*, September 7, 1887.

8. *Herald*, September 8, 1887

9. *Prescott JM*, September 9, 1877. Samuel A. Haught's reflection: "The Grahams were doomed from the start. The governor of the territory said, 'Kill them, and no one will be hurt for it.' W.A. Clark of Jerome, who was worth forty million dollars, said, 'Kill them [meaning the Grahams]. They will soon be robbing trains.' When the war was over Clark gave [Jim] Roberts a good job as a reward."

10. Faulk, op. cit.

11. *Herald*, July 23, 1887.

12. Mulvenon biography, typescript, Sharlot Hall Historical Society, Prescott.

13. *Prescott Courier*, July 7, 1906.

14. *Prescott JM*, September 9, 1887. Forrest, Woody, and others have this name as "Bristow," but the newspapers of this date clearly spell it "Burton."

15. *Herald,* September 14, 1887.
16. Hazelton.
17. Woody papers. She quotes Samuel A. Haught.
18. Frederick Russell Burnham, *Scouting on Two Continents.*
19. Voris.
20. Charley Duchet, dying declaration transcribed by secretary of Dr. H.A. Hughes, March 1925. For many early decades of the twentieth century, this document was kept from the public by the State Historian. The why of it escapes the author.
21. *Kansas City Star,* March 25, 1925.
22. Voris.
23. Hazelton.
24. ADBG.
25. Tom Horn, *Life of Tom Horn.*
26. Barnes, AHR. In ADBG, Forrest speculates that Mrs. Elliot's next husband may have been W.H. Bishop, veteran Tewksbury loyalist.
27. Voris.
28. Ibid.
29. Barnes, AHR. Charles Perkins told Barnes that Joe Ellenwood was riding with Billy Graham the day Billy was shot, and he helped the lad home.
30. Woody papers.
31. Voris.
32. Woody papers.
33. Barnes, AHR.
34. Globe, AZ.
35. Barnes, AHR. Also, in a letter to the Arizona [Pioneers] Historical Society January 16, 1929, Joe T. McKinney stated, "[Jim] Roberts showed me where Tewksbury and Jacobs were killed. . . .He also showed me the battleground where Middleton was killed. Middleton was with the Grahams. Roberts killed him, or rather, as he said, 'shot him and let him squall himself to death.' "
36. Woody papers; *Silver Belt,* January 14, 1887.
37. U.S. Weather Bureau records.
38. Barnes, AHR, "When Mulvenon came through the valley on his second trip he coaxed Roberts to join his posse, which he did."; Flake; Woody papers; *Globe, AZ; Prescott JM,* September 9, 1887; and *Silver Belt,* October 1, 1887, all touch upon the makeup of the posse. Haught says, "Mulvenon came from Prescott by way of Tunnel Creek under the Rim. He passed S.A. Haught's house, and only had six men with him. There never was a man from Payson who took part in the war." On this last point, the record seems to dispute Jim Sam Haught.
39. Voris.
40. Barnes, AHR.

BOOK III
Chapter I
1. Clues to Al Rose's life exist on his headstone and footstone, Young Cemetery, the Arizona Great Register, 1884, and a feature story by Frank A. Littlefield, *The Arizona Republic,* November 29, 1964; also, Woody papers.
2. Harvey Samuel, conversations with author, mid-1950s. A highway patrolman, Harvey was a grandson of Liz Rose and Robert Samuel.
3. Strawberry precinct court records, Woody papers, Horton—all vibrate with the feistiness of Al Rose. Haught: "Al Rose was the agitator who got the Grahams into all this trouble."

4. Voris.

5. Sidney Kartus, "Helen Duette Ellison," *Arizona Historical Review*, July 1931.

6. Ellison collection, Arizona Historical Society, Tucson.

7. Voris.

8. No verification came to the author that J.W. Ellison ever held the rank of Confederate colonel.

9. Glenn Ellison, conversations and letters, 1963.

10. Voris.

11. Ibid; Roscoe G. Willson, *Pioneer Cattlemen of Arizona.*

12. Samuel, op. cit.

13. Ellison collection, Phoenix newspaper clipping, n.d., Arizona Historical Society, Tucson.

14. Fred W. Croxon, "History of Grazing on the Tonto National Forest."

15. Voris.

16. Woody papers.

17. Kartus, op. cit.

18. Glenn Ellison, in a handwritten photo caption, Ellison Collection, Arizona Historical Society, Tucson.

19. Bob Housholder, *The Grizzly Bear in Arizona.*

20. Croxon, op. cit.

21. In time, J.W. Ellison would hold office as supervisor in both Yavapai and Gila counties.

22. Mrs. Rose Maret, conversations with author, 1987. The Ellison ranches were noted for hospitality—three thousand overnight "stayers" per year. Ellison built for security: stout rock forts with gun slots, masonry walls, and earthen roofs. There was reason. During the mid-1880s, renegade Apaches were tying down half the combat troops of the U.S. Army. A typical raid: a band of eleven braves went on the warpath in November 1885. In a month they traveled a thousand, two hundred miles, stole and wore out two hundred fifty horses, slaughtered thirty-eight settlers, and escaped into Mexico. This was in a region patrolled by eighty-three companies of American troops.

23. Samuel Graham's funeral eulogy, *Boone County Democrat* (Iowa), September 3, 1897.

24. *Boone County Standard* (Iowa), October 1, 1887.

25. *Boone County Democrat* (Iowa), October 5, 1887.

26. *Boone County Democrat*, October 12, 1887.

27. *The Daily Arizonan*, Phoenix, October 6, 1887. This piece in its entirety was reprinted in the *Boone County Democrat.*

28. Exactly $3,168.78 "for his services, expenses and fees in Pleasant Valley for these two trips," according to Barnes, AHR.

29. *Silver Belt*, October 15, 1887.

30. *Herald*, November 3, 1887.

31. *Globe, AZ*; Woody papers; Hazelton

32. *St. Johns Herald*, October 20, 1887.

33. James T. McClintock adorned the margins of a Horton manuscript. draft with critical notes concerned largely with dates.

34. *Tombstone Epitaph*, November 5, 1887.

35. Estella Converse Hill shared her copy of this letter with the author during conversations in 1962.

36. Ibid.

37. Hazelton.

38. *Silver Belt*, May 19, 1888.

39. Voris.

40. Woody papers. Reference is made to an undated letter from Norman Rose to Jess G. Hayes.

41. ADBG.
42. *Prescott Courier,* November 7, 1887.
43. Fish.
44. McKinney.
45. Voris. Statements of Bill Voris are rejected by some students of the war. Bob Carlock's one word characterization: "Windbag."
46. Ibid.
47. *Silver Belt,* June 1, 1889.
48. Not even John Black Blevins, who had fired point-blank at Sheriff Owens, went to prison. He was given a full pardon by Governor Zulick and set free. Arizona Department of Library, Archives and Public Records.
49. *Globe, AZ.*
50. Helen Duette Ellison died April 18, 1931; J.W. Ellison, January 21, 1934.
51. Woody papers.
52. Ibid.
53. *Silver Belt,* August 10, 1888.
54. *Silver Belt,* August 25, 1888.
55. Through several August 1888 issues, the *Silver Belt* pieces together a mosaic of terror: thirty-five men and sixty people in all, huddled in tent camps around Perkins Store.
56. *Herald,* August 22, 1888. The only evidence found in print, the author considers this item of covert military intervention of great significance.
57. Barnes, AHR; See also, Roscoe G. Willson, *The Arizona Republic,* March 11, 1951.

Chapter II
1. Hazelton.
2. ADBG.
3. Will C. Barnes, *Apaches and Longhorns*; Barnes papers. The versions of one of Arizona's revered historians differ substantially.
4. G.W. Shute, "Pleasant Valley War," wrote that a large number of the Committee were from the Salt River Valley, and the leader was 'Captain Watkins.' Haught: "The Committee was organized and the men sworn in. The twenty-three remaining [?] men were joined by Jim Houck. They went upon the mountain and three men were hung upon one limb." In another paragraph, Haught states: "When the Vigilante Committee returned from the hanging. . .Captain Watkins rode to Robbers Roost on Gun Creek for the men who had stolen [Jim?] Roberts's horses. Finding seven men there, he advised them that they were no longer wanted in this community and they left and were never heard from again."
5. Ibid., Shute.
6. ADBG.
7. Barnes, *Apaches and Longhorns.*
8. ADBG.
9. Ibid.
10. ADBG. Forrest had before him letters provided by the Stott family.
11. Barnes papers.
12. McKinney, AHR.
13. Tom Horn, *Life of Tom Horn*; ADBG; Hazelton explores at length the possible connection of Billy Wilson with Billy the Kid.
14. ADBG. Motte Clymer was what the elder Stotts understood the name to be; Sam Brown remembered the name as Floyd Clymer.
15. Ibid.
16. Roscoe G. Willson, *The Arizona Republic,* July 8, 1951. Woody papers: "Why hang Stott, Scott and Wilson?" Mrs. Woody asked Bill Colcord in an interview. She quotes his reply, "We didn't want to waste ammunition. It was cheaper to hang them."

17. Barnes papers.
18. Woody papers.
19. Fish; also, Roberta Flake Clayton typescript largely buttresses Fish, and "it was generally believed and was doubtless the fact that Houck acted in accordance with the plan to get the men into the power of the mob, and was so implicated and even assisted in the hanging."
20. Barnes, *Apaches and Longhorns.*
21. The graves were opened and contents examined in 1942 in the presence of Fred A. Turley, prominent rim country rancher. The ghoulish sifting of the burials was detailed by Turley in his letter mailed to Leslie G. Gregory in March 1946. Justification for the exhumation was not made clear, and resulted in not much more than confirmation of the number and size of the men and the recovery of a few swatches of cloth and pocket trinkets, which were taken as souvenirs. The original oak sapling gravestakes were replaced in later years with more substantial markers. A copy of the Turley letter is at the Arizona Historical Society.
22. Barnes, *Apaches and Longhorns;* Barnes papers.
23. Ibid.
24. Flake.
25. ADBG.
26. Voris.

Chapter III

1. Prescott newspapers during the lethal summer of 1887 scorched Meadows for holding legal, fee-supported hearings into homicides and other high crimes within his jurisdiction.
2. Don Dedera, *The Cactus Sandwich,* Budge Ruffner anecdote about Judge John J. Hawkins.
3. Ibid, anecdote told by Supreme Court Justice Levi S. Udall.
4. *Silver Belt,* June 1, 1889; McKinney, AHR; Barnes papers.
5. *Herald,* July 12, 1892.
6. Dyer's "Bird's Eye View of Phoenix," 1885.
7. Mountain Bell archives.
8. John R. Murdock, *Arizona Characters in Silhouette.*
9. C.C. Colley, "Carl T. Hayden—Phoenician," *Journal of Arizona History,* August 1977.
10. In the legislature's parceling of plums in this political deal, Phoenix got the insane asylum.
11. Ernest J. Hopkins and Alfred Thomas Jr., *The Arizona State University Story.* Let the record show that into its second century ASU was educating more than 42,000 enrollees at the nation's sixth-largest core campus. Of secondary, yet noteworthy importance, the Sun Devil football team emerged victorious in Pasadena's 1987 Rose Bowl. Those who would criticize inclusion of this note by the author might better expend ink and breath elsewhere.
12. Estella Converse Hill, interviews, 1962. Her mother never went to Pleasant Valley until the 1920s, then as a tourist. The source of Forrest's ADBG Chapter XVIII—in which Annie rides and shoots and lives in the valley—is not given.
13. Undoubtedly the Graham quarter-section had been cultivated along with 50,000 other Salt River Valley acres by the HoHoKam people a thousand years before.
14. Hill, op. cit.
15. Letter dated July 31, 1888, Phoenix, provided author by Tom's daughter, Estella. If true, the audacious visit to his ranch refutes the conclusion of Tewksbury-slanted historians, particularly Mrs. Woody, that Tom Graham was a coward who fled Sheriff Mulvenon and abandoned a brother to a friendless end.
16. Boone, Iowa, newspapers, autumn 1887.
17. Hill, op. cit.

18. Horton. He likened the celebration to that which followed the defeat of the Apaches at Big Dry Wash. Although unreliable as to dates, Horton's manuscript gives the year as 1888 and describes the triumphant bacchanal in believable detail.
19. *Silver Belt,* May 12, 1888.
20. *Silver Belt,* May 26, 1888.
21. Graham probate, Maricopa County.
22. ADBG; Woody papers.
23. Pat Jahns, *The Frontier World of Doc Holliday.*
24. ADBG.
25. *Silver Belt,* June 16, 1888.
26. *Herald,* December 4, 1888.
27. Hill, op. cit.
28. Woody papers; Barnes papers.
29. Ed was entrusted with the settlement of Newton's estate.
30. Haught: "George Newton was killed on Salt River because he was loaded with ammunition for the Tewksburys. There is a grave in a thicket on Salt River where he was supposed to have crossed, but who sleeps there I do not know."
31. Hill, op. cit.; *Gazette,* June 1, 1892.
32. Letters, shared by Estella Converse Hill, 1962.
33. *Globe, AZ.*
34. Woody papers. Interview with L.L. Harmon, May 24, 1931.
35. *Herald,* August 12, 1887. The interview "this morning" occurred ten days after Graham was assassinated. Bill Colcord years later stated to Clara Woody (her papers) that Graham and Duchet spent but one night in Pleasant Valley, as their man, S.W. Young, managed the roundup. Colcord said, "[Graham] would have been killed if he'd rode the range or stayed longer. The *Globe, AZ,* book credits Harvey Colcord, Bill's brother, for this opinion.
36. *Gazette,* July 19, 1892.
37. *Gazette,* August 14, 1892.
38. *Herald,* August 4, 1892.

Chapter IV
1. Harvey L. Mott, "Fifty Year History of the *Arizona Republic*," transcript in possession of Phoenix Newspapers, Inc.
2. *Herald,* August 3, 1892.
3. Ibid.
4. *Herald,* August 4, 1892.
5. In later years, Ed Cummings, twelve years of age when Graham was shot, ostensibly claimed he saw the crime, recognized the murderer, and was a "chief witness at Ed Tewksbury's trial." To the contrary, Ed Cummings was not mentioned in the press or court records of the 1890s as a witness; yet Forrest in ADBG drew heavily upon Cummings ("all the vividness of childhood") for a comprehensive account.
6. ADBG.
7. *Herald,* July 30, 1892.
8. *Gazette,* August 4, 1892.
9. *Herald,* August 2, 1892.
10. *Herald,* June 14, 1892.
11. *Herald,* June 19, 1892.
12. ADGB.
13. Respectively, *Gazette,* June 21; *Herald,* June 1; and *Herald,* August 5, 1892.
14. *Herald,* August 2.
15. *Gazette,* August 3.

16. Tewksbury examination.
17. Ibid.
18. Ibid.
19. Estella Converse Hill, interviews, 1962.
20. Tewksbury examination. For prosecution exhibits, the views are westward with buttes and Double Buttes School showing. Today, the intersection of Priest and Broadway is a major Tempe center.
21. Ibid.
22. *Gazette,* August 6, 1892.
23. *Herald,* August 4, 1892.

Chapter V
1. *Gazette,* August 5, 1892.
2. Between Tempe Butte and Pikers Peak, today's Sun Devil Stadium is located. At the time of Graham's murder the population of Arizona was about ninety thousand. With some standing on the sidelines, more than that number filled Sun Devil Stadium to greet His Holiness Pope John Paul II in the late summer of 1987.
3. Tempe, 1890, "Birdseye Sketch" by C.J. Dyer published by Schmidt Label & Lithography, San Francisco, author's collection.
4. James Barney, *The Phoenix Gazette,* April 25, 1959.
5. Barnes, AHR. This ranks not among Barnes's worthy efforts. It is replete with sophomoric gaffes and murky research, and reveals more of Barnes's bias in the Graham-Tewksbury feud than likely he wanted to show. Forrest in ADBG furthers the characterization of Rhodes as "a jovial man, popular among his neighbors at that time and respected by all, not the type you would pick for a killer; and it was always hard for me to believe that he had any connection with the Graham murder."
6. Unidentified newspaper clipping, May 5, 1888, McClintock papers.
7. *Tempe News,* August 18, 1892.
8. *Herald,* August 8, 1892.
9. *Herald,* August 5, 1892.
10. *Herald,* August 8, 1892; Estella Converse Hill, interviews, 1962.
11. *Gazette,* August 9, 1892.
12. Mrs. Mollie Cummings McTaggert, interview, 1962.
13. *Herald,* August 8, 1892.
14. Mrs. Bettie Gregg Adams, interview with author, 1962.
15. *Herald,* August 9, 1892.
16. *Herald,* August 10, 1892.
17. *The Arizona Republican,* August 10, 1892.
18. Woody papers.
19. If Annie inherited Tom's handgun as he left it, possibly the chamber beneath the firing pin held no cartridge, but rather a rolled-up banknote. Too many westerners had been wounded by six-guns discharging by accident. That summer, Newell Herrick, pioneer Phoenix blacksmith, met an untimely end: ". . .sleeping in the yard on a cot, and had started with his pistol to shoot a noisy cat. . .when he fell over a little child's express wagon, discharging the .44 calibre revolver into his bowels. . . ."
20. *The Arizona Republican,* August 10, 1892.
21. *Herald,* August 9, 1892.
22. *Arizona Daily Star* (Tucson), August 9, 1892.
23. *Gazette,* August 10, 1892.
24. Ibid.
25. *Herald,* August 10, 1892.
26. *Gazette,* August 11, 1892.

27. *Herald,* August 11, 1892.
28. Ibid.
29. Ibid.
30. *The Arizona Republican,* August 11, 1892.
31. *Herald,* August ll, 1892.
32. Ibid.
33. *The Arizona Republican,* August 13, 1892.
34. *Gazette,* August 13, 1892.
35. Ibid.
36. *Herald,* August 13, 1892.
37. *Herald,* August 15, 1892.
38. *Gazette,* August 16, 1892.
39. *Gazette,* August 19, 1892.
40. *Herald,* August 19, 1892.
41. *Gazette,* August 20, 1892.
42. *Gazette,* August 28, 1892.
43. ADBG.
44. McKinney, AHR.
45. Compare with letter, corroborating, of Mrs. Mary Ann Tewksbury Rhodes to her son, November 13, 1924, Arizona Historical Society. Also, Hazelton.

Chapter VI
1. *Gazette,* August 3, 1892.
2. ASU Alumni Society archives.
3. Testimony of Lon Forsee, Tempe justice of the peace.
4. Primarily through three Phoenix daily newspapers and wire reports.
5. Gila County, minutes of the Board of Supervisors, canvass of elections, November 17, 1890.
6. Woody papers.
7. *The Arizona Republican,* August 3, 1892.
8. *Arizona Daily Star,* Tucson, August 3, 1892.
9. *Gazette,* August 5, 1892. The sarcastic parody unexpectedly came true. Ed indeed surrendered, but the damage done by a carping press cost Montgomery reelection.
10. *Gazette,* August 4, 1892.
11. *Herald,* August 4, 1892.
12. Ibid.
13. *Herald,* August 3, 1892.
14. Hazelton.
15. *Arizona Daily Star,* Tucson, August 12, 1892.
16. *Arizona Daily Star,* Tucson, August 13, 1892.
17. Only a historical researcher could fully empathize with the blind alley problem created by Ed in this remark to the *Star.* Apparently Ed did not mean *English* as a surname, rather *English* as a national origin. In his testimony later at Tewksbury's trials, Duchet revealed that early in his life he had used his stepfather's name, Ingram, an *English* name.
18. *Tempe Daily News,* August 20, 1892.
19. Barnes, AHR.
20. Barnes papers.
21. The complete six hundred, forty-eight-page indexed record of this hearing is preserved in the University of Arizona Library Special Collections, which kindly provided the author with a copy.
22. For good cause, many a reader may quarrel with the author's gross abridgment of the Tewksbury transcript. But that document alone makes a stack of paper in legal format

about seven inches thick: about 350,000 words.

23. Woody papers.

24. *Gazette,* August 30, 1892.

25. Petersen's splendid Queen Anne home at Priest and Southern became Tempe's restored historic pride.

26. *Herald,* August 29, 1892. Interview with author, 1962.

27. Ibid.

28. *Herald,* August 30, 1892.

29. Ibid.

30. Tewksbury transcript.

31. *Gazette,* August 31.

32. Ibid.

33. *Herald,* September 2, 1892.

34. *Herald,* September 3, 1892.

35. J.W. (Bill) Voris was the father of Bob Voris, informant to Clara Woody and Dale S. King.

36. *Herald,* September 3, 1892.

37. Ibid. It seems certain that George Wilson was in the Middleton cabin when John Paine and Hamp Blevins were shot out of their saddles. Bill Voris was named by J.W. Ellison as a member of the lynch gang that hanged Stott, Scott, and Wilson.

38. *Gazette,* September 7, 1892.

39. *Herald,* September 2, 1892.

40. *Gazette,* September 1, 1892.

41. *Gazette,* September 10, 1892.

42. Maricopa County court records.

43. Hazelton.

44. Voris.

45. Maricopa County court records.

46. *Gazette,* December 23, 1893.

47. *Gazette,* December 29, 1893.

48. *Arizona Daily Star* (Tucson), March 5, 1894.

49. *Arizona Daily Star,* January 3-11, 1895.

50. *Herald,* January 11, 1895, quoting the *Arizona Daily Citizen.*

51. *Herald* (weekly edition), January 3, 1895, quoting the *Arizona Daily Star.*

52. The Rhodes/Tewksbury experience mocks modern preoccupation with pre-trial publicity and court news coverage. American law, wrought in the real world, awaited these two celebrities. Convicted in the press, Rhodes nonetheless was freed almost immediately. Trial by jury of peers was deemed the least objectionable means of determining Tewksbury's guilt. The law assumed some press would be irresponsible. . .that wild rumor would be passed. . .that vigilante meetings might be held. . .that witnesses would remain free to spread truth and falsehood. . .that the sheriff and deputies would be accountable at all times to the electorate. . .that defense counsel might grab at every advantage. . .that prosecutors might play to the audience. . .that judges might feel criticism before, during, and after a trial. . .and that an entire territorial population before trial could synthesize the most intimate detail regarding a crime. It was assumed from veniremen involved with life, and exposed to workaday mix of fact and fiction, could be screened twelve jurors capable of rising above their prejudices. Not today. Our radically changed law seeks jurors who stay out of touch with events, stand aloof from their neighbors, remain blissfully ignorant of social change, and possess an unrealistically uncontaminate psyche. For better or for worse, it's different.

Afterword

1. Tom Graham's letters, shared by his daughter Estella.
2. ADBG.
3. Probate of Tom Graham's estate.
4. Frank W. and Ruth D. Roach Medley, *A Roach Family History,* a copy of this private printing provided by a descendant and esteemed friend, Wally Perry of Phoenix. Hazelton says Philley's tombstone makes him twenty-one at his death. Haught: "John Pool beat his wife to death and then he killed [Horace] Philley, who was supposed to take charge of the Graham cattle. This happened on Reno Hill. Then he killed one man in Tonto Basin. This was his deathbed confession."
5. Probate of Graham estate.
6. Ibid.
7. Estella Converse Hill, interviews, 1962.
8. *Gazette,* June 1, 1961.
9. John Hughes, communication to author, 1986.
10. Hazelton.
11. ADBG.
12. *The Arizona Republic,* August 28, 1955.
13. ADBG; Hazelton.
14. ADBG.
15. *Prescott JM,* September 10, 1887.
16. ADBG.
17. Barnes, AHR.
18. Ruth Blevins Simpson, conversations with author. Evelyn (Eva) Blevins died January 17, 1952, in Arizona Pioneers Home, Prescott.
19. *The Arizona Republic,* June 1, 1961.
20. *The Arizona Republic,* November 27, 1962. Those interested in the love story of Braulia and Ed Tewksbury: Hazelton tells a charming story, "Edwin Tewksbury Takes a Wife, Literally."
21. *Herald,* March 30, 1891.
22. Tewksbury papers, Sharlot Hall Historical Society.
23. Ibid.
24. *Arizona Daily Star,* April 6, 1904. Ed's decline was chronicled in the press, one agonizing paragraph at a time. Examples: Has to give up a job with the Union Pacific, *Silver Belt,* September 14, 1899; returns from medical treatment in Chicago, *Silver Belt* quoted in the *Tombstone Prospector,* August 11, 1903; hospitalized with advanced paralysis and consumption, *Silver Belt,* March 31, 1904. Impoverished, Braulia for years eked out a living selling tamales to friends.
25. Woody papers.
26. Ibid. "John Rhodes narrowly escaped death when his horse was shot out from under him on a trail near the Verde River." *The Arizona Enterprise,* April 19, 1894.
27. ADBG. She had borne a daughter and son by John Tewksbury, and four daughters and two sons by John Rhodes.
28. Minutes of the Arizona Pioneers Historical Society, February 2, 1919.
29. Hazelton.
30. *The Arizona Republic,* January 1, 1936.
31. Tom Power, who had been a prisoner more than forty years, personal communication to author.
32. *The Arizona Republican,* October 15, 1907.

33. *Arizona Daily Star,* January 11, 1934.
34. Flake.
35. ADBG.
36. Tom Horn, *Life of Tom Horn.*
37. McClintock papers.
38. *The Arizona Republican,* March 31, 1921.
39. *Silver Belt,* July 16, 1896.
40. Glenn Ellison, inked on back of Campbell portrait, Arizona Historical Society, "A white man killed him but the Apaches got the blame."
41. *The Arizona Republic,* January 22, 1934.
42. Hazelton.
43. Larry Schweikart, *A History of Arizona Banking.*
44. Tonto National Forest records.
45. Robert L. Thomas, *The Arizona Republic,* November 11, 1978.
46. McClintock papers.
47. Horton.
48. Fred W. Croxon, *History of Grazing on Tonto National Forest.*
49. Jo Johnson, "The Hashknife Outfit," *Arizona Highways Magazine,* June 1956.
50. Robert L. Thomas, *The Arizona Republic,* November 11, 1978.
51. *Prescott Courier,* October 15, 1887.

Bibliography

Adams, Ramon F. *Cowboy Lingo.* Boston: Houghton Mifflin, 1956.

_____ . "The Old-Time Cowhand," *Arizona Highways Magazine,* April 1962.

Allison, Robert, rewritten by L.L. Lathrop. *The Blevins Family: An Episode in the Pleasant Valley War.* Unpublished typescript, Arizona Pioneers' Historical Society, August 1936.

American Quarter Horse Association, editors. *Ride a Quarter Horse.* Amarillo, Texas: American Quarter Horse Association, 1960.

Arizona Livestock Sanitary Board. *Brands and Marks of Cattle. . .as they Appear of Record in the Office of the Live Stock Sanitary Board of Arizona.* Phoenix: McNeil Printing Company, 1908.

Arnold, Oren. "Romance of the Brands," *Arizona Highways Magazine,* November 1941.

_____ . "How to Read a Brand," *Arizona Highways Magazine,* March 1949.

_____ . *Irons in the Fire: Cattle Brand Lore.* New York: Abelard-Schuman, 1965.

Arnold, Oren and John P. Hale. *Hot Irons: Hearldry of the Range.* New York: Macmillan, 1940.

Bancroft, Hubert Howe. *History of Arizona and New Mexico, 1830–1888.* San Francisco: The History Company, 1889.

Banta, Alfred F. *Alfred Franklin Banta: Arizona Pioneer,* memoirs edited by Frank Reeve. Albuquerque: University of New Mexico Press, 1953.

Barnard, Edward S., editor. *Story of the Great American West.* Pleasantville: Reader's Digest, 1977.

Barnes, Frank C. *Cartridges of the World,* fourth edition, Chicago: Follett Publishing Company, 1980.

Barnes, Will C. *Arizona Place Names.* University of Arizona General Bulletin No. 2. Tucson: University of Arizona, 1935. Revised and enlarged by Byrd H. Granger. Tucson: University of Arizona Press, 1960.

_____ . *Apaches and Longhorns.* Los Angeles: Ward Richie Press, 1941; reprint Tucson: University of Arizona Press, 1982.

_____ . "The Pleasant Valley War of 1887," *The Arizona Historical Review,* volume IV, number three and number four. Tucson: The Arizona Pioneers' Historical Society, October 1931, January 1932.

_____ . *Biography of Commodore Perry Owens,* typescript. Tucson: Arizona Historical Society, no date.

Bartholomew, Ed. *Western Hard-Cases, or, Gunfighters Named Smith.* Ruidoso, New Mexico: Frontier Book Company, 1960.

Bean, Amelia. *The Feud.* Garden City: Doubleday & Company, 1960.

Blair, Wink. "Our Shepherds of the Desert," *Outdoor Arizona Magazine,* April 1972.

Bourke, John G. *On the Border with Crook.* New York: Charles Scribner's Sons, 1891, reprint Glorieta, New Mexico: Rio Grande Press, 1960.

Boyer, Mary G., editor. *Arizona in Literature.* Glendale, California: Arthur H. Clark, 1934.

Bradley, Glenn D. *The Story of the Santa Fe.* Boston: R.G. Badger Company, circa 1920.

Brandes, Ray. *Frontier Military Posts of Arizona.* Globe: Dale Stuart King, 1960.

Brown, Dee and Martin Schmidt. *Trail Driving Days.* New York: Charles Scribner's Sons, 1952.

Brown, Mark H. and W.R. Felton. *Before Barbed Wire.* New York: Bramhall House, 1956.

Bunnell, Dick. "Arizona Roundup, 1951," *Arizona Highways Magazine,* September 1951.

Burke, J.F. "Jim Roberts, Old Hand with a Gun," *Frontier Times Magazine,* June–July 1980.

Burnham, Frederick Russell. *Scouting on Two Continents.* Garden City, New York: Doubleday, Page & Company, 1926.

Carlton, Frances C. "J.D. Houck, the Sheep King of Cave Creek," *Journal of Arizona History,* Spring 1980.

Cary, Lucian. *Lucian Cary on Guns.* Greenwich, Connecticut: Fawcett Publications, 1950.

Clark, Walter Van Tilburg. *The Ox-bow Incident.* New York: Random House, 1940.

Clayton, Roberta. "Commodore Owens and the Blevins Gang," chapter in *Life of J.A. Hunt,* typescript duplicate, author's collection.

Cline, Platt. *They Came to the Mountain.* Flagstaff: Northern Arizona University with Northland Press, 1976.

Clum, John P., with foreword and notes by John D. Gilchriese. *It All Happened in Tombstone,* reprinted from the *Arizona Historical Review,* October 1929. Flagstaff: Northland Press, 1965.

Colley, Charles C. "Carl T. Hayden—Phoenician," the *Journal of Arizona History,* Autumn 1977.

Cook, James E. "Battle of Big Dry Wash" three-part series, *The Arizona Republic,* July 12, 14, and 16, 1987.

Coolidge, Dane. *The Man Killers.* New York: E.P. Dutton, 1921.

_____ . *Fighting Men of the West.* New York: E.P. Dutton, 1932.

_____ . *Arizona Cowboys.* New York: E. P. Dutton and Co., 1938.

Clum, Woodworth. *Apache Agent: The Story of John P. Clum.* Boston: Houghton Mifflin Company, 1936.

Croxon, Fred W. *History of Grazing on Tonto National Forest,* speech, Tonto Grazing Conference, Phoenix, Arizona, November 4–5, 1926.

_____ . "Dark Days in Central Arizona," as told to James E. Serven for the *Smoke Signal Magazine,* Tucson Corral of Westerners, Number 34, 1977.

Davisson, Lori. "New Light on the Cibicue Fight," *Journal of Arizona History,* 1979.

Decker, Jeremy. "Drinkers of the Wind," *Continental Airlines Magazine,* April 1986.

Dedera, Don. *A Mile in His Moccasins.* Phoenix: McGrew Printing & Lithographing, 1960.

_____ . "Camp Reno," *The Arizona Republic,* February 14, 1962.

_____ . *Arizona the Beautiful.* New York: Doubleday and Company, 1974.

_____ . "Gila Trail—Pathway in the Desert," *Trails West.* Washington: The National Geographic Society, 1979.

_____ . "They Died with Their Boots On—The Pleasant Valley War Revisited," *Arizona Highways Magazine,* August 1984.

_____ . *The Cactus Sandwich, and Other Tall Tales of the Southwest.* Flagstaff, Arizona: Northland Press, 1986.

_____ . "The Gold Star Mothers of the Pleasant Valley War," *Arizona Highways Magazine,* September 1987.

Dobie, J. Frank. *The Longhorns.* Boston: Little, Brown and Co., 1941.

Drago, Harry Sinclair. *The Great Range Wars.* New York: Dodd, Mead & Company, 1970.

Durham, Philip and Everett L. Jones. *The Negro Cowboy.* Cornwall, New York: Cornwall Press, 1965.

Eggenhoffer, Nick. *Wagons, Mules and Men.* New York: Hastings House, 1961.

Elliott, Wallace W. & Company, editors. *History of Arizona Territory.* San Francisco: Wallace W. Elliott & Company, 1884; reprint, Flagstaff, Arizona: Northland Press, 1964.

Ellison, Glenn. *Cowboys Under the Mogollon Rim.* Tucson: University of Arizona Press, 1968.

_____ . *Back Trackin'.* Globe, Arizona: Tyree Publishing, 1975.

_____ . *More Tales from Slim Ellison.* Tucson: University of Arizona Press, 1981.

Evans, Edna Hoffman. *Written with Fire: The Story of Cattle Brands.* New York: Holt, Rinehart and Winston, 1962.

Farish, Thomas Edwin. *History of Arizona,* eight volumes. San Francisco: Filmer Brothers Electrotype Company, 1916, 1917, 1918.

Faulk, Odie B. *Land of Many Frontiers, a History of the American Southwest.* New York: Oxford University Press, 1968.

Fish, Joseph. *History of Arizona,* parts I and II, unpublished typescript, Arizona State Department of Library, Archives and Public Records, circa 1896.

Flake family. *William J. Flake, Pioneer-Colonizer.* Snowflake, Arizona: privately published, circa 1966.

Flake, Osmer D. *Some Reminiscenses of the Pleasant Valley War and Causes That Led Up to It,* typescript edited by Levi S. Udall, Arizona State Department of Library, Archives and Public Records, received April 13, 1958.

Flayderman, Norm. *Flayderman's Guide to Antique American Firearms,* second edition. Northfield, Illinois: DBI Books, 1980.

Forrest, Earle R. *Arizona's Dark and Bloody Ground.* Caldwell: The Caxton Printers, Ltd., 1936; revised and expanded, 1952; reprint, Tucson: University of Arizona Press, 1984.

_____ . "Red Years on the Arizona Frontier," *Travel Magazine,* October, 1927, reprinted in *Arizona Peace Officer's Magazine,* February–March 1937.

Fraser, James. *Cattle Brands in Arizona.* Flagstaff, Arizona: Northland Press, 1968.

Gard, Wayne. *Frontier Justice.* Norman: University of Oklahoma Press, 1949.

Gillette, Frank. *Pleasant Valley.* Young, Arizona: privately published, 1984.

Goff, John S. *Arizona Territorial Officials,* two volumes. Cave Creek: Black Mountain Press, 1978.

Grant, Bruce. *The Cowboy Encyclopedia.* New York, Chicago, San Francisco: Rand McNally, 1951.

Green, Ben K. *The Color of Horses.* Flagstaff, Arizona: Northland Press, 1974.

Gregory, Leslie E., and Earle R. Forrest. "Arizona's Haunted Walls of Silence," *Arizona Highways Magazine,* October 1947.

Grey, Zane. *The Hash Knife Outfit.* New York: Harper & Row, 1933; reprint, New York: Pocket Books, 1975.

_____ . *To the Last Man.* New York: Harper & Row, 1922; reprint, New York: Pocket Books, 1971.

_____ . *Under the Tonto Rim.* New York: Grosset & Dunlap, 1926.

Gruber, Frank. *Zane Grey, a Biography.* New York and Cleveland: World Publishing Company, 1970.

Haskett, Bert. "Early History of the Cattle Industry in Arizona," *Arizona Historical Review,* October 1935.

_____ . "History of the Sheep Industry in Arizona," *Arizona Historical Review,* July 1936.

Haught, Samuel A. Untitled typescript duplicate, author's collection, undated.

Hayes, Jess G. *Apache Vengeance.* Albuquerque: University of New Mexico Press, 1954.

_____ . *Boots & Bullets, The Life and Times of John W. Wentworth.* Tucson: University of Arizona Press, 1967.

_____ . *Sheriff Thompson's Day.* Tucson: University of Arizona Press, 1968.

Hazelton, Drusilla. *The Tonto Basin's Early Settlers,* unpublished typescript, copy at the Arizona Historical Society, Tucson.

Henry, Will. *The Fourth Horseman.* New York: Bantam Books, 1954.

Henson, Pauline. *Founding a Wilderness Capital.* Flagstaff, Arizona: Northland Press, 1965.

Hertzog, Peter. *Outlaws of New Mexico.* Santa Fe: Sunstone Press, 1984.

Hill, Myles E. and John H. Goff. *Arizona Past and Present.* Cave Creek, Arizona: Black Mountain Press, 1970.

Hinton, Richard J., editor. *The Hand-book to Arizona.* San Francisco: Payot, Upham & Company, 1878; reprint, Phoenix: Arizona Silhouettes, 1954.

Hodge, Hiram C. *Arizona As It Is, or The Coming Country.* New York: Hurd and Houghton, 1877; reprint, Glorieta, New Mexico: Rio Grande Press, 1965.

Hooper, Mildred and C.R. Hooper, "Pleasant Valley: an Unpleasant Past," *Outdoor Arizona Magazine,* August 1974.

Hopkins, Ernest J. *Financing the Frontier.* Phoenix: The Valley National Bank, 1950.

Hopkins, Ernest J. and Alfred Thomas Jr. *The Arizona State University Story.* Phoenix: Southwest Publishing, 1960.

Horn, Tom. *Life of Tom Horn, Government Scout and Interpreter, Written by Himself, Together with His Letters and Statements by His Friends; A Vindication.* Denver: for J. C. Coble by the Louthan Book Company, 1904; reprint, Norman: University of Oklahoma Press, 1964.

Horton, L.J. *The Pleasant Valley War,* unpublished typescript, Sharlot Hall Historical Society, Prescott, circa 1925.

Houck, Martha. *An Arizona Pioneer's Reminiscenses: A Report on Pioneer Life in Arizona, Based on Information Given by Mr. and Mrs. J.D. Houck, Including Relations with Indians, and the Pleasant Valley War,* unpublished typescript, Arizona Historical Foundation, Arizona State University, 1916.

Hughes, Stella. *Hashknife Cowboy.* Tucson: University of Arizona Press, 1985.

Hunt, Frazier. *The Long Trail from Texas.* New York: Doubleday, Doran & Company, 1940.

Huntington, Dan. *Fort McDowell in the Eighties.* Unpublished typescript, Arizona State Library, Archives and Public Records, 1957.

Jahns, Pat. *The Frontier World of Doc Holliday.* New York: Hastings House, 1957.

Johnson, Annie Richardson and Elva Richardson Shumway, in collaboration with Enola

Johnson Mangelson. *Charles Edmund Richardson.* Tempe: Publication Services, 1982.

Johnson, G. Wesley Jr. *Phoenix: Valley of the Sun.* Tulsa, Oklahoma: Continental Heritage Press, 1982.

Johnson, Jo. "The Hashknife Outfit," *Arizona Highways Magazine,* June 1956.

_____ . "Commodore Perry Owens," *Arizona Highways Magazine,* October 1960.

_____ . "Tales of the Little Colorado," *Arizona Highways Magazine,* September 1965.

Kant, Candace. *Zane Grey's Arizona.* Flagstaff, Arizona: Northland Press, 1984.

Kartus, Sidney. "Helen Duette Ellison Hunt," *Arizona Historical Review,* July 1931.

Keleher, William A. *Violence in Lincoln County, 1869-1881.* Albuquerque: University of New Mexico Press, 1957.

King, Frank M. *Wranglin' the Past.* Privately printed, 1935; Pasadena: Trail's End Publishing, 1946.

Kuykendall, Ivan Lee. *Ghost Riders of the Mogollon.* San Antonio: The Naylor Company, 1954.

Lake, Stuart N. *Wyatt Earp, Frontier Marshal.* Boston and New York: Houghton Mifflin Company, 1931.

Line, Francis Raymond. "Arizona Sheep Trek," *National Geographic Magazine,* April 1950.

_____ . "Sheep, Stars and Solitude," *Arizona Highways Magazine,* April 1955.

Lockwood, Frank C. *Arizona Characters.* Los Angeles: The Times-Mirror Press, 1928.

_____ . *Pioneer Days in Arizona; From the Spanish Occupation to Statehood.* New York: The Macmillan Company, 1932.

_____ . *More Arizona Characters,* University of Arizona General Bulletin No. 6. Tucson: University of Arizona, 1943.

Lowe, Charles H. *Arizona's Natural Environment.* Tucson: University of Arizona Press, 1964.

Lutrell, Estelle. *Newspapers and Periodicals, 1859-1911,* University of Arizona General Bulletin no. 15, vol. XX no. 3. Tucson: University of Arizona, July 1949.

McClintock, James Harvey. *Arizona: Prehistoric, Aboriginal; Pioneer; Modern,* three volumes. Chicago: The S.J. Clarke Publishing Company, 1916.

_____ . "The Pleasant Valley War," *Arizona Cattleman Magazine,* March 11, 1918.

_____ . *Mormon Settlement in Arizona.* Phoenix: no publisher, 1921; reprint, Tucson: University of Arizona Press, 1985.

_____ . Papers of James Harvey McClintock, Phoenix Public Library.

McKinney, Joe T. "Reminiscenses," *The Arizona Historical Review,* volume V, number one, volume V, number two, volume V, number three, Tucson: The Arizona Pioneers' Historical Society, April, July, and October 1932.

McLaughlin, Herb and Dorothy. *Phoenix 1870-1970 in Photographs.* Phoenix: Arizona Photographic Associates, 1970.

Mahan, Frances Jones. "Unique Day," *Arizona Cattlelog Magazine,* October 1953.

Marshall, James. *Santa Fe: The Railroad That Built an Empire.* New York: Random House, 1945.

Marshall, Otto Miller. *The Wham Paymaster Robbery.* Pima, Arizona: Pima Chamber of Commerce, 1967.

Middleton, Hattie (Mrs. G.M. Allison). "Account of Indian Fight in Pleasant Valley" (no title), *Frontier Times Magazine,* June 1928; reprinted, *True West Magazine,* March –April 1964.

Miller, Joseph. *Arizona: A State Guide,* revised. New York: Hastings House, 1965.

_____ . *Arizona: The Last Frontier.* New York: Hastings House, 1956.

_____ . *Arizona Cavalcade.* New York: Hastings House, 1962.

_____. *Arizona Rangers.* New York: Hastings House, 1972.

Mott, Harvey L. *Fifty Year History of The Arizona Republic,* unpublished typescript, Phoenix Newspapers, Inc., circa 1944.

Murdock, John R. *Arizona Characters in Silhouette.* Privately printed from articles appearing in *The Arizona Republic,* April–May 1933.

Murphy, Ira A. *Brief History of Payson, Arizona.* Payson, Arizona: Payson Public Library, 1983.

_____, editor. *Rim Country History.* Payson, Arizona: Northern Gila County Historical Society, 1984.

Murphy, Merwin L. "W.J. Murphy and the Arizona Canal Company," *The Journal of Arizona History,* Summer 1982.

Myers, John Myers. *The Last Chance: Tombstone's Early Years.* New York: E.P. Dutton & Company, 1950.

_____. *Print in a Wild Land.* Garden City: Doubleday & Company, Inc., 1967.

_____. *The Westerners.* Englewood Cliffs: Prentice-Hall, Inc., 1969.

Myrick, David. *Pioneer Arizona Railroads.* Golden, Colorado: Colorado Railroad Museum, 1968.

National Archives. Microcopy files of records, returns and communications, Fort McDowell, Arizona Territory. Sacks Collection, Arizona Historical Foundation, Arizona State University.

Noble, Marguerite. *Filaree.* New York: Random House, 1979; reprint, Albuquerque: University of New Mexico Press, 1985.

Ogle, Ralph H. *Federal Control of Western Apaches: 1848–1886.* reprint, Albuquerque: University of New Mexico Press, 1940 and 1969.

Palmer, Hollis B. "Great Sheep Drive," *Arizona Highways Magazine,* October 1941.

Paré, Madeline Ferrin. *Arizona Pageant, a Short History of the Forty-eighth State.* Phoenix: Arizona Historical Foundation, 1965.

Peace, Jayne. *The History of Gisela.* Payson, Arizona: privately published, 1981.

Penfield, Thomas. *Western Sheriffs and Marshals.* New York: Grossett & Dunlap, 1955.

Peplow, Edward H. Jr. *History of Arizona.* New York: Lewis Historical Publishing Company, 1958.

_____. "Arizona's Famous Pleasant Valley War," *Phoenix Magazine,* June 1974.

Peplow, Elizabeth W. and Edward H., Jr. *When the Cow Jumped over the Moon: The Story of Cattle Growing in Yavapai County, Arizona.* Prescott: Yavapai Cattle Growers, 1952.

Peterson, Sue. "Shepherds of the Open Range," *Arizona Highways Magazine,* August 1978.

Potter, Alvina N. *The Many Lives of the Lynx.* Prescott: privately printed, 1964.

Powell, Donald M. *An Arizona Gathering.* Tucson: Arizona Pioneers' Historical Society, circa 1960.

Powell, Lawrence Clark. *From the Heartland: Profiles of People and Places of the Southwest and Beyond.* Flagstaff, Arizona: Northland Press, 1976.

Prassel, Frank Richard. *The Western Peace Officer: A Legacy of Law and Order.* Norman: University of Oklahoma Press, 1972.

Provence, Jean. *Bloody Pleasant Valley.* Typescript, Phoenix Public Library, 1975.

Raine, William MacLeod. *Famous Sheriffs and Western Outlaws.* Garden City, New York: Doubleday, Doran & Company, Inc., 1929.

_____. "The War for the Range," *Frank Leslie's Popular Monthly,* February 1903.

Raine, William MacLeod and Will C. Barnes. *Cattle.* Garden City, New York: Doubleday, Doran & Company, Inc., 1930.

Reed, Alan C. "Apache: Cattle, Horses, and Men," *Arizona Highways Magazine,* July 1954.

Reed, Bill. *The Last Bugle Call, a History of Fort McDowell, Arizona Territory 1865–1890.* Parsons, West Virginia: McClain Printing Company, 1977.

Rickey, Don Jr. *$10 Horse, $40 Saddle: Cowboy Clothing, Arms, Tools and Horse Gear of the 1880s.* Fort Collins, Colorado: Old Army Press, 1976.

Ridgway, W.R. "The Not-So-Pleasant Pleasant Valley War," *The Arizona Republic,* August 28, 1955.

Roach, Frank W. and Ruth D. Roach Medley. *A Roach Family History.* Lubbock: Keels & Company, 1974.

Rollins, Philip Aston. *The Cowboy; His Characteristics, His Equipment, and His Part in the Development of the West.* New York: Charles Scribner's Sons, 1922.

Savage, Pat. *One Last Frontier.* New York: Exposition Press, 1964.

Santee, Ross. *Cowboy.* New York: Cosmopolitan Book Corporation, 1928.

_____. *Apache Land.* New York: Charles Scribner's Sons, 1947.

_____. *Lost Pony Tracks.* New York: Charles Scribner's Sons, 1953.

Schmidt, Elaine Field. "Basque Shepherds in Arizona," *Outdoor Arizona Magazine,* November 1976.

Schmookler, Andrew. *The Parable of Tribes: The Problem of Power in Social Evolution.* Berkeley: University of California Press, 1984.

Schweikart, Larry. *A History of Banking in Arizona.* Tucson: University of Arizona Press, 1982.

Serven, James E. *Conquering the Frontiers.* La Habra, California: Foundation Press, 1974.

_____. "Winchester 1886 Repeater Provided Plenty of Punch," *American Rifleman Magazine,* March 1972.

Shadegg, Steven C. *The Phoenix Story, An Adventure in Reclamation.* Phoenix: privately published, 1958.

Shelton, Charles E. *Photo Album of Yesterday's Southwest.* Palm Desert, California: Desert Magazine, 1961.

Shute, G.W. "Pleasant Valley War, Revised," *Arizona Cattlelog,* April 1956.

Sloan, Richard E. *Memories of an Arizona Judge.* Palo Alto, California: Stanford University Press, 1932.

Smith, Cornelius C. Jr. *A Southwestern Vocabulary: The Words They Used.* Pasadena: Arthur C. Clark, 1950.

Smith, Howard V. *The Climate of Arizona.* Tucson: University of Arizona Agricultural Experiment Station Bulletin number 279, 1956.

Sonnichsen, Charles Leland. *I'll Die Before I Run: The Story of the Great Feuds of Texas.* New York: Harper & Row, 1951.

Spude, Robert L. "A Land of Sunshine and Silver," *The Arizona Journal of History,* Spring 1975.

Stanley, F. (Stanley Francis Lewis Crocchioli). *Desperadoes of New Mexico.* Denver: World Press, 1953.

Stevens, Robert C. *Echoes of the Past.* Prescott: Yavapai Cowbelles, 1964.

Summerhayes, Martha. *Vanished Arizona: Recollections of My Army Life.* reprint, Chicago: The Lakeside Press, 1939.

Sutton, Fred. "Gunmen I Have Known," *Winners of the West Magazine,* March 30, 1935.

Tanner, George S. and J. Morris Richards. *Colonization of the Little Colorado.* Flagstaff, Arizona: Northland Press, 1977.

Theobald, John and Lillian. *Arizona Territory: Post Offices and Postmasters.* Phoenix: Arizona Historical Foundation, 1961.

_____. *Wells Fargo in Arizona Territory.* Tempe: Arizona Historical Foundation, 1978.

Thrapp, Dan L. *Al Sieber, Chief of Scouts.* Norman: University of Oklahoma Press, 1964.

_____. *The Conquest of Apacheria.* Norman: University of Oklahoma Press, 1967.

Trimble, Marshall. *Arizona, a Panoramic History of a Frontier State.* Garden City: Doubleday and Company, Inc., 1977.

_____ . *Arizona Adventure*. Phoenix: Golden West Publishers, 1982.

_____ . *In Old Arizona*. Phoenix: Golden West Publishers, 1985.

Turner, Frederick Jackson. *The Frontier in American History*. New York: Henry Holt & Company, 1920.

Tucker, Edwin A. and George Fitzpatrick. *Men Who Matched the Mountains*. Washington, D.C.: United States Department of Agriculture, 1972.

Voris, Robert. Unpublished typescript of interview conducted May 20 and July 29, 1957, by Clara T. Woody and Dale Stuart King, Woody Collection, Arizona Historical Society, Tucson.

Wagoner, J.J. *History of the Cattle Industry in Southern Arizona, 1540–1940*. Tucson: University of Arizona Bulletin volume 23, number 2, 1952.

Wallace, Andrew W. *Sources & Readings in Arizona History*. Tucson: Arizona Pioneers' Historical Society, 1965.

Ward, Fay E. *The Cowboy at Work: All About His Job and How He Does It*. New York: Hastings House, 1958.

Watkins, Dwight. "Arizona Sheep Drives," *Arizona Highways Magazine*, October 1949.

Watrous, George R. *The History of Winchester Firearms, 1866–1966*. New Haven: Winchester-Western Press, 1966.

Way, Thomas E. *Sergeant Fred Platten's Ten Years on the Trail of the Redskins*. Williams, Arizona: Williams News Press, 1959.

Weed, William. Court reporter's transcript, preliminary hearing, August 29–September 8, 1892, Territory of Arizona vs. Edwin Tewksbury, two volumes, University of Arizona Library, 1892.

Wentworth, Edward Norris. *America's Sheep Trails: History, Personalities*. Ames: Iowa State College Press, 1948.

Wilhelm, C. Leroy and Mabel R. Wilhelm. *A History of St. Johns Stake*. Orem, Utah: Historical Publications, 1982.

Acknowledgments

Professor Ernest J. Hopkins promised little more than "intensive living" to those of us in the first journalism classes he convened after World War II at the college now maturing as Arizona State University. I inferred he meant we would have a hell of a good time and not make much money. For most of us, Hoppy's predictions proved true on both counts. Even today, few reporters get rich, so the prospect of intensive living must explain why twelve hundred aspirants at present are enrolled in the Walter Cronkite School of Journalism and Telecommunication, a department of Arizona State's College of Public Programs. A career in journalism persists as an attractive prospect: consuming, contributory, vital involvement in current events.

But our mentor cautioned against preoccupation with the present and future. By example, Professor Hopkins, trailblazing investigative reporter who had raked muck for Lincoln Steffens, devoted much of the last third of his life to history—to the past's lessons in economics, in literature, in social equity. Long after Hoppy committed his cadres of journalists to the coverage of daily news, he encouraged them to cultivate historical perspective. Hoppy would quote Ben Hecht: "Trying to determine what is going on in the world by reading the newspapers is like trying to tell time by watching the second hand of a clock." That probably holds true today for television, too.

Through his own industrious decades as professor emeritus, Hoppy urged me to finish my rear-view book. For his unflagging support I am most grateful.

Twenty-five years ago, another professor, Dr. C.L. Sonnichsen of the University of Texas at El Paso, in response to my presumptuous letter, responded with characteristic generosity and directness. "By all means write the book," he said. That Doc Sonnichsen in his eighty-seventh year would risk reading and commenting upon the product is a satisfying happenstance, indeed. John Orr Theobald considered history also to be "intensive living," and in demonstration, dozens of times we'd wheel a Jeep off into some hidden intersection of wild nature and westering humanity. For John Theobald, history was a participation sport.

As if we needed another example, Clara T. Woody's fate serves to remind us that books must be written as well as researched. Age, poor health, and mindless vandals overtook her and her work—leaving *Outlaw Valley* largely unsynthesized, and her papers hopelessly scrambled. In transferring her research library to the Arizona Historical Society, I have gratefully perused pockets of coherence; the reorganization of her homogeneous mass of data awaits the commitment of a younger, more patient scholar.

In two lengthy interviews and associated correspondence, Earle Forrest encouraged renewed inquiry into his baseline publication, *Arizona's Dark and Bloody Ground*. I owe considerable debt to the man and his work. Almost from the beginning Bob Allison, Ruth Blevins Simpson, and Joe Miller shared everything they learned of the Tonto feud. Fred Eldean some day may be fully recognized for what he preserved of Arizona land history. I was aided by some of the war's surviving eyewitnesses—mostly women: Bertha Acton, Bettie Adams, Estella Hill, Mollie McTaggert, Emma Sears, and Betty and Ola Young. As this work drew to a close, warmly appreciated also was the splendid company and professional collaboration of artist Bill Ahrendt and editor Susan McDonald.

A cynic might say that historical establishments are in the business of furthering historical projects, but that isn't always so. Thus, my thanks to the ever-helpful assistance of the Arizona Department of Library, Archives and Public Records; the Arizona Historical Foundation, Arizona State University; the Arizona Historical Society; Arizona Room, Phoenix Public Library; the library of Phoenix Newspapers, Incorporated; the Sharlot Hall Historical Society; the Tempe Historical Society; and the University of Arizona Library. Court and administrative officials of

Apache, Coconino, Gila, Greenlee, Maricopa, Mohave, Navajo, Pinal, Pima, and Yavapai counties invariably were helpful whenever asked.

In large and small ways, I am obliged to individuals: Sue Abbey, Bob Allison, Ernesto Arbizu, Charles Armer, Oren Arnold, Ben Avery, Marcy Bagley, James Barney, Eddie Basha Jr., Susan Berry, Jean Bock, Wes Bolin, Ethel Bouton, Barbara Boyle, Jay Brashear, Margaret Bretharte, Bing Brown, F.V. (Bud) Brown, Isabelle Brown, Don Bufkin, Dana Burden, John Caffrey, Bob Capps, Bob Carlock, Fran Carlson, Raymond Carlson, Ed Carson, Frank Carson, Jack Cavness, Don Chambers, Frank Chapman, Perl Charles, Dick Charnock, Lloyd Clark, Aaron Cohen, Frank Colcord, George Collins, James E. Cook, Marguerite Cooley, Bonnie Conkle, Norman Conkle, Frank Connelly, Inez Connelly, Bob Courtney, Josephine Craig, Jennie Daggs, Willard Daws, Ed Delph, Anna Mae Deming, Bud Dewald, Bruce Dinges, Don Dotts, Carol Downey, Fred Dove, Lisa Dunning, Kearney Egerton, Slim Ellison, Bill Epler, Bob Farrell, Orien W. Fifer Jr., Bert Fireman, Ed Fitzhugh, Eugene Flake, Glenn Flake, Sank Flake, Jerry Foster, Sam Freedman, Zena Friedman, Freddy Fritz, Kay Gammage, John Gilchriese, Frank Gillette, Bill Goettl, Barry Goldwater, Frank X. Gordon, Giles Goswick, Bonnie Greer, Dick Greer, Fred Guirey, John Haldiman, Hugh Harelson, Richard Harris, Homer Haught, Jess Hayes, Drusilla Hazelton, Louis Heib, Frank Helmich, Lloyd Henning, William Hermann, Lyle Hiner, Bob Hirsch, Wes Holden, Frank Honsik, Jean Hopkins, Bob Housholder, Betsy Howard, Paul Hubbard, John Hughes, Al Jacoby, Pat Jahns, David Jenney, Carol Jensen, Louie Jurwitz, Jack Karie, Danny Kovel, Ken Kimsey, Rachel Lamb, Cameron Laughlin, Pat Laughlin, Nyle Leatham, Louie Lechuga, Fred Leftwich, Mary Leonard, Herb Lindner, John Low, Bill Lyon, Bill McCune, Bill McGrath, Dan McGrew, Dorothy McLaughlin, Herb McLaughlin, Reg Manning, Garland Maret, Rose Maret, Bebe May, Jack May, Downs Matthews, Dick Miller, Harry Mitchell, Neil Morgan, Jim Moss, Ed Murray, Jack Myers, Lou Myers, Brian Neumeister, Marguerite Noble, William H. O'Brien, Sada O'Brien, Bill Passey, Wally Perry, Charlie Pickrell, Collice Portnoff, Tom Power, Joanne Ralston, Lily Ramsey, Glen Randall, Margaret Jane Rice, Roy Rice, J. Morris Richards, Hal Richardson, Sterling Ridge, Bill Ridgway, Mary Rittenhouse, Bill Roberts, Dick Royko, Morris Rozar, Budge Ruffner, Harvey Samuel, Tom Sanford, Susie Sato, Steve Shadegg, Bill Schulz, Leland Shelley, Tom Sherlock, Chuck Sherrill, Bill Shover, Maury Sizer, Dean Smith, Morgan Smith, Sam Steiger, Joe Stocker, Glendon Swarthout, Jim Tallon, Lillian Theobald, Dick Totman, Rosemary Totman, Joanne Twining, Marshall Trimble, Stan Turley, Stewart Udall, Sam Vaughan, Jim Wallace, Carla Warrick, Dick Waters, Jack Williams, Roscoe Willson, Maggie Wilson, Manya Winsted, Merrill Windsor, Sharon Womack, John Woody, Doc Wright, Jo Wykoff, Jack

Yelverton, Earl Zarbin, and Ed Zumach.

Family tie, family endeavor, family tragedy unified the people of this story. My own family humored decades of the moods and maunderings of an obsessed historical sleuth, and for that I have thanked them all in private. Especially Annabeth.

Index